Lecture Notes in Economics and Mathematical Systems

Managing Editors: M. Beckmann and W. Krelle

265

Dynamic Games and Applications in Economics

Edited by T. Başar

Springer-Verlag
Berlin Heidelberg New York Tokyo

Managing Editors

Prof. Dr. M. Beckmann
Brown University
Providence, RI 02912, USA

Prof. Dr. W. Krelle
Institut für Gesellschafts- und Wirtschaftswissenschaften
der Universität Bonn
Adenauerallee 24-42, D-5300 Bonn, FRG

Editor

Prof. Dr. Tamer Başar
Department of Electrical and Computer Engineering
and Coordinated Science Laboratory
University of Illinois, 1101 W. Springfield Avenue
Urbana, Illinois 61801, USA

ISBN 3-540-16435-9 Springer-Verlag Berlin Heidelberg New York Tokyo
ISBN 0-387-16435-9 Springer-Verlag New York Heidelberg Berlin Tokyo

Printing and binding: Beltz Offsetdruck, Hemsbach/Bergstr.
2142/3140-543210

PREFACE

This volume contains eleven articles which deal with different aspects of dynamic and differential game theory and its applications in economic modeling and decision making. All but one of these were presented as invited papers in special sessions I organized at the 7th Annual Conference on Economic Dynamics and Control in London, England, during the period June 26-28, 1985.

The first article, which comprises Chapter 1, provides a general introduction to the topic of dynamic and differential game theory, discusses various noncooperative equilibrium solution concepts, including Nash, Stackelberg, and Consistent Conjectural Variations equilibria, and a number of issues such as feedback and time-consistency. The second chapter deals with the role of information in Nash equilibria and the role of leadership in Stackelberg problems. A special type of a Stackelberg problem is the one in which one dominant player (leader) acquires dynamic information involving the actions of the others (followers), and constructs policies (so-called incentives) which enforce a certain type of behavior on the followers; Chapter 3 deals with such a class of problems and presents some new theoretical results on the existence of affine incentive policies. The topic of Chapter 4 is the computation of equilibria in discounted stochastic dynamic games. Here, for problems with finite state and decision spaces, existing algorithms are reviewed, with a comparative study of their speeds of convergence, and a new algorithm for the computation of nonzero-sum game equilibria is presented.

Chapter 5 of the volume illustrates the open-loop Stackelberg equilibrium solution by means of specific economic examples arising in a regional investment allocation problem. The study leads to interesting economic interpretations, and a number of theoretical questions. Chapter 6 provides an in-depth survey on the applications of dynamic game theory to macroeconomics, covering primarily areas such as economic growth and income distribution, macroeconomic stabilization, modeling of interaction between government and private sector, international policy coordination, and conflicts among sectors of an economy. Chapter 7 deals with the analysis of a number of issues in international policy making, by applying the framework of dynamic game theory to a dynamic inflationary model of two independent economies.

In this model, the objective of each policy maker is taken to reflect a trade-off between the rate of inflation and unemployment in his country, and the equilibrium is studied under feedback Nash, feedback Stackelberg and feedback consistent conjectural variations type of behavior, comparatively and numerically.

Chapter 8 is a comprehensive survey on optimal dynamic pricing in oligopolistic markets, and it provides a critical evaluation of the role of differential game theory in such applications. Chapter 9 deals with a specific model of dynamic advertising and pricing in an oligopoly, and obtains open-loop Nash equilibrium solutions. Chapter 10 surveys some dynamic game theory models of fishery management, and discusses the noncooperative feedback Nash and the cooperative Nash bargaining solutions in this context. The final chapter, Chapter 11, is devoted to a differential game theoretic modeling and analysis of the problem of common property exploitation under random hazards of extinction. The focus is on long run behavior, stationary policies, and a comparison of noncooperative and cooperative solutions, using a differential game model involving a jump process.

Even though this volume is not exhaustive in the choice of topics on economic applications of dynamic games, it does cover a rather broad spectrum in both theory and applications, and should therefore be useful to researchers in mathematical economics, operations research, systems and control, and differential games. I would like to thank the authors for their contributions both to this volume and to the invited sessions on "Dynamic Game Theory and Applications in Economics" at the 7th Annual Conference on Economic Dynamics and Control in London. I am sure every chapter in this volume has benefited from the stimulating discussions conducted during and after the paper presentations at the Conference.

My sincere thanks also go to Ms. Dixie Murphy for the secretarial undertaking and the editorial assistance during all phases of this project.

October 1985
Urbana, Illinois, USA

Tamer Başar

LIST OF CONTRIBUTING AUTHORS

BAGCHI, A.
Twente University of Technology, Dept. of Applied Math
7500 AE Enschede Netherlands

BAŞAR, T.
University of Illinois, Coordinated Science Laboratory
Urbana, Illinois 61801 USA

BRETON, M.
GERAD, École des Hautes Études Commerciales
Montreal, Quebec H3T 1V6 Canada

CLEMHOUT, S.
Cornell University
Ithaca, New York 14853 USA

de ZEEUW, A.
Tilburg University
5000 LE Tilburg Netherlands

DOCKNER, E.
University of Economics, Institute of Economic Theory
and Policy, Augasse 2-6, Vienna Austria

d'OREY, V.
University of Illinois, Department of Economics
Champaign, Illinois 61820 USA

EHTAMO, H.
Helsinki University of Technology, Systems Analysis Lab
02150 Espoo Finland

FEICHTINGER, G.
University of Technology, Institute of Econometrics
and Operations Research, A-1040,
Argentinierstraße 8, Vienna Austria

FILAR, J. A.
The Johns Hopkins University, Dept. of Mathematical
Sciences
Baltimore, Maryland 21218 USA

HÄMÄLÄINEN, R. P.
Helsinki University of Technology, Systems Analysis Lab
02150 Espoo Finland

HAURIE, A.
GERAD, École des Hautes Études Commerciales
Montreal, Quebec H3T 1V6 Canada

JØRGENSEN, S.
Institute of Theoretical Statistics, Copenhagen School
of Economics and Business Administration
DK-1925, Frederiksberg C (Copenhagen) Denmark

KAITALA, V.
Helsinki University of Technology, Systems Analysis Lab
02150 Espoo Finland

MEIJDAM, L.
Tilburg University
5000 LE Tilburg Netherlands

POHJOLA, M.
University of Helsinki, Department of Economics
00100 Helsinki Finland

SCHULTZ, T. A.
The Johns Hopkins University, Dept. of Mathematical
Sciences
Baltimore, Maryland 21218 USA

TURNOVSKY, S. J.
University of Illinois, Department of Economics
Champaign, Illinois 61820 USA

WAN, JR., H.
Cornell University
Ithaca, New York 14853 USA

TABLE OF CONTENTS

A TUTORIAL ON DYNAMIC AND DIFFERENTIAL GAMES

Tamer Başar
Coordinated Science Laboratory
University of Illinois
1101 W. Springfield Avenue
Urbana, Illinois 61801/USA

Abstract

A general formulation of dynamic and differential games is given, which includes both discrete and continuous time problems as well as deterministic and stochastic games. Solution concepts are introduced in two categories, depending on whether the dynamic game is defined in normal or extensive form. For the former, we present the Nash, Stackelberg and Consistent Conjectural Variations (CCV) equilibria, with considerable discussion devoted to the CCV solution, including comparisons with other more specific definitions found in the literature. For games in extensive form, we discuss the feedback solution concepts, and elaborate on the time consistency issue, which is currently of major interest in the economics literature. The chapter concludes with a discussion which puts into proper perspective the topics and contributions of the ten papers to follow, and their relationships with each other.

1. Introduction and Main Ingredients

Dynamic game theory provides a framework for a quantitative modeling and analysis of the interactions of economic agents among themselves and with the (uncertain) environment, and sets the appropriate mathematical tools for arriving at "optimal" decisions under varying behavioral stipulations. The basic ingredients of such a quantitative theory are the following:

(1) The number of economic agents (synonymously, decision makers or players): $(1,2,\ldots,n) \triangleq \mathbf{N}$, where $\mathbf{N}$ will be called the *player set*, and each agent will be denoted generically by i.

(2) The *time interval* on which the decision process is defined: $\Xi = [0,t_f]$. This could be a discrete interval, which corresponds to the situation when decisions are made at discrete instants of time: $0 = t_0, t_1, t_2, \ldots, t_f$; or it could be a continuous interval, which corresponds to the case when decisions are made throughout

the time interval $[0,t_f]$. The former characterizes, along with other ingredients, a "discrete-time (dynamic) game" (synonymously, "difference game"), whereas the latter leads to a "continuous-time (dynamic) game" also known as a "differential game."

(3) *Decision* (control) *variable* for each agent: $u_i \in \mathbb{U}_i$, $i \in \mathbb{N}$, where $\mathbb{U}_i$ is the decision space of agent i. In a dynamic game, u_i depends on the time variable t, $u_i = u_i(t)$, and for each $t \in \Xi$, $u_i(t) \in U_i$, where U_i is also called the decision or action space; this is the set in which the decision variable takes values for each fixed $t \in \Xi$.

(4) *Disturbance variable*, $w \in \mathbb{W}$, which is not under the control of the agents, but whose probabilistic description is common knowledge to all agents. For each $t \in \Xi$, we will let $w(t) \in W$, where W is some appropriate set.

(5) *Information structure*, $\eta = (\eta_1, \ldots, \eta_n)$, which is an appropriate mapping defined on the product space $(\underset{i \in \mathbb{N}}{X} \mathbb{U}_i) X \mathbb{W}$, satisfying some causality requirements. Here $\eta_i(t)$ represents the precise information acquired by agent i on $(u_1, \ldots, u_n, w)$ by the time point $t \in \Xi$.

(6) *Policy* (strategy) *variables*, $\gamma_i \in \Gamma_i$, $i \in \mathbb{N}$, where Γ_i is known as the policy space of agent i. It is the collection of all appropriately chosen mappings $\gamma_i : \eta \to u_i$.

(7) *Objective* (loss) *functionals*, L_i, $i \in \mathbb{N}$, which map $(\underset{i \in \mathbb{N}}{X} \mathbb{U}_i) X \mathbb{W}$ into the real line; L_i stands for the loss (or minus payoff) accrued to agent i as a result of actions taken by all the agents, and as a function of the realized value of $w \in \mathbb{W}$. These loss functionals can be transformed into cost functionals defined on the product policy space $\underset{i \in \mathbb{N}}{X} \Gamma_i$, using the relationship

$$J_i(\gamma_1, \ldots, \gamma_n) = \underset{w}{E}\{L_i(\gamma_1(\eta_1(u,w)), \ldots, \gamma_n(\eta_n(u,w)), w)\}$$

where the expectation is taken with respect to the statistics of w, defined on $\mathbb{W}$. The functionals J_i thus generated are also called objective functionals, and they correspond to the so-called *strategic* (synonymously, *normal*) form of the dynamic game.

Even though the above seven ingredients provide a complete description of an n-agent stochastic dynamic game (other than the solution concept), it has been common practice (for several reasons) to introduce an intermediate variable x, called the *state variable*, which carries some aggregate information concerning the evolution of the decision process. Such a (stochastic) variable would be defined by

$$x(t) = T_t(x(\tau),u_1(\tau),\ldots,u_n(\tau);w(\tau);\tau < t)$$

$$t > 0 \quad , \quad x(0) = x_0$$

where T is some causal (nonanticipative) mapping from $(\underset{i\in \mathbb{N}}{X} \mathbb{U}_i) X \bar{\mathbb{X}} X \mathbb{D}$ into $\bar{\mathbb{X}}$, where the latter is the so-called "state space" where the state x belongs. The variable x_0 is the initial state, which may be taken, in this general formulation, as a component of w. For each fixed t, $x(t) \in X$, where X may also be called the state space. Associated with x, is another (stochastic) variable $y_i \in \mathbb{Y}_i$, $i \in \mathbb{N}$, which is the measurement (observation) process of agent i; it is given by

$$y_i(t) = S_{it}(x(\tau),u_1(\tau),\ldots,u_n(\tau);w(\tau);\tau \leq t) \quad , \quad i \in \mathbb{N} \quad ,$$

where $S_i : (\underset{i\in \mathbb{N}}{X} \mathbb{U}_i) X \bar{\mathbb{X}} X \mathbb{D} \to \bar{\mathbb{X}}$ is some nonanticipatory mapping for each $i\in\mathbb{N}$. Let us denote by Y_i the set in which $y_i(t)$ takes values. Now, the information acquired by agent i can be expressed in terms of the measurement process $y = (y_1,\ldots,y_n)$:

$$\eta_i(t) = C_{it}(y(\tau);\tau \leq t)$$

where C_i is some appropriate nonanticipative mapping. The intermediate variable x introduced above generally admits a physical or economic interpretation, and thus it becomes more appropriate to define the loss functionals, say $\tilde{L}_i$, $i\in\mathbb{N}$, on $(\underset{i\in \mathbb{N}}{X} \mathbb{U}_i) X \bar{\mathbb{X}} X \mathbb{D}$; however, since x can in turn be expressed in terms of (u,w), this can again be transformed into functionals L_i, $i\in\mathbb{N}$, defined on the original space. The *strategic* (normal) *form* of the dynamic game, which involves only the strategy spaces $\Gamma_1,\ldots,\Gamma_n$ and the functionals $J_1,\ldots,J_n$, therefore remains intact, regardless of whether $\tilde{L}_i$ or L_i are chosen as loss functionals of the so-called *extensive form* of the game.

Two special cases of this general formulation are Differential and Difference Games with Perfect State Information (PSI):

<u>Differential Game with PSI</u>

$$\Xi = [0,t_f]$$

$$T_t(\alpha(\tau);\tau < t) = \int_0^t \alpha(\tau)d\tau$$

$$S_{it}(x(\tau),u_1(\tau),\ldots,u_n(\tau);\tau \leq t) = x(t)$$

$$L_i(\alpha) = \int_0^{t_f} f^i_\tau(\alpha(\tau))d\tau, \text{ for some } f^i.$$

Difference Game with PSI

$$\Xi = \{0,1,2,\ldots,t_f\}$$

$$T_t(\alpha(\tau),\tau < t) = \alpha(t-1)$$

$$S_{it}(x(\tau),u_1(\tau),\ldots,u_n(\tau);w(\tau);\tau \le t) = x(t)$$

$$L_i(\alpha) = \sum_{t\in\Xi} f_t^i(\alpha(t))$$

In each case the probability measure on $\mathbb{W}$ associated with the random variable w is taken to be one-point, this being common information to all agents. Hence, here we are in the realm of so-called *deterministic games*, for which three types of information structures (IS) have been prevelant in the literature during the last twenty or so years. These are:

1. $C_{it}(y(\tau);\tau \le t) = x(t)$: closed-loop no-memory or feedback IS.
2. $C_{it}(y(\tau);\tau \le t) = \{x(\tau),\tau \le t\}$: closed-loop IS (this incorporates memory).
3. $C_{it}(y(\tau);\tau \le t) = x_0$: open-loop IS.

Various extensions of these are possible in the case of stochastic dynamic games (where w is a "nonsingular" random variable or process): For stochastic games with perfect state measurements, the above three IS's are still valid, and arise frequently in applications. Other information structures involve explicitly the noisy measurements y_i, $i\in\mathbb{N}$, and are classified according to whether the measurements are shared with other agents or not. Some examples are:

4. $C_{it}(y(\tau);\tau \le t) = \{y(\tau),\tau \le t\}$: closed-loop IS with memory and total sharing of measurements.
5. $C_{it}(y(\tau);\tau \le t) = y(t)$: noisy feedback IS with total sharing of measurements.
6. $C_{it}(y(\tau);\tau \le t) = y_i(t)$: noisy feedback IS with no sharing of measurements.
7. $C_{it}(y(\tau);\tau \le t) = \{y_i(\tau),\tau \le t; y_j(\tau),\tau \le t-\varepsilon, j\in\mathbb{N}, j\ne i\}$: closed-loop IS with memory and sharing of measurements with a delay of ε time units.

2. Solution Concepts

There are two categories of solution concepts applicable to dynamic games; one of these uses the normal form of the game whereas the other one uses the extensive form. Recall that the normal (strategic) form suppresses all the informational aspects of the game and is characterized completely by policy spaces and cost functionals:

$$(\gamma_1, \gamma_2, \ldots, \gamma_n) \in \Gamma_1 X \ldots X \Gamma_n$$

$$J_i(\gamma_1, \ldots, \gamma_n) \quad , \quad i \in N \quad .$$

Hence, the solution concepts to be introduced for this form are valid irrespective of whether the game is static or dynamic, or whether it is deterministic or stochastic. We have basically three kinds of non-cooperative equilibrium solutions in the first category, as delineated below:

Solution Category 1: Normal Form Description

1. NASH EQUILIBRIUM: $(\gamma_1^*, \ldots, \gamma_n^*) \triangleq \gamma^* \in \underset{i \in N}{X} \Gamma_i$

The policy n-tuple γ^* is in *Nash equilibrium* if (and only if)

$$\gamma_i^* = \underset{\gamma_i \in \Gamma_i}{\arg\min}\, J_i(\gamma^{i*}, \gamma_i)$$

where

$$(\gamma^{i*}, \gamma_i) \triangleq (\gamma_1^*, \ldots, \gamma_{i-1}^*, \gamma_i, \gamma_{i+1}^*, \ldots, \gamma_n^*) \quad .$$

A Nash equilibrium solution is stable if it can be obtained through an iterative procedure (in policy space) and regardless of what initial choice starts the iteration. One such recursion is

$$\begin{cases} \gamma_i^* = \lim_{k \to \infty} \gamma_i^{(k)} \quad , \quad \forall \gamma_i^{(0)} \in \Gamma_i \quad , \quad i \in N \\ \gamma_i^{(k+1)} = \underset{\gamma_i \in \Gamma_i}{\arg\min}\, J_i(\gamma_1^{(k)}, \ldots, \gamma_{i-1}^{(k)}, \gamma_i, \gamma_{i+1}^{(k)}, \ldots, \gamma_n^{(k)}) \end{cases}$$

which corresponds to the scheme whereby agents update their policies simultaneously, using the most recent policies of other agents. Yet another scheme is

$$\begin{cases} \gamma_i^* = \lim_{k \to \infty} \gamma_i^{(k)} \quad , \quad \forall \gamma_i^{(0)} \in \Gamma_i \quad , \quad i \in N \\ \gamma_i^{(k+1)} = \underset{\gamma_i \in \Gamma_i}{\arg\min}\, J_i(\gamma_1^{(k+1)}, \ldots, \gamma_{i-1}^{(k+1)}, \gamma_i, \gamma_{i+1}^{(k)}, \ldots, \gamma_n^{(k)}) \end{cases}$$

where the agents update their policies in a predetermined order, using the most recent available information.

Remark 1: A Nash equilibrium solution is unique if it is stable according to any one of these two schemes; however, we should note that even a unique Nash equilibrium solution is not necessarily stable, and stability under one scheme does not imply stability under the other, unless there are only two agents. □

2. STACKELBERG EQUILIBRIUM: $n=2$; $(\gamma_1^*,\gamma_2^*) \triangleq \gamma^* \in \Gamma_1 x \Gamma_2$

A pair of policies γ^* is in Stackelberg equilibrium with Agent 1 as the <u>leader</u> (and Agent 2 as the <u>follower</u>) if (and only if)

$$\gamma_1^* = \arg\min_{\gamma_1\in\Gamma_1} J_1(\gamma_1, T_2(\gamma_1))$$

$$\gamma_2^* = T_2(\gamma_1^*)$$

$$T_2(\gamma_1) \triangleq \arg\min_{\gamma_2\in\Gamma_2} J_2(\gamma_1,\gamma_2) \quad , \quad \forall\gamma_1\in\Gamma_1 \quad ,$$

where the underlying assumption has been that the mapping $T_2 : \Gamma_1 \to \Gamma_2$ as defined above (called the "reaction function of the follower") is unique. If this uniqueness assumption does not hold, an alternative definition is

$$\gamma_1^* = \arg\min_{\gamma_1\in\Gamma_1} \sup_{\gamma_2\in R_2(\gamma_1)} J_1(\gamma_1,\gamma_2)$$

$$\gamma_2^* \in R_2(\gamma_1^*)$$

where $R_2(\gamma_1) \subset \Gamma_2$ is the reaction set for Agent 2, defined by

$$R_2(\gamma_1) = \{\hat{\gamma}_2\in\Gamma_2 : J_2(\hat{\gamma}_2,\gamma_1) \le J_2(\gamma_2,\gamma_1) \ , \ \forall\gamma_2\in\Gamma_2\}$$

Note that this refers to a "worst case" approach for the leader, which safeguards the leader's losses against worst choices out of the set $R_2(\gamma_1)$.

Remark 2: If the mapping T_2 is unique, it can be shown that the Stackelberg solution for the leader leads to no worse performance (for him) than any one of the Nash solutions; however, this property does not necessarily hold when R_2 is not a singleton [see, Başar and Olsder (1982)]. □

Remark 3: The Stackelberg solution can be extended to the case of $n>2$ agents, by introducing several levels of hierarchy and appropriate solution concepts among agents occupying the same level of hierarchy. See, Başar and Olsder (1982) for details. □

It may seem at the outset that the Stackelberg solution is not an "equilibrium solution." However, it can be shown that [see, Başar and Haurie (1984)] the Stackelberg solution of a static (or dynamic) game is equivalent to one of the Nash equilibrium solutions (so-called <u>strong</u> (feedback) <u>Nash equilibrium solution</u>) of a related dynamic game. To see this relationship, let us consider the following two illustrative examples.

Example 1: Here we have a static two player finite game with cost matrix

$u_1 \backslash u_2$	0	1
0	(1,3)	(0,2) *
1	(2,0)	(-1,1)

were the agents have two choices each and the ordered pairs of each entry of the matrix denote the corresponding costs to Agents 1 and 2. The game has no Nash equilibrium solution (in pure policies), but admits a unique Stackelberg solution with Agent 1 as the leader:

$$(u_1^*, u_2^*) = (0,1)$$

which corresponds to the cost pair (0,2).

Now, to construct the related dynamic game for which this constitutes a Nash equilibrium solution, we take the strategies as

γ_1 : constant

γ_2 : $U_1 \to U_2$

which involves a dynamic information pattern for the second agent (the follower). The extensive form of the original game under this (Stackelberg) information pattern is

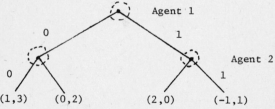

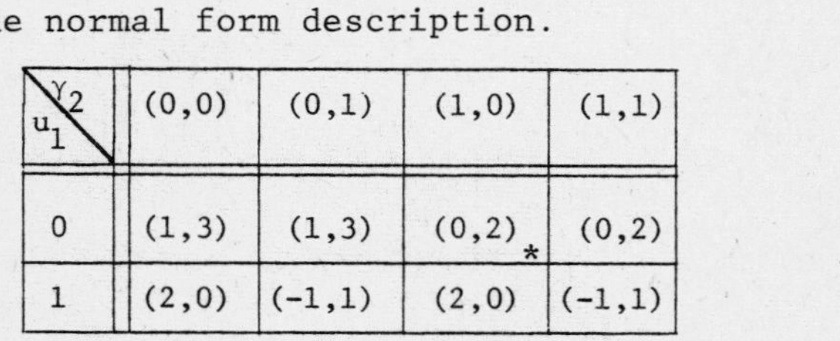

which admits the normal form description.

$u_1 \backslash \gamma_2$	(0,0)	(0,1)	(1,0)	(1,1)
0	(1,3)	(1,3)	(0,2) *	(0,2)
1	(2,0)	(-1,1)	(2,0)	(-1,1)

where $\gamma_2 = (a,b)$ stands for the convention that Agent 2 plays $u_2 = a$ when Agent 1 chooses $u_1 = 0$, and $u_2 = b$, otherwise. This (2x4) bi-matrix game admits a unique Nash equilibrium solution as indicated, which corresponds to the Stackelberg solution of the static 2x2 bi-matrix game.

This is also the so-called "feedback Nash equilibrium solution" of the extensive form, which is a solution concept belonging to Category 2, yet to be introduced.

Example 2: Consider again a bi-matrix game, namely,

u_1 \ u_2	L	M	R
L	$(0,-1)_*$	(2,1)	$(\frac{3}{2}, -\frac{2}{3})$
R	(1,2)	$(1,0)_N$	(3,1)

This static game admits a unique Stackelberg solution with Agent 1 as leader:

$$(u_1^*, u_2^*) = (L,L) \Rightarrow (0,-1) \quad ;$$

and a unique Nash solution:

$$(u_1^*, u_2^*) = (R,M) \Rightarrow (1,0) \quad .$$

Its dynamic version, under the Stackelberg information pattern, admits the extensive form description

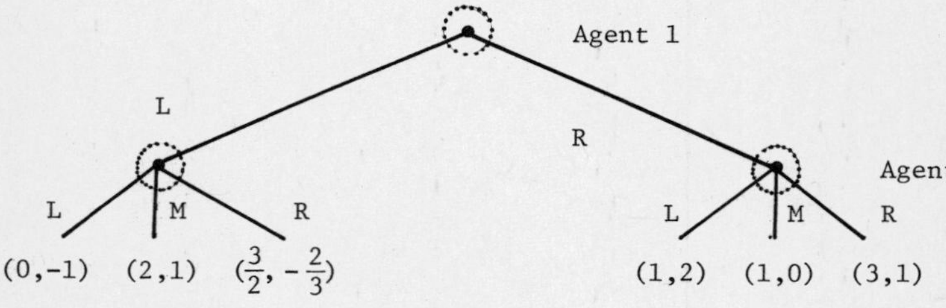

whose normal (strategic) form description is the 2x9 bi-matrix game

u_1 \ γ_2	LL	LM	LR	ML	MM	MR	RL	RM	RR
L	(0,-1)	$(0,-1)_*$	(0,-1)	(2,1)	(2,1)	(2,1)	$(\frac{3}{2}, -\frac{2}{3})$	$(\frac{3}{2}, -\frac{2}{3})$	$(\frac{3}{2}, -\frac{2}{3})$
R	(1,2)	(1,0)	(3,1)	(1,2)	$(1,0)^\dagger$	(3,1)	(1,2)	$(1,0)^\dagger$	(3,1)

The Stackelberg solution of the static version is indeed a Nash equilibrium solution of this bi-matrix game (the "starred" entry); however, the game admits two other Nash equilibria, both corresponding to the Nash equilibrium solution of the original static game (those indicated by "asterisks"). The "starred" one can be singled out as being the only feedback (strong) Nash equilibrium of the extensive form.

3. CONSISTENT CONJECTURAL VARIATIONS (CCV) EQUILIBRIUM: $n=2$; $(\gamma_1^c, \gamma_2^c) \triangleq \gamma^c \in \Gamma_1 x \Gamma_2$.

The CCV solution which is defined primarily for two-player games, has attracted considerable attention in the economics literature in recent years, and different versions of it have been introduced by different authors. The debate still continues.

Introduction of the CCV equilibrium concept stems from a dissatisfaction with the Nash solution concept, the claim being that the Nash equilibrium concept is contradictory within itself, making certain assumptions initially and not checking validity of these after the solution has been computed. More specifically, in the two-agent case, assuming existence of a unique Nash equilibrium solution γ^*, this can be computed as the unique fixed point of the equation

$$\begin{cases} \gamma_1 = T_1(\gamma_2) \\ \gamma_2 = T_2(\gamma_1) \end{cases}$$

where

$$\begin{cases} T_1(\gamma_2) = \arg\min_{\gamma_1 \in \Gamma_1} J_1(\gamma_1, \gamma_2) \\ T_2(\gamma_1) = \arg\min_{\gamma_2 \in \Gamma_2} J_2(\gamma_1, \gamma_2) \end{cases} .$$

Equivalently,

$$\gamma_1 = T_1 o T_2(\gamma_1)$$

$$\gamma_2 = T_2 o T_1(\gamma_2) \qquad ;$$

in other words, in computing his Nash equilibrium policy, each agent assumes a certain rationality in the way his co-player will respond to his policy choices. However, this working assumption is not utilized in the actual construction of policies, leading to an apparent inconsistency. This feature is more pronounced if the Nash equilibrium solution is stable and is computed according to

$$\gamma_i^* = \lim_{k\to\infty} \gamma_i^{(k)} \quad , \quad i=1,2,$$

where

$$\gamma_i^{(k+1)} = T_i(\gamma_j^{(k)}) \quad , \quad i,j=1,2 \; ; \; j\neq i \quad .$$

Here, at each step of the iteration, each agent acts under the assumption that the other agent will stick to his policy computed at the previous step, while such an assumption is clearly violated in the actual play. Hence, the initial behavioral assumption is not consistent with the actual moves and their consequences. An alternative behavioral assumption on the part of each agent, which would also retain consistency, is the following:

Let $\tau_1 x \tau_2$ be the class of all mappings (T_1, T_2), $T_1 : \Gamma_2 \to \Gamma_1$, $T_2 : \Gamma_1 \to \Gamma_2$, with the property that composite maps $T_1 o T_2$ and $T_2 o T_1$ have unique fixed points. For a given pair $(T_1^c, T_2^c) \in \tau_1 x \tau_2$, let $(\gamma_1^c, \gamma_2^c) \in \Gamma_1 x \Gamma_2$ denote the unique fixed points, satisfying

$$\gamma_1^c = T_1^c o T_2^c(\gamma_1^c)$$

$$\gamma_2^c = T_2^c o T_1^c(\gamma_2^c) \quad .$$

Introduce $(\hat{\gamma}_1, \hat{\gamma}_2) \in \Gamma_1 x \Gamma_2$ through

$$\hat{\gamma}_1 = \arg\min_{\gamma_1 \in \Gamma_1} J_1(\gamma_1, T_2^c(\gamma_1))$$

$$\hat{\gamma}_2 = \arg\min_{\gamma_2 \in \Gamma_2} J_2(T_1^c(\gamma_2), \gamma_2) \quad .$$

Since

$$T_1^c(\gamma_2) = \gamma_1^c + \underbrace{T_1^c(\gamma_2) - T_1^c(\gamma_2^c)}_{\Delta T_1^c(\gamma_2)}$$

$$T_2^c(\gamma_1) = \gamma_2^c + \underbrace{T_2^c(\gamma_1) - T_2^c(\gamma_1^c)}_{\Delta T_2^c(\gamma_1)} \quad ,$$

we can rewrite $\hat{\gamma}_1$ and $\hat{\gamma}_2$ in the functional form

$$\hat{\gamma}_1 = g_1^{\Delta T_2^c}(\gamma_2^c)$$

$$\hat{\gamma}_2 = g_2^{\Delta T_1^c}(\gamma_1^c)$$

where

$$g_1^{\Delta T_2^c} = \arg\min_{\gamma_1 \in \Gamma_1} J_1(\gamma_1, \gamma_2 + \Delta T_2^c(\gamma_1))$$
$$: \Gamma_2 \to \Gamma_1$$

$$g_2^{\Delta T_1^c} = \arg\min_{\gamma_2} J_2(\gamma_1 + \Delta T_1^c(\gamma_2), \gamma_2)$$
$$: \Gamma_1 \to \Gamma_2$$

which could again be interpreted as reaction functions of Agents 1 and 2, respectively. We are now in a position to introduce a CCV equilibrium in general terms:

Using the preceding notation, a pair of reaction functions $(T_1^c, T_2^c) \in \tau_1 x \tau_2$, along with their unique fixed point $(\gamma_1^c, \gamma_2^c) \in \Gamma_1 x \Gamma_2$, constitute a *consistent conjectural variations equilibrium* if (and only if)

$$\left.\begin{aligned} g_1^{\Delta T_2^c} &= T_1^c \\ g_2^{\Delta T_1^c} &= T_2^c \end{aligned}\right\} \qquad \text{consistency of reaction functions}$$

and

$$\left.\begin{aligned} \hat{\gamma}_1 &= \gamma_1^c \\ \hat{\gamma}_2 &= \gamma_2^c \end{aligned}\right\} \qquad \text{consistency of policies} \quad .$$

Remark 4: In the most general case, it may be impossible to validate consistency of the reaction functions, though this may be possible to any "order" under appropriate smoothness conditions on J_1 and J_2 (this will be further discussed in the sequel). Consistency of policies, on the other hand, is more readily testable. □

To gain more insight into our definition of CCV equilibrium, let us take $\Gamma_1 = \Gamma_2 = \mathbb{R}$, and J_1 and J_2 to be continuously differentiable and strictly convex (jointly) in their arguments. Furthermore, let $\tau_1 x \tau_2$ be chosen such that $J_1(\cdot, T_2(\cdot))$ and $J_2(T_1(\cdot), \cdot)$ are strictly convex in their arguments, for every pair $(T_1, T_2) \in \tau_1 x \tau_2$. To save from indices, let $\gamma_1 = u$, $\gamma_2 = v$. Then, a pair of reaction functions $(T_1^c, T_2^c) \in \tau_1 x \tau_2$ are in CCV equilibrium if (and only if)

$$\frac{\partial J_1(u,v)}{\partial u} + \frac{\partial J_1(u,v)}{\partial v} \cdot \frac{\partial T_2^c(u)}{\partial u} \equiv 0 \quad , \quad \text{for } u = T_1^c(v) \tag{i}$$

$$\frac{\partial J_2(u,v)}{\partial v} + \frac{\partial J_2(u,v)}{\partial u} \cdot \frac{\partial T_1^c(v)}{\partial v} \equiv 0 \quad , \quad \text{for } v = T_2^c(u) \quad . \tag{ii}$$

Note that these are two coupled partial differential equations which are, in general, difficult to solve. To gain some further insight, we expand these around the CCV solution (u^c, v^c) and perform a local analysis. Firstly, to third order in v:

$$T_1^c(v) \cong u^c + \frac{dT_1^c(v^c)}{dv}(v - v^c) + \frac{1}{2}\frac{d^2T_1^c(v^c)}{dv^2}(v - v^c)^2 + \frac{1}{6}\frac{d^3T_1^c(v^c)}{dv^3}(v - v^c)^3$$

and likewise, to third order in u:

$$T_2^c(u) \cong v^c + \frac{dT_2^c(u^c)}{du}(u - u^c) + \frac{1}{2}\frac{d^2T_2^c(u^c)}{du^2}(u - u^c)^2 + \frac{1}{6}\frac{d^3T_2^c(u^c)}{du^3}(u - u^c)^3 \quad .$$

Now, rewriting (i)

$$\frac{\partial J_1(T_1^c(v), v)}{\partial u} + \frac{\partial J_1(T_1^c(v), v)}{\partial v} \cdot \frac{\partial T_2^c(T_1^c(v))}{\partial u} \equiv 0 \quad , \quad v \in \mathbb{R} \quad ,$$

and using the above expansion for $T_1^c(v)$ around $v = v^c$, we arrive at:
zero'th order

$$\frac{\partial J_1(u^c, v^c)}{\partial u} + \frac{\partial J_1(u^c, v^c)}{\partial v} \cdot \frac{dT_2^c(u^c)}{du} = 0 \quad ; \qquad (0)$$

first order (arguments at $u = u^c$, $v = v^c$)

$$\frac{\partial^2 J_1}{\partial u^2} \cdot \frac{dT_1^c}{dv} + \frac{\partial^2 J_1}{\partial u \partial v}\left[1 + \frac{dT_1^c}{dv} \cdot \frac{dT_2^c}{du}\right] + \frac{\partial^2 J_1}{\partial v^2} \cdot \frac{dT_2^c}{du} + \frac{\partial J_1}{\partial v} \cdot \frac{d^2T_2^c}{du^2} \cdot \frac{dT_1^c}{dv} = 0 \quad ; \qquad (1)$$

second order (arguments at $u = u^c$, $v = v^c$)

$$\frac{\partial^3 J_1}{\partial u^3} \cdot \left(\frac{dT_1^c}{dv}\right)^2 + \frac{\partial^3 J_1}{\partial u^2 \partial v} \cdot \frac{dT_1^c}{dv} + \frac{\partial^2 J_1}{\partial u^2} \cdot \frac{d^2T_1^c}{dv^2} + \left[\frac{\partial^3 J_1}{\partial u^2 \partial v}\frac{dT_1^c}{dv} + \frac{\partial^3 J_1}{\partial u \partial v^2}\right] \cdot \left[1 + \frac{dT_1^c}{dv}\frac{dT_2^c}{du}\right] + \frac{\partial^2 J_1}{\partial u \partial v}\left[\frac{d^2T_1^c}{dv^2} \cdot \frac{dT_2^c}{du} + \left(\frac{dT_1^c}{dv}\right)^2 \cdot \frac{d^2T_2^c}{du^2}\right] \qquad (2)$$

$$+ \frac{dT_2^c}{du} \cdot \left[\frac{\partial^3 J_1}{\partial v^3} + \frac{\partial^3 J_1}{\partial v^2 \partial u} \cdot \frac{dT_1^c}{dv}\right] + \left[2\frac{\partial^2 J_1}{\partial v^2} + \frac{\partial^2 J_1}{\partial u \partial v} \cdot \frac{dT_1^c}{dv}\right] \frac{d^2 T_2^c}{du^2} \cdot \frac{dT_1^c}{dv}$$

$$+ \frac{\partial J_1}{\partial v} \cdot \frac{d^3 T_2^c}{du^3} \left(\frac{dT_1^c}{dv}\right)^2 + \frac{\partial J_1}{\partial v} \cdot \frac{d^2 T_2^c}{du^2} \cdot \frac{d^2 T_1^c}{dv^2} = 0 \quad ;$$

where we assume that derivatives of all required orders exist. Likewise, rewriting (ii)

$$\frac{\partial J_2(u, T_2^c)u))}{\partial v} + \frac{\partial J_2(u, T_2^c(u))}{\partial u} \cdot \frac{\partial T_1^c(T_2^c(u))}{\partial v} \equiv 0 \quad , \quad u \in \mathbb{R} \quad ,$$

and using the expansion for $T_2^c(u)$ around $u = u^c$, we have:

zero'th order

$$\frac{\partial J_2(u^c, v^c)}{\partial v} + \frac{\partial J_2(u^c, v^c)}{\partial u} \cdot \frac{dT_1^c(v^c)}{dv} = 0 \quad ; \qquad (0')$$

first order (arguments at $u = u^c$, $v = v^c$)

$$\frac{\partial^2 J_2}{\partial v^2} \cdot \frac{dT_2^c}{du} + \frac{\partial^2 J_2}{\partial u \partial v}\left[1 + \frac{dT_2^c}{du} \cdot \frac{dT_1^c}{dv}\right] + \frac{\partial^2 J_2}{\partial u^2} \cdot \frac{dT_1^c}{dv} + \frac{\partial J_2}{\partial u} \cdot \frac{d^2 T_1^c}{dv^2} \cdot \frac{dT_2^c}{du} = 0 \; ; \qquad (1')$$

second order (arguments at $u = u^c$, $v = v^c$)

$$\frac{\partial^3 J_2}{\partial v^3} \cdot \left(\frac{dT_2^c}{du}\right)^2 + \frac{\partial^3 J_2}{\partial v^2 \partial u} \cdot \frac{dT_2^c}{du} + \frac{\partial^2 J_2}{\partial v^2} \cdot \frac{d^2 T_2^c}{du^2} + \left[\frac{\partial^3 J_2}{\partial u \partial v^2} \cdot \frac{dT_2^c}{du} + \frac{\partial^3 J_2}{\partial v \partial u^2}\right]$$

$$\left[1 + \frac{dT_1^c}{dv} \cdot \frac{dT_2^c}{du}\right] + \frac{\partial^2 J_2}{\partial u \partial v}\left[\frac{d^2 T_2^c}{du^2} \cdot \frac{dT_1^c}{dv} + \left(\frac{dT_2^c}{du}\right)^2 \cdot \frac{d^2 T_1^c}{dv^2}\right] \qquad (2')$$

$$+ \left[\frac{\partial^3 J_2}{\partial u^3} + \frac{\partial^3 J_2}{\partial u^2 \partial v} \cdot \frac{dT_2^c}{du}\right] \cdot \frac{dT_1^c}{dv} + \left[2\frac{\partial^2 J_2}{\partial u^2} + \frac{\partial^2 J_2}{\partial u \partial v} \cdot \frac{dT_2^c}{du}\right] \cdot \frac{d^2 T_1^c}{dv^2} \cdot \frac{dT_2^c}{du}$$

$$+ \frac{\partial J_2}{\partial u} \cdot \frac{d^3 T_1^c}{dv^3}\left(\frac{dT_2^c}{du}\right)^2 + \frac{\partial J_2}{\partial u} \cdot \frac{d^2 T_1^c}{dv^2} \cdot \frac{d^2 T_2^c}{du^2} = 0 \quad .$$

In view of these relationships, we now refine the definition of CCV equilibrium for thrice continuously differentiable cost functions J_1 and J_2:

Definition (0): A pair of conjectured response functions (T_1^c, T_2^c) is in CCV equilibrium to zero'th order if (and only if) (0) and (0´) are satisfied. □

Definition (1): A pair of conjectured response functions (T_1^c, T_2^c) is in CCV equilibrium to <u>first order</u> if (and only if) (0)-(1) and (0´)-(1´) are satisfied. □

Definition (2): A pair of conjectured response functions (T_1^c, T_2^c) is in CCV equilibrium to <u>second order</u> if (and only if) (0)-(2) and (0´)-(2´) are satisfied. □

It should be clear from the above how these definitions for the CCV equilibrium can be extended to arbitrary order, provided that J_1 and J_2 are continuously differentiable up to that order.

We now make a number of observations which are essential for the proper understanding (and interpretation) of the available results in the literature on CCV equilibrium, in our general context.

Observation 1: The (Cournot) Nash equilibrium (u^*, v^*) where each player takes the policy of the other player as given (and fixed) is a zero'th order CCV equilibrium, with

$$T_1^c(v) \equiv u^* \quad , \quad T_2^c(u) \equiv v^* \quad .$$

It is also a first order CCV equilibrium under the set of restrictive conditions

$$\frac{\partial^2 J_1(u^*, v^*)}{\partial u \partial v} = 0 \quad ; \quad \frac{\partial^2 J_2(u^*, v^*)}{\partial u \partial v} = 0 \quad .$$

For (u^*, v^*) to be a second order CCV equilibrium, also the set of conditions

$$\frac{\partial^3 J_1(u^*, v^*)}{\partial u \partial v^2} = 0 \quad ; \quad \frac{\partial^3 J_2(u^*, v^*)}{\partial v \partial u^2} = 0 \quad ,$$

has to be satisfied. Since the latter two of conditions are overly restrictive, we can comfortably say that generically the Nash equilibrium solution defined earlier in this paper is a zero'th order CCV equilibrium; hence, the open-loop, closed-loop and feedback Nash equilibria for dynamic games (using the terminology of Başar and Olsder (1982)) are all zero'th order CCV solutions [see, also Fershtman and Kamien (1985) for some discussion on why these equilibria are CCV solutions, where CCV is defined in some other (more restrictive) way].

Observation 2: If we take J_1 and J_2 to be jointly quadratic in (u,v), and $T_1^c(v)$ and $T_2^c(u)$ to be affine in their arguments, then (2) and (2´) become identically zero (and so do higher (than two) order conditions), thus implying that for quadratic games one may search CCV equilibrium in the class of affine reaction functions. Note that for such functions, the convexity restriction imposed earlier on $\tau_1 x \tau_2$ is also satisfied.

Now, for quadratic games and with affine reaction functions, (1) and (1´) take the simpler forms

$$(*)\quad \begin{cases} \dfrac{\partial^2 J_1}{\partial u^2}\cdot\dfrac{dT_1^c}{dv}+\dfrac{\partial^2 J_1}{\partial u\partial v}\left[1+\dfrac{dT_1^c}{dv}\cdot\dfrac{dT_2^c}{du}\right]+\dfrac{\partial^2 J_1}{\partial v^2}\cdot\dfrac{dT_2^c}{du}=0 \\[2ex] \dfrac{\partial^2 J_2}{\partial v^2}\cdot\dfrac{dT_2^c}{du}+\dfrac{\partial^2 J_2}{\partial u\partial v}\left[1+\dfrac{dT_2^c}{du}\cdot\dfrac{dT_1^c}{dv}\right]+\dfrac{\partial^2 J_2}{\partial u^2}\cdot\dfrac{dT_1^c}{dv}=0 \end{cases},$$

from which $\dfrac{dT_1^c(v^c)}{dv}$ and $\dfrac{dT_2^c(u^c)}{du}$ have to be solved. Many authors [e.g. Kamien and Schwartz (1983), Bresnahan (1981)] have introduced and used the CCV equilibrium concept through the above set of equations, and have asserted that this is applicable in the general class of games; our analysis above shows that if the conjectured response function are not affine, this is not the correct set of equations, because there are additional terms representing the contribution of higher order derivatives of T_1^c and T_2^c to the CCV solution. Furthermore, if J_1 and J_2 are not quadratic, first-order equations do not completely characterize the solution, and higher order equations have to be solved.

Returning back to (*) for quadratic J_1 and J_2, we substitute dT_1^c/dv from the first into the second, to obtain the quadratic equation

$$(dT_2^c/du)^2 + b(dT_2^c/du) + c = 0$$

where

$$b = \frac{(\partial^2 J_1/\partial u^2)(\partial^2 J_2/\partial v^2) - (\partial^2 J_2/\partial u^2)(\partial^2 J_1/\partial v^2)}{(\partial^2 J_1/\partial u\partial v)(\partial^2 J_2/\partial v^2) - (\partial^2 J_1/\partial v^2)(\partial^2 J_2/\partial u\partial v)}$$

$$c = \frac{(\partial^2 J_1/\partial u^2)(\partial^2 J_2/\partial u\partial v) - (\partial^2 J_2/\partial u^2)(\partial^2 J_1/\partial u\partial v)}{(\partial^2 J_1/\partial u\partial v)(\partial^2 J_2/\partial v^2) - (\partial^2 J_1/\partial v^2)(\partial^2 J_2/\partial u\partial v)} .$$

Depending on the relative magnitudes of b^2 and $4c$, this quadratic equation may or may not admit a real solution. If it does not, then this implies that either the problem does not admit a CCV solution, or the CCV response functions are nonlinear in their arguments.

Observation 3: As we have discussed earlier, the zero'th order CCV solution can be obtained iteratively, under a condition of "stability." It is not at all clear, even for quadratic games, whether such an iterative computation exists for the first-order CCV solution, and what the corresponding conditions are. □

Remark 5: One could envision extensions of the CCV equilibrium as given here to games with more than two players. In this case a player's reaction function depends on the policies or actions of more than one player, thus compounding the difficulty of developing a "clean" characterization of the CCV solution whenever it exists. □

Solution Category 2: Extensive Form Description

There exist a number of solution concepts developed for dynamic games, which make explicit use of the extensive form description. Before presenting these, we first introduce a general (appealing) feature shared by some of these solutions — what we call a "time consistency" property. Toward this end, let $\mathbb{G}(0,t_f)$ denote a dynamic game defined on the time interval $[0,t_f]$, and $\mathbb{G}(s,t_f)$ denote exactly the same game, but defined on a shorter time interval $[s,t_f]$. Note that an underlying implicit assumption here is that the truncation of the original game to the time interval $[s,t_f]$ is a well-defined operation — this being so for all s, $0 < s < t_f$.

Let S be an operator which produces for each such game a unique policy n-tuple belonging to the appropriate policy space of the agents; that is

$$S(\mathbb{G}(s,t_f)) = (\gamma_1,\ldots,\gamma_n)_{(s)} \triangleq \gamma_{(s)}$$

where subscript (s) indicates that the corresponding game is defined on $[s,t_f]$. We call S a *solution operator.*

Definition (3): Let $\mathbb{G}(0,t_f)$ be a dynamic game whose truncated version for every s, $0 < s < t_f$, is well-defined. A solution operator S for $\mathbb{G}$ is said to generate a <u>time-consistent</u> solution $\gamma_{(0)}$ if, for every s, $0<s<t_f$, S acting on $\mathbb{G}(s,t_f)$ generates $\gamma_{(s)}$ which is a truncated version of $\gamma_{(0)}$, that is

$$(\gamma_1(t,\eta_1(t),\ldots,\gamma_n(t,\eta_n(t)))_{(0)} \equiv (\gamma_1(t,\eta_1(t)),\ldots,\gamma_n(t,\eta_n(t)))_{(s)}$$

for all t, $s \leq t \leq t_f$.

An equilibrium solution concept is *time-consistent* if its associated solution operator S generates a time-consistent solution. □

Intuitively, time-consistent solution concepts yield equilibrium policies with the property that at no point during the course of the game would any agent (given the option of revising his policy) find it to his benefit, under the adopted solution concept, to deviate from the adopted equilibrium policy; in other words; a time-consistent equilibrium solution retains its equilibrium property throughout the course of the game. In single agent deterministic dynamic game (or synonymously, optimal control) problems, for example, the optimal open-loop solution (obtained using the minimum principle) is not time-consistent, while the optimal feedback (closed-loop) control law (obtained using the dynamic programming approach) is time-consistent. Hence, time-consistency of the solution depends very much on (i) the nature of the dynamics of the problem, (ii) the information pattern, and (iii) the structure of the cost functional(s). Again referring to optimal control problems, the one defined by

$$\left.\begin{array}{lll} \text{state equation:} & x(t+1) = f(t,x(t),u(t)) \quad , & t=0,1,2,\ldots \\ \text{information pattern:} & \eta(t) = x(t) & \\ \text{loss functional:} & \tilde{L}(x,u) = \sum_t g(t,x(t+1),u(t)) & \end{array}\right\}$$

has every $\tilde{L}$-minimizing solution time-consistent, whereas if we change the state equation to:

$$x(t+1) = f(t,x(t),x(t-1),u(t))$$

which includes an extra lag variable, the solution is no longer time-consistent. It would be time consistent if we also change the information pattern to

$$\eta(t) = \{x(t),x(t-1)\}$$

The implication of the above discussion for dynamic games is that in order to be able to come up with time-consistent equilibrium solutions, we have to impose some restrictions on the extensive form of the game in terms of the state equation, information patterns, loss functionals and the probabilistic description of the random quantities w. Toward this end, we henceforth take the information pattern to be closed-loop no-memory (synonymously, state feedback) for all agents:

$$\eta_i(t) = x(t) \quad , \quad i \in \mathbf{N} \quad ,$$

and confine our attention, for lucidity of the presentation, to deterministic games defined in discrete time. Let the time interval $[0,t_f]$ be $\{0,1,2,\ldots,t_f\}$ and the loss functionals be additively decomposed as

$$\tilde{L}_i = \sum_t g_i(t,x(t+1),u(t))$$

where

$$u \triangleq \{u_1,\ldots,u_n\} \quad .$$

Note that the game $\mathfrak{G}(s,t_f)$, defined earlier, has the loss functionals

$$\sum_{t\geq s} g_i(t,x(t+1),u(t)) \quad .$$

Now, let $\hat{S}$ denote the solution operator applied to a single stage game (such as $\mathfrak{G}(t_f-1,t_f)$), producing any one of the equilibrium solutions introduced under Category 1 (namely; Nash, Stackelberg or CCV equilibria), and consider the following recursion (with $t_f-1 = \bar{1}$, $t_f-2 = \bar{2},\ldots,t_f-m = \bar{m},\ldots,$).

Recursion (1):

$$\hat{\gamma}_{\bar{I}} \triangleq (\hat{\gamma}_{1,\bar{I}},\ldots,\hat{\gamma}_{n,\bar{I}}) = \hat{S}(\mathbb{G}(\bar{I},t_f))$$

$$\hat{\gamma}_{\bar{2}} \triangleq (\hat{\gamma}_{1,\bar{2}},\ldots,\hat{\gamma}_{n,\bar{2}}) = \hat{S}(\mathbb{G}(\bar{2},t_f)\Big|_{\gamma_{\bar{I}}=\hat{\gamma}_{\bar{I}}})$$

$$\vdots$$

$$\hat{\gamma}_{\bar{m}} = \hat{S}(\mathbb{G}(\bar{m},t_f)\Big|_{\gamma_{\bar{m}}=\hat{\gamma}_{\bar{m}},\ldots,\gamma_{\bar{I}}=\hat{\gamma}_{\bar{I}}})$$

$$\vdots$$

$$\hat{\gamma}_{\bar{0}} = \hat{S}(\mathbb{G}(0,t_f)\Big|_{\gamma_1=\hat{\gamma}_1,\ldots,\gamma_{\bar{I}}=\hat{\gamma}_{\bar{I}}}) .$$

Definition (4): For a dynamic game $\mathbb{G}(0,t_f)$ which is stagewise decomposable, a solution operator S leads to a feedback equilibrium solution if there exists an $\hat{S}$ such that

$$S(\mathbb{G}(0,t_f)) = \hat{\gamma}$$

where the latter is obtained via *Recursion (1)*. Such a solution is called feedback Nash equilibrium (respectively, feedback Stackelberg and feedback consistent conjectural variations) if $\hat{S}$ generates at each stage a Nash equilibrium (respectively, Stackelberg and CCV) solution. □

Observation 4: Feedback equilibrium solution is, by construction, time-consistent, regardless of what equilibrium concept is adopted for each individual static game encountered in the recursion. □

Remark 6: As shown in Başar and Olsder (1982), under fairly general conditions, the feedback Nash equilibrium solution is also a Nash solution for the corresponding normal form of the dynamic game under the perfect state feedback information pattern. However, this property does not hold for the feedback Stackelberg and feedback CCV solutions, and hence these two solutions cannot be obtained using the normal form of the game. As a by-product of this discussion comes out the fact that the Stackelberg and CCV solutions obtained on the normal form of a dynamic game are not time-consistent. □

The concept of feedback equilibrium (with the time-consistency property) is not necessarily restricted to deterministic games and to those with additively decomposable loss functionals. The concept is equally applicable to stochastic problems with proper correlation properties between the random variables affecting the system dynamics at different stages, and to problems with loss functionals which can be decomposed stagewise multiplicatively. Furthermore, an extension of the feedback equilibrium concept to continuous-time problems is possible, by converting the original problem to a sequence of discrete-time problems, and requiring that a proper limit exists to that sequence. Such an approach leads to the conclusion that the Nash equilibrium solution obtained for the normal form of a differential game under the perfect state feedback information pattern is also a feedback Nash equilibrium, having the time-consistency feature. The feedback Stackelberg solution (cf. Başar and Haurie (1984)), however, is different from the Stackelberg solution, with the latter not being time-consistent.

3. Mathematical Tools and General Discussion

The solution concepts introduced in the previous section directly suggest the mathematical tools which are most appropriate for dynamic/differential games under various information structures. These all involve optimization of functionals, either over time or stagewise at each point in time. The former requires results from optimal control theory to be used in this context, whereas for the latter, nonlinear programming techniques become indispensable tools. Applications of these dynamic and static optimization techniques in the deviation of Nash and Stackelberg equilibria, and the ensuing necessary and/or sufficient conditions to be satisfied by the corresponding solutions have been discussed extensively in Başar and Olsder (1982). Here we provide a nutshell description of these results and identify some outstanding challenging issues, also with reference to the contents of the following chapters.

A prime example of direct application of optimal control theory (specifically the minimum principle of Pontryagin) in dynamic game theory is the derivation of conditions for open-loop Nash equilibria in differential games. The discrete-time counterpart of the minimum principle is likewise applicable to open-loop Nash equilibria of multi-stage (discrete-time) games. In both cases, each player faces a standard optimal control problem, which is arrived at by fixing the other players' policies as some arbitrary functions. Hence, each such optimal control problem is parameterized in terms of some open-loop control policies which, however, do not alter the structure of the underlying optimization problems because of their open-loop character. Therefore, in principle, the necessary and/or sufficient conditions for open-loop Nash equilibria can be obtained by listing down the conditions required by each optimal control problem (via the minimum principle) and then requiring that these all be satisfied simultaneously. Because of the couplings that exist between these various conditions, each one corresponding to the optimal control problem faced by one player, to solve for the corresponding equilibria analytically or numerically is several orders of magnitude more difficult than to solve optimal control problems. Very few closed-form solutions exist for these game problems, one of which pertains to the case when cost functions are quadratic and the state equation is linear. There are other specially structured, one or two-dimensional problems, for which properties of the solution (such as switching behavior, asymptotic stability, finite cost, etc.) can be read off from the conditions provided by the minimum principle, through some analyses. Results along these lines have been reported in Chapter 9 by Dochner and Feichtinger, in the context of a specific problem arising in oligopolistic markets, involving dynamic advertising and pricing. Other economic applications of the open-loop Nash equilibrium concept have been discussed in Chapters 6 and 8, by Pohjola and Jørgensen, respectively, who survey the literature on the application of dynamic game theory in macroeconomics (such as economic growth and income distribution, macroeconomic stabilization, interaction between government and private sector, international policy coordination and conflicts among sectors in the economy), and optimal dynamic pricing in oligopolistic markets.

When the players have access to closed-loop state information, the feedback Nash equilibrium solution introduced in the previous section becomes more relevant, which is also appealing because of time consistency. Here, since we are dealing with feedback policies, dynamic programming takes over the role of the minimum principle, leading to a recursive derivation of the solution for finite horizon multi-stage games. This involves the solution of static Nash games at each time step, and an appropriate updating mechanism which is basically a set of difference equations. In continuous-time problems (differential games) these difference equations are replaced by partial differential equations, and the finite number of static Nash games are replaced by static games to be solved for each time point in a finite interval. Hence the numerical computation of the feedback Nash solution is much more difficult in differential games than in difference games, requiring inevitably the use of discretization (or numerical approximation) techniques. This difficulty can be mitigated, on the surface, by restricting attention to stationary policies (which are constant over time) in an attempt to capture the essence of long-term behavior of Nash equilibria in infinite horizon problems (with or without a discount factor in the cost functions). Since the resulting set of conditions are now time-invariant, and the search is over all time-invariant policies depending only on the current value of the state, the numerical computations are relatively simpler, especially for differential games. However, now additional issues such as asymptotic stability of the overall system, and finiteness of the resulting costs arise, which have to be addressed properly in the derivation of the policies. There is also the further question of whether the stationary Nash equilibrium policies (provided that they exist) can be obtained as the limit of the Nash solutions of finite horizon dynamic games. These issues have been addressed and extensively discussed in Chapter 7 by Başar, Turnovsky and d'Orey for discrete-time games, first in a general context and then in the specific context of international monetary policy making. The chapter also includes a number of numerical results on the solutions of finite and infinite-horizon Nash games, which indicate an interesting convergence pattern. Feedback Nash equilibrium has also been adopted as an appropriate solution concept in Chapter 10 (Kaitala) and Chapter 11 (Clemhout and Wan), which are devoted to dynamic game theory models and analyses arising in the exploitation of renewable resources.

The feedback and the open-loop are not the only two Nash solutions that arise in dynamic and differential games; there is a whole range of other possibilities that involve mixed information structures (incorporating memory). Derivation of Nash equilibria with memory is much more difficult than open-loop or feedback Nash equilibria, since standard techniques of optimal control and nonlinear programming do not alone provide a complete package for such derivations. Furthermore, since Nash equilibria under different information patterns lead in general to different Nash cost values for all players, with no clear rank ordering, the question of the choice of the best solution among possibly an uncountable number of them becomes an important relevant issue. This is particularly so in view of the fact that better information for one player does not necessarily imply better Nash performance for that player. Some of these issues have been discussed in Chapter 2 by Meijdam and de Zeeuw.

A second general solution concept we have introduced in the previous section is the Stackelberg solution. For the problem with two levels of hierarchy, the definition given in Section 2 directly leads to a set of necessary conditions for open-loop Stackelberg equilibrium, again by using the minimum principle. The difference from the case of the open-loop Nash equilibria is that while one set of players (the followers) solve standard open-loop optimal control problems, the others (the leaders) are confronted with a nonstandard one which takes the solutions of the former as constraints. Numerical algorithms for such problems are still in their infancy, and no general satisfactory theory (of existence, uniqueness and computation) exists today. In Chapter 5, Bagchi discusses some of these issues in the context of a number of illustrative examples which involve economic models where hierarchy arises very naturally.

Under the feedback information structure, the most appropriate "Stackelberg" solution concept is the feedback Stackelberg (FBS) solution introduced by Definition 4 in Section 2. As indicated there, this is not really a Stackelberg solution, in the sense that if the leader were able to announce his strategy at all stages (or time points) from the very beginning, then he could achieve a better performance than the one incurred under the FBS solution. However, the FBS solution is most appropriate if the leader can dominate the decision process only stage-wise and if the only information available to the leader is the current value of the state (and no memory). Furthermore, as in the case of the feedback Nash solution, the derivation of the FBS equilibrium involves the solution of a sequence of static Stackelberg games and an appropriate updating scheme. The kind of questions we raised while discussing the feedback Nash solution are also valid here, questions such as asymptotic stability of the overall system under the FBS solution (for the infinite-horizon problem), and the possibility of obtaining the FBS solution of the infinite-horizon dynamic game as the limit of solutions of a sequence of finite-horizon games. These issues have been addressed in Chapter 7, first in general terms and then through numerical computation in the context of an economic model arising in international monetary policy making.

In a Stackelberg situation, if the leader can announce and dictate his entire sequence of policies from the very beginning, then the feedback information structure is not compatible with this type of a domination structure, leading, in general, to a problem with no solution (see, Başar and Selbuz (1979)). To make this a meaningful problem, the leader will have to be endowed with some memory on the past values of the state. With such an enlarged information structure, dynamic games could admit global Stackelberg equilibrium, but the mathematical techniques needed to derive such equilibria are not of the standard type; see, for example, Papavassilopoulos and Cruz (1979) for the derivation of necessary conditions for Stackelberg solutions of differential games with memory information structures, and Başar and Selbuz (1979) for the actual derivation of global Stackelberg policies for a class of dynamic games with memory. In some cases, by using memory strategies the leader can achieve the best possible performance, as though the follower(s) was (were) cooperating with him, in which case the actual policy for the leader is some memory representation of his feedback team solution. Such closed-loop Stackelberg games are intimately related to incentive decision problems where one of the decision makers announces incentives for the other decision maker in order to influence the outcome of the decision process biased towards his desires. In order to be enforceable, such incentive policies necessarily involve the actions of the "following" decision makers as well as the information available to him, which make them both dynamic and of the memory type. Hence, deterministic incentive decision problems can be viewed as closed-loop Stackelberg games with a certain type of information structure and can be treated as such; see, for example, Ho, Luh and Olsder (1982), Zheng and Başar (1982) and Başar (1985). Some further theoretical results along these directions have been presented in Chapter 3 by Ehtamo and Hämäläinen. For counterparts of some of these results in stochastic decision problems, see Başar (1984), and Cansever and Başar (1985).

One area of research on dynamic and differential games, which requires special attention, is the development of computational algorithms for Nash, Stackelberg and CCV equilibria. For Nash equilibria, one possible class of schemes is the "iteration in policy space," introduced in Section 2 in the context of *stable* Nash equilibria. This is valid not only for deterministic games but also for stochastic ones, and the schemes introduced in Section 2 could be extended to cover cases where the decision makers update their policies under some random or chaotic ordering, provided that some conditions are fulfilled to ensure that none of the players is left out of the iteration for an "extended" period of time. To prove convergence of such schemes, one will have to adopt the framework of fixed point computations as in Baudet (1978) and Bertsekas (1983), and utilize some convergence results from Ortega and Rheinboldt (1970).

"Iteration in policy space" is an off-line scheme for the computation of Nash equilibria in dynamic/differential games. This would not be applicable to cases when the players have updated state information, (especially in stochastic decision problems) and use this information on-line to improve upon their earlier decisions by iterating in the decision space. New ideas and approaches are needed to attack these problems and to obtain implementable algorithms, for both Nash and Stackelberg equilibria, as well as for CCV equilibrium. Breton et al. review in Chapter 4 some of the existing algorithms for computation of equilibria in stochastic dynamic games with discounted cost functions, present a comparative study on speeds of convergence of these algorithms, and also develop a new algorithm.

A topic which has not been covered in this chapter, and to which little has been devoted in this volume, is "cooperative games." This is also an area of current interest for applications in economics, and development of bargaining solutions and algorithms for dynamic/differential games is a timely and important research topic. Some discussion on cooperative solutions and Nash's bargaining scheme has been included in Chapters 10 and 11.

References and Selective Bibliography

Başar, T. (1984), "Affine Incentive Schemes for Stochastic Systems with Dynamic Information," SIAM J. Control and Optimization, vol. 22, no. 2, pp. 199-210.

Başar, T. (1985), "Dynamic Games and Incentives," in Systems and Optimization, Lecture Notes in Control and Information Sciences, A. Bagchi and H. Th. Jongen (edts.), Springer-Verlag, vol. 66, pp. 1-13.

Başar, T. and A. Haurie (1984), "Feedback Equilibria in Differential Games with Structural and Modal Uncertainties," in Advances in Large Scale Systems, vol. 1, J. B. Cruz, Jr. (ed.) JAI Press Inc., pp. 163-201.

Başar, T., A. Haurie and G. Ricci (1985), "On the Dominance of Capialists Leadership in a Feedback Stackelberg Solution of a Differential Game Model of Capitalism," J. Economic Dynamics and Control, to appear.

Başar, T. and G. J. Olsder (1982), Dynamic Noncooperative Game Theory, Academic Press, London/New York.

Başar, T. and H. Selbuz (1979), "Closed-Loop Stackelberg Strategies with Applications in the Optimal Control of Multilevel Systems," IEEE Transactions on Automatic Control, vol. AC-24, no. 2, pp. 166-179.

Baudet, G. M. (1978), "Asynchronous Iterative Methods for Multiprocessors," J. Association for Computing Machines, vol. 25, no. 2, pp. 226-244.

Bertsekas, D. P. (1983), "Distributed Asynchronous Computation of Fixed Points," Mathematical Programming, vol. 27, North-Holland, pp. 107-120.

Bresnahan, T. F. (1981), "Duopoly Models with Consistent Conjectures," American Economic Review, vol 71, pp. 934-945.

Cansever, D. H. and T. Başar (1985), "Optimum/Near-Optimum Incentive Policies for Stochastic Decision Problems in the Presence of Parametric Uncertainty," Automatica, vol. 24, no. 5.

Feichtinger, G. and S. Jørgensen (1983), "Differential Game Models in Management," European J. Operational Research, vol. 14, pp. 137-155.

Fershtman, C. and M. I. Kamien (1985), "Conjectural Equilibrium and Strategy Spaces in Differential Games," in Optimal Control Theory and Economic Analysis, vol. 2, G. Feichtinger (ed.), North-Holland.

Hallett, A. J. H. (1984), "Non-cooperative Strategies for Dynamic Policy Games and the Problem of Time Inconsistency," Oxford Economic Papers, vol. 36, pp. 381-399.

Ho, Y. C., P. B. Luh and G. J. Olsder, "A Control Theoretic View on Incentives," Automatica, vol. 18, pp. 167-179.

Kamien, M. I. and N. L. Schwartz (1983), "Conjectural Variations," Canadian J. Economics, vol. 16, pp. 191-211.

Miller, M. and M. Salmon (1983), "Dynamic Games and Time Inconsistency of Optimal Policies in Open Economies," preprint.

Ortega, J. M. and W. C. Rheinboldt (1970), Iterative Solution of Nonlinear Equations in Several Variables, Academic Press, New York.

Papavassilopoulos, G. P. and J. B. Cruz, Jr. (1979), "Nonclassical Control Problems and Stackelberg Games," IEEE Transactions on Automatic Control, vol. AC-24, no. 2, pp. 155-166.

Zheng, Y. P. and T. Başar, "Existence and Derivation of Optimal Affine Incentive Schemes for Stackelberg Games with Partial Information: A Geometric Approach," International J. Control, vol. 35, no. 6, pp. 997-1012.

ON EXPECTATIONS, INFORMATION AND DYNAMIC GAME EQUILIBRIA

Lex Meijdam and Aart de Zeeuw
Tilburg University
P.O. Box 90153
5000 LE Tilburg
the Netherlands

Abstract

This paper deals with information and policy announcements in non-cooperative dynamic games. It fits in the discussion on time inconsistency of optimal policy under forward looking expectations. For some simple examples results are derived in the field of memory strategies and in the field of consistent, credible and cheating strategies.

1. Introduction

Optimization techniques developed for physical and engineering systems are often applied to the control of economic systems. The objective functional of the controller (e.g. the government) is minimized given a passive economic system. However, as Lucas (1976) has stressed, an economy is not a passive system. In an economy there are, in general, several independently acting controllers. The actions of these controllers depend on their expectations with respect to the actions of the other decision makers. Forward looking expectations ruin the standard non-anticipation property of a system. As Kydland and Prescott (1977) have noticed the optimal policy is time inconsistent.

Kydland and Prescott (1977) came more or less to the conclusion that the optimal control approach as such was under reconsideration. Later on, however, it became the common idea that the optimal control approach had to be placed in a game theory framework. The revival of dynamic game theory in economic literature was a fact. The famous result of Simaan and Cruz (1973b) that Bellman's principle of optimality does not generalize to the Stackelberg solution became known as time inconsistency.

What is actually the problem? The answer to this question has a technical side and a conceptual side. Technically speaking the problem is that dynamic programming can not be used to find the closed loop no memory Stackelberg solution. Conceptually speaking the problem is that the global Stackelberg decision model yields policies which become sub-optimal in the course of the game when reoptimizing is allowed for: in the future there can be an incentive to change the policy which was originally established. Furthermore, it is hard to defend a decision model in which the follower believes such a time inconsistent announcement of the leader.

The Stackelberg solution concept is a sequential concept: the players act one after another. The follower knows the action of the leader when he acts himself. However, the follower does not know the leaders future actions. He has to decide on the basis of the leaders announcement. Incentives to cheat arise for the leader because of the time inconsistency. Two solutions can be distinguished. Firstly, the follower believes the announcement and the leader does not cheat or reoptimize. This situation results in the global Stackelberg outcome. Secondly, a reoptimization in the future is to be expected. Oudiz and Sachs (1984) give a nice interpretation: a change in government. This outcome has to be consistent. That is to say, a future reoptimization will not lead to a change in policy. Otherwise the announcement will not be believed. The feedback stagewise Stackelberg solution, which is found by means of dynamic programming, is consistent by construction. It is also possible to formulate a consistent open-loop Stackelberg solution. The reputation of the government plays an important role here. It is an interesting idea to try to formalize the concept of reputation (see e.g. Kreps and Wilson (1982) and Barro and Gordon (1983)). In dynamic finite horizon games the loss of reputation in the course of the game can be formalized by an end-penalty.

It is important to note that these problematic aspects of the Stackelberg concept can also occur in a game where the players have to perform their actions at the same time. One of the players (e.g. the government) can try to become a Stackelberg leader by announcing his policy before it is actually played. In this type of game additional incentives to cheat arise! Generally, the leader can gain by cheating on his announcement at the time of action. It is reasonable to assume that the effect of cheating will be that the follower will not believe the announcements anymore. Three solutions can be distinguished. Firstly, the follower believes the announcement and the leader does not cheat or reoptimize. This situation results again in the Stackelberg outcome. Secondly, a reoptimization in the future is to be expected. This outcome has to be consistent. Finally, cheating is expected. In this case the announcement has to be "cheating-proof". Therefore it is necessary, but not sufficient, that the announcement is consistent. It will be shown that the Nash concept seems to be the only reasonable concept for this game. For this reason the Nash announcement can be called a credible announcement. When cheating is not expected, but occurs anyhow, several outcomes are possible. For example, the follower believes the announcement, consistent or not, but the leader cheats on his announcement. It is reasonable to assume that after this has happened the follower stops believing. All possible outcomes have to be evaluated by the leader against his expected loss of reputation.

The paper is organized as follows. Section 2 elaborates on information. Some papers (e.g. Backus and Driffill (1985)) jump very quickly from an open-loop Stackelberg framework to a feedback stagewise or dynamic programming framework in order to achieve consistency. It is true that the feedback stagewise solution concept has very nice properties (like sub-game perfectness). It presupposes, however, information on the state of the system. A change in information structure should not be justified alone on the strive for time consistency. Section 2 shows the impact of the information structure on the outcome with the help of some simple examples. Section 3 elaborates on announcements, consistency and cheating. A simple linear quadratic example is used to illustrate some possible outcomes which were described in this introduction. Section 4 is a conclusion. Definitions and propositions are brought together in an appendix.

2. On information

This section discusses the impact of the information structure on the outcome of Nash and Stackelberg games with the help of some simple examples. Papers by Starr and Ho (1969a), (1969b), Simaan and Cruz (1973a), (1973b) and Basar (1976) have particularly initiated understanding in this field. The section is organized as follows. Firstly, the terminology is briefly summarized. Secondly, some results are called to mind. Thirdly, a few examples illustrate these results and show some of the typical problems and facts outside these results.

For the moment, two types of information structures are distinguished:

- the open-loop information structure, where the players have no information on the actual state of the system; controls are a function of time and initial state.
- the closed-loop no memory or feedback information structure, where the players have perfect information on the actual state of the system; controls are a function of time and actual state.

For a fixed initial state an open-loop control is in fact only a function of time. In this case it belongs to the set of feedback controls.

Two modes of play are distinguished. In the global mode the players lay down their strategies at the beginning of the planning period. This mode is compatible with both the open-loop and the feedback information structure. In the stagewise mode the players decide at each point of time. For each state which can be reached at that point of time a strategy is formulated such that the expected loss for the remainder of the planning period is minimized. Stagewise solutions are sub-game perfect (see Selten (1975)) where a sub-game is a game over the remainder of the planning period. This mode is only compatible with the feedback information structure.

Pontryagin's minimum principle solves global open loop problems and dynamic programming solves feedback stagewise problems (see e.g. de Zeeuw (1984)). The other problems are mostly difficult to solve (see examples).

Two more rules of a non-cooperative game are distinguished:

- the players act at the same time (simultaneously); they do not know each others actions in the current and future periods when they act.
- the players act one after another (sequentially); in contrast to the simultaneous concept one of the players (the follower) knows the action of the other player (the leader) in the current period.

So far as a player does not know the actions of the other player he has to decide on the basis of expectations with respect to these actions. When these expectations turn out to be right a solution (an equilibrium) for the game results. In the simultaneous case this equilibrium is called the Nash equilibrium. In the sequential case this equilibrium is called the Stackelberg equilibrium.

In the case of two players the Stackelberg outcome is better for the leader than the Nash outcome. For the follower the outcome can be worse, but does not have to be worse.

In a strict convex linear quadratic framework the (unique) linear feedback global Nash equilibrium coincides with the feedback stagewise Nash equilibrium (see de Zeeuw (1984)). However, for a fixed initial state the open-loop Nash solution is also a feedback global solution! As will be seen below the feedback global Stackelberg concept causes problems.

Three examples will enlighten this material.

<u>Example 1</u>

Starr and Ho (1969b) constructed the game represented by figure 1. There are two players and two stages. At each stage each player has two possible controls: 0 and 1. Figure 1 shows the possible transitions and the associated costs.

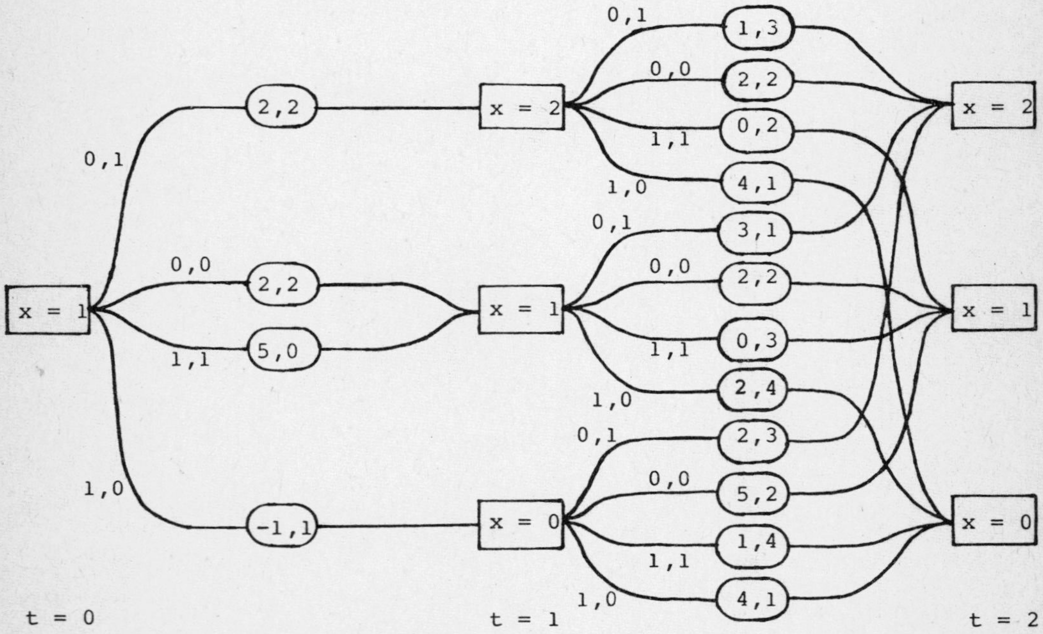

<u>Figure 1</u>

Starr and Ho end up with the following results:

a) open-loop Nash solution:

$u_1(0) = 1,\ u_2(0) = 0,$

$u_1(1) = 1,\ u_2(1) = 0,$

with costs (3,2),
where $u_i(t)$ is the action of player i at stage t.

b) feedback stagewise Nash solution:

$u_1(0,1) = 0,\ u_2(0,1) = 1,$

$u_1(1,2) = 0,\ u_2(1,2) = 0,$

$u_1(1,1) = 1,\ u_2(1,1) = 1,$

$u_1(1,0) = 1,\ u_2(1,0) = 0,$

with costs (4,4),
where $u_i(t,x)$ is the action of player i at time t in state x.

c1) feedback global Nash solution:

$u_1(0,1) = 0,\ u_2(0,1) = 1,$

$u_1(1,2) = 0,\ u_2(1,2) = 0,$

$u_1(1,1) = 1,\ u_2(1,1) = 1,$

with costs (4,4).

The last result is not completely correct. Properly speaking there are two more feedback global Nash solutions:

c2) $u_1(0,1) = 1,\ u_2(0,1) = 0,$

$u_1(1,1) = 1,\ u_2(1,1) = 0,$

$u_1(1,0) = 1,\ u_2(1,0) = 0,$

C3) $u_1(0,1) = 0,\ u_2(0,1) = 1,$

$u_1(1,2) = 0,\ u_2(1,2) = 0,$

$u_1(1,1) = 1,\ u_2(1,1) = 0.$

The solution (c2) is in fact the open-loop solution (a). Because the initial state is fixed, the open-loop strategies are only a function of time! This implies that they can be conceived as feedback strategies. The solution (c3) differs only outside the equilibrium trajectory from (c1). However, if for some reason the trajectory passes through state 1

at stage 1, only the solution (cl) will yield a Nash equilibrium for the remainder of the game. If this argument is extended to all possible states at stage 1, the feedback stagewise solution (b) results. This is the only solution which remains Nash after all possible mistakes. That is to say, this is the only solution which is sub-game perfect (see Selten (1975)) where the sub-game is the game over the remainder of the planning period.
Finally, an interesting aspect of this example is that the open-loop solution dominates the feedback solution. That is to say, the outcome is better for both players.

Example 2 (see de Zeeuw (1984)).

Consider the following two-stage linear quadratic game:

$$J_1 := \frac{1}{2}\,(u_1^2(0)+x^2(2)),$$

$$J_2 := \frac{1}{2}\,(x^2(1)+u_2^2(1)),$$

$$x(2) = x(1) + u_2(1),$$

$$x(1) = x(0) + u_1(0),$$

$$x(0) = x_0.$$

Player 2 is the leader and player 1 is the follower.

Open-loop Stackelberg solution:

$$u_1(0) = -\frac{3}{5}\,x_0,\; u_2(1) = \frac{1}{5}\,x_0,$$

with costs $(0.36\ x_0^2,\ 0.1\ x_0^2)$.

Feedback stagewise Stackelberg solution:

$$u_1(0,x) = -\frac{1}{2}\,x,\; u_2(1,x) = 0,$$

with costs $(0.25\ x_0^2,\ 0.125\ x_0^2)$.
The open-loop Stackelberg solution is time inconsistent.

Linear feedback global Stackelberg game:

suppose $u_2(1,x) = ax$;
rational reaction of the follower:

$$u_1(0,x) = -\frac{(1+a)^2}{1+(1+a)^2}\,x;$$

the leader faces the problem:

$$\text{minimize } \frac{1}{2}\left(\frac{1+a^2}{(1+(1+a)^2)^2}\,x_0^2\right);$$

it follows that the leader can enforce as low costs as he wants by choosing "a" big enough; a big "a" can be considered as an incentive for the follower to steer $x(1)$ close to zero.

There are more information structures than the two mentioned above. For example, there is the <u>closed-loop-memory</u> information structure, where controls are a function of time and the state of the system in present and past. Even in a strict convex linear quadratic framework this information structure leads to infinitely many Nash solutions (see Basar and Olsder (1982)). As will be seen in example 3 below there are closed loop memory solutions which dominate both the open-loop and feedback solution! That is to say, the outcome is better for both players. A closed loop memory Stackelberg solution can be found in Basar and Selbuz (1979).

<u>Example 3</u> (see de Zeeuw (1984)).

Consider the following two-stage strict convex linear quadratic game:

$$J_1 := \frac{1}{2}\,(x^2(0)+u_1^2(0)+x^2(1)+u_1^2(1)+x^2(2)),$$

$$J_2 := \frac{1}{2}\,(2x^2(0)+u_2^2(0)+2x^2(1)+u_2^2(1)+2x^2(2)),$$

$$x(2) = x(1) + u_1(1) + u_2(1),$$

$$x(1) = x(0) + u_1(0) + u_2(0),$$

$$x(0) = x_0.$$

Open-loop Nash solution:

$$u_1(0) = -\frac{5}{19}x_0, \; u_2(0) = -\frac{10}{19}x_0,$$

$$u_1(1) = -\frac{1}{19}x_0, \; u_2(1) = -\frac{2}{19}x_0,$$

with costs $(0.56\, x_0^2,\ 1.191\, x_0^2)$.

Feedback stagewise Nash solution:

$$u_1(0,x) = -\frac{1}{4}x, \; u_2(0,x) = -\frac{19}{36}x,$$

$$u_1(1,x) = -\frac{1}{4}x, \; u_2(1,x) = -\frac{1}{2}x,$$

with costs $(0.559\, x_0^2,\ 1.198\, x_0^2)$.

The open-loop Nash solution is time consistent in the sense that the actions $u_1(1)$ and $u_2(1)$ relate to the state $x(1)$ in the way as prescribed by the results of dynamic programming.

Consider the following class of linear closed-loop memory strategies:

$$u_1(0,x) = cx, \qquad u_2(0,x) = fx,$$

$$u_1(1,x,y) = ay + bx, \qquad u_2(1,x,y) = dy + ex,$$

where x is the observed state at stage 0 and y is the observed state at stage 1.

The Nash solutions are represented by tuples (a,b,c,d,e,f) which fit the following set of equations:

$$4q = 1 + c + f,$$

$$2qa = -10q - f,$$

$$qd = -5q - c,$$

$$b = 19q + 2f,$$

$$e = 18q + 4c.$$

For all (c,f) such that $1 + c + f \neq 0$ this set of equations yields one closed loop memory Nash solution.
For $b = e = 0$ the linear feedback global Nash solution results. It coincides with the feedback stagewise solution.
Some closed-loop memory solutions are dominated by others. The sub-set of undominated solutions is given by:

$$(c,f) = \frac{-10\mu + 19}{8\mu^2 + 2\mu - 19}(1-\mu,\mu),\ \mu \in (0,1).$$

For example, for $\mu = \frac{2}{3}$, the result is

$$u_1(0,x) = -\frac{37}{127}x, \qquad u_2(0,x) = -\frac{74}{127}x,$$

$$u_1(1,x,y) = \frac{17}{4}y - \frac{72}{127}x,\ u_2(1,x,y) = \frac{17}{4}y - \frac{76}{127}x,$$

with costs $(0.551\ x_0^2,\ 1.189\ x_0^2)$.

This closed-loop memory Nash solution dominates both the open-loop Nash solution and the feedback stagewise Nash solution!
Whatever nice properties the feedback stagewise solution may have, the fact that it can be dominated by solutions with a comparable type of information structure should at least be a matter of concern. A reconciling approach could lie in the definition of the state of the system (see e.g. Tenney (1981)).

3. On announcements, consistency and cheating.

Two earlier conclusions motivate this section. Firstly, in the global Stackelberg solution concept the leader is better off than in the Nash concept. Secondly, the Stackelberg solution is time inconsistent (except for the feedback stagewise case which is time consistent by construction).

From the first conclusion the idea was born that in the case of simultaneous acting one of the players (e.g. the government) can try to become a Stackelberg leader by making an announcement before the actual play. When the other player is "naive" and believes the announcement, the Stackelberg solution may result. However, when the other player does not give in to the attempt of the first player, he can try to force the first player back to the Nash solution by playing Nash himself.

The introduction of an announcement implies the introduction of two possibilities to cheat on the announcement. The first possibility emanates from time inconsistency. The optimal announcement generally becomes sub-optimal after some actions are performed. An incentive arises to change the original plan in the course of the game. Only a time consistent strategy is "cheating-proof" in this respect. A time consistent strategy is a strategy with the property that future reoptimizations will not lead to a change in strategy. The second possibility occurs even in a static context. The announcement generally differs from "the optimal reaction to the optimal reaction to the announcement". Only the Nash announcement is "cheating-proof" in this respect. Moreover, the Nash announcement is consistent. Therefore it will be called <u>credible.</u>

When cheating is possible the question rises whether cheating is expected. Suppose that the second player expects the first player to cheat and suppose the first player expects this, etc. A process results of optimal reactions to and fro starting from the initial considerations of the first player. The credible solution concept is the only reasonable concept for this situation.

Suppose that the second player does not expect the first player to cheat. If the first player cheats anyhow, several outcomes are possible depending on at what point of time he cheats. It is reasonable to assume that after cheating has occurred the game falls back in the Nash mode.

The player who can cheat on his announcement has a choice. If he cheats, from then on the Nash mode which is "cheating-proof" is the result. If he does not cheat, he can benefit from the Stackelberg mode and from future possibilities to cheat. After all this player has to compare a cheating gain with a loss in reputation. The loss in reputation can be conceived as a penalty on cheating. This aspect should lead to a change in the concept of credibility. Furthermore, the expectation of the other player with respect to this reputation should play a role here.

In the case of sequential acting the only cheating possibility emanates from time inconsistency in the <u>global</u> mode. The credible announcement is the consistent Stackelberg announcement.

The feedback stagewise Stackelberg solution (FBS) is consistent by construction. A reoptimization or a reconsideration of strategy in the course of the game will not lead to a change in strategy. In the case of simultaneous acting the claim for credibility yields the feedback stagewise Nash (FBN) solution.

In an open-loop information structure the claim for consistency tends to a contradictio in terminis. A reoptimization in the course of the game seems to require information on the state of the system in the course of the game which contradicts open-loop information. However, in this case the state of the system has to be seen as solely a function of the initial state and the performed actions. A consistent open-loop Stackelberg (COLS) solution can be defined along the lines of the model in Kydland and Prescott (1977). It will be clear that stochastic modelling will find difficulties here. In the case of sequential acting the claim for consistency or credibility yields the consistent open-loop Stackelberg (COLS) solution. In the case of simultaneous acting the claim for consistency gives the same solution. However, the claim for credibility leads to the open-loop Nash (OLN) solution.

It is time to schematize these considerations and to give an example.

Table 1 shows the classical point of view. Two rules of the dynamic game are emphasized:

- what information is available to the players?
- do the players act simultaneously or sequentially?

Table 2 introduces where necessary the claim for consistency.

Table 3 extends the columns of table 1 to several possibilities that emanate from considering one player to announce his strategy before the actual play. In addition, where possible, outcomes can be considered in which somewhere cheating has occurred.

	simultaneous	sequential
open-loop	OLN	OLS
feedback/stagewise	FBN	FBS

Table 1. Classical

	simultaneous	sequential
open-loop	OLN	COLS
feedback/stagewise	FBN	FBS

Table 2. Consistency

sequential	reputation	consistent	credible
open-loop feedback/stagewise	OLS FBS cheating possible	COLS FBS	COLS FBS
simultaneous	**reputation**	**consistent**	**credible**
open-loop feedback/stagewise	OLS FBS cheating possible	COLS FBS cheating possible	OLN FBN

Table 3. Announcements

OLN : open-loop Nash;
OLS : open-loop Stackelberg;
COLS: consistent open-loop Stackelberg;
FBN : feedback/stagewise Nash;
FBS : feedback/stagewise Stackelberg.

Example 4

The two-stage strict convex linear quadratic game from example 3 in section 2 is considered again. Player 2 is the player who makes the announcement.
Table 4 lists the possible solutions.

	$u_2(0)$	$u_2(1)$	$u_1(0)$	$u_1(1)$	$x(1)$	$x(2)$	J_2 (in x_0^2)	J_1 (in x_0^2)
OLS	-0.286	0	-0.429	-0.143	0.286	0.143	1.143	0.653
COLS	-0.286	-0.102	-0.408	-0.102	0.306	0.102	1.150	0.641
OLN	-0.526	-0.105	-0.263	-0.053	0.211	0.053	1.191	0.560
FBS	-0.321	-0.102	-0.374	-0.102	0.306	0.102	1.160	0.627
FBN	-0.528	-0.111	-0.25	-0.056	0.222	0.056	1.198	0.559

Table 4

It is always true in two player games that the Stackelberg outcomes are better for the leader than the Nash outcomes. In this example the follower is better off in the Nash concept.
When the information structures are compared, player 2 has lower costs in the open-loop structure and player 1 has lower costs in the feedback/stagewise structure in this example.
Suppose that the players act sequentially and player 2 announces the open-loop Stackelberg solution. In this case there is only one cheating possibility due to time inconsistency. The outcome is:

$$u_2(0) = -0.286,\ u_1(0) = -0.429\ x(1) = 0.286,\ J_2 = 1.136\ x_0^2,$$

$$u_2(1) = -0.095,\ u_1(1) = -0.095\ x(2) = 0.095,\ J_1 = 0.642\ x_0^2.$$

The cheating gain for player 2 is 0.007 x_0^2. This gain has to be compared with his loss in reputation. Note that cheating is also better for player 1!
Suppose that the players act simultaneously. In this case there are several cheating possibilities, when cheating is not expected. Table 5 lists the outcomes. The numbers I and II refer to cheating in the first and second period, respectively.

	$u_2(0)$	$u_2(1)$	$u_1(0)$	$u_1(1)$	$x(1)$	$x(2)$	J_2 (in x_0^2)	J_1 (in x_0^2)
OLS-I	-0.402	-0.085	-0.429	-0.085	0.169	0.042	1.115	0.608
OLS-II	-0.286	-0.095	-0.429	-0.142	0.286	0.048	1.129	0.644
COLS-I	-0.416	-0.088	-0.408	-0.044	0.175	0.044	1.123	0.601
COLS-II	-0.286	-0.136	-0.408	-0.102	0.306	0.068	1.148	0.638
FBS-I	-0.441	-0.093	-0.374	-0.046	0.186	0.046	1.138	0.589
FBS-II	-0.321	-0.136	-0.374	-0.102	0.306	0.068	1.159	0.624

Tabel 5.

In the open-loop information structure the best possibility for player 2 is the open-loop Stackelberg announcement with cheating in the first period. The cheating gain is 0.028 x_0^2. He should not cheat, when the penalty on cheating or the loss in reputation is equal or higher than 0.028 x_0^2. Note that player 1 has the second to lowest costs, when player 2 announces the consistent open-loop Stackelberg solution and cheats

in the first period. He achieves the lowest costs when Nash is announced (and played).
In the feedback/stagewise information structure cheating in the first period is also the best possibility. The gain is 0.022 x_0^2. The same remarks for player 1 apply.

4. Conclusion

This paper deals primarily with the possible role of information and announcements in non-cooperative dynamic games where players act simultaneously.

Open-loop and feedback/stagewise information structures, which are directly linked to the minimum principle and dynamic programming, are well understood. It is felt, however, that feedback/global and memory information structures should still be subject of concern. For example, by means of a simple two stage game it is shown that there exist many equilibria in these information structures which dominate both the classical solutions.

The analysis of announcements fits very well in the present discussion in the literature with respect to the interaction between a policy declaration by the government and the actual play by both the private sector and the government. It is tried to conceptualize when and to what extent the classical sequential solution concepts reappear. Furthermore, for a simple example the several cheating possibilities for the leader are evaluated against his loss of reputation.

All things considered the feedback/stagewise Nash solution concept seems still the most appropriate concept for applications. It is a consistent, credible or cheating-proof and sub-game perfect equilibrium. However, it presupposes state information. Moreover, when the concept of reputation can be formalized further, the leader role of the government may reappear.

5. References

Backus, D. and J. Driffill (1985), "Dynamically Consistent Policy with Forward-Looking Expectations", Discussion Papers in Economics and Econometrics, No. 8502, University of Southampton.

Barro, R.J. and D.B. Gordon (1983), "Rules, Discretion and Reputation in a Model of Monetary Policy", Journal of Monetary Economics, vol. 12, pp. 101-121.

Basar, T. (1976), "On the Uniqueness of the Nash Solution in Linear-Quadratic Differential Games", International Journal of Game Theory, vol. 5, pp. 65-90.

Basar, T. and G.J. Olsder (1982), "Dynamic Noncooperative Game Theory", Academic Press, New York.

Basar, T. and H. Selbuz (1979), "Closed-Loop Stackelberg Strategies with Applications in the Optimal Control of Multilevel Systems", IEEE Transactions on Automatic Control, vol. AC 24, no. 2, pp. 166-178.

Kreps, D.M. and R. Wilson (1982), "Reputation and Imperfect Information", Journal of Economic Theory, vol. 27, pp. 253-279.

Kydland, F. and E. Prescott (1977), "Rules rather than discretion: the inconsistency of optimal plans", Journal of Political Economy, vol. 85, pp. 473-492.

Lucas, R.E., jr. (1976), "Econometric Policy Evaluation: a Critique", Journal of Monetary Economics: Supplement I, pp. 19-46.

Oudiz, G. and J. Sachs (1984), "International Policy Coordination in Dynamic Macroeconomic Models", Working Paper No. 1417, National Bureau of Economic Research.

Selten, R. (1975), "Reexamination of the Perfectness Concept for Equilibrium Points in Extensive Games", International Journal of Game Theory, vol. 4, pp. 25-55.

Simaan, M. and J.B. Cruz, jr. (1973a), "On the Stackelberg Strategy in Nonzero-Sum Games", Journal of Optimization Theory and Applications, vol. 11, no. 5, pp. 533-555.

Simaan, M. and J.B. Cruz, jr. (1973b), "Additional Aspects of the Stackelberg Strategy in Nonzero-Sum Games", Journal of Optimization Theory and Applications, vol. 11, no. 6, pp. 613-626.

Starr, A.W. and Y.C. Ho (1969a), "Nonzero-Sum Differential Games", Journal of Optimization Theory and Applications, vol. 3, no. 3, pp. 184-206.

Starr, A.W. and Y.C. Ho (1969b), "Further Properties of Nonzero-Sum Differential Games", Journal of Optimization Theory and Applications, vol. 3, no. 4, pp. 207-219.

Tenney, R.R. (1981), "On the Concept of State in Decentralized Control", Information and Control, vol. 50, pp. 1-12.

de Zeeuw, A.J. (1984), "Difference Games and Linked Econometric Policy Models", Doctorate Thesis, Tilburg University.

Appendix

Let:

(i) $T := \{0,1,2,\ldots,t_f-1\}$ be the time axis.

(ii) $x(t) \in X$ be the state of the system at time t, $t \in \{0,1,\ldots,t_f\}$

(iii) Ω be the information set (note that $\Omega=X$ for the open-loop and the feedback information structure)

(iv) V_i be the set of input values for player i (i=1,2)

(v) $[u_i:T\times\Omega\to V_i] \in U_i$ be the control law for player i (i=1,2)

(vi) $J_i : X \times U_1 \times U_2 \to \mathbb{R}$ be the function that determines the outcome of the game for player i (i=1,2)

(vii) $[u_{i,t}:\Omega\to V_i] \in U_{i,t}$ be the restriction of the control law u_i to the time point t ($i=1,2,\ t \in T$)

(viii) $\underline{u}_{i,t} := (u_{i,o},u_{i,1},\ldots,u_{i,t-2},u_{i,t-1}) \in \underline{U}_{i,t}$ be the restriction of the control law u_i to the time interval $[0, t-1]$ ($i=1,2,\ t \in T$)

(ix) $\bar{u}_{i,t} := (u_{i,t},u_{i,t+1},\ldots,u_{i,t_f-2},u_{i,t_f-1}) \in \bar{U}_{i,t}$ be the restriction of the control law u_i to the time interval $[t, t_f-1]$ ($i=1,2,\ t \in T$)

Note that:

$$(u_{i,t},\ \bar{u}_{i,t+1}) = \bar{u}_{i,t}$$

$$(\underline{u}_{i,t},\ u_{i,t}) = \underline{u}_{i,t+1}$$

$$(\underline{u}_{i,t},\ \bar{u}_{i,t}) = u_i$$

Definition 1 (see Basar and Olsder (1982) p. 94)

$(u_1^*,\ u_2^*)$ is a *global Nash equilibrium* for $x(0) = x_0$ if

a) $J_1(x_0,\ u_1^*,\ u_2^*) \leq J_1(x_0,\ u_1,\ u_2^*) \quad \forall u_1 \in U_1$

b) $J_2(x_0,\ u_1^*,\ u_2^*) \leq J_2(x_0,\ u_1^*,\ u_2) \quad \forall u_2 \in U_2$

Definition 2 (see Basar and Olsder (1982) p. 127-128)

$(u_1^*,\ u_2^*)$ is a *global Stackelberg equilibrium* for $x(0) = x_0$ if

a) $$\max_{u_1 \in F(x_0,u_2^*)} J_2(x_0,u_1,u_2^*) \leq$$

$$\max_{u_1 \in F(x_0,u_2)} J_2(x_0,u_1,u_2) \quad \forall u_2 \in U_2$$

b) $u_1^* \in F(x_0,u_2^*)$

where $F(x_0,u_2) := \{u_1 \in U_1 \mid J_1(x_0,u_1,u_2) \leq J_1(x_0,\hat{u}_1,u_2)\ \forall \hat{u}_1 \in U_1\}$

Definition 3 (see Basar and Olsder (1982) p. 116-117)

(u_1^*,u_2^*) is a *stagewise feedback Nash equilibrium* if

a) $$J_1(x(0),(\underline{u}_{1,t},\bar{u}^*_{1,t}),(\underline{u}_{2,t},\bar{u}^*_{2,t})) \leq$$

$$J_1(x(0),(\underline{u}_{1,t},u_{1,t},\bar{u}^*_{1,t+1}),(\underline{u}_{2,t},\bar{u}^*_{2,t})) \quad \forall u_{1,t} \in U_{1,t}$$

b) $J_2(x(0),(\underline{u}_{1,t},\bar{u}^*_{1,t}),(\underline{u}_{2,t},\bar{u}^*_{2,t})) \leq$

$J_2(x(0),(\underline{u}_{1,t},\bar{u}^*_{1,t}),(\underline{u}_{2,t},u_{2,t},\bar{u}^*_{2,t+1}))\ \forall u_{2,t} \in U_{2,t}$

$\forall t \in T,\ \forall x(0) \in X,\ \forall \underline{u}_{1,t} \in \underline{U}_{1,t},\ \forall \underline{u}_{2,t} \in \underline{U}_{2,t}$

Note that the last line of this definition can be interpreted as "at any time, at any reachable state of the system".

Definition 4 (see Basar and Olsder (1982) p. 131)

(u^*_1,u^*_2) is a stagewise feedback Stackelberg equilibrium if:

a) $\max_{u_{1,t} \in \hat{F}_t(\bar{u}^*_{1,t+1},\bar{u}^*_{2,t})} J_2(x(0),(\underline{u}_{1,t+1},\bar{u}^*_{1,t+1}),(\underline{u}_{2,t},\bar{u}^*_{2,t})) \leq$

$\max_{u_{1,t} \in \hat{F}_t(\bar{u}^*_{1,t+1},(u_{2,t},\bar{u}^*_{2,t+1}))} J_2(x(0),(\underline{u}_{1,t+1},\bar{u}^*_{1,t+1}),$

$(\underline{u}_{2,t},u_{2,t},\bar{u}^*_{2,t+1}))\ \forall u_{2,t} \in U_{2,t}$

b) $u^*_{1,t} \in \hat{F}_t(\bar{u}^*_{1,t+1},\bar{u}^*_{2,t})$

$\forall t \in T,\ \forall x(0) \in X,\ \forall \underline{u}_{1,t} \in \underline{U}_{1,t},\ \forall \underline{u}_{2,t} \in \underline{U}_{2,t}$

where $\hat{F}_t(\bar{u}_{1,t+1},\bar{u}_{2,t}) := \{u_{1,t} \in U_{1,t} \mid J_1(x(0),u_1,u_2) \leq$

$J_1(x(0),(\underline{u}_{1,t},\hat{u}_{1,t},\bar{u}_{1,t+1}),\ (\underline{u}_{2,t},\bar{u}_{2,t}))\ \forall \hat{u}_{1,t} \in U_{1,t}\}$

Proposition 1

(u^*_1,u^*_2) is a global feedback Nash equilibrium (for $x(0)=x_0$) if it is a stagewise Nash equilibrium.

Proof: The system player i (i=1,2) controls given u^*_j (j=1,2,i≠j) is causal. Bellman's principle of optimality is valid so the (global) optimal value of the objective functional can be found by dynamic programming (see Basar and Olsder (1982) p. 117)

Proposition 2

In a strict convex linear quadratic framework the global linear feedback Nash equilibrium $\forall x(0) \in X$ exists and is unique.
This is also the unique stagewise feedback Nash equilibrium.

Proof: see de Zeeuw (1984) p. 100.

Definition 5 (see Kydland and Prescott (1977))

A control law u_i is consistent if $\forall t \in T$, $\bar{u}_{i,t}$ minimizes the objective functional (in the class of admissable control laws) given $x_0 \in X$, $\underline{u}_{i,t}$, $\underline{u}_{j,t}$ and player j's (re)action $\bar{u}_{j,t}$.

In the stagewise mode, that is based on the idea of optimization at any moment in time, every equilibrium control law is consistent by construction. A global Stackelberg-leader control law is, in general, inconsistent. A consistent global Stackelberg equilibrium can be defined as follows:

let (for $t \in T$) :

(i) $G_{1,t}(x(0),\underline{u}_{1,t},u_2) :=$

$$\{\bar{u}_{1,t} \in \bar{U}_{1,t} \mid \bar{u}_{1,t+1} \in H_{1,t+1}(x(0),(\underline{u}_{1,t},u_{1,t}),u_2)\} \quad \text{if } t < t_{f-1}$$

$$U_1 \quad \text{if } t = t_{f-1}$$

(ii) $H_{1,t}(x(0),\underline{u}_{1,t},u_2) :=$

$$\{\bar{u}_{1,t} \in G_{1,t}(x(0),\underline{u}_{1,t},u_2) \mid J_1(x(0),(\underline{u}_{1,t},\bar{u}_{1,t}),u_2) \leq J_1(x(0),(\underline{u}_{1,t},\hat{\bar{u}}_{1,t}),u_2)\ \forall \hat{\bar{u}}_{1,t} \in G_{1,t}(x(0),\underline{u}_{1,t},u_2)\}$$

(iii) $M_t(x(0),\underline{u}_{1,t},\underline{u}_{2,t}) :=$

$$\{\bar{u}_{2,t} \in \bar{U}_{2,t} | \bar{u}_{2,t+1} \in N_{t+1}(x(0),(\underline{u}_{1,t},u_{1,t}), (\underline{u}_{2,t},u_{2,t}))$$

$$\forall \bar{u}_{1,t} \in H_{1,t}(x(0),\underline{u}_{1,t},u_2)\} \quad \text{if } t < t_{f-1}$$

$$U_2 \quad \text{if } t = t_{f-1}$$

(iv) $N_t(x(0),\underline{u}_{1,t},\underline{u}_{2,t}) :=$

$$\{\bar{u}_{2,t} \in M_t(x(0),\underline{u}_{1,t},\underline{u}_{2,t}) |$$

$$\max_{\bar{u}_{1,t} \in H_{1,t}(x(0),\underline{u}_{1,t},u_2)} J_2(x(0),(\underline{u}_{1,t},\bar{u}_{1,t}),u_2) \leq$$

$$\max_{\bar{u}_{1,t} \in H_{1,t}(x(0),\underline{u}_{1,t},(\underline{u}_{2,t},\bar{u}_{2,t}))} J_2(x(0),(\underline{u}_{1,t},\bar{u}_{1,t}),(\underline{u}_{2,t},\bar{u}_{2,t}))$$

$$\forall \hat{\bar{u}}_{2,t} \in M_t(x(0),\underline{u}_{1,t},\underline{u}_{2,t})\}$$

<u>Definition 6</u>
(u_1^*,u_2^*) is a <u>consistent Stackelberg equilibrium</u> for $x(0) = x_0$ if

a) $u_2^* \in N_0(x_0)$

b) $u_1^* \in H_{1,0}(x_0,u_2^*)$

ON AFFINE INCENTIVES FOR DYNAMIC DECISION PROBLEMS

Harri Ehtamo and Raimo P. Hämäläinen
Systems Analysis Laboratory
Helsinki University of Technology
02150 Espoo, Finland

Abstract

Construction of optimal incentive strategies for continuous time two-person game problems described by integral convex cost criteria is considered. The strategies are affine in the data available and they are represented by means of Stieltjes measures.

1. Introduction

Various incentive problems have become an area of active research in the last few years (see e.g. Ehtamo and Hämäläinen 1985, Ho 1983, Ho, Luh and Olsder 1982, Zheng and Başar 1982, Zheng, Başar and Cruz 1984). One of the most popular incentive problems is related to an asymmetric game situation and can be stated as follows. Consider a two-person deterministic dynamic game problem with a hierarchical decision structure, where Player 1 is the leader and Player 2 is the follower. Let $J_1(u,v)$ and $J_2(u,v)$ be the cost functionals for the players, where u and v are the leader's and the follower's decision variables, respectively; the corresponding decision spaces are denoted by U and V which are assumed to be appropriate Banach spaces. The problem then is to find an incentive strategy $\gamma: V \to U$ for the leader which, by taking into account rational responses of the follower, leads to a most favourable decision pair for the leader. This pair, denoted by (u^*,v^*), may be defined, for example, as a pair which globally minimizes $J_1(u,v)$ on $U \times V$, provided such a pair exists, or it could be chosen according to some other suitable criterion. A strategy solving this problem is called an optimal incentive strategy (OIS) for the leader.

Recently Zheng, Başar and Cruz (1984) have extensively studied existence and construction of optimal affine incentive schemes for dynamic games formulated in appropriate Hilbert spaces. In the context of continuous time problems they studied memory strategies of the form

$$u(t) = \gamma(v)(t) = u^*(t) - \int_{t_0}^{t} R(t,\tau)(v-v^*)(\tau)d\tau, \quad t \in [t_0,t_f], \tag{1}$$

where $u \in L_2^{m_1}[t_0,t_f]$, $v \in L_2^{m_2}[t_0,t_f]$, and (u^*,v^*) is the team optimal solution. The problem then is to find R, $\|R\| < \infty$, such that γ is an OIS for the leader. Zheng *et al.* constructed such R's in terms of the gradients of the follower's cost functional calculated at the team optimal point (u^*,v^*). However, rather strong assumptions on the game parameters were needed to guarantee that $\|R\| < \infty$. One way to develop the approach of Zheng *et al.* is to represent the admissible strategies by means of Stieltjes measures; i.e., one can assume that the leader adopts a strategy of the form

$$\gamma(v)(t) = u^{o}(t) - \int_{t_0}^{t} [d_\theta \eta(t,\theta)]v(\theta), \tag{2}$$

where the integral is Lebesgue-Stieltjes integral. Strategies of this form have earlier been considered, in the case of linear quadratic Stackelberg games, by Papavassilopoulos and Cruz (1980), and by Ehtamo and Hämäläinen (1985).

In the present paper we adopt the function-space approach of Zheng *et al.* (1984), and construct OIS's of the form (2) for a general class of continuous time incentive problems described by integral convex cost criteria. It will be shown that for most problems there exists an optimal strategy, or an ε-strategy, of the form (2) for the leader, provided certain continuity and differentiability conditions hold. By the existence of an ε-strategy we mean the following: For every $\varepsilon > 0$ there exists an incentive strategy by which the leader can induce a decision pair, say $(u^\varepsilon,v^\varepsilon)$, such that $|J_1(u^*,v^*) - J_1(u^\varepsilon,v^\varepsilon)| < \varepsilon$.

The contents of the paper are as follows. Section 2 deals with existence and construction of optimal strategies of the form (2). In Section 3 we compute explicit examples and in Section 4 ε-strategies are considered. In some cases an incentive strategy can be realized as a cheating strategy. This case is considered in Section 5. Finally, in Section 6 Nash games with incentive strategies are briefly discussed.

We denote by B_∞^n the Banach space $B_\infty([t_0,t_f],R^n)$ of R^n-valued, Borel measurable, bounded functions with the sup topology. By $B_\infty^{n\times m}$ we mean the Banach space $B_\infty([t_0,t_f],R^{n\times m})$. The sup norm is denoted by $\|\cdot\|$, while the Euclidean norm (or the corresponding matrix norm) is denoted by $|\cdot|$. All integrals will be Lebesgue or Lebesgue-Stieltjes integrals.

2. Construction of optimal incentive strategies

A. *The Model*

Let us consider a two-person dynamic game problem with a hierarchical decision structure, where Player 1 is the leader and Player 2 is the follower. The decision variables of the leader and the follower are denoted by $u \in U$ and $v \in V$, respectively. In the following $U = B_\infty^{m_1}$, $V = B_\infty^{m_2}$ are the decision spaces for the players. The cost functionals for the players are denoted by $J_1(u,v)$ and $J_2(u,v)$; $J_i: U \times V \to R$, $i = 1,2$. (We assume that the initial state $x_0 \in R^n$ is fixed, and the state vector x is expressed as a function of the decision variables $(u,v) \in U \times V$). We further make the following assumptions.

Assumption 2.1. $J_2(u,v)$ is Fréchet-differentiable and strictly convex on $U \times V$.

Assumption 2.2. There exist mappings $T_1: U \times V \to U$, and $T_2: U \times V \to V$ such that for all $(u,v) \in U \times V$

$$\langle h_1, \nabla_u J_2(u,v)\rangle = \int_{t_0}^{t_f} h_1'(t)T_1(u,v)(t)dt, \; h_1 \in U, \tag{3}$$

$$\langle h_2, \nabla_v J_2(u,v)\rangle = \int_{t_0}^{t_f} h_2'(t)T_2(u,v)(t)dt, \; h_2 \in V, \tag{4}$$

where $\nabla_u J_2(u,v) \in U^*$ is the gradient of J_2 with respect to u at (u,v), and $\nabla_v J_2(u,v) \in V^*$ is the gradient of J_2 with respect to v at (u,v).

Adopting the terminology used by Zheng *et al.* (1984), the function $T_1(u,v)(t)$ $(T_2(u,v)(t))$ represents the leader's (the follower's) ability to influence J_2 by changing his decision variable $u(t)$ $(v(t))$ at time t.

Assumption 2.3: The leader has perfect information on the follower's actions.

We next assume that the admissible strategies $\gamma: V \to U$ for the leader are of the form

$$u(t) = \gamma(v)(t) = u^o(t) - \int_{t_0}^{t} [d_\theta \eta(t,\theta)]v(\theta), \; t \in [t_0,t_f], \tag{5}$$

where the integral is Lebesgue-Stieltjes integral (see e.g. Royden 1969), and the following standing hypotheses is made on $\eta: [t_0,t_f] \times \times R \to R^{m_1 \times m_2}$.

Assumption 2.4: $\eta(t,\theta) = 0$, for $\theta \geq t$, $t \in (t_0,t_f]$; $\eta(t,\theta)$ is

Borel measurable in (t,θ) and continuous from the right in θ on (t_0,t_f); $\theta \to \eta(t,\theta)$ is of bounded variation on $[t_0,t_f]$ for all t; the mapping $t \to \int_{t_0}^{t} [d_\theta \eta(t,\theta)]\varphi(\theta)$ is Borel measurable on $[t_0,t_f]$ for each fixed $\varphi \in B_\infty^{m_2}$, and there is a constant c, such that

$$|\int_{t_0}^{t} [d_\theta \eta(t,\theta)]\varphi(\theta)| \leq c\|\varphi\|, \tag{6}$$

for all $t \in [t_0,t_f]$, and for all $\varphi \in B_\infty^{m_2}$.

Observe that $Q: V \to U$, $(Qv)(t) = \int_{t_0}^{t} [d_\theta \eta(t,\theta)]v(\theta)$, is a bounded linear operator as is implied by Inequality (6). Moreover, by Inequality (6),

$$|\eta(t,\theta)| = |\int_{t_0}^{t} [d_s \eta(t,s)]\chi_{[\theta,t_f]}(s)| \leq c, \tag{7}$$

for all (t,θ), $t_0 \leq \theta \leq t \leq t_f$, where $\chi_{[\theta,t_f]}(s)$ is the characteristic function of $[\theta,t_f]$. We denote the space of admissible strategies for the leader by Γ, and let the follower's strategy space be $B_\infty^{m_2}$.

Let now $(u^*,v^*) \in U \times V$ be a pair which is chosen according to some criterion and is considered to be most favourable to the leader. This pair may be defined, for example, as a pair which globally minimizes $J_1(u,v)$ on $U \times V$, provided such a pair exists. The incentive problem can then be stated as follows.

(P1) Find $\gamma \in \Gamma$ such that v^* uniquely solves the minimization problem

$$\min_{v \in V} J_2(\gamma(v),v), \tag{8}$$

and

$$\gamma(v^*) = u^*. \tag{9}$$

If $\gamma \in \Gamma$ solves (P1), it is called an optimal incentive strategy (OIS) for the leader. Note that OIS clearly is a Stackelberg strategy for the leader under the given information structure.

Remark 2.1: If the minimization problem (8) admits a solution, it is unique, since, by Assumption 2.1, $J_2(\gamma(v),v)$ is strictly convex when γ is of the form (5).

B. Existence and Construction of OIS's

Let a pair $(u^*,v^*) \in U \times V$ be given. Let us seek the strategy in the form

$$u(t) = \gamma(v)(t) = u^*(t) - \int_{t_0}^{t} [d_\theta \eta(t,\theta)](v-v^*)(\theta), \tag{10}$$

since this form automatically satisfies $\gamma(v^*) = u^*$; i.e., when the follower's decision is $v = v^*$, the leader's decision is $u = u^*$. Thus it remains to choose η such that (10) is an OIS. We proceed as Zheng *et al.* (1984).

Since, by Assumption 2.1, the set

$$\Omega^* = \{(u,v) \in U \times V \mid J_2(u,v) \leq J_2(u^*,v^*)\} \tag{11}$$

is strictly convex, with (u^*,v^*) as a boundary point, there exists a supporting hyperplane Π^* passing through (u^*,v^*), provided that Ω^* contains an interior point (Luenberger 1969). If an interior point does not exist, (u^*,v^*) globally minimizes J_2. In this case $\gamma(v) = u^*$, $v \in V$, is an optimal incentive strategy for the leader. If there is η such that the set of decision pairs (u,v), defined by the incentive scheme (10), lies on Π^*, then it has the unique common point (u^*,v^*) with Ω^*. Hence, the unique solution to the follower's minimization problem is v^*, and the strategy given by (10) becomes an optimal incentive strategy for the leader.

Set

$$y(t) = T_1(u^*,v^*)(t) \tag{12}$$

$$z(t) = T_2(u^*,v^*)(t), \quad t \in [t_0,t_f]. \tag{13}$$

Then the equation of the supporting hyperplane Π^* may be written as

$$\langle u-u^*,\nabla_u J_2(u^*,v^*)\rangle + \langle v-v^*,\nabla_v J_2(u^*,v^*)\rangle$$
$$= \int_{t_0}^{t_f} (u-u^*)'(t)y(t)dt + \int_{t_0}^{t_f} (v-v^*)'(t)z(t)dt = 0. \tag{14}$$

Then we have

Proposition 2.1: Under Assumptions 2.1-2.4 let η satisfy

$$\int_{t}^{t_f} \eta'(\tau,t)y(\tau)d\tau = -\int_{t}^{t_f} z(\tau)d\tau, \quad t \in [t_0,t_f]. \tag{15}$$

Then

$$u(t) = \gamma^*(v)(t) = u^*(t) - \int_{t_0}^{t} [d_\theta \eta(t,\theta)](v-v^*)(\theta), \tag{16}$$

is an optimal incentive strategy for the leader.

Proof: Since $\gamma(v^*) = u^*$, it suffices to show that the submanifold denined by (16) lies on the hyperplane (14). The unsymmetric Fubini theorem (see Cameron and Martin 1941) asserts that for every $\omega \in B^{m_2}$

$$\int_{t_0}^{t_f} \left(\int_{t_0}^{t} w'(\theta) d_\theta \eta'(t,\theta)\right) y(t)dt = \int_{t_0}^{t_f} w'(\theta) d_\theta \left(\int_{\theta}^{t_f} \eta'(t,\theta)y(t)dt\right)$$

$$= -\int_{t_0}^{t_f} w'(\theta) d_\theta \left(\int_{\theta}^{t_f} z(t)dt\right) = \int_{t_0}^{t_f} w'(\theta)z(\theta)d\theta, \tag{17}$$

where in the second step we used (15). Using (16) and (17) we get

$$0 = \int_{t_0}^{t_f} (u-u^*)'(t)y(t)dt + \int_{t_0}^{t_f} \left(\int_{t_0}^{t} (v-v^*)'(\theta) d_\theta \eta'(t,\theta)\right) y(t)dt$$

$$= \int_{t_0}^{t_f} (u-u^*)'(t)y(t)dt + \int_{t_0}^{t_f} (v-v^*)'(t)z(t)dt. \tag{18}$$

Thus (16) lies on the hyperplane (14) and defines an optimal incentive strategy for the leader. □

Remark 2.2: If, instead of strict convexity, we assume that $J_2(u,v)$ is convex on $U \times V$, and η satisfies (15), then v^* still solves Problem (8), but not necessarily uniquely, since Ω^* is only convex.

Remark 2.3: Let $J_2(u,v)$ be of the form

$$J_2(u,v) = I_1(u,v) + I_2(v), \quad (u,v) \in U \times V. \tag{19}$$

Then the requirement of strict convexity can be replaced by the following milder condition without affecting the validity of Proposition 2.1: $I_1(u,v)$ is convex on $U \times V$, and $I_2(v)$ is strictly convex on V (cf. the LQ-problem in Section 3.A). Since, in this case, $J_2(\gamma(v),v)$ is strictly convex on V, the solution to the follower's problem (8) is unique.

We will close this section by constructing analytically η's satisfying Eq. (15) for given y and z.

(i) Let

$$\eta(t,\theta) = \begin{cases} -H_{>}(t-\theta)\eta(t), & t \in (t_0,t_f], \\ -H_{\geq}(t_0-\theta)\eta(t_0), & t = t_0, \end{cases} \tag{20}$$

where $\eta \in B_{\infty}^{m_1 \times m_2}$, and the step functions $H_{>}(\sigma)$, $H_{\geq}(\sigma)$ are defined by

$$H_{>}(\sigma) = \begin{cases} 1, & \sigma > 0, \\ 0, & \sigma \leq 0, \end{cases} \qquad H_{\geq}(\sigma) = \begin{cases} 1, & \sigma \geq 0, \\ 0, & \sigma < 0. \end{cases} \tag{21}$$

Equation (15) simplifies to

$$\int_t^{t_f} \eta'(\tau)y(\tau)d\tau = \int_t^{t_f} z(\tau)d\tau, \quad t \in [t_0,t_f]. \tag{22}$$

This equation has a bounded solution if and only if there is c such that

$$|z(t)| \leq c|y(t)|, \quad t \in [t_0,t_f]. \tag{23}$$

If this is the case, set

$$\eta'(t) = z(t)\frac{y'(t)}{y'(t)y(t)}, \tag{24}$$

when $y(t)$ does not vanish. Then η is Borel measurable and bounded, and solves Eq. (22). Using representation (20) γ^* can be written as

$$\gamma^*(v)(t) = u^*(t) - \eta(t)(v-v^*)(t). \tag{25}$$

Hence in this case the leader's decision at time t only depends on the current value of the follower's decision.

(ii) Let us assume that $y(t)$, $z(t)$ are Lipschitz continuous at $t = t_f$, and

$$y(t_f) = T_1(u^*,v^*)(t_f) \neq 0. \tag{26}$$

Then there exists an optimal incentive strategy for the leader. Namely, set

$$\eta(t,\theta) = \begin{cases} -H_{>}(t-\theta)y(t)h'(\theta), & t \in (t_0,t_f], \\ -H_{\geq}(t_0-\theta)y(t_0)h'(t_0), & t = t_0, \end{cases} \tag{27}$$

where

$$h(\theta) = \frac{1}{\int_{\theta}^{t_f} y'(\tau)y(\tau)d\tau} \int_{\theta}^{t_f} z(\tau)d\tau, \qquad \theta \in [t_0,t_f), \tag{28}$$

$$h(t_f) = \lim_{\theta \to t_f} h(\theta) = \frac{z(t_f)}{y'(t_f)y(t_f)} . \tag{29}$$

Then $\eta(t,\theta)$ solves Eq. (15). Moreover, Assumption 2.4 holds, since $h(\theta)$ is continuous on $[t_0,t_f]$, Lipschitz continuous at $\theta = t_f$, differentiable on $[t_0,t_f)$, and by a simple computation one gets that $(d/d\theta)h(\theta)$ is uniformly bounded. In this case γ^* can be written as

$$\gamma^*(v)(t) = u^*(t) + y(t) \int_{t_0}^{t} [\frac{d}{d\theta} h'(\theta)](v-v^*)(\theta)d\theta$$

$$- y(t)h'(t)(v-v^*)(t). \tag{30}$$

Remark 2.4: Lipschitz continuity of $y(t)$ and $z(t)$ at $t = t_f$ can be replaced by Hölder continuity of $y(t)$ and $z(t)$ at $t = t_f$. In this case $h(\theta)$ is Hölder continuous at $\theta = t_f$, and there are constants k and α, $0 < \alpha < 1$, such that $|\frac{d}{d\theta} h(\theta)| \leq k(t_f-\theta)^{-\alpha}$ for $\theta \to t_f$. Hence the integral in (30) is well defined.

(iii) Consider the case $y(t_f) = 0$. Let $y(t)$ and $z(t)$ be Lipschitz continuous at $t = t_1$, $t_0 < t_1 < t_f$, and assume that $y(t_1) \neq 0$, and $|z(t)| \leq c|y(t)|$, $t \in [t_1,t_f]$. Then one can use the results of (i) and (ii) to construct optimal incentive policies for the leader. One choice for the optimal η is e.g.

$$\eta(t,\theta) = \begin{cases} -H_{>}(t-\theta)(H_{>}(t-t_1)\eta(t) + H_{\geq}(t_1-t)y(t)h'(\theta)), & t \in (t_0,t_f], \\ -H_{\geq}(t_0-\theta)y(t_0)h'(t_0), & t = t_0, \end{cases} \tag{31}$$

where $\eta(t)$, $t_1 < t \leq t_f$, is as in (24), and $h(\theta)$, $t_0 \leq \theta \leq t_1$, is as in (28), (29), but with t_f replaced by t_1.

Remark 2.5: Assume the leader needs some time to detect and infer the available information. Then his decision can only depend on the values of $v(\theta)$, for $t_0 \leq \theta \leq t-h$, where $h > 0$. Let the admissible (time lag) strategies for the leader be e.g. of the form

$$\gamma(v)(t) = u^*(t) - \int_{t_0}^{t-h} [d_{\theta}\eta(t,\theta)](v-v^*)(\theta), \quad t \in [t_0,t_f], \tag{32}$$

where $\eta(t,\theta) = 0$ for $t < t_0+h$, and for $\theta \geq t-h$, $t \in (t_0+h,t_f]$. Condition (15) for optimal incentive strategies then reads

$$\int_{t+h}^{t_f} \eta'(\tau,t)y(\tau)d\tau = -\int_{t}^{t_f} z(\tau)d\tau, \quad t_0 \leq t \leq t_f-h, \tag{33}$$

$$z(t) = 0, \quad t > t_f-h. \tag{34}$$

3. Examples

A. A Linear Quadratic Problem

Consider the dynamic system

$$\dot{x}(t) = Ax(t) + B_1u(t) + B_2v(t), \; x(t_0) = x_0, \; t \in [t_0,t_f], \tag{35}$$

and the cost functionals

$$J_i(u,v) = \frac{1}{2} x'(t_f)F_ix(t_f) + \frac{1}{2}\int_{t_0}^{t_f} (x'(t)Q_ix(t)$$

$$+ u'(t)R_{i1}u(t) + v'(t)R_{i2}v(t))dt, \quad i = 1,2, \tag{36}$$

where $x(t) \in R^n$, $u(t) \in R^{m_1}$, $v(t) \in R^{m_2}$. The matrices A, B_i, $Q_i = Q_i' \geq 0$, $R_{ij} = R_{ij}' \geq 0$, $R_{11} > 0$, $R_{12} > 0$, $R_{22} > 0$, are Borel measurable and bounded on $[t_0,t_f]$, and the constant matrices $F_i = F_i' \geq 0$. The team solution minimizing J_1 is

$$u^*(t) = -R_{11}^{-1}B_1'Kx^*(t), \; v^*(t) = -R_{12}^{-1}B_2'Kx^*(t), \tag{37}$$

$$J_1^* = \frac{1}{2} x_0'K(t_0)x_0, \tag{38}$$

where K is the solution of the Riccati equation

$$\dot{K} = -KA - A'K - Q_1 + K[B_1R_{11}^{-1}B_1' + B_2R_{12}^{-1}B_2']K,$$

$$\text{a.e. } t \in [t_0,t_f], \quad K(t_f) = F_1, \tag{39}$$

and the optimal trajectory x^* is given by

$$x^*(t) = \phi_\Lambda(t,t_0)x_0, \tag{40}$$

$$\frac{\partial\phi_\Lambda}{\partial t}(t,t_0) = \Lambda\phi_\Lambda(t,t_0), \text{ a.e. } t \in [t_0,t_f], \; \phi_\Lambda(t_0,t_0) = I, \tag{41}$$

where

$$\Lambda = A - B_1R_{11}^{-1}B_1'K - B_2R_{12}^{-1}B_2'K. \tag{42}$$

To calculate the gradients of J_2 with respect to u and v we write

$$x(t) = \phi_A(t,t_0)x_0 + \int_{t_0}^{t} \phi_A(t,\tau)B_1(\tau)u(\tau)d\tau$$

$$+ \int_{t_0}^{t} \phi_A(t,\tau)B_2(\tau)v(\tau)d\tau, \tag{43}$$

where

$$\frac{\partial\phi_A}{\partial t}(t,t_0) = A(t)\phi_A(t,t_0), \quad \phi_A(t_0,t_0) = I. \tag{44}$$

Then we find that

$$\langle h_1,\nabla_u J_2(u,v)\rangle = x'(t_f)F_2 \int_{t_0}^{t_f} \phi_A(t_f,\tau)B_1(\tau)h_1(\tau)d\tau$$

$$+ \int_{t_0}^{t_f} (x'(t)Q_2(t) \int_{t_0}^{t} \phi_A(t,\tau)B_1(\tau)h_1(\tau)d\tau + u'(t)R_{21}(t)h_1(t))dt$$

$$= \int_{t_0}^{t_f} h_1'(t)T_1(u,v)(t)dt, \tag{45}$$

where

$$T_1(u,v)(t) = R_{21}(t)u(t) + B_1'(t)[\phi_A'(t_f,t)F_2x(t_f)$$

$$+ \int_{t}^{t_f} \phi_A'(\tau,t)Q_2(\tau)x(\tau)d\tau], \quad t \in [t_0,t_f]. \tag{46}$$

In a similar way we get

$$\langle h_2,\nabla_v J_2(u,v)\rangle = \int_{t_0}^{t_f} h_2'(t)T_2(u,v)(t)dt, \tag{47}$$

where

$$T_2(u,v)(t) = R_{22}(t)v(t) + B_2'(t)[\phi_A'(t_f,t)F_2x(t_f)$$

$$+ \int_{t}^{t_f} \phi_A'(\tau,t)Q_2(\tau)x(\tau)d\tau], \quad t \in [t_0,t_f]. \tag{48}$$

At the team optimal point (37) we have

$$T_1(u^*,v^*)(t) = -R_{21}R_{11}^{-1}B_1'K\phi_\Lambda(t,t_0)x_0 + B_1'[\phi_A'(t_f,t)F_2\phi_\Lambda(t_f,t)$$

$$+ \int_t^{t_f} \phi_A'(\tau,t)Q_2(\tau)\phi_\Lambda(\tau,t)d\tau]\phi_\Lambda(t,t_0)x_0. \tag{49}$$

Let P be the solution of

$$\dot{P} = -P\Lambda - A'P - Q_2, \quad P(t_f) = F_2,$$

i.e.

$$P(t) = \phi_A'(t_f,t)F_2\phi_\Lambda(t_f,t) + \int_t^{t_f} \phi_A'(\tau,t)Q_2(\tau)\phi_\Lambda(\tau,t)d\tau. \tag{50}$$

Then

$$y(t) = T_1(u^*,v^*)(t) = [B_1'P - R_{21}R_{11}^{-1}B_1'K]x^*(t). \tag{51}$$

In a similar way we obtain

$$z(t) = T_2(u^*,v^*)(t) = [B_2'P - R_{22}R_{12}^{-1}B_2'K]x^*(t). \tag{52}$$

Next, assume that $y(t)$, $z(t)$ are Lipschitz continuous at $t = t_f$. Since K, P and x^* are Lipschitz continuous on $[t_0,t_f]$ (the game parameters are bounded), the Lipschitz continuity of B_i, R_{ij} at $t = t_f$ guarantee the validity of this assumption. Then there exists an optimal affine incentive strategy of the form (30) for the leader, provided

$$y(t_f) = [B_1'(t_f)F_2 - R_{21}(t_f)R_{11}^{-1}(t_f)B_1'(t_f)F_1]x^*(t_f) \neq 0. \tag{53}$$

Note that if $F_1 = F_2 = 0$, then $y(t_f) = z(t_f) = 0$. To handle this case, see Case (iii) of Section 2.B.

B. *A More General Problem*

Let

$$x(t) = \phi_A(t,t_0)x_0 + \int_{t_0}^{t} \phi_A(t,\sigma)f(u(\sigma),v(\sigma),\sigma)d\sigma, \quad t \in [t_0,t_f], \tag{54}$$

$$J_2(u,v) = g(x(t_f)) + \int_{t_0}^{t_f} L(x(t),u(t),v(t),t)dt, \tag{55}$$

define a strictly convex function on $U \times V$, where $\phi_A(t,t_0)$ is as in (44). We assume that $g: R^n \to R$ is continuously differentiable; $f(u,v,t)$ is continuous in u,v,t and continuously differentiable with respect to u,v; $L(x,u,v,t)$ is continuous in x,u,v,t and continuously differentiable with respect to x,u,v. Then $J_2(u,v)$ is Fréchet-differentiable on $U \times V$ (see e.g. Girsanov 1972). $J_2(u,v)$ is strictly convex on $U \times V$ if e.g. $f(u,v,t)$ is affine in u and v, $g(x)$ is convex, and $L(x,u,v,t)$ is of the form $L_1(x,t) + L_2(u,v,t)$, where $L_1(x,t)$ is convex in x, and $L_2(u,v,t)$ is strictly convex in (u,v).

One can now proceed as in previous sections to construct optimal incentive policies for the leader. Thus, by differentiating and using the Fubini theorem it is easy to verify that $y(t)$ and $z(t)$ are given by

$$y(t) = T_1(u^*,v^*)(t) = L_u'(x^*,u^*,v^*,t) + f_u'(u^*,v^*,t)\mu(t), \tag{56}$$

$$z(t) = T_2(u^*,v^*)(t) = L_v'(x^*,u^*,v^*,t) + f_v'(u^*,v^*,t)\mu(t), \tag{57}$$

where μ is the solution of

$$\dot{\mu}(t) = -A'(t)\mu(t) - L_x'(x^*,u^*,v^*,t),\ \mu(t_f) = g_x'(x^*(t_f)), \tag{58}$$

and is given by

$$\mu(t) = \phi_A'(t_f,t)g_x'(x^*(t_f)) + \int_t^{t_f} \phi_A'(\tau,t)L_x'(x^*,u^*,v^*,\tau)d\tau,$$

$$t \in [t_0,t_f]. \tag{59}$$

4. ε-strategies

We next study the case, where $y(t)$ and $z(t)$, Eqs. (12), (13), are Lipschitz continuous at $t = t_f$, $y(t_f) = 0$, $z(t_f) \neq 0$. It is easy to see that in this case there does not exist η, satisfying Inequality (7), such that Eq. (15) holds for $t \to t_f$. However, under certain conditions, there still exists an affine ε-strategy for the leader. That is, for every $\varepsilon > 0$ there exists an affine incentive strategy $\gamma^\varepsilon: V \to U$ for the leader by which he is able to achieve the cost, say J_1^ε, such that

$$|J_1^* - J_1^\varepsilon| < \varepsilon, \tag{60}$$

where $J_1^* = J_1(u^*,v^*)$ is a most favourable performance for the leader.

We assume that $J_1(u,v)$ is continuous at (u^*,v^*). Let us further assume that $T_1(\cdot,\cdot)(t_f): U \times V \to R^{m_1}$ is Gateaux differentiable at (u^*,v^*), and there exists $(q,r) \in U \times V$ such that

$$\frac{d}{d\alpha} T_1(u^* + \alpha q, v^* + \alpha r)(t_f)\Big|_{\alpha=0} \neq 0. \tag{61}$$

Since $T_1(u^*,v^*)(t_f) = 0$, (61) implies that there exists $\delta > 0$ such that

$$T_1(u^\alpha,v^\alpha)(t_f) \neq 0, \text{ for } 0 < \alpha < \delta, \tag{62}$$

where

$$u^\alpha \hat{=} u^* + \alpha q, \quad v^\alpha = v^* + \alpha r. \tag{63}$$

Hence (recall Eq. (26)) there exists an affine ε-strategy for the leader, provided there exists δ' such that for every $\alpha \in (0,\delta')$ $T_i(u^\alpha,v^\alpha)(t)$ is Lipschitz (Hölder) continuous at $t = t_f$, $i = 1,2$.

Remark 4.1: Consider, for example, the linear-quadratic problem defined in Section 3.A, and assume B_i, R_{ij} are Lipschitz continuous at $t = t_f$. Then there exists an affine ε-strategy for the leader, provided there exists (q,r) $U \times V$, q,r Lipschitz continuous at $t = t_f$, such that

$$R_{21}(t_f)q(t_f) + B_1'(t_f)F_2 \Big[\int_{t_0}^{t_f} \phi_A(t_f,\tau)B_1(\tau)q(\tau)d\tau$$
$$+ \int_{t_0}^{t_f} \phi_A(t_f,\tau)B_2(\tau)r(\tau)d\tau\Big] \neq 0. \tag{64}$$

5. Perfect cheating with incentive strategies

Let (u^*,v^*) be the most favourable decision pair for the leader. Let $u^c \in U$ be any vector such that

$$T_1(u^c,v^*)(t_f) \neq 0. \tag{65}$$

Then there exists an incentive strategy γ^c for the leader of the form

$$\gamma^c(v)(t) = u^c(t) - \int_{t_0}^{t} [d_\theta \eta(t,\theta)](v-v^*)(\theta), \quad t \in [t_0,t_f], \tag{66}$$

such that v^* solves the follower's problem, and $\gamma^c(v^*) = u^c$, provided $T_i(u^c,v^*)(t)$ is Lipschitz continuous at $t = t_f$, $i = 1,2$.

One realization of the strategy (66) might be as follows: Assume the follower is unable to detect the values of the state and the values of the leader's control, i.e. he implements an open-loop strategy. Assume then that the leader announces the strategy γ^c to the follower who reacts to this by choosing the control v^* and expects the leader to implement the control $u^c = \gamma^c(v^*)$. However, since the follower is unable to detect the leader's actions the leader can as well implement the control $u = u^*$. In literature this kind of realization is known as perfect cheating (see Hämäläinen 1981, where open-loop cheating in linear-quadratic games has been studied). Consider again the linear-quadratic game of Section 3, where the Lipschitz continuity of B_i, R_{ij} is understood. Let $q \in U$ be any vector such that q is Lipschitz continuous at $t = t_f$, and

$$R_{21}(t_f)q(t_f) + B_1'(t_f)F_2 \int_{t_0}^{t_f} \phi_A(t_f,\tau)B_1(\tau)q(\tau)d\tau \neq 0. \tag{67}$$

Then there exists $u^c \in U$, and an incentive strategy γ^c for the leader of the form (66) such that v^* solves the follower's problem, and $\gamma^c(v^*) = u^c$. Note that in this case there also exists an affine ε-strategy for the leader, cf. Eq. (64).

6. Nash games with incentive strategies

Consider two players, Player 1 and Player 2, with decision spaces U and V, and cost functionals $J_i: U \times V \to R$, $i = 1,2$. Here U and V are assumed to be appropriate function spaces. Assume that the players have perfect information on each other's actions, and let $\Gamma_1 = \{\gamma_1 \mid \gamma_1: V \to U\}$, $\Gamma_2 = \{\gamma_2 \mid \gamma_2: U \to V\}$ be the strategy spaces for the players.

Definition 6.1: A strategy pair $(\gamma_1^N,\gamma_2^N) \in \Gamma_1 \times \Gamma_2$ is called a Nash equilibrium if there exists a pair $(u^N,v^N) \in U \times V$ such that

$$u^N = \gamma_1^N(v^N), \qquad v^N = \gamma_2^N(u^N), \tag{68}$$

$$J_1(u^N,v^N) \leq J_1(u,\gamma_2^N(u)), \quad \text{for all} \quad u \in U,$$
$$J_2(u^N,v^N) \leq J_2(\gamma_1^N(v),v), \quad \text{for all} \quad v \in V. \tag{69}$$

Observe that if Γ_i's consist of constant mappings, i.e. the players play open loop, then Definition 6.1 is the standard definition of the open-loop Nash equilibrium.

Next, given a decision pair $(u^d,v^d) \in U \times V$, one may try to find a strategy pair $(\gamma_1^d,\gamma_2^d) \in \Gamma_1 \times \Gamma_2$, such that Eqs. (68) and (69) hold. In some situations the pair (u^d,v^d) could be, for example, a bargaining solution. In such cases it is natural that each player wants to safeguard himself against any attempts by the other player to break the agreement in order to improve his outcome. One possibility then, is to construct incentive strategies for the players such that when each player implements his own strategy, the best result the other player can get is just (u^d,v^d).

As before, let $U = B_\infty^{m_1}$, $V = B_\infty^{m_2}$. Assume that $J_i(u,v)$ is Fréchet-differentiable and strictly convex on $U \times V$, $i = 1,2$, and there exist mappings $T_{i1}: U \times V \to U$, and $T_{i2}: U \times V \to V$, such that for all $(u,v) \in U \times V$

$$\langle h_1,\nabla_u J_i(u,v)\rangle = \int_{t_0}^{t_f} h_1'(t)T_{i1}(u,v)(t)dt, \quad h_1 \in U, \tag{70}$$

$$\langle h_2,\nabla_v J_i(u,v)\rangle = \int_{t_0}^{t_f} h_2'(t)T_{i2}(u,v)(t)dt, \quad h_2 \in V, \tag{71}$$

$i = 1,2$. Let the pair (u^d,v^d) be such that

$$T_{21}(u^d,v^d)(t_f) \neq 0, \quad T_{12}(u^d,v^d)(t_f) \neq 0. \tag{72}$$

If further $T_{ij}(u^d,v^d)(t)$ are Lipschitz continuous at $t = t_f$, there exists a strategy pair (γ_1^d,γ_2^d) of the form

$$u(t) = \gamma_1^d(v)(t) = u^d(t) - \int_{t_0}^{t} [d_\theta\eta_1(t,\theta)](v-v^d)(\theta), \tag{73}$$

$$v(t) = \gamma_2^d(u)(t) = v^d(t) - \int_{t_0}^{t} [d_\theta\eta_2(t,\theta)](u-u^d)(\theta), \tag{74}$$

$t \in [t_0,t_f]$, where η_1 and η_2 are as in Assumption 2.4, such that Eqs. (68) and (69) hold.

7. Conclusions

In this paper derivation of affine incentive strategies for continuous time hierarchical and symmetric decision problems described by integral convex cost criteria have been discussed. The main assumption we have made is that the players (or, in the case of hierarchical decision structure, just one of them) have perfect knowledge of each other's actions, although the approach we have taken can also be generalized to the case where the players have only partial dynamic information on each other's actions (see e.g. Zheng and Başar 1982). We have not discussed the information gathering mechanisms underlying this assumption, but mention only that in many applications the players can have information on each other's actions, for example, by observing the system state. Also, in real world problems, information gathering mechanisms always have time lags which must to be taken into account when calculating the optimal strategies. Our results can be generalized to various problems having multilevel of hierarchy. This will be discussed in a forthcoming publication.

8. References

Ehtamo, H. and R.P. Hämäläinen (1985), "Construction of optimal affine incentive strategies for linear-quadratic Stackelberg games," Helsinki University of Technology, Systems Research Report A12.

Ho, Y.C. (1983), "On incentive problems," Syst. and Contr. Lett. 3, pp. 63-68.

Ho, Y.C., P.B. Luh and G.J. Olsder (1982), "A control theoretic view on incentives," Automatica, vol. 18, pp. 167-179.

Hämäläinen, R.P. (1981), "On the cheating problem in Stackelberg games", Int. J. Systems Sci., vol. 12, pp. 753-770.

Papavassilopoulos, G.P. and J.B. Cruz, Jr. (1980), "Sufficient conditions for Stackelberg and Nash strategies with memory," J. Optimiz. Theory Appl., vol. 31, pp. 233-260.

Zheng, Y.P. and T. Başar (1982), "Existence and derivation of optimal affine incentive schemes for Stackelberg games with partial information: A geometric approach," Int. J. Control, vol. 35, no. 6, pp. 997-1011.

Zheng, Y.P., T. Başar and J.B. Cruz, Jr (1984), "Stackelberg strategies and incentives in multiperson deterministic decision problems," IEEE Trans. Syst., Man, Cybern., vol. SMC-14, no. 1, pp. 10-24.

Cameron, R.H. and W.T. Martin (1941), "An unsymmetric Fubini theorem," Bull. Am. Math. Soc., vol. 47, pp. 121-125.

Girsanov, I.V. (1972), "Lectures on Mathematical Theory of Extremum Problems," Lecture Notes in Economics and Mathematical Systems, vol. 67, Springer, Berlin.

Luenberger, D.G. (1969), Optimization by Vector Space Methods, Wiley, New York.

Royden, H.L. (1969), Real Analysis, Macmillan, New York.

ON THE COMPUTATION OF EQUILIBRIA IN DISCOUNTED STOCHASTIC DYNAMIC GAMES

Michèle Breton[*], Jerzy A. Filar[**], Alain Haurie[*] and Todd A. Schultz[**]

[*]GERAD, École des Hautes Études Commerciales,
5255 avenue Decelles, Montréal,
Québec, Canada, H3T 1V6.

[**]Department of Mathematical Sciences,
The Johns Hopkins University,
Baltimore, Md 21218.

Abstract

Various algorithms for numerical solutions of discounted stochastic games are presented. For zero-sum two-person games, the existing algorithms are compared on randomly generated games and a hybrid algorithm is proposed. For general-sum N-person games, a new mathematical programming formulation which permits the numerical solution of a game by using a non-linear programming code is presented.

Acknowledgements: This research has been supported by the «Direction de la recherche, École des H.E.C., Montréal» and by the «Centre de calcul de l'Université de Montréal» to the first author, NSF grant #ECS-8503440 to the second and fourth author and SSHRC grant #410-83-1012 to the third author.

1. INTRODUCTION

The purpose of this paper is to report on a continuing research aimed at deriving numerical solutions of the Dynamic Programming Equations (DPE) associated with equilibria of discounted sequential games.

We can say that the theory of dynamic games stems from two important seminal works: Shapley (1953) introduced the concept of Markov game and Isaacs (1965) introduced the concept of differential game. In both cases the game considered was a duel (two-player and zero-sum), and the dynamic programming approach was intimately associated with the characterization of the solution.

The theory initiated by Isaacs was extended (Case (1969)) to non-cooperative nonzero-sum dynamic games and the current state of development of the theory of differential and multistage games is well presented in the book of Başar and Olsder (1982). Most of the results obtained are qualitative in nature, very little has been done towards the derivation of general purpose algorithms for the computation of equilibria in such games. By and large one could say that the only nonzero-sum differential or multistage game models which lend themselves to a complete resolution are (i) the Linear Quadratic Gaussian differential games, (ii) the games with an affine structure with respect to the state variables (Clemhout and Wang (1974)), and the games with an affine structure with respect to the control variables which then lead to bang-bang strategies. The picture is a little bit more attractive for two-player zero-sum games where a more complete existence theory has been developed (Friedman (1971)).

The situation is somewhat different for the theory of discounted Markov games that developed after Shapley's original paper. One important aspect of the dynamic programming approach for zero-sum discounted sequential games is that it leads to the computation of a fixed point for a contraction mapping. Thus the existence results are constructive and provide natural algorithms for the computation of the solution. In the case of non-cooperative sequential games, the existence results are not so easily related to a numerical technique.

Raghavan (1984) recently surveyed the existing algorithms for two-person stochastic games with finite state and action sets, but did not report on the relative performances of the various algorithms in terms of computational efficiency. In fact, even for zero-sum Markov games, very few numerical experiments have been reported.

There is a parallel between the theory of differential games vs. the theory of Markov games, and the theory of optimal control vs. the theory of Markov decision processes. Recent developments of stochastic control of discrete systems (Rishel (1977), Boel and Varayia (1977)) and on Markovian decision processes (Whitt (1978, 1979), Bertsekas and Shreve (1978)) have established a link between the two areas which can be exploited for the design of efficient computation methods based on approximation techniques (Haurie and L'Ecuyer (1982, 1985)). Our long term objective in this research is to reach a similar state of cross-fertilisation between sequential game theory and differential game theory. The development steps considered for the implementation of efficient computational algorithms in dynamic games are: (i) extension of the theory of Markov games to the case of continuous states and action sets and random jump times, (ii) implementation of approximation techniques in a general dynamic programming algorithm which should permit a continuous problem to be solved through a sequence of approximating discrete problems, and, finally, (iii) selection of performant discrete state and action algorithms for the solution of the large scale problems which would result from the approximation of continuous state and action models. The present paper is entirely devoted to the third task, as it surveys the existing algorithms for zero-sum discounted Markov games, compares them on randomly generated test problems, and proposes a new general algorithm for nonzero-sum Markov games.

The paper is organized as follows: In Section 2, the notation and the dynamic programming formalism «à la Denardo» (1967) are introduced. In Section 3, the existing algorithms for the computation of saddle points are compared. In Section 4, a new mathematical programming formulation which permits the numerical solution of the DPE for N-person game equilibria is proposed. Finally in Section 5, the existing algorithms for specially structured stochastic games are surveyed rapidly.

2. NOTATION AND PRELIMINARIES

We consider finite stochastic games played in discrete stages. At stage 0, the state of the system is observed by the players; each one then chooses an action from a set of admissible actions, independently from the others. This choice can be made by random sampling from a selected distribution. The players then receive a reward and the system moves to a new state, according to a transition law. The process is then repeated from stage 1, and so on, for an infinite number of stages.

Let

I : finite player set , $\mathrm{Card}(I) = N$

S : finite state space

B_{is} : finite space of admissible actions of player i in state s, with $B_s \triangleq X_I B_{is}$ and $B \triangleq X_S B_s$

$r(s,i,\underline{b})$: (one-step) reward to player i in state s when actions are $\underline{b}$; $i \in I$, $s \in S$, $\underline{b} \in B_s$

$q(s'|s,\underline{b})$: transition probability from s to s' when actions are $\underline{b}$; $s', s \in S$, $\underline{b} \in B_s$.
We assume that $\sum_{s' \in S} q(s'|s,b) = 1$ for all $s \in S$.

β $(0 \leq \beta < 1)$: one step discount factor.

A <u>policy</u> $\delta_i : S \to (B_{is})$ is a function associating a probability distribution on the action space of player i (also called a mixed action for player i) with each state s in S. Let Δ_i be the space of all policies for player i, $\Delta = X_I \Delta_i$. A <u>Markov strategy</u> $\pi_i \in \Pi_i$ is a sequence of policies for each stage $\{\delta_i^0, \delta_i^1, \delta_i^2, \ldots\}$. A <u>stationary strategy</u> is a sequence of identical policies for all stages; we still use the notation δ_i to represent the stationary strategy $\{\delta_i, \delta_i, \delta_i, \ldots\}$ and the notation $\underline{\delta}$ to represent the N-player stationary strategy vector $(\delta_1, \delta_2, \ldots, \delta_N)$. Throughout this paper, we only consider stationary and Markov strategies and we restrict the analysis to the so-called β-discounted game, where the reward at stage t is discounted to stage 0 by a factor β^t, $\beta \in [0,1)$. The objective of each player is to maximize the sum of the expected discounted rewards.

Let $v_{\underline{\pi}}(s,i)$ represent the infinite horizon sum of expected discounted rewards for player i when the initial state is s and the players use the strategy vector $\underline{\pi}$. If there exists a stationary strategy vector $\underline{\delta}^*$ such that for a given $\varepsilon \geq 0$, for each player i and for all $\gamma_i \in \Pi_i$,

$$v_{\underline{\delta}^*}(s,i) \geq v_{[\underline{\delta}^{*-i},\gamma_i]}(s,i) + \varepsilon \qquad (1)$$

where $[\underline{\delta}^{*-i},\gamma_i]$ is a strategy vector $\underline{\delta}$ such that $\delta_j = \delta_j^*$ for $i \neq j$ and $\delta_i = \gamma_i$, then the strategy vector $\underline{\delta}^*$ is called a <u>stationary ε-equilibrium</u> (<u>equilibrium</u> if $\varepsilon = 0$).

In zero-sum two-person games, the reward to player 1 is paid by player 2, so that $r(s, 1, \underline{b}) = -r(s, 2, \underline{b})$. Consequently, $v_{\underline{\delta}}(s,1) = -v_{\underline{\delta}}(s,2)$ and if there exists an equilibrium stationary strategy pair $\underline{\delta}^*$, the quantity $v^*(s) \triangleq v_{\underline{\delta}^*}(s,1)$ is called the value of the game starting in state s.

Finally, let us introduce the following dynamic programming formalism first proposed by Denardo (1967).

Let V be the space of bounded functions $v : S \times I \to \mathbb{R}$ and $h : S \times I \times B \times V \to \mathbb{R}$ be the local income function, i.e. the (expected discounted) reward to player i when the state of the system is s, the actions of the players are $\underline{b}$ and all future rewards are described by the function v. We define the dynamic programming operator $H_{\underline{\delta}} : V \to V$ by

$$(H_{\underline{\delta}}v)(s,i) = h(s,i,\underline{\delta}(s),v) \tag{2}$$

where

$$h(s,i,\underline{\delta}(s),v) = \sum_{\underline{b}\in B_s} h(s,i,\underline{b},v)\, p_{\underline{\delta}(s)}(\underline{b}) \tag{3}$$

and

$$h(s,i,\underline{b},v) = r(s,i,\underline{b}) + \beta \sum_{s'\in S} v(s',i)q(s'|s,\underline{b}) \tag{4}$$

where $p_{\underline{\delta}(s)}(\underline{b})$ is the joint probability of the N-tuple of actions $\underline{b}$ with marginal probabilities $\delta_i(s)$ for each i.

3. COMPARISON OF ALGORITHMS FOR FINITE STATE AND ACTION ZERO-SUM GAMES

Stochastic games were introduced by Shapley (1953) who considered what are now called two-person zero-sum discounted games with finite state and action spaces and proved that such games have a value obtained through stationary strategies. We briefly present in this section some of the available algorithms for the computation of equilibrium stationary strategies in zero-sum games (also called saddle points). The main feature of this section is the report on numerical experiments appearing in Subsection 3.5 .

Here, since the game is zero-sum, the argument i is not necessary; $v : S \to \mathbb{R}$ is the future reward function for player 1. Let $F : V \to V$ be the operator defined by

$$(Fv)(s) = \min_{\delta_2\in\Delta_2} \max_{\delta_1\in\Delta_1} (H_{\underline{\delta}}v)(s) \tag{5}$$

and let $v^*(s)$ be the value of the game when the state of the system is s.

3.1 Shapley's (1953) value iteration algorithm

The algorithm proposed by Shapley (denoted SH) is based on the contraction property of the operator F. Successive approximations of v^* are obtained by the value iterations

$$v^{n+1}(s) = (Fv^n)(s) \qquad \text{for all } s \in S . \tag{6}$$

At each iteration, Card(S) matrix games are solved. The procedure stops when the difference between two successive approximations of v^* is small enough. The algorithm converges from any v^0 if F is contracting, which is the case when $\beta < 1$.

Shapley's algorithm is related to the value iteration algorithm in Markov Decision Processes; it does not utilize the information contained in the optimal strategies at each iteration. The two algorithms presented in Subsections 3.2 and 3.3 could be related to the policy iteration approach.

3.2 Hoffman and Karp (1966) and Van der Wal (1978) policy improvement

Define the operator $F_{\delta_2} : V \to V$ by

$$(F_{\delta_2} v)(s) = \max_{\delta_1 \varepsilon \Delta_1} (H_{\underline{\delta}} v)(s) \qquad \text{for all } s \in S \tag{7}$$

associating with any function v and policy δ_2 of player 2, the maximum local reward to player 1.

The algorithm proposed by Hoffman and Karp (denoted HK) iterates as follows: starting with $v^0 \geq v^*$ (componentwise), for a given function v^n it finds the stationary strategy $\underline{\delta}(n)$ such that

$$(H_{\underline{\delta}(n)} v^n)(s) = (F\, v^n)(s) \qquad \text{for all } s \in S \tag{8}$$

where F is the operator defined in (5); for the fixed strategy $\delta_2(n)$ it finds a fixed point of the operator $F_{\delta_2(n)}$, then sets it as the next iterate, that is:

$$v^{n+1}(s) = (F_{\delta_2(n)}\, v^{n+1})(s) \qquad \text{for all } s \in S . \tag{9}$$

The procedure stops when the difference between two successive approximations of v^* is small enough. This algorithm has been shown to converge by Rao, Chandrasekaran and Nair (1973). At each step, Card(S) matrix games and Card(S) Markov Decision Processes (MDPs) are solved; however, the convergence rate towards v^* is improved, with respect to Shapley's algorithm, by utilizing information contained in the optimal strategy of player 2 at each iteration.

The algorithm proposed by Van der Wal (denoted VDW) is an extension of this algorithm where one uses approximate solution to the MDPs at each iteration, thus reducing the amount of work in one iteration: Starting with $v^0 \geq v^*$, for a given v^n, again it finds the strategy $\underline{\delta}(n)$ such that (8) holds, and for the fixed strategy $\delta_2(n)$, it determines the next iterate as:

$$v^{n+1}(s) = (F_{\delta_2(n)}^{\;k}\, v^n)(s) \qquad \text{for all } s \in S \tag{10}$$

the k-fold iterate of $F_{\delta_2(n)}$ on v^n, where $k \geq 1$. Notice that $k = 1$ corresponds to Shapley's algorithm and that $k = \infty$ corresponds to Hoffman and Karp's algorithm.

3.3 Pollatschek and Avi-Itzhak's (1969) policy iteration algorithm

Pollatschek and Avi-Itzhak suggested a Newton-Raphson technique, (denoted PA), which proceeds as follows: starting with $v^0 \geq v^*$, for a given function v^n, it finds $\underline{\delta}(n)$ such that (8) holds, then computes the fixed point

$$v^{n+1}(s) = (H_{\underline{\delta}(n)} v^{n+1})(s) = v_{\underline{\delta}(n)}(s) \qquad \text{for all } s \in S \tag{11}$$

(this reduces to the solution of a set of linear equations), and stops when the difference between two successive approximations of v is small enough. At each iteration, Card(S) matrix games and a linear equation system of size Card(S) are solved. Pollatschek and Avi-Itzhak proved that this algorithm converges under the very restrictive condition

$$\max_{s \in S} \{ \sum_{s' \in S} \max_{\underline{b} \in B_s} q(s'|s,\underline{b}) - \min_{\underline{b} \in B_s} q(s'|s,\underline{b})\} \leq \frac{1-\beta}{\beta} \tag{12}$$

but used it successfully on problems not satisfying this condition.

Van der Wal (1978) showed that the algorithm does not converge in general. The conditions for convergence of this algorithm, which required notably less computing time than the two previous ones in test problems, as shown in section 3.5, are still not known.

3.4 Vrieze and Tijs (1980) fictitious play algorithm

Vrieze and Tijs have proposed a different solution method (denoted VT) based on the method of fictitious play for the solution of matrix games of Robinson (1950) and Brown (1951).

At each iteration, each player looks at past history and chooses an action optimizing a one-step reward, given a fictitious policy for the other player obtained as a randomized policy based on the frequency distribution of this player's previous actions observed in the past. The algorithm computes an upper and a lower bound on the value function and stops when these bounds are close enough.

The convergence of this method is very slow, as it can be observed from the numerical results of Section 3.5, but it requires only, at each iteration, the computation of the minimum and the maximum of the Card(S) components of a vector.

3.5 Numerical results

The algorithms presented in Sections 3.1 to 3.4 were used to solve a number of test problems; These test problems were randomly generated, with various numbers of states, numbers of actions in each state and various discount factors. The transition matrices contained various percentages (denoted PR) of non-zero elements, uniformly distributed and randomly scattered. The rewards were uniformly distributed on $(0,2(1-\beta))$. In Figures 1-4 we present for nine of those test problems, the CPU times in seconds on a CYBER-835 computer, to obtain various precisions. A precision of ε means that the stationary strategy obtained is an ε'-equilibrium with $\varepsilon' < \varepsilon$ (see Remark 3.1). Notice that the order of magnitude of v^* in all the problems is 1, so that 100 ε can be interpreted as an approximation of the error in percentage points of the value.

For each problem, the ratio of the left hand side over the right hand side of (12) was computed and appears next to its identification; recall that this ratio should be less than one in order to guarantee the convergence of the PA algorithm. Also appearing (in brackets) on Figures 1-4 are the number of iterations performed with each algorithm to reach the final precision.

Remark 3.1

At iteration n, let the strategy $\underline{\delta}(n)$ be such that, for a given $\varepsilon' \geq 0$,

$$|v^*(s) - v_{\underline{\delta}(n)}(s)| \leq \varepsilon' \qquad \text{for all } s \in S . \tag{13}$$

Then what we call the precision ε of the solution is a bound for ε'. The bound ε was computed in the same way for all the algorithms : at iteration n, let

$$U_n = \max_{s \in S} \{(Fv^n)(s) - v^n(s)\} \tag{14}$$

$$L_n = \min_{s \in S} \{(Fv^n)(s) - v^n(s)\} \tag{15}$$

then

$$\varepsilon = \frac{(U_n - L_n) \beta}{1-\beta} . \tag{16}$$

Remark 3.2

Notice that the convergence criterion for all the algorithms was thus based on the obtainment of an ε-optimal strategy rather that the obtainment of a sufficiently precise approximation of v^*. This has a very significant impact on the relative performances of SH and HK algorithms.

In the literature, it is assumed that using HK algorithm improves the rate of convergence with respect to SH algorithm by utilizing the information contained in the optimal strategies at each iteration. It is a fact that, if instead of (13) the convergence criterion is replaced by

$$|v^*(s) - v^n(s)| \leq \varepsilon' \qquad \text{for all } s \in S \tag{17}$$

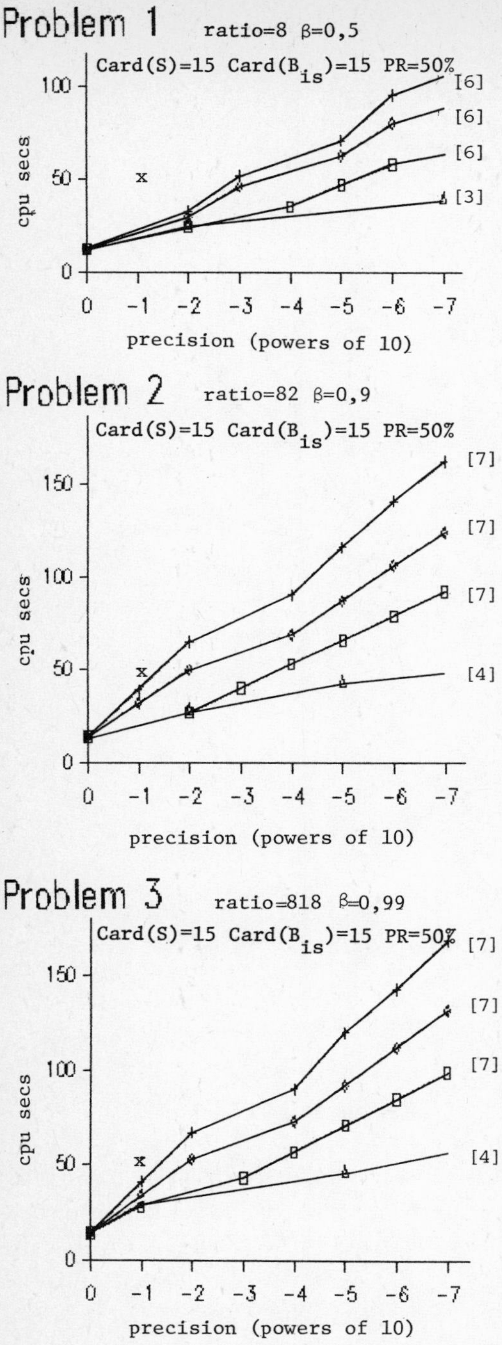

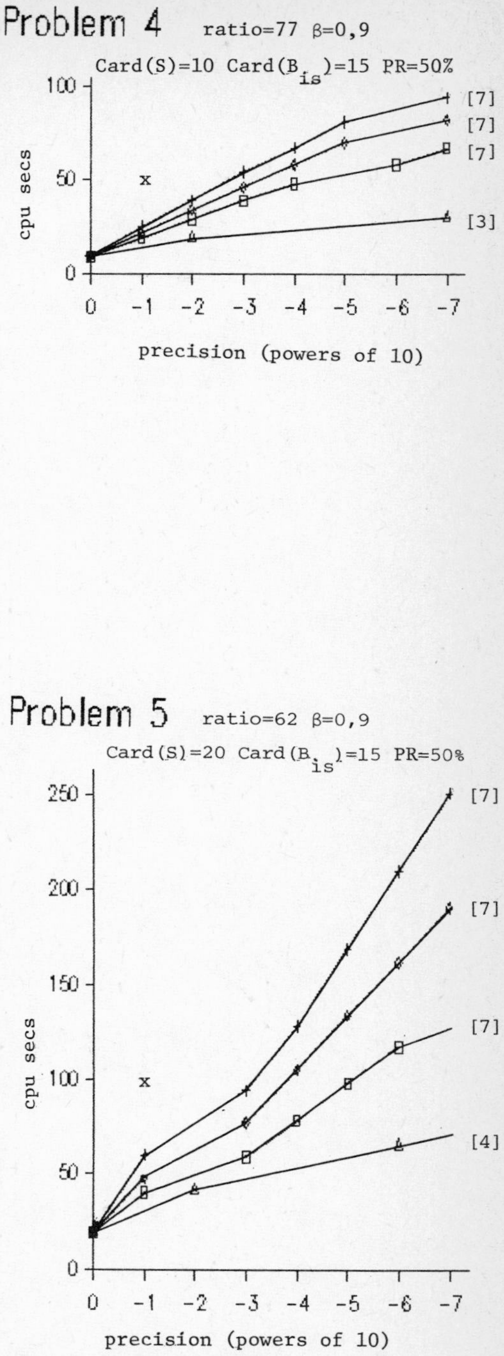

□ SH + HK ◊ VDW △ PA x VT

Figure 1: Effect of β

Figure 2: Effect of Card(S)

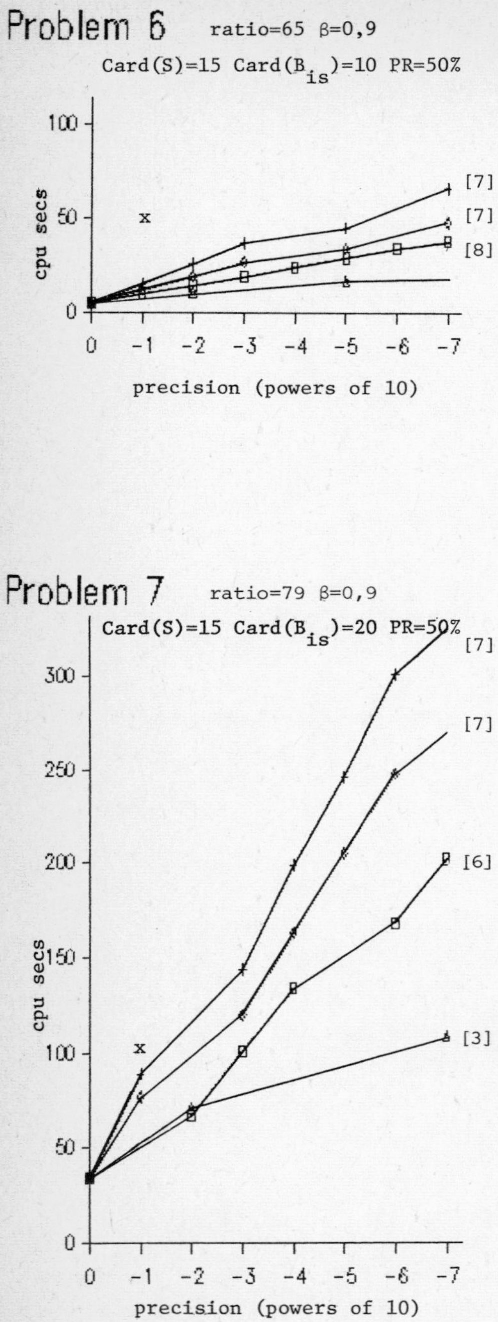

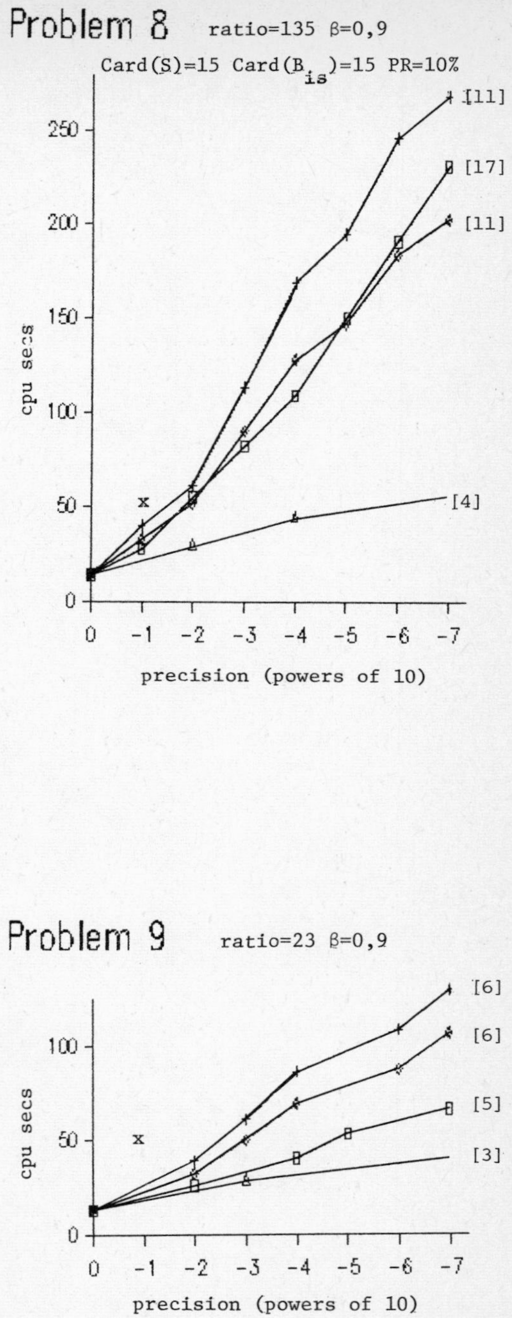

□ SH + HK ◇ VDW △ PA x VT

Figure 3: Effect of Card(B_{is})

Figure 4: Effect of PR

then the convergence of SH algorithm is much slower. For example, in test problem 2, it takes 300 CPU seconds with the convergence criterion (17) to reach a bound on ε' of 0,01 for the SH algorithm, compared with 65 CPU seconds for the HK algorithm.

This is due to the fact that a value iteration algorithm is not a very efficient way to determine $v_{\underline{\delta}}$ for a given $\underline{\delta}$. In almost all the test problems, the SH algorithm did converge to an ε-optimal strategy in no more iterations than the HK algorithm; even when that was not the case (see Problem 8), since each iteration of HK involves more work than one of SH, Shapley's algorithm, where the stopping criterion is the convergence to an ε-optimal strategy, is computationally more efficient than the HK algorithm. In order to obtain an estimate of the value of the game, it then suffices to solve the linear system (12).

Remark 3.3

In all the test problems, we found that the VDW algorithm, with k as small as 3, did converge to an ε-optimal strategy in the same number of iteration as the HK algorithm. For problems with sparse transition matrices VDW was computationally more efficient than SH.

Remark 3.4

The PA algorithm was consistently much faster than the others in all test problems. The condition (12) is very restrictive (it was not satisfied in any of the test problems); it is satisfied when the transition probabilities are independent of the actions of the players; it is likely to be satisfied when the discount factor is small and when the transition probabilities are not strongly dependent on the choice of actions. PA algorithm did converge in test problems with ratio as high as 1500. However, it has been shown that PA algorithm does not converge in general (Van Der Wal (1978)).

Remark 3.5

For the VT algorithm, although the amount of work needed in one iteration is small, the convergence is so slow that it cannot even be compared in CPU execution time with the other algorithms. Moreover, the bounds that are computed by VT algorithm are not tight and cannot be used as a stopping criterion. In Figures 1-4, for VT algorithm, we give the bound ε computed by (16) for the strategy obtained after 50 seconds and 100 seconds of CPU time.

Remark 3.6

With these algorithms it is already possible to solve fairly large problems; in fact, the limitation in the size of the problems was due to the size of the reward and transition matrices (data); the memory requirement to keep the data becomes very large as Card(S) and Card(B) grow. This means that by using functions $r(\cdot)$ and $q(\cdot|\cdot)$ instead of matrices, the size of the problems that could be solved by these algorithms could be augmented.

Remark 3.7

An hybrid algorithm can be used in order to avoid cycling that could eventually occur in the PA algorithm: at each iteration of PA algorithm, compute the bound $\varepsilon(n)$ given by (16). Continue to iterate using PA while the ε values are decreasing. If, at iteration n, $\varepsilon(n) > \varepsilon(n-1)$, then change to SH algorithm, using v^{n-1} as the starting point. Since for SH algorithm, the ε values are decreasing, global convergence is assured.

4. ALGORITHMS FOR NONZERO-SUM STOCHASTIC GAMES

Fink (1964), Rogers (1969) and Sobel (1971) extended Shapley's model to nonzero-sum games with finite state and action spaces. For the finite state and action spaces case, they showed the existence of stationary equilibrium strategies.

For nonzero-sum stochastic games, there is not much available in terms of algorithms. We present here a new result which can be used for the computation of equilibrium strategies in the general case (N-person, general-sum).

4.1 Failure of a dynamic programming method in the two-person nonzero-sum case

One could again try to solve a two-person nonzero-sum stochastic game through a value iteration or a policy iteration approach.

The first approach would be to solve a finite horizon game, starting with for example $v^0 \equiv 0$ as the final reward, and working backwards in time. If, as $n \to \infty$, the equilibrium reward function for the n-step game converges to a fixed point $v_{\underline{\delta}^*}$, then $\underline{\delta}^*$ is a stationary equilibrium strategy satisfying (1). This corresponds to the value iteration method of Markov Decision Processes and is an analog of Shapley's method for zero-sum games.

In the zero-sum case, the convergence of the value iteration algorithm follows from the monotonicity and contraction properties of the operator F. However, in the nonzero-sum case, an equilibrium dynamic programming operator G such that, for all $\gamma_i \in \Delta_i$, all $i \in I$ and all $s \in S$,

$$(Gv)(s,i) = (H_{\underline{\delta}^*} v)(s,i) \geq (H_{[\underline{\delta}^{*-1},\gamma_i]} v)(s,i) \tag{18}$$

is neither uniquely determined nor monotone, as it can be seen from the following one-state game:

(10,20)	5,5
5,5	(20,10)

where an entry (r_1,r_2) in position (j,k) corresponds to the payoffs $r_1 \triangleq r(1,j,k)$ and $r_2 \triangleq r(r,j,k)$.

At iteration 1, starting with $v^0 = 0$, there are two equilibria in pure strategies for this bimatrix game, and the two equilibrium rewards differ. In that case, the terminal reward at iteration 2 is not uniquely determined for the 2-stage game.

Choosing arbitrarily any one of the two equilibrium policies, let r_1^* and r_2^* represent the corresponding equilibrium rewards for players 1 and 2. Solving the 2-stage game amounts to solving the bimatrix game:

$10+\beta r_1^*$, $20+\beta r_2^*$	$5+\beta r_1^*$, $5+\beta r_2^*$
$5+\beta r_1^*$, $5+\beta r_2^*$	$20+\beta r_1^*$, $10+\beta r_2^*$

which again admits two equilibria in pure strategies. It is easily seen that in this one-state example, at each iteration there will be two equilibria in pure strategies and that the process need not converge to any fixed point v_{δ}. Also, letting $\beta < 1/2$, $r_1^* = 10$, $r_2^* = 20$, by using the policy $(2,\bar{2})$ in the 2-stage game, player 2 would get a smaller reward than in the one-stage game, and non-monotonicity of the operator G follows.

The following algorithm has been proposed by Rao, Chandrasekaran and Nair (1973). For a given function v^n find $\underline{\delta}(n)$ such that

$$(Gv^n)(s,i) = H_{\underline{\delta}(n)}v^n(s,i)) \qquad \text{for all } s \in S \text{ and all } i \in I \tag{19}$$

then compute the fixed point $v_{\underline{\delta}(n)}$ and use it as the next iterate, that is:

$$v^{n+1}(s,i) = (H_{\underline{\delta}(n)}v^{n+1})(s,i) = v_{\underline{\delta}(n)}(s,i) \tag{20}$$

This is the procedure of Pollatschek and Avi-Itzhak (1969), extended to nonzero-sum games. It corresponds to the policy iteration approach for Markov Decision Processes. The first step of the algorithm could be solved by e.g. Lemke-Howson (1964) algorithm, and the second step is the solution of a linear equations system of size Card(S) × N.

If this procedure converges, then $\underline{\delta}(n)$ is an equilibrium strategy pair for the game. However, even for the zero-sum case, this algorithm does not converge in general.

4.2 A fixed point algorithm for the general N-person game

Sobel (1971) proved the existence of a fixed point of the mapping $\Psi : \Delta \to 2^{\Delta}$ where $\Psi(\underline{\delta}) = X_I\ \Psi_i(\underline{\delta})$ and where

$$\Psi_i(\underline{\delta}) = \{\gamma_i \in \Delta_i : (F_{\underline{\delta}}\, v_{\underline{\delta}})(s,i) = \max_{\gamma_i \in \Delta_i} (H_{[\underline{\delta}^{-i},\gamma_i]}\, v_{\delta})(s,i)\ \forall s \in S\} \tag{21}$$

A fixed point of Ψ, i.e. a policy $\underline{\delta}^*$ such that $\underline{\delta}^* \in \Psi(\underline{\delta}^*)$ corresponds to a stationary equilibrium strategy.

Hence one could, at least in principle, apply one of the existing algorithms proposed for the computation of fixed point; for instance, see Karmadian (1976) or Van der Laan and Talman (1982). In the latter work two static three person games with three actions for each player were successfully solved. The potential of these techniques for finding equilibria of stochastic games remains unexplored.

4.3 A nonlinear programming approach for the general N-person nonzero-sum game

Filar and Schultz (1985) used a nonlinear program to solve discounted or undiscounted zero-sum games with special structure. In this section, we generalize this approach to the N-person, nonzero-sum case and associate with a noncooperative game a mathematical program, with non linear objective, and linear constraints. This technique can also be viewed as a natural consequence of Theorem 3 of Sobel (1971).

The solution of the following mathematical program yields an ε'-equilibrium stationary strategy ($\varepsilon' \geq 0$) for the N-person noncooperative game:

$$\min \psi(\underline{x}) = \sum_{s \in S} \sum_{i \in I} \{[c(i,s) - r_{\underline{\delta}}(s,i)]^2 + [d(i,s) - \sum_{s' \in S} q_{\underline{\delta}}(s'|s)\, v(s',i)]^2 + \sum_{j \in B_{is}} [u(i,j,s) - \sum_{s' \in S} q_{[\underline{\delta}^{-i},j]}(s'|s)\, v(s',i)]^2\} \qquad (22)$$

s.t. $\underline{x} \in D_\varepsilon$, the constraint set defined by:

$$v(s,i) \geq r_{[\underline{\delta}^{-i},j]}(s,i) + \beta\, u(i,j,s) - \varepsilon \qquad (23)$$

$$|v(s,i) - c(i,s) - \beta\, d(i,s)| \leq \varepsilon \qquad (24)$$

$$\sum_{j \in B_{is}} \delta_{ij}(s) = 1 \qquad (25)$$

$$\delta_{ij}(s) \geq 0\ ; \qquad \forall j \in B_{is},\ \forall i \in I,\ \forall s \in S \qquad (26)$$

where we have denoted $\underline{x}$ the vector of variables ($\underline{v}$, $\underline{c}$, $\underline{d}$, $\underline{u}$, $\underline{\delta}$),

$$r_{\underline{\delta}}(s,i) = \sum_{\ell \in I} \sum_{j_\ell \in B_{\ell s}} r(s,i,\underline{j})\, \delta_{\ell j_\ell} \qquad (27)$$

$$q_{\underline{\delta}}(s'|s) = \sum_{\ell\varepsilon I} \; \sum_{j_\ell \varepsilon B_{\ell s}} q(s'|s,\underline{j})\, \delta_{\ell j_\ell} \tag{28}$$

and $[\underline{\delta}^{-i},j]$ is the strategy vector $\underline{\delta}'$ such that

$$\delta'_{\ell m}(s) = \delta_{\ell m}(s) \qquad \ell \neq i$$

$$\delta'_{im}(s) = 0 \qquad m \neq j$$

$$\delta'_{ij}(s) = 1 \ ,$$

Here $r_{\underline{\delta}}(\cdot)$ and $q_{\underline{\delta}}(\cdot)$ are respectively the expected one-step reward and expected transition probability functions when the players use the policy $\underline{\delta}$.

<u>Theorem 4.1</u>. Consider a noncooperative, N-person discounted stochastic game, and the mathematical program (22)-(26).

Then

(1) There exists a $\underline{x}^* = (\underline{v}^*, \underline{c}^*, \underline{d}^*, \underline{u}^*, \underline{\delta}^*)$, $\underline{x}^* \varepsilon D_0$, such that $\psi(x^*) = 0$

(2) $\psi(\underline{x}) \geq 0$ for all $\underline{x} \varepsilon D_\varepsilon$

(3) $\underline{\delta}^*$ is a stationary equilibrium.

(4) Let $\hat{\underline{x}} = (\hat{v}, \hat{c}, \hat{d}, \hat{u}, \hat{\delta})$ be such that $\hat{\underline{x}} \varepsilon D_\varepsilon$ and $\psi(\hat{\underline{x}}) \leq \varepsilon^2$; then $\hat{\underline{\delta}}$ is a $\frac{\varepsilon(3+2\beta)}{(1-\beta)}$ -equilibrium.

<u>Proof</u>

(1) By Theorem 1 of Sobel (1971), there exists a stationary equilibrium $\underline{\delta}^*$. Let

$$v^*(s,i) = v_{\underline{\delta}^*}(s,i) \qquad \forall s\varepsilon S,\ \forall i\varepsilon I \tag{29}$$

$$c^*(i,s) = r_{\underline{\delta}^*}(s,i) \qquad \forall s\varepsilon S,\ \forall i\varepsilon I \tag{30}$$

$$d^*(i,s) = \sum_{s'\varepsilon S} q_{\underline{\delta}^*}(s'|s)\, v^*(s',i) \qquad \forall s\varepsilon S,\ \forall i\varepsilon I \tag{31}$$

$$u^*(i,j,s) = \sum_{s'\varepsilon S} q_{[\underline{\delta}^{*-i},j]}(s'|s)\, v^*(s',i) \quad \forall j\varepsilon B_{is},\ \forall s\varepsilon S,\ \forall i\varepsilon I \tag{32}$$

The above define a vector $\underline{x}^* = (\underline{v}^*, \underline{c}^*, \underline{d}^*, \underline{u}^*, \underline{\delta}^*)$ such that, by construction, $\psi(\underline{x}^*) = 0$.

Furthermore, also by construction, $\underline{\delta}^*$ satisfies constraints (25) and (26). Since $\underline{\delta}^*$ is an equilibrium, we have

$$v_{\underline{\delta}^*}(s,i) \geq v_{[\underline{\delta}^{*-i},\gamma_i]}(s,i) \qquad \forall s\varepsilon S, \quad \forall \gamma_i \varepsilon \Pi_i, \quad \forall i \varepsilon I \tag{33}$$

Let γ_i be the strategy $\{\delta_i', \delta_i^*, \delta_i^*, \delta_i^*, \ldots\}$, with $\delta_{ij}'=1$ and $\delta_{ik}' = 0$, $k \neq j$.

Then

$$v_{\underline{\delta}^*}(s,i) \geq r_{[\underline{\delta}^{*-i},j]}(s,i) + \beta \sum_{s'\varepsilon S} q_{[\underline{\delta}^{*-i},j]}(s'|s)\, v_{\underline{\delta}^*}(s',i)$$

$$= r_{[\underline{\delta}^{*-i},j]} + \beta\, u^*(i,j,s) \qquad \forall s\varepsilon S \quad \forall i\varepsilon I \quad \forall j\varepsilon B_{is} \tag{34}$$

so constraints (23) are satisfied with $\varepsilon = 0$.

Finally, $\forall s\varepsilon S \quad \forall i\varepsilon I$

$$v_{\underline{\delta}^*}(s,i) = r_{\underline{\delta}^*}(s,i) + \beta \sum_{s'\varepsilon S} q_{\underline{\delta}^*}(s'|s)\, v_{\underline{\delta}^*}(s',i)$$

$$= c^*(i,s) + \beta\, d^*(i,s)$$

and constraints (24) are satisfied with $\varepsilon = 0$. Hence $\underline{x}^* \varepsilon D_0$ and $\psi(x^*)=0$.

Part (2) is obvious. This assures that the global minimum of ψ is 0.

(3) Let $\underline{x}^* \varepsilon D_0$ be such that $\psi(\underline{x}^*) = 0$, so that the equalities (30), (31) and (32) hold.

Substituting in the constraints (24) and (23), we obtain, $\forall j\varepsilon B_{is}$, $\forall s\varepsilon S$, $\forall i\varepsilon I$

$$v^*(s,i) = r_{\underline{\delta}^*}(s,i) + \beta \sum_{s'\varepsilon S} q_{\underline{\delta}^*}(s'|s)\, v^*(s',i) = v_{\underline{\delta}^*}(s,i) \tag{35}$$

$$v^*(s,i) \geq r_{[\underline{\delta}^{*-i},j]}(s,i) + \beta \sum_{s'\varepsilon S} q_{[\underline{\delta}^{*-i},j]}(s'|s)\, v^*(s',i)\,. \tag{36}$$

Define the vectors

$$\underline{v}(i) = [v(s,i) : s \varepsilon S]$$

$$\underline{v}_{\underline{\delta}}(i) = [v_{\underline{\delta}}(s,i) : s \in S]$$

$$\underline{r}_{\underline{\delta}}(i) = [r_{\underline{\delta}}(s,i) : s \in S]$$

and the transition matrix

$$\underline{Q}_{\underline{\delta}} = [q_{\underline{\delta}}(s'|s) : s \in S \ , \ s' \in S] \ .$$

Let $\gamma_i \varepsilon \Delta_i$ be any stationary strategy for player i; from (36), we get, $\forall \gamma_i \varepsilon \Delta_i$, $\forall i \varepsilon I$

$$v^*(i) \geq \underline{r}_{[\underline{\delta}^{*-i},\gamma_i]}(i) + \beta \, \underline{Q}_{[\underline{\delta}^{*-i},\gamma_i]} \underline{v}^*(i)$$

$$\geq \underline{r}_{[\underline{\delta}^{*-i},\gamma_i]}(i) + \beta \, \underline{Q}_{[\underline{\delta}^{*-i},\gamma_i]} \Big(\underline{r}_{[\underline{\delta}^{*-i},\gamma_i]}(i) + \beta \, \underline{Q}_{[\underline{\delta}^{*-i},\gamma_i]} \underline{v}^*(i) \Big)$$

$$\vdots$$

$$\geq \sum_{t=1}^{\infty} \beta^{t-1} \, \underline{Q}^{t-1}_{[\underline{\delta}^{*-i},\gamma_i]} \underline{r}_{[\underline{\delta}^{*-i},\gamma_i]}(i) = \underline{v}_{[\underline{\delta}^{*-i},\gamma_i]}(i) \ . \tag{37}$$

Combining (37) and (35), we obtain

$$v_{\underline{\delta}^*}(s,i) \geq v_{[\underline{\delta}^{*-i},\gamma_i]}(s,i) \qquad \forall \gamma_i \varepsilon \Delta_i, \ \ \forall i \varepsilon I \ . \tag{38}$$

Using Hordijk, Vrieze and Wanrooij (1982), (38) can be shown to hold for all $\gamma_i \ \varepsilon \Pi_i$, for all $i \varepsilon I$, and $\underline{\delta}^*$ is an equilibrium.

(4) Let $\underline{\hat{x}} \ \varepsilon \ D_\varepsilon$ be such that $\psi(\underline{\hat{x}}) \leq \varepsilon^2$.

Then, $\forall j \varepsilon B_{is}$, $\forall s \varepsilon S$, $\forall i \varepsilon I$

$$\left| r_{\hat{\underline{\delta}}}(s,i) - \hat{c}(i,s) \right| \leq \varepsilon \tag{39}$$

$$\left| \hat{d}(i,s) - \sum_{s' \varepsilon S} q_{\hat{\underline{\delta}}}(s'|s) \, \hat{v}(s',i) \right| \leq \varepsilon \tag{40}$$

$$\left| \hat{u}(i,j,s) - \sum_{s' \varepsilon S} q_{[\hat{\underline{\delta}}^{-i},j]}(s'|s) \, \hat{v}(s',i) \right| \leq \varepsilon \ . \tag{41}$$

Substituting (39)-(41) in constraint (24), we obtain, $\forall s \varepsilon S$, $\forall i \varepsilon I$

$$\left| \hat{v}(s,i) - r_{\hat{\underline{\delta}}}(s,i) - \beta \sum_{s' \varepsilon S} q_{\hat{\underline{\delta}}}(s'|s) \, \hat{v}(s',i) \right| \leq \varepsilon \, (2+\beta),$$

so that

$$\left| v_{\hat{\underline{\delta}}}(s,i) - \hat{v}(s,i) \right| \leq \frac{\varepsilon(2+\beta)}{1-\beta} \quad \forall s \varepsilon S, \ \forall i \varepsilon I \ . \tag{42}$$

Substituting (39)-(41) into constraint (23), we obtain, $\forall j\in B_{is}$, $\forall s\in S$, $\forall i\in I$

$$\hat{v}(s,i) \geq r_{[\underline{\hat{\delta}}^{-i},j]}(s,i) + \beta \sum_{s'\in S} q_{[\underline{\hat{\delta}}^{-i},j]}(s'|s)\,\hat{v}(s',i) - \varepsilon(1+\beta) \tag{43}$$

Let $\gamma_i\in\Delta_i$ be any stationary strategy of player i; from (43), we get for all $i \in I$

$$\underline{\hat{v}}(i) \geq \underline{r}_{[\underline{\hat{\delta}}^{-i},\gamma_i]}(i) + \beta\, \underline{Q}_{[\underline{\hat{\delta}}^{-i},\gamma_i]}\,\underline{\hat{v}}(i) - \varepsilon(1+\beta)\,\underline{e}$$

$$\geq \underline{r}_{[\underline{\hat{\delta}}^{-i},\gamma_i]}(i) + \beta\, \underline{Q}_{[\underline{\hat{\delta}}^{-i},\gamma_i]}\Big(\underline{r}_{[\underline{\hat{\delta}}^{-i},\gamma_i]}(i) + \beta\, \underline{Q}_{[\underline{\hat{\delta}}^{-i},\gamma_i]}\,\underline{\hat{v}}(i) - \varepsilon(1+\beta)\,\underline{e}\Big) - \varepsilon(1+\beta)\,\underline{e}$$

$$\vdots$$

$$\geq \sum_{t=1}^{\infty} \beta^{t-1} Q^{t-1}_{[\underline{\hat{\delta}}^{-i},\gamma_i]}\big(\underline{r}_{[\underline{\hat{\delta}}^{-i},\gamma_i]}(i) - \varepsilon(1+\beta)\,\underline{e}\big)$$

$$= \underline{v}_{[\underline{\hat{\delta}}^{-i},\gamma_i]}(i) - \frac{\varepsilon(1+\beta)}{1-\beta}\,\underline{e} \tag{44}$$

where $\underline{e}$ is a vector with 1 in every entry.

Combining (42) and (44), we obtain, $\forall s\in S$, $\forall i\in I$, $\forall \gamma_i\in\Delta_i$

$$v_{\underline{\hat{\delta}}}(s,i) \geq \hat{v}(s,i) - \frac{\varepsilon(2+\beta)}{1-\beta} \geq v_{[\underline{\hat{\delta}}^{-i},\gamma_i]}(s,i) - \frac{\varepsilon(3+2\beta)}{1-\beta} \tag{45}$$

and $\underline{\hat{\delta}}$ is a $\frac{\varepsilon(3+2\beta)}{1-\beta}$ - equilibrium □

Let $T = \sum_{i\in I} \sum_{s\in S} \mathrm{Card}(B_{is})$ represent the total number of actions. Thus we can find an equilibrium point by minimizing a polynomial function of degree 2(N+1) of 3N×Card(S)+2T variables, subject to 2N×Card(S) linear and T polynomial constraints. Indeed, by similar methods we can obtain an equivalent formulation with only linear constraints, but at the cost of introducing T more variables. Of course, in the two-player case, all the constraints are linear.

We have not yet proceeded to an extensive numerical experimentation of this algorithm. As a preliminary result let us mention that we have used the non-linear programming package SOL/NPSOL (Gill et al (1983)) to solve the mathematical program (22)-(26) associated with the <u>static</u>

3-player game of example 2 in Van Der Lan (1982) and obtained the equilibrium strategy (with $\varepsilon^2 = 0{,}2 \times 10^{-8}$) in 150 CPU seconds on a VAX-11 computer. In a static game the mathematical programming problem is much easier to solve.

5. STRUCTURED STOCHASTIC GAMES

It is known that the general class of discounted stochastic games is in a certain mathematical sense «too large». It has been shown that this class does not possess «the ordered field property»; for instance, even in the zero-sum case when all the data of the game are rational the value vector can have irrational entries. The importance of this property was first noted in Parthasarathy and Raghavan (1981), since it is this property which is the most natural indicator that the game may be solvable by finite methods. The latter paper initiated the search for «Structured Markov Games» which are not only solvable in stationary strategies but also possess the ordered field property. Four such classes have now been identified and studied: 1. the Single-Controller Stochastic Games, 2. the Switching-Controller Stochastic Games, 3. the Games with State Independent Transitions and Separable Rewards, 4. the Games with Additive Reward and Transition Structure.

The ordered field property has, at least partially, fulfilled its promise for all of the above classes, in the sense that finite solution methods are now known for many of them. In the case of the single-controller zero-sum stochastic games (and also of the games in class 3.) the known methods are efficient and easy to implement (e.g., see Hordijk and Kallenberg (1981), Vrieze (1981), Parthasarathy, Tijs and Vrieze (1984), Filar (1985) and Mohan and Raghavan (1983)).

The case of switching-controller games is, however, one of a much greater order of difficulty, as indicated by the methods of Vrieze, Tijs, Raghavan and Filar (1983). For the zero-sum switching-controller, and the additive reward transition games, Filar and Schultz (1985) exploited the special structure to derive bilinear programming algorithms for computing equilibrium strategies. The latter results, as well as the single-controller results of Filar (1985), Hordijk and Kallenberg (1981) and Vrieze (1983) can all be viewed as naturally leading to the unified mathematical programming formulation of Section 4.4, which treats the general-sum, N-person games.

Another advantage of the latter formulation is that in many cases it generalizes to undiscounted stochastic games. For these games the stationary equilibrium strategies need not exist (e.g., see Blackwell and Fergusson (1968)); however, often when they exist, they can be shown to be part of global solution of appropriate mathematical programs (e.g., see Filar and Schultz (1985), Filar (1985), Hordijk and Kallenberg (1981) and Vrieze (1981)).

6. Conclusion

This paper has briefly reviewed the existing algorithms for computing equilibria in discounted stochastic dynamic game (zero and nonzero-sum), and a new general algorithm for the computation of nonzero-sum game equilibria has been proposed.

For zero-sum two-person games it clearly appears that the Pollatschek and Avi-Itzhak algorithm, when it converges, is the fastest. The Shapley algorithm always converges with a relatively good performance in terms of CPU time. This leads to the conclusion that, to solve a zero-sum stochastic dynamic game, a good strategy should be to implement the hybrid algorithm described in Remark 3.7.

For nonzero-sum two-player games, the Rao and Chandrasekaran algorithm, implemented with the Lemke-Howson algorithm for the computation of static bimatrix game equilibria, is a first alternative. However, the convergence is not guaranteed. For N-person games, a general solution procedure has been proposed in section 4.3. It uses a nonlinear programming auxiliary problem. As shown in preliminary tests the speed of convergence of the procedure will probably be affected by the usual problems of ill-conditionning encountered in non convex mathematical programming problems.

7. REFERENCES

Başar, T. and G.J. Olsder (1982), Dynamic Noncooperative Game Theory, Academic Press.

Bertsekas, D.P. and S.E. Shreve (1978), Stochastic Optimal Control : The Discrete Time Case, Academic Press.

Blackwell, D. and T.S. Ferguson (1968), «The Big Match», Ann. of Math. Stat., vol. 39, pp. 159-163.

Boel, R. and P. Varayia (1977), «Optimal Control of Jump Process», SIAM Journal on Control and Optimization, vol. 15, pp. 385-394.

Brown, G.W. (1951), «Iterative Solution of Games by Fictitious Play» in: Activity Analysis of Production and Allocation, Koopmans, T.C. (ed.) John Wiley, N.Y., pp. 374-376.

Case, J.H. (1969), «Toward a Theory of Many Player Differential Games», SIAM Journal on Control, vol. 7, no. 2, pp. 179-197

Clemhout, S. and H.Y. Wang (1974), «A Class of Trilinear Differential Games», Journ. of Opt. Theory and Applications, vol. 14, pp. 419-424.

Denardo, E.V. (1967), «Contraction Mappings in the Theory Underlying Dynamic Programming», Siam Rev. vol. 9, pp. 165-177.

Filar, J.A. (1985), «Quadratic Programming and the Single-Controller Stochastic Game», to appear in Journal of Math. Analysis and Appl.

Filar, J.A. and T. Schultz (1985), «Bilinear Programming and Structured Stochastic Games», to appear in Journ. of Opt. Theory and Applications.

Fink, A.M. (1964), «Equilibrium in a Stochastic n-Person Game», J. Sci. Hiroshima Univ. Ser., vol. A1;28, pp. 89-93.

Friedman, A. (1971), Differential Games, Wiley-Interscience, N.Y.

Gill, P.E., W. Murray, M.A. Saunders and M.H. Wright (1983), «Users' Guide for SOL/NPSOL : A Fortran Package for Non Linear Programming», Technical Report SOL 83-12, Stanford University, Stanford, California.

Haurie, A. and P. L'Écuyer (1982), «A Stochastic Control Approach to Group Preventive Replacement in a Multi-Component System», IEEE Trans. on Automatic Control, vol. AC-27, pp. 387-393.

Haurie, A. and P. L'Écuyer (1985), «Approximation and bounds in Discrete Event Dynamic Programming», to appear in IEEE Transactions.

Hoffman, A. and R. Karp (1966), «On Non-Terminating Stochastic Games», Man. Science vol. 12, pp. 359-370.

Hordijk, L. and Kallenberg, L.C.M. (1981), «Linear Programming and Markov Games I», in: Game Theory and Mathematical Economics, O.Moeschlin, D. Pallaschke (eds.), North-Holland, pp. 291-305.

Hordijk, L. and Kallenberg, L.C.M. (1981), «Linear Programming and Markov Games II», in: Game Theory and Mathematical Economics, O.Moeschlin, D. Pallaschke (eds.), North-Holland, pp. 307-319.

Hordijk, L., O.J. Vrieze and G.L. Wanrooij (1982), «Semi Markov Strategies in Stochastic Games», Intl. Journ. of Game Theory, vol. 12, pp. 81-89.

Isaacs, R. (1965), Differential Games, Wiley, New-York.

Karmadian, S. (1976), Fixed points : Algorithms and Applications, Academic Press, N.Y.

Lemke, C.E. and J.T. Howson (1964), «Equilibrium Points of Bimatrix Games», SIAM Journal on Applied Math., vol. 12, pp. 413-423.

Mohan, S.R. and Raghavan, T.E.S. (1983), An Algorithm for Switching Control Discounted Stochastic Games, Tech. Report., University of Illinois at Chicago.

Parthasarathy, T., S.H. Tijs and O.J. Vrieze (1984), «Stochastic Games with State Independant Transitions and Separable Rewards», In: Selected Topics in OR and Math. Economics, G. Hammer and D. Pollaschke (eds) Springer-Verlag Notes Series #226.

Parthasarathy, T. and T.E.S. Raghavan (1981), «An Ordered Field Property for Stochastic Games when One Player Controls Transition Probabilities», JOTA, vol. 33, pp. 375-392.

Pollatschek, M. and B. Avi-Itzhak (1969), «Algorithms for Stochastic Games with Geometrical Interpretation», Man. Science vol. 15, pp. 399-415.

Raghavan, T.E.S., (1984), Algorithms for Stochastic Games, A Survey, Technical Report, University of Illinois at Chicago.

Rao, S., R. Chandrasekaran and K. Nair (1973), «Algorithms for discounted Stochastic Games», JOTA vol. 11, pp. 627-637.

Rishel, R. (1977), «Optimality for Completely Observed Controlled Jump Processes», IEEE Trans. Autom. Cont., vol. AC-22, pp. 906-908.

Robinson, J. (1950), «An Iterative Method of Solving a Game», Ann. of Math., vol. 54, pp. 296-301.

Rogers, P.D. (1969), Nonzero-sum Stochastic Games, Ph. D. Thesis, University of California at Berkeley.

Shapley, L.S. (1953), «Stochastic Games», Proc. Nat. Acad. Sci. USA, vol. 39, pp. 1095-1100.

Sobel, M.J. (1971), «Noncooperative Stochastic Games», Annals of Math. Stat. vol. 42, pp. 1930-1935.

Van der Wal, J. (1978), «Discounted Markov Games : Generalized Policy Iteration Method», JOTA vol. 25, pp. 125-138.

Vrieze, O.J. (1981), «Linear Programming and Undiscounted Stochastic Games in Which One Player Controls Transitions», OR Spektrum, vol. 3, pp. 29-35.

Vrieze, O.J. (1983), Stochastic Games with Finite State and Action Spaces, Ph. D. Thesis, Free University of Amsterdam, The Netherlands.

Vrieze, O.J. and S.H. Tijs (1980), «Fictitious Play Applied to Sequences of Games and Discounted Stochastic Games», Intl. Journ. of Game Theory vol. 11, pp. 71-85.

Vrieze, O.J., S.H. Tijs, T.E.S. Raghavan and J.A. Filar (1983), «A Finite Algorithm for the Switching Control Stochastic Game», OR Spektrum, vol. 5, pp. 15-24.

Whitt, W. (1978), «Approximations of Dynamic Programs I», Math. of Oper. Res. vol. 2, pp.297-302.

Whitt, W. (1979), «Approximations of Dynamic Programs II», Math. of Oper. Res. vol. 3, pp. 231-243.

SOME ECONOMIC APPLICATIONS OF DYNAMIC STACKELBERG GAMES

Arunabha Bagchi
Department of Applied Mathematics
Twente University of Technology
P.O. Box 217, 7500 AE Enschede
The Netherlands

1. Introduction

Two equilibrium concepts are frequently used in connection with noncooperative games. When there is no cooperation among the players and they make decisions independently, the natural solution concept is the Nash equilibrium solution where no single player has an incentive to deviate unilaterally from that solution. On the other hand, when one or several player(s) has (have) dominant role(s) vis-a-vis the rest of the players, one has to introduce a hierarchical equilibrium concept, known as the Stackelberg equilibrium solution.

In many economic games, there is a structural hierarchy or domination in the decision making process. Multilevel planning is an obvious example of hierarchy, while financial or institutional power often enable some decision makers to impose their decisions on others. In this paper, we consider some economic models where economic games with hierarchy or domination arise naturally. They illustrate dynamic Stackelberg games in economic models and their methods of solutions. A thorough introduction to dynamic noncooperative games may be found in Başar and Olsder (1982).

2. Hierarchical Decision Maker: Regional Allocation of Investment

We illustrate hierarchical decision making by means of an example arising in the regional investment allocation problem (see Bagchi (1984) for details). We consider an economy consisting of two regions, 1 and 2, both of which want to grow optimally according to their own choice, but the savings they make in the process of growth are redistributed by the central planning board in order to reduce any disparity between the regions. There is an inherent conflict between the two regions in the optimization process and we assume that the regions play a noncooperative game between them. The planning board is the higher level decision maker and can impose its decision on the regions. However, a wrong decision on the part of the planning board could conceivably make everybody worse off - a situation which the planning board would naturally try to avoid. We can illustrate this by considering the extreme case when region 2 is so poor that it has to consume everything it produces in order to maintain the minimum level of consumption. The planning board may like, for equitable growth, to transfer a large part of the savings of region 1 to region 2. But, then, region 1 will have hardly any incentive to save at all and, inspite of all the good intentions, there will be no savings to be transferred. With hardly any saving for the economy as a whole, there will be disastrous consequences for the amount of total capital at the end of the planning period.

Let us formulate the problem mathematically. Consider an economy consisting of two regions which are administratively separated. Let K_i denote the capital, L_i the working population and Y_i the output of region i, i = 1,2. With Cobb-Douglas production function for each region,

$$Y_i = AK_i^{\alpha} L_i^{1-\alpha} \tag{2.1}$$

The population of each region grows exogenously at the rate n. Thus,

$$\dot{L}_i = nL_i \ , \ L_i(0) = L_{i0}, \ i = 1,2 \tag{2.2}$$

Let c_i denote the fraction of the output of region i used for consumption in that region and the planning board allocates a constant fraction $\beta(\gamma)$ of the savings of region 1(2) back to the same region. The system dynamics is then given by (with $k_i = K_i/L_i$, and $L_r = L_{10}/L_{20}$)

$$\dot{k}_1 = \beta Ak_1^{\alpha}(1-c_1) + (1-\gamma)\frac{1}{L_r} Ak_2^{\alpha}(1-c_2) - nk_1 \tag{2.3}$$

$$k_1(0) = k_{10}$$

$$\dot{k}_2 = (1-\beta)L_r Ak_1^{\alpha}(1-c_1) + \gamma Ak_2^{\alpha}(1-c_2) - nk_2 \tag{2.4}$$

$$k_2(0) = k_{20}$$

The planning board, which acts as a higher level decision maker, chooses β and γ. For fixed β and γ, the local authorities of the two regions act as lower level decision makers and use their consumption decisions as control variables to optimize their respective welfare criteria. Thus, for example, region i may want to choose c_i so as to maximize

$$J_i = \int_0^T \frac{1}{1-\nu}(c_i Ak_i^{\alpha} - \bar{x})^{1-\nu} dt + b_i k_i(T) \tag{2.5}$$

where $0 < \nu < 1$, $\bar{x}$ is the subsistence level of consumption, b_i,

$i = 1,2$, are constants and T is an appropriate planning horizon. Regions 1 and 2, for fixed β and γ, are interested in maximizing their respective criteria J_1 and J_2 subject to the dynamic constraints (2.3)-(2.4). With no cooperation and independent decision making by the regions, we have a Nash game at the lower level of the decision making process.

The next question is the policy issue confronting the planning board. It has to take basically two factors into account, while choosing an appropriate criterion. One is to reduce economic disparities between the regions at the end of the planning period and the other is to maximize the end capital available for future investment in the economy as a whole. One plausible choice of criterion is:

$$J = \varepsilon \frac{L_{1T}L_{2T}|k_{1T}-k_{2T}|}{(L_{1T}+L_{2T})(L_{1T}k_{1T}+L_{2T}k_{2T})} + (1-\varepsilon)\frac{L_{10}k_{10}+L_{20}k_{20}}{L_{1T}k_{1T}+L_{2T}k_{2T}} \tag{2.6}$$

where $L_{iT} \triangleq L_i(T)$ and $k_{iT} = k_i(T)$, $i = 1,2$ and $0 < \varepsilon < 1$.

The following questions arise immediately:

(a) The existence of a Nash equilibrium solution for the game played between the regions;
(b) the uniqueness of a Nash solution; and
(c) existence of a unique minimum of J defined above for $0 \leq \beta, \gamma \leq 1$.

Let us first suppose that J is minimized only on the boundary $\beta = 1$ or $\gamma = 1$. Then the Nash game played at the lower level reduces to a sequence of two optimal control problems. If, for example, $\gamma = 1$, region 1 can optimize its own consumption pattern independent of region 2. The optimal c_1 and k_1, thus obtained, can then be substituted in the optimization problem for region 2 where they appear only as exogenous quantities. The existence and uniqueness of Nash equilibrium solution is then assured using standard results in control theory (see e.g. van Long and Vousden (1977)).

What happens when $\beta < 1$ and $\gamma < 1$? In this case, both the regions give to and receive from the other region a part of their savings. This distribution mechanism is clearly unnecessary, since the region that gives more to the other region than what it receives back from it can only give this extra amount to the other region and avoid this obvious redundancy. There is also a more fundamental reason why the optimal β and γ cannot lie strictly inside the square $0 < \beta, \gamma < 1$. This has to do with the noncooperative game played at the regional level. Even if a region gets back some amount given from that region to the other one by the planning board, the consumption decision of that region is based on an implicit mistrust that any amount will at all be given back to the region and it reacts by consuming more than what it would do otherwise. This reduces the amount that can be transferred to the other region and both the regions become worse-off, without any noticable improvement in the income disparity between them. Extensive simulation studies have confirmed the validity of this intuition.

It is easy to extend our previous analysis to the n-region investment allocation problem. We may conclude that, for the optimal decision of the planning board, the following rule must prevail: "any region which has to give up part of its savings during the redistribution process cannot get any parts of the savings of the other regions". Suppose that out of the savings of region i, a fraction $\gamma_{i,j}$ is given to the region j for investment in that region. In terms of $\gamma_{i,j}$'s we can formulate our conclusion as follows: "$\gamma_{i,i} \neq 1 \Longrightarrow \gamma_{j,i} = 0$ for $j = 1,\ldots,n$, $j \neq i$". Of course, $\sum_{j=1}^{n} \gamma_{i,j} = 1$, $i = 1,\ldots,n$, always holds. Thus, the criterion for the planning board is optimized only on some edges of the parallelopiped $0 \leq \gamma_{i,j} \leq 1$, $j \neq 1$, $i,j = 1,\ldots,n$. It readily follows that at the regional level, for γ's on such edges, the game problem reduces to a sequence of n optimal control problems. The existence and uniqueness of the Nash equilibrium solution are assured for those γ's. We can also give a graph theoretic characterization of the optimal decisions, γ's, of the planning board. We denote a region by a node of a graph and the capital flow (via redistribution) from one region to another by a directed line It is, then, not possible for two nodes to be connected by directed lines in both the directions.

3. Dominant Decision Maker: An Embarge Game

We discuss a differential game model of oil embargo studied by Hauptman (1982). Player 1 is a cartel of oil producing countries that group together to decide on a possible embargo against another group of countries, denoted by player 2. The cartel acts first and the countries threatened by a possible embargo can only react to the decision of the cartel. Thus, Stackelberg solution concept is appropriate for such games.

It is assumed that the countries threatened with possible embargo have built up oil reserve. Let Y(t) denote the gross national product

(GNP) of player 2 at time t. Empirical studies have been carried out in the United States to consider the effect of the '73-'74 oil embargo on the GNP-loss caused by the shortfall of oil supply. Based on one such study, the rate of change of GNP can be described by

$$\dot{Y}(t) = (\alpha - cS(t)^2)Y(t), \tag{3.1}$$

$$Y(t_0) = Y_0 \tag{3.2}$$

where Y_0 is the GNP of the unit period ending at t_0 and $S(t)$ is the shortfall in the rate of oil supply. The control variable $u_1(t)$ of the cartel is its production cutback decision. There is a maximum technically feasible limit of production cutback:

$$0 \leq u_1(t) \leq \bar{z}_1, \quad t \in [t_0, t_1] \tag{3.3a}$$

where $u_1(t) = 0$ means full production and $u_1(t) = \bar{z}_1$ means total embargo.

The control variable of player 2 is clearly the drawdown policy from its reserve, which we denote by $u_2(t)$. This is also constrained by

$$0 \leq u_2(t) \leq \bar{z}_2 \tag{3.3b}$$

with $\bar{z}_2 \leq \bar{z}_1$, in general. If drawdown poses no technical problem, we can assume that $\bar{z}_1 = \bar{z}_2$. In terms of $u_1(t)$ and $u_2(t)$, we can write $S(t) = u_2(t) - u_1(t)$. It is realistic to impose the additional constraint

$$0 \leq u_2(t) \leq u_1(t) \tag{3.3c}$$

Finally, let R be the size of the oil stock in reserve. Then

$$\int_{t_0}^{t_1} u_2(t)dt \leq R \tag{3.3d}$$

We transform the integral constraint (3.3d) to a terminal state constraint by introducing an additional state variable. Thus, let $x_1(t) \triangleq Y(t)$ and $x_2(t) \triangleq \int_{t_0}^{t} u_2(s)ds$. The system is described by

$$\dot{x}_1 = (\alpha - c(u_2(t) - u_1(t))^2)x_1 \ , \ x_1(t_0) = x_0 \tag{3.4a}$$

$$\dot{x}_2 = u_2 \ , \ x_2(t_0) = 0 \tag{3.4b}$$

subject to the constraints (3.3a) - (3.3d).

Let us now specify the optimizing criteria for the two players. We suppose that player 1 wants to minimize

$$J_1(u_1,u_2) = -\int_{t_0}^{t_1} c(u_1(t) - u_2(t))^2 x_1(t) l_1(t)dt$$

$$+\int_{t_0}^{t_1} \tilde{c}u_2(t) l_2(t)dt, \quad \tilde{c} > 0 \tag{3.5a}$$

where l_1 is strictly decreasing and l_2 is strictly increasing positive convex functions of time in $[t_0,t_1]$. Criterion (3.5a) can be interpreted as follows: the first integrand describes the ability of the cartel to cause GNP-loss of player 2 and the second integral represents income losses to player 1 due to export cutbacks. Player 2, in turn, is assumed to be interested only in minimizing its total GNP-loss and the criterion for player 2 can be expressed as

$$J_2(u_1,u_2) = -\int_{t_0}^{t_1} x_1(t)dt \tag{3.5b}$$

We first solve the optimization problem for the follower (player 2). Consider the system (3.4a) - (3.4b) subject to the constraints (3.3a) - (3.3d) and with cost functional (3.5b). The Hamiltonian for this problem is

$$H_2(t,x_1,x_2,u_1,u_2,p_{02},p_{12},p_{22}) = -p_{02}x_1 + p_{12}(\alpha - c(u_1-u_2)^2)x_1 + p_{22}u_1 \tag{3.6}$$

with the set of terminal points $T = \{t_0, x_1(t_0) = x_0,\ x_2(t_0) = 0,\ t_1,\ 0 \le x_1(t_1),\ 0 \le x_2(t_1) \le R\}$. Pontryagin's maximum principle gives the following optimal control, given the decision $u_1(t)$ of player 1, as follows:

$$u_2^0(t) = \begin{cases} \min.(\bar{z}_2, u_1(t)) & \text{for } t \le t_r \text{ with } \int_{t_0}^{t_r} u_1(t)dt = R \\ 0 & \text{for } t > t_r \end{cases} \tag{3.7}$$

Turning now to the decision of the leader, we consider the state equation (3.4a) and the minimizing criterion (3.5a). The Hamiltonian now is

$$H_1(t,x_1,u_1,u_2,p_{01},p_{11}) = -p_{01}cl_1(t)(u_2 - u_1)^2 x_1$$

$$+ p_{01}\tilde{c}l_2(t)u_2 + p_{11}(\alpha - c(u_2 - u_1)^2)x_1 \tag{3.8}$$

Using the maximum principle again, one can conclude that the optimal decision for the cartel is $u_1^0(t) \equiv 0$ for $t_1 \in [t_0,t_r]$. Thus, the only case of interest is when the terminal time $t_1 > t_r$. In this case

$$u_1^0(t) = \bar{z}_1 \tag{3.9}$$

as long as

$$\bar{z}_1 \geq \frac{\tilde{c}l_2(t_1)}{cl_1(t_1)x_1(t_1)} \tag{3.10}$$

But, in this situation, $x_1(t_1) = x_{1_n}(t_r)$ exp. $(\alpha - c\bar{z}_1^2)(t_1 - t_r)$ and eq^n. (3.10) can be checked. When eq^n. (3.10) ceases to hold, $u_1^0(t)$ switches back to 0. Taking t_1 as a variable, one can determine the time t^* at which $u_1^0(t)$ switches back from $\bar{z}_1$ to 0. Thus, for $t_1 < t_r$, no embargo is the optimal solution. For $t_1 > t_r$, total embargo of limited duration is the best policy.

In the real embargo situation, t_1 is not predetermined. Thus, if the cartel wants the decision for an embargo, $t_r < t^*$ has to be fulfilled and $t_1 \in (t_r, t^*)$ has to be chosen. The choice of terminal time causing the greatest loss to player 2 is t^*. The decision of imposing an embargo depends heavily on the ratio of the two weighting functions l_1 and l_2.

4. Dominant Decision Maker: A World Industrialization Model

In the late sixties, in a U.N.I.D.O. conference held at Lima, it was agreed that, by the year 2000, the industrial production of the less developed countries should be at least one-fourth the total industrial production of the world as a whole. As a follow-up to this declaration, a dynamic, multisectoral, multiregional linear input-output world industrialization model has been developed by Opdam and Ten Kate (1978) and the feasibility of the "Lima target" has been studied within the production and trade possibilities. The approach we discuss here differs from Opdam and Ten Kate (1978) in the role of the different regions in the optimization process and in assuming that each region has its own optimization criterion which may be in conflict with one another. This leads to a multicriteria Stackelberg game of which we give two possible formulations: one as a linear-quadratic game and the other in the linear programming set up.

4.1 Linear-Quadratic Stackelberg Game

The model described in Opdam and Ten Kate (1978) was slightly modified by Moraal (1980) to give a state space description of the system, where the control and state variables have been specified. Thus, we divide the world into R regions, in each of which there are n different production sectors, m(≤n) of which may be traded in the world market (world goods). Each region can decide on its savings and imports from other regions, so that they can be assumed to be control variables. The population in each region and intraregional trade are assumed to be exogenously specified in this model. The state variables are gross national products and new investments, the evolution of which are described by

$$x_{rt} = A^1_{rt} x_{\overline{rt-1}} + A^2_{rt} i^{new}_{\overline{rt-1}} + \sum_{i=1}^{R} B^1_{rt} m^{wi}_{rt} + B^2_{rt} S_{rt} + \sum_{i=1}^{R} B^3_{rt} m^{wr}_{it} + C^1_{rt} m^{wr}_{rt} + C^2_{rt} P_{rt} \qquad (4.1)$$

$$i^{new}_{rt} = A^3_{rt} x_{\overline{rt-1}} + A^4_{rt} i^{new}_{\overline{rt-1}} + \sum_{\substack{i=1 \\ i\neq r}}^{R} B^4_{rt} m^{wi}_{rt} + B^5_{rt} S_{rt} + \sum_{\substack{i=1 \\ i\neq r}}^{R} B^6_{rt} m^{wr}_{it} + C^3_{rt} m^{wr}_{rt} + C^4_{rt} P_{rt} \qquad (4.2)$$

$$(r = 1,\ldots,R;\ t = 1,\ldots,T)$$

where

x_{rt} = n-vector with components denoting GNP per sector in region r at time t;

i^{new}_{rt} = n-vector with components denoting new investments per sector of origin in region r at time t;

m^{wi}_{rt} = m-vector of control (instrument) variables with components denoting imports of world goods per sector in region r at time t from region i(i≠r);

S_{rt} = scalar control (instrument) variable, denoting the controllable part of the savings of region r at time t;

m^{wr}_{rt} = m-vector of exogenous variables with components denoting intraregional imports of world goods per sector in region r at time t;

P_{rt} = scalar exogenous variable, the population of region r at time t.

Define

$$z_{rt} = [x'_{rt}\, i^{new'}_{rt}]' \quad , \quad e_{rt} = [m^{wr'}_{rt}\, P_{rt}]'$$

$$u_{rt} = [m^{w1'}_{rt} \ldots m^{\overline{wr-1}'}_{rt} \quad m^{\overline{wr+1}'}_{rt} \ldots m^{wR'}_{rt}\, S_{rt}]'$$

$$z_t = [z'_{1t} \ldots z'_{Rt}]' \quad , \quad e_t = [e'_{1t} \ldots e'_{Rt}]'$$

Then, we can write (4.1) and (4.2) together as

$$z_t = A_t z_{t-1} + \sum_{j=1}^{R} B_{jt} u_{jt} + C_t e_t \tag{4.3}$$

with appropriate block diagonal matrices A_t, B_{jt} and C_t.

Suppose that region r wants to minimize its own criterion which we denote by J_r. We assume quadratic form for J_r and take, in general,

$$J_r = \sum_{t=1}^{T} \{(z_t - \hat{z}_t^r)' Q_{rt} (z_t - \hat{z}_t^r) + \sum_{j=1}^{R} (u_{jt} - \hat{u}_{jt}^r)' R_{rjt} (u_{jt} - \hat{u}_{jt}^r)\} \tag{4.4}$$

where $\hat{z}_t^r$, $\hat{u}_{1t}^r, \ldots, \hat{u}_{Rt}^r$ are the desired nominal paths of the state and control variables for region r. Similar "tracking" criteria in the context of Nash games have been studied by Pindyck (1977), where the two players were the fiscal and monetary authorities in the United States.

It is only realistic to assume that some regions play a dominant role in the multicriteria optimization problem formulated above. We divide the world into 3 regions of the developed market economies (DME's, r = 1), the less developed market economies (LME's, r = 2) and the centrally planned economies (CPE's, r = 3). The purpose is to use this model to study the development possibilities of the modern industrial sector of LME's. The LME's must import industrial goods for rapid industrialization, but are heavily dependent for this purpose on their exports to pay for the needed imports.But their exports are controlled by the import policies of the rest of the world economies. LME's, therefore, should realistically be considered as followers in the game formulated above.

The CPE's trade mostly in barter fashion with the LME's and are interested in balancing the account. One can, with some justification, treat it as exogenous to the model. In this situation, the DME's play the role of the leader. One can, as well, treat both the DME's and CPE's as leaders in this game. Here we assume dat DME's act as a leader, LME's as a follower and CPE's are treated as exogenous to the model.

As regards the criteria for the regions, it is obvious that in the first place, they aim at optimizing their own welfare; for example, maximizing the consumption, minimizing the balance-of-payments deficits and so on. At the same time, however, there is a general consensus between the DME's and LME's on the desirability of sufficient industrial development of the latter. The Lima target is one such common goal which can be incorporated in the criteria of both the regions. The solution of this Stackelberg game will depend upon the information available to the regions during the decision making process. We did not bother with this aspect in the preceding sections since we were only interested in open-loop Stackelberg solutions. Depending on the information structure, one may study open-loop, feedback and closed-loop Stackelberg games. These are discussed in detail in Basar and Olsder (1982), where explicit solutions for linear-quadratic Stackelberg games under some information structures are also given.

A new situation arises if we assume, that the OPEC countries have dominant roles in some decision variables, while the DME's dominate in others. An equilibrium solution concept in such situations is an interesting area for investigation.

4.2 Stackelberg Games in Linear Programming Context

One serious drawback in converting input-output models in economics into state space form is that, in the latter situation, the state variables will not automatically be nonnegative. If we impose nonnegativity as state constraints, the resulting linear-quadratic Stackelberg games cannot be explicitly solved anymore. An alternative approach is to proceed directly with the original model and this we now discuss. The details of what follows may be found in Bagchi (1984).

For the Stackelberg linear programming problem to be of managable dimension, we consider a simple aggregated model consisting only of 3 sectors:

1. The "Traditional" sector, composed of sectors producing agricultural, mining and food products;
2. The "Modern Industry" sector, composed of sectors producing chemicals, metals and equipment;
3. The "Services" sector, consisting of transport, communication, construction and services.

For convenience, we list all the symbols used below:

x : vector of gross output by sector
$\bar{A}$: technology matrix of input-output coefficients
c : vector of final consumption by sector
i : vector of total investments by sector of origin
e : vector of exports by sector
m : vector of imports by sector
Y : gross national product by region
α : vector of gross value added coefficients
P : total population by region
C : total consumption expenditures by region

γ_0 : vector of coefficients with the sum of elements equal to 0
S : controllable part of savings
σ_0 : scalar coefficients giving autonomous part of per capita savings
$i^{repl.}$: vector of replacement investment by sector of origin
i^{new} : vector of new investments by sector of origin
h : vector of accumulated new investments over a period of θ (time steps) years by sector of destination
$\hat{\kappa}$: diagonal matrix of marginal sectoral capital-output ratios
$\hat{\omega}_0, \hat{\omega}_1$: diagonal matrix of weights; $\hat{\omega}_0 + \hat{\omega}_1 = I$
k : vector of capital stocks
$\hat{\delta}_0$: diagonal matrix of replacement ratios
γ_1 : vector of coefficients with the sum of elements equal to 1.

The input-output model of Opdam and Ten Kate (1978), aggregated for 3 sectors, can now be expressed as the following two basic model constraints:

$$R_r x_{rt} \geq (\hat{\delta}_{or} - \hat{\omega}_1^{-1} \tfrac{1}{\theta})\bar{K}_r x_{r\,\overline{t-1}} - \hat{\omega}_1^{-1} \hat{\omega}_0 i_{r\,\overline{t-1}}^{new}$$

$$+ (B_3-B_1)m_{rt}^{wi} - \gamma_{1r}S_{rt} + B_2 m_{it}^{wr} + (\gamma_{0r}-\gamma_{1r}\sigma_{0r})P_{rt} \qquad (4.5)$$

and

$$i_{rt}^{new} = \hat{\omega}_1^{-1} \tfrac{1}{\theta} \bar{K}_r x_{rt} - \hat{\omega}_1^{-1} \tfrac{1}{\theta} \bar{K}_r x_{r\,\overline{t-1}} - \hat{\omega}_1^{-1} \hat{\omega}_0 i_{r\,\overline{t-1}}^{new} \qquad (4.6)$$

$$r = 1,2;\ i = 1,2;\ i \neq r,\ t = 1,2,3$$

where

$$R_r = I - \bar{A}_r - \gamma_{1r}\alpha_r' - \hat{\omega}_1^{-1} \tfrac{1}{\theta} \bar{K}_r.$$

We take θ = 10 years, 1970 as the base year and the terminal year is 2000.

To make the model realistic, we have to impose some additional constraints. Let x_{rtj} denote the j-th component of the vector x_{rt} and use similar notations for other vectors. There must be some allowable limits to balance-of-payments deficits and surpluses. Assume that CPE's have perfect balance of trade with other regions. We can express this by

$$B_{rt}^{l} \leq [1\ 1]\ (m_{it}^{wr} - m_{rt}^{wi}) \leq B_{rt}^{u} \qquad (4.7)$$

There is also a limit to import substitution, which we represent by

$$m^{wi}_{rtj} \geq \{(1-\varepsilon^{i}_{rj})^{t} \, m^{wi}_{r0j} \big/ x_{r0j}\} x_{rtj} \tag{4.8}$$

with ε^{i}_{rj}, $i \neq r$, $i,j,r = 1,2$, constants.

There is obviously a limit to export growth for world goods by region of destination which we take to be of geometric type:

$$m^{wr}_{it} \leq (1+\hat{\pi}^{i}_{r})^{t\theta} \, m^{wr}_{i0} \tag{4.9}$$

There is also savings constraint which we take as

$$S_{rt} \leq 0.25 \, Y_{rt} \tag{4.10}$$

Finally, we take the Lima target as a constraint in the model. In our notation, we can express this as

$$x_{232} \geq \alpha(x_{132}+x_{232}) \tag{4.11}$$

Equations (4.5) - (4.11) constitute the model constraints. There are altogether 51 inequalities in the model. Control variables for regions r, $r = 1,2$, are x_{rt}, i^{new}_{rt}, m^{wi}_{rt}, S_{rt}, $i = 1,2$, $i \neq r$, $t = 1,2,3$. Both DME's and LME's have altogether 27 control or instrumental variables.

We consider the linear criterion of discounted total consumption for both the regions. Thus, region r, $r = 1,2$, wants to minimize

$$J_r = -\sum_{t=1}^{3} C_{rt} \big/ (1+\eta_r)^{\theta(t-1)}, \quad \eta_r \text{ specified constant.}$$

Choosing η_r so that $(1+\eta_r)^{\theta} = 2$, we have the simplified criterion

$$J_r = \{\sigma_{0r}P_{r1} + \tfrac{1}{2}\sigma_{0r}P_{r2} + \tfrac{1}{4}\sigma_{0r}P_{r3}\}$$

$$+ \{-\alpha'_r x_{r1} + S_{r1} - \tfrac{1}{2}\alpha'_r x_{r2} + \tfrac{1}{2}S_{r2} - \tfrac{1}{4}\alpha'_r x_{r3} + \tfrac{1}{4}S_{r3}\} \tag{4.12}$$

The Stackelberg problem we are faced with can be abstractly described as follows:
We have two players, the leader (1) and the follower (2). Decision variables for the leader, $u_1 \in \mathbb{R}^{m_1}$ and those for the follower, $u_2 \in \mathbb{R}^{m_2}$. The leader chooses u_1 and the follower chooses u_2 to minimize respectively

$$J_1(u_1,u_2) = c'_{11}u_1 + c'_{12}u_2 \text{ and } J_2(u_1,u_2) = c'_{21}u_1 + c'_{22}u_2.$$

Decisions of both the players are restricted to a feasible set

$$FS = \{(u_1,u_2) \mid A_1u_1+A_2u_2 \leq b; \; u_1 \geq 0, \; u_2 \geq 0\}.$$

Follower's LP problem (P1):

With announced u_1^0,

$$\text{minimize } c_{21}'u_1^0 + c_{22}'u_2$$

$$\text{subject to } A_2u_2 \le b - A_1u_1^0;\ u_2 \ge 0.$$

Assume that, given $u_1 \in \mathbb{R}^{m_1}$, there exists a unique optimal $u_2^0(u_1)$ for problem (P1).

Leader's optimization problem (P2):

$$\text{minimize } c_{11}'u_1 + c_{12}'u_2$$

$$\text{subject to } A_1u_1 + A_2u_2 \le b;\ u_1 \ge 0,\ u_2 \ge 0$$

$$u_2 = u_2^0(u_1).$$

Define the reaction curve

$$RC = \{(u_1,u_2)\,|\,u_1 \text{ is admissible and } u_2 = u_2^0(u_1)\}$$

Problem (P2) is then equivalent to

$$\text{minimize } J_1(u_1,u_2) \text{ subject to } (u_1,u_2) \in RC.$$

Problem (P2) is nonstandard since RC is not convex anymore. It is possible, however, to develop a simplex-type algorithm to solve this Stackelberg linear programming (SLP)-problem. The algorithm depends crucially on the following two properties:

Property 1. If a team solution (for the leader) exists, a Stackelberg solution also exists (a Team solution for the leader is a minimum point for $J_1(u_1,u_2)$ on FS). Moreover, if (u_1^0,u_2^0) is a Team solution and $(u_1^0,u_2^0) \in RC$, then (u_1^0,u_2^0) is a Stackelberg solution.

Property 2. If a Stackelberg solution exists, there is a Stackelberg solution at an extreme point of FS.

Briefly, the algorithm works as follows: start by computing a Team solution for the leader. If it is on RC, we stop. Otherwise move from one extreme point of FS to an adjacent extreme point, just as in the simplex algorithm. This algorithm has been used for simulation studies of the simple world industrialization model described above. Based on the simulation runs, one can make the following observations:

(1) In all the simulation runs, results for the year 1980 are identical. Both regions have maximum savings and no overproduction. The DME's have maximum trade deficit possible and this is effected by

maximum trade deficit in the traditional sector and a slight trade surplus in the industrial sector.

(2) Differences in the results for different α's start to appear in the year 1990. Savings are still maximum and no overproduction takes place. Trade deficit for DME's is not maximum possible for $\alpha = 0.2$, but is again maximum for $\alpha = 0.3$. The effect of "Lima target" set for the year 2000 is already noticeable in the year 1990. The LME's have strong tendency to increase their industrial production, while the DME's pay some more attention to their traditional sector.

(3) In the year 2000, the effect of "Lima target" is clear. There is still no overproduction while savings for LME's is maximum in all the simulation runs. For $\alpha = 0.3$, however, the DME's do not use their maximum growth possibilities. The LME's have maximum trade deficit possible, effected through maximum allowed trade deficit in the traditional sector and a slight trade surplus in the industrial sector, an exact replica of the trade pattern of the DME's in the year 1980.

5. Conclusion

By means of specific economic models, various kinds of Stackelberg differential games have been analyzed in the present survey. The economic models discussed lead to theoretical questions of considerable complexity not all of which have yet been resolved satisfactorily. Stackelberg set-up leads to another interesting area of research in economics- the theory of incentives. A survey of the incentives problem may be found in Ho, Luh and Olsder (1982).

6. References

Bagchi, A. (1984), Stackelberg Differential Games in Economic Models, Lecture Notes in Control and Information Sciences, Springer-Verlag, Berlin.

Başar, T. and G.J. Olsder (1982), Dynamic Noncooperative Game Theory, Academic Press, London.

Hauptman, H. (1982), "Stackelberg Strategies and An Embargo Game", in Optimal Control Theory and Economic Analysis, G. Feichtinger (Ed.), North-Holland, Amsterdam.

Ho, Y.C., P. Luh and G.J. Olsder (1982), "A Control Theoretic View of Incentives", Automatica, vol. 18, pp. 167-179.

Moraal, M. (1980), "State Space Representation and Simulation of a Simple World Industrialization Model", TW Memorandum, no. 300, Dept. of Applied Mathematics, Twente University of Technology, Enschede, The Netherlands.

Opdam, H . and A. Ten Kate (1978), "A Simple World Industrialization Model", Internal Report, Centre for Development Planning, Erasmus University, Rotterdam.

Long, N. van and N. Vousden, "Optimal Control Theorems", in _Applications of Control Theory to Economic Analysis_, J.D. Pitchford and S.J. Turnovsky (Eds.), North-Holland, Amsterdam.

Pindyck, R.S. (1977), "Optimal Planning for Economic Stabilization Policies Under Decentralized Control and Conflicting Objectives", _IEEE Transactions on Automatic Control_, vol. AC-22, pp. 517-530.

APPLICATIONS OF DYNAMIC GAME THEORY TO MACROECONOMICS

Matti Pohjola*
Department of Economics
University of Helsinki
Aleksanterinkatu 7
00100 Helsinki, Finland

Abstract

This paper surveys some macroeconomic applications of dynamic game theory. We begin by defining dynamic games and their solution concepts. We then turn to the applications and cover the following areas: economic growth and income distribution, macroeconomic stabilization, interaction between the government and the private sector, international policy co-ordination and conflicts among sectors in the economy.

1. Introduction

Modern macroeconomic modelling has reached a level of sophistication which is unprecedented in the fifty-year history of macroeconomic thought. In the first four decades following Frisch's introduction in 1933 of the term "macroeconomics" and the publication in 1936 of Keynes's General Theory, analyses of relations between broad economic aggregates were based on models in which the decisions of the mass of private agents were subsumed in simple ad hoc rules of behaviour. Von Neumann's and Morgenstern's pioneering contribution to the strategic behaviour of economic actors remained unnoticed by macroeconomists. The works of Nyblén (1951) and Faxén (1957) are the exceptions needed to prove this rule. Modern models have much firmer microeconomic foundations. They are designed for analyses of the dynamics arising from the interactions among different rational decision-makers such as private agents, interest groups, fiscal and monetary authorities as well as present and future governments. Discussions are conducted in terms like cooperative and noncooperative strategies, information structures and Nash and Stackelberg equilibria. Macroeconomic theory has essentially been rewritten in the past ten years. Dynamic game theory has here played an important

---

*I wish to thank Pertti Haaparanta, Seppo Honkapohja and Raimo P. Hämäläinen for helpful comments. Financial support from the Yrjö Jahnsson Foundation is also gratefully acknowledged. The usual disclaimer applies.

role which was first implicit but has recently been explicitly recognized. For example, Lucas (1985, p. 11), who is one of the main contributors to the new macroeconomics, states that "... the main criticism of Keynesian models and their use in formulating policies that one associates with the idea of 'rational expectations' are all straightforward consequences of the acceptance of the general formalism of dynamic games ..."

Macroeconomic applications of dynamic game theory are quite recent, but their number is rapidly increasing. As far as I know, no survey of them has yet been made. Given that we can view dynamic game theory as a child of the parents game theory and optimal control theory [Başar and Olsder (1982, p.2)], it is natural to look for one in the existing macroeconomic biographies of the parents. The recent surveys by Schotter and Schwödiauer (1980) and Shubik (1982) of game theory models contain no macroeconomic applications. Kendrick's (1976, 1981) and Pau's (1979) surveys of optimal control theory models do have some references to early applications of dynamic game theory, but these are not given the consideration they deserve. The biographies by Case (1979), Clemhout and Wan (1979) and Başar and Olsder (1982) of the grown-up child are equally terse on its achievements in macroeconomics.

In this paper I shall try to trace the first macroeconomic steps taken by dynamic game theory. This will be done by making first a portrait of the child in section 2 and then by describing in sections 3 and 4 its achievements in the shadow of the parent optimal control theory in the fields of economic growth and stabilization policy. The more independent life in the modelling of government - private sector interactions, international policy coordination problems and interdependence between sectors in the economy are covered in sections 5, 6 and 7.

When I began to work on this survey, I had in mind a more technical presentation. The great variety of existing models led me to reject this idea soon. I instead decided to characterize questions posed, approaches taken, results obtained and future work suggested in each of the fields of application covered in this paper. As I have personally worked in only one of these areas, my views must be biased. There must also exist many models which I am not aware of. All omissions are, however, unintentional.

2. Dynamic games: concepts and solutions

To illustrate dynamic games and their solution concepts, let us here consider two-player nonzero-sum differential (i.e. continuous-time) games only and refer to Başar and Olsder (1982) for a comprehensive treatment. To keep the analysis simple, let us assume that each player has only one control variable and that the system can be described by scalar state variable $x(t)$ in which t denotes time. The evolution of the state is governed by the differential equation

$$\dot{x}(t) = f(t,x(t),u_1(t),u_2(t)) \; ; \; x(0) = x_0 , \tag{1}$$

where $u_i(t)$ is player i's control variable belonging to a prescribed control region. Player i is assumed to choose his strategy so as to maximize the objective function

$$J_i(u_1,u_2) = {}_0\int^T L_i(t,x(t),u_1(t),u_2(t))dt , \tag{2}$$

in which T denotes the horizon date.

Playing open-loop strategies, the players announce and commit themselves to control variables which are functions of time and the initial state: $u_i(t) = u_i(t,x_0)$. Playing feedback strategies, they announce and commit to control laws which make the control variables depend on time and the current state: $u_i(t) = u_i(t,x(t))$. It is also possible for them to apply more general closed-loop strategies with memory. These are, however, more difficult to analyse because of the informational nonuniqueness of equilibria based on them.

A strategy pair (u_1^*,u_2^*) is said to constitute an open-loop Nash equilibrium of the differential game defined in equations (1) and (2) if, and only if,

$$\begin{aligned} &J_1(u_1^*,u_2^*) \geqq J_1(u_1,u_2^*) , \\ &J_2(u_1^*,u_2^*) \geqq J_2(u_1^*,u_2) \end{aligned} \tag{3}$$

for all admissible open-loop strategies u_1 and u_2. These inequalities mean that the path to which each player commits himself is an optimal response to the opponent's choice when viewed from the initial (date, state) pair. The continuation of this strategy is not, however, required to be an optimal response when viewed from any intermediate (date, state) pair. This more stringent condition is also met if the players apply feedback strategies. The feedback Nash equilibrium is defined by inequalities (3) added with the requirement that they hold for all $(t,x(t))$. It is thus subgame perfect [Selten (1975)] because the equilibrium conditions are satisfied in every subgame of the original game.

As the concept of time consistency of an equilibrium will be discussed in sections 5 and 6, let us here observe that although the open-loop Nash equilibrium is not subgame perfect, it is nevertheless time consistent. By this we mean that the continuation of the equilibrium solution remains a Nash equilibrium along the optimal path. This property follows directly from inequalities (3), whereby, given the opponent's choice, each player's optimization problem is a standard control problem satisfying the principle of optimality. The subgame perfectness of an equilibrium is thus a stronger requirement than its time consistency, and their difference relates to the specification of nonequilibrium behaviour.

It is not necessary here to go into the details of the derivation of either open-loop or feedback Nash equilibria since they have been well documented by, for example, Başar and Olsder (1982). Let us just recall that the two solutions are not equivalent in general. An intuitive explanation is as follows: playing feedback strategies, each player knows that his decision will affect the state variable, which will in turn have an impact on the opponent's decision in the future. This link between the players' choices is missing if they apply open-loop strategies. There do, however, exist games for which an open-loop Nash equilibrium also qualifies as a feedback equilibrium. An important class of them are state-separable games [Dockner, Feichtinger and Jørgensen (1985)], in whose set of necessary conditions neither the costate equations nor the Hamiltonian - maximizing conditions depend on the state variable.

The Stackelberg solution is the relevant noncooperative equilibrium concept for the differential game defined in equations (1) and (2) if the roles of the players are asymmetric. There are two types of asymmetry to be considered. The first one is the case in which one of the players, the leader, is able to announce his whole course of action, i.e. strategy, first and impose it on the other player, the follower. The players can apply either open-loop or feedback strategies. The important thing to notice here is that we can use this kind of global open- or closed-loop Stackelberg solution to characterize an equilibrium between the players only if the leader can commit himself to his announcement. This observation follows from the fact that the leader's optimal strategy is time inconsistent, as will be demonstrated below, and consequently credible only under precommitment.

The second type of asymmetry arises if one of the players, the leader, is able to (or has to) act before the follower in every stage of the game. No strategic commitment is possible in this case. The players are assumed to have access to the current state information. They thus have asymmetric information structures. The leader knows the state and time whereas the follower knows the state, time and the control chosen by the leader. This feedback Stackelberg solution, introduced by Simaan and Cruz (1973b), can be shown to correspond to an equilibrium in a differential game having the described asymmetric information structure [Başar and Haurie (1984)]. The solution can be obtained via a dynamic programming approach. It is therefore subgame perfect and time consistent.

As the global Stackelberg solution has been widely applied in the modelling of the government - private sector interaction (see section 5), we here pause to explain briefly its derivation and the source of time inconsistency. Let us assume for simplicity that the players apply open-loop strategies u_1 and u_2 belonging to the strategy spaces U_1 and U_2 respectively. Assume that the reaction set of player 2

$$R_2(u_1^o) = \{u_2^o \varepsilon U_2 \; : \; J_2(u_1^o, u_2^o) = \max_{u_2 \varepsilon U_2} J_2(u_1^o, u_2)\} \qquad (4)$$

is a singleton for every decision u_1^o of player 1, so that it defines a mapping $T_2 \colon U_1 \to U_2$. Then a strategy pair $(\hat{u}_1, \hat{u}_2)$ constitutes an open-loop Stackelberg solution for the differential game (1) - (2) if

$$\begin{aligned} \hat{u}_1 &= \arg\max_{u_1 \varepsilon U_1} J_1(u_1, T_2 u_1) \, , \\ \hat{u}_2 &= T_2 \hat{u}_1 \, . \end{aligned} \qquad (5)$$

Assuming that the leader has announced a strategy u_1^o, the follower obtains his rational reaction according to (4) by solving the standard control problem of maximizing his payoff (2) subject to (1) and $u_1 = u_1^o$. The solution to this problem can be described by a set of necessary conditions consisting of the follower's costate equation and Hamiltonian-maximizing condition. This set as well as the state equation (1) form the constraints of the leader's control problem, whose solution yields the Stackelberg strategy according to (5). Consequently, the leader's problem contains two state variables: x(t) and the follower's costate variable y(t). This problem differs from a standard control problem in that the initial value of the 'state' y(t) is not given. The leader determines it through his choice of controls in an optimal way, i.e. so that his costate variable z(t) corresponding to y(t) satisfies z(0) = 0. The variable z(t) evolves according to $\dot{z} = -\partial H_1/\partial y$ where H_1 denotes the leader's Hamiltonian. Since $\dot{z} \neq 0$ in general, we have $z(t) \neq 0$ for $t > 0$. This means that the leader is willing to reoptimize at each date t, i.e. to announce a new plan which would yield $y(t)$ such that $z(t) = 0$. Consequently, the principle of optimality does not hold and the leader's strategy is time inconsistent. Credibility can be obtained under precommitment only.

A time-consistent, open-loop Stackelberg solution can be obtained by allowing the leader to revise his plans constantly and by assuming the follower to be aware of this. Such a solution, introduced by Cruz (1975), is obtained recursively via a dynamic programming approach. Leadership is here a property which applies to each stage of the game at a time. The leader is being forced to regard the state $x(t)$ as given at each date. This strategy is secure against potential changes by the leader during the game and we can safely call it an equilibrium. It is identical with the feedback Stackelberg equilibrium if the players apply feedback strategies instead of open-loop ones. The time-consistent solution obtained in this way, however, yields a lower payoff to the leader than the time-inconsistent Stackelberg solution indicating the importance to him of a period of commitment.

A time- consistent Stackelberg solution is also obtained if, by applying closed-loop (memory) strategies, the leader is able to force the follower to the team-optimal solution maximizing the leader's objective function. The leader formulates his strategy as a disguised threat, under which the follower then maximizes his own criterion. Such games were introduced by Başar and Selbuz (1979) as well as Papavassilopoulos and Cruz (1980). The leader's information set may also contain the follower's past controls, in which case the former can directly formulate incentives designed to induce the latter to behave in a desired way [see, for example, Zheng, Başar and Cruz (1984) as well as Ehtamo and Hämäläinen (1985)]. These memory or incentive strategies essentially turn the game into a team decision problem whose solution is time consistent (but not subgame perfect).

The two noncooperative solution concepts defined in the preceding paragraphs are not in general Pareto-optimal. In Pareto games the players have to make an agreement to cooperate. No player is allowed to deviate from the agreed-upon strategy. Pareto-optimal solutions are obtained by devising u_1 and u_2 so as to maximize

$$J(u_1,u_2) = \alpha J_1(u_1,u_2) + (1-\alpha) J_2(u_1,u_2) \,, \tag{6}$$

where α, $0 < \alpha < 1$, is an index of the bargaining strength of player 1.

The players may here choose to play open-loop strategies since, as the agreement is binding, there is no reason why they should not commit themselves to fixed functions of time at the start of the game.

The Pareto game leaves open the choice of α. Further rules are needed for this selection. The standard game-theoretic approach to model this choice is to formulate a set of axioms which state directly what the payoffs to the players should be under circumstances in which the outcome is obvious. These self-evident situations embody elementary principles of equity and basic restrictions on the use of power when a compromise is the objective. One of the solutions based on such axioms is the Nash bargaining solution. Under this scheme the payoffs to the players are obtained by devising u_1 and u_2 so as to maximize the Nash product

$$I(u_1,u_2) = [J_1(u_1,u_2) - J_1(\bar{u}_1,\bar{u}_2)]\,[J_2(u_1,u_2) - J_2(\bar{u}_1,\bar{u}_2)], \qquad (7)$$

where $\bar{u}_1$ and $\bar{u}_2$ are the status quo strategies applied in the case of no agreement. For example, noncooperative Nash solutions may be applied to define the status quo situation.

The strategies $\bar{u}_1$ and $\bar{u}_2$ can alternatively be defined as threats. It is clear from (7) that they define the outcome of negotiations between the players in a direct way. Knowing this, the players may derive them noncooperatively to satisfy the equilibrium conditions (3) and to maximize their negotiated payoffs. Sufficient conditions for this threat bargaining solution in differential games have been produced by Liu (1973).

We are now ready to turn to consider what applications the solution concepts introduced in this section have found in macroeconomics.

3. Games of economic growth and distribution

Nearly sixty years ago Frank Ramsey (1928) pioneered in a new field of economic theory which we nowadays call optimal economic growth. His work was more or less ignored during the rise of Keynesian macroeconomics when unemployment and inflation were regarded as the pressing issues. In many respects Ramsey's analysis was already quite general and it was extended in a number of ways, for example, by allowing for many capital goods, population growth, technical progress and uncertainty in the 1960's [for a survey see, for example, Wan (1971, Ch 10)]. This new theoretical interest in the issues of optimal economic growth arose as a direct consequence of the advances made in growth theory and control theory. Pontryagin's maximum principle was quickly adopted by economists.

In the heydays of the applications of optimal control theory to the modelling of economic growth, distributional issues were much neglected. This must have reflected the bias of the general economics profession to questions of growth as well as the immaturity of the methods which were available to deal with dynamic conflicts.

The first game-theoretic approach to distributional issues was formulated by Phelps and Pollak (1968), who viewed economic growth and distribution as an intergenerational conflict. Assuming that the present generation derives its utility from the consumption pattern of infinitely many nonoverlapping generations but that it can only control its own saving rate, they demonstrated that the Nash equilibrium of this intergenerational game results in under-saving. Their model cannot, however, be expressed in the form of equations (1) - (2) and, therefore, we shall not review the works based on this approach.

The first study applying dynamic game theory to the modelling of growth and distribution is due to Lancaster (1973). He took up the issues, studied by the classical economists Malthus, Ricardo and Marx, of capital accumulation and the distribution of income between the social classes and formulated them as a simple two-player noncooperative differential game between workers and capitalists. Lancaster's model has both a (neo-)Marxian and a Keynesian flavour. It is distinctly Marxian in the sense that he studies a labour-surplus economy and assumes that the workers can control income distribution in any given period by being able to set the share of their consumption in total output. Thus, distribution is prior to accumulation. The capitalists are assumed to control accumulation by being able to choose the share of investment in the surplus, i.e. in output which is not consumed by the workers. This disjunction of saving and investment decisions brings in some Keynesian flavour. Both social classes devise their strategies so as to maximize their own consumption over a finite horizon. By assuming technology to be linear, the game can be expressed in a form whose state equation (1) and criterion functions (2) are linear in the state variable $x(t)$, the capital stock. The game is relatively easy to solve and since it is state-separable its open-loop equilibrium also qualifies as the feedback Nash solution.

By comparing the noncooperative equilibrium with the cooperative solution which was obtained under the assumption that saving and investment decisions are derived so as to maximize total (worker plus capitalist consumption, Lancaster demonstrated that both social classes could obtain more consumption under cooperation. His important conclusion was that the Keynesian separation of saving and investment decisions results in dynamic inefficiency. Later Hoel (1978) showed that the game solution does not usually belong to the set of Pareto-optimal solutions and that it results in lower capital accumulation than all the cooperative solutions.

Table 1 summarizes the dynamic game models based on the Lancaster approach. It also contains the contributions of Hamada (1967), Marglin (1976), Stanley (1978) and Hammer (1981), in which the framework is somewhat different from Lancaster's. In these studies the government chooses the time path of income redistribution from workers to capitalists whose fixed saving rate is higher than that of the former class so as to maximize a weighted average of the worker and capitalist welfare. I have included these applications of optimal control theory in the Pareto-optimal solutions of "capitalism games".

The original Lancaster model has been technically extended in a number of ways. Hoel (1978) studied the implications of diminishing returns to capital, which make the state equation (1) nonlinear in the capital stock. Infinite horizon, nonlinear utility functions and the full-employment constraint have been introduced in Pohjola (1985).

Assuming that the general specification of a two-class society in which each class acts as a single decision-making unit is acceptable, the model can be further extended in a number of technical ways. First, to get rid of the assumption that there is only a single technique of production in existence, the fixed-coefficient production function should be replaced by a standard neoclassical one. The production technique would then be determined by the capitalists by choosing the level of employment and the rate of investment so as to maximize their objective function. The workers' control variable would now be the wage rate rather than the share of their consumption in output. Second, instead of assuming that there is no technical change or that it is exogenous and of the labour-augmenting type as in Pohjola (1985), we could assume that the capitalists can choose the rate as well as the direction of technical change subject to the innovation possibility frontier, which defines the trade-off between labour-augmenting and capital-augmenting technical progress. As dynamic games have not yet achieved the maturity of optimal control methods which have been extensively applied in growth theory, these extensions are not easy to carry out. Consequently, various authors (see Table 1) have chosen the alternative route of generalizing the institutional framework of the Lancaster model.

Information structure	Noncooperative solutions		Cooperative solutions	
	Nash	Stackelberg	Pareto	Nash's threat bargaining
Open loop	Lancaster (1973) Hoel (1978) Pohjola (1983b, 1984a, 1985) Buhl & Machaczek (1985)	Pohjola (1983a)	Hamada (1967) Lancaster (1973) Marglin (1976) Hoel (1978) Stanley (1978) Hammer (1981) Pohjola (1985)	Pohjola (1984b)
Feedback	Lancaster (1973) Pohjola (1983b, 1984a, 1985) Başar, Haurie & Ricci (1985)	Başar, Haurie & Ricci (1985)		

<u>Table 1</u>: Capitalism games

The explanation for the dynamic inefficiency displayed in these studies is a dynamic externality. One group's decision to save and invest for the future is affected by the fact that the accumulated amount may be consumed by some other group. Rationally acting players take into account this public good nature of provision for the future and, consequently, save and invest less than they would do under cooperation. Externalities also arise under other specifications of growth and distribution similar to those arising from the worker-capitalist conflict. An example is an economy where the working class is not a single decision-making unit but has organized itself in a number of competing unions [Pohjola (1984a)]. I have argued in Pohjola (1985) that we can explain in terms of this externality many current economic problems, such as high real wages, slow growth and unemployment, from a new viewpoint.

Ways of reducing the welfare loss which arises from the lack of cooperation between the social classes have been examined in a few studies. In Pohjola (1983b) it is demonstrated that a partial transfer of control over the investment decision from capitalists to workers improves both player's welfare. Such a transfer of economic power is an essential feature of the worker investment funds established recently in Sweden. Buhl and Machaczek (1985) have extended this approach by considering the implications of the worker ownership of capital. In Pohjola (1983a) I have compared the Nash solution to the Lancaster game with the open-loop Stackelberg solution. It turned out that both players prefer the Stackelberg formulation but that neither workers nor capitalists want to act as the leader. This means that the game is in a stalemate. The conclusion is, however, sensitive to the assumption about the information structure, as Başar, Haurie and Ricci (1985) have pointed out. They showed that both players want the capitalists to act as the leader if feedback strategies are applied. Under the workers' leadership the Stackelberg solution is equivalent to the feedback Nash equilibrium. In economic terms this conclusion follows from the neo-Marxian assumption concerning income distribution and it demonstrates the importance to the workers of a period of commitment. It is interesting to observe that in the practice of incomes policy it is the workers who apply open-loop strategies. The Nash bargaining solution and the optimal threats announced by the social classes to affect the negotiated solution to their own advantage are examined in Pohjola (1984b). It is demonstrated that the workers' threat takes the form of refusing to accept low wages while capitalists threaten to refrain from investing. The threats as well as the possible gains from cooperation determine the players' relative importance, or bargaining power, and it is shown that capitalists are in general in a stronger position than workers.

The games of distribution and growth surveyed here have not yet reached the maturity of optimal growth theory models. Much technical work is needed before we will be able to characterize the solutions to these problems without having to resort to special utility and production functions. Other possible avenues of future research might also include attempts to generalize the distribution theory applied in the Lancaster type models. An obvious alternative to the Marxian approach is the Keynesian theory in which effective demand plays a crucial role. Attempts by growth theorists to explain the distribution of wealth between the social classes would also benefit from a game-theoretic approach.

4. Macroeconomic stabilization games

In the 1970's control theory gained widespread application by economists in their analyses of macroeconomic stabilization problems [for surveys see Chow (1975) and Kendrick (1976, 1981)]. The research strategy followed was to estimate more and more realistic econometric macromodels and to apply more and more sophisticated control techniques to design better and better fiscal and monetary policies to be executed in perfect coordination by a single benevolent decision-maker, the government. This "Keynesian" approach can be summarized in Wan's (1985) pseudochemical reaction formula:

Econometric model	+	Control theory	→	Optimal stabilization

Even a parliamentary committee was established to report on the prospects of these new techniques [Committee on Policy Optimisation (1978)].

The view whereby fiscal and monetary policies are not coordinated and may sometimes be acting at cross purposes is old [see Mundell (1962) for a discussion of the assignment problem] and always timely [see, for example, Blinder (1983) for the current debate in the United States]. Consequently, given the increase in interest in the macroeconomic applications of optimal control theory which was experienced in the early 1970's, it comes as no surprise that the current wave of macroeconomic applications of dynamic game theory was initiated by the studies [Kydland (1975, 1976), Pindyck (1976, 1977)], in which the policy coordination issue was tackled. The approach taken was simply to replace the single policy-maker, the government, of the optimal control theory applications by two independent decision-makers, i.e. by the fiscal and monetary authorities.

We can give at least the following three reasons for the lack of coordination between fiscal and monetary policies:

(i) The two authorities may have different objective functions because either they have different conceptions of what is best for society or they have to act under different political pressures.

(ii) The policy-makers may have different models of the economy, which means that their opinions about the likely effects of monetary and fiscal policies differ.

(iii) Even if the authorities agree upon the working of the economy, their views about the likely effects of given policy measures may differ because they have different information in the form of measurements and forecasts available to them.

As far as I know, only case (i) has so far been considered in the literature. It can be handled by applying game theory. Case (iii) belongs to the realm of team decision theory. Case (ii) is, I believe, the most difficult one to model, but it might be tackled along the lines suggested in Başar (1985).

The analysis of the conflict between the fiscal and monetary authorities arising from different objectives was initiated by Kydland (1975, 1976) and Pindyck (1976, 1977). The dynamic game applications that I am familiar with are presented in Table 2. The approach taken and the results obtained in these works can be summarized by the following formula:

Econometric model	+	Game theory	→	Sub-optimal stabilization

The econometric model forms the state equations (1) of the game, where now the state vector x contains the policy-makers' target variables, u_1 denotes the fiscal policy instruments and u_2 the monetary policy variables. In all the studies reported on here f(.) is linear with respect to both state and control variables. It is specified in discrete-time form, except in Neck (1985). The authorities' objective functions (2) are quadratic loss functions in all studies except Neck (1985), in which they are linear. Pindyck (1976, 1977) as well as Neese and Pindyck (1984) applied an estimated model of the U.S. economy, Kydland (1976) and Hämäläinen (1978) used an ad hoc numerical model, whereas Kydland (1975) and Neck (1985) preferred theoretical formulations.

Information structure	Noncooperative solutions		Cooperative solutions	
	Nash	Stackelberg	Pareto	Nash Bargaining
Open loop	Kydland (1975) Pindyck (1976, 1977) Neese & Pindyck (1984) Neck (1985)	Kydland (1975)	Neese & Pindyck (1984) Neck (1985)	Neese & Pindyck (1984)
Feedback	Kydland (1975, 1976) Pindyck (1977) Neese & Pindyck (1984) Neck (1985)[b]	Kydland (1975, 1976)		
Periodic open loop-feedback	Hämäläinen (1978)			

Table 2: Macroeconomic stabilization games[a]

[a] All are linear-quadratic multi-stage games except Neck (1985), which is a linear-linear differential game.

[b] Neck actully derived only the open-loop solution, but since his game is state separable, it also qualifies as the feedback equilibrium.

These applications teach us the following:

(i) The relative timing of fiscal and monetary expansion is as important as the amounts of expansion [Pindyck (1976, 1977)]. This result follows from the fact that fiscal and monetary policies operate with different lags, making it necessary to study the policy conflict in an explicitly dynamic setting.

(ii) The conflict can indeed be severe [Pindyck (1976, 1977), Neese and Pindyck (1984)] and the policies may be working in exactly opposite directions because of the lack of cooperation between the authorities [Neck (1985)].

(iii) Both authorities can benefit from having more information, which is obtained by adopting feedback strategies instead of open-loop ones [Neese and Pindyck (1984)], but this result may be sensitive to the assignment of instruments to targets [Hämäläinen (1978)].

(iv) Both authorities can benefit from leader - follower arrangements [Kydland (1975, 1976)]. As casual observation suggests that in any given year the fiscal authority acts first and the monetary second, the role of leadership here falls in a natural way on the shoulders of the former.

(v) More sophisticated noncooperative behaviour makes both authorities worse off than less sophisticated strategies. Simple modes of behaviour, for example, nonreactive rules, may be Pareto-superior to sophisticated strategies [see Neese and Pindyck (1984) as well as Fair's (1978) control theory application; a discussion of rules suggested by macroeconomists can be found in Blinder (1983)].

Avenues of future research should, in my opinion, include the modelling of the effects of other reasons than the conflict in objectives for the lack of coordination between fiscal and monetary policy. Some possible reasons were mentioned in the preceding. What we need is an explanation to the existence of separate policy-makers. Blinder (1983) raises the possibility that greater coordination may actually make things worse if neither of the authorities knows the true model. Even the specification of the conflict in objectives needs further clarification. If it is a consequence of the fact that the fiscal and monetary authorities have to operate under different political pressures, the integration of macroeconomic stabilization games with political business cycle models [see, for example, Nordhaus (1975)] might prove fruitful. The latter types of models specify the political pressures in an explicit way. Finally, the leader - follower relationship is a bit more complicated than what is assumed in the existing models because monetary policy instruments can be changed more frequently than fiscal ones, so sometimes the monetary authority is the leader. The variable leadership Stackelberg game of Başar and Haurie (1984) could be applied to capture this phenomenon.

5. Games between the government and the private sector

Faxén's (1957) book contains, as far as I know, the first dynamic game formulation of the government - private sector interaction. Being influenced by von Neumann's and Morgenstern's (1944) book and Nash's (1951) paper, he produced a numerical example in which the relation between macroeconomic policy and business firms' investment planning is modelled as a noncooperative multi-stage finite game. What interests us here more than the details of this example is Faxén's general conclusion whereby firm's reaction patterns should not be regarded as fixed but should be derived from an optimization model. This means that the decisions of economic agents depend not only on the past development but also on expectations of the future and thus on anticipated macroeconomic policy. Faxén, whose thoughts were much influenced by the Stockholm School economists, concluded that the conduct of monetary and fiscal policies should be based on a consistent, long-term strategy so that firm's expectations are fulfilled, for otherwise their effect will be more or less erratic.

The mainstream macroeconomic theory in the 1950's and 1960's was, however, not based on the works of the Stockholm School economists but on those of Keynes. Keynesian macroeconomics does not, or at least did not in those days, pay much attention to the microeconomic foundations of macroeconomic relations. The decisions of the mass of private economic agents are subsumed in simple ad hoc rules of behaviour. These rules are fixed, independent of future economic policy, and they form the econometric model, discussed in the previous section, which the government can then control. It took twenty years under the dominance of the Keynesian School before ideas quite similar to Faxen's were independently and forcefully put forward by Lucas (1976). An interesting coincidence is that his analysis is also based on earlier work on firms' investment behaviour. Lucas's message is that the theory of economic policy based on the Keynesian econometric tradition is in need of a revision, because the structure of the econometric model depends on the government's policy rules. This follows from the fact that private agents optimize in a dynamic environment. To do this they have to form expectations about the way other economic actors, including the government, are going to behave. Because the government is also a player in this game, the analysis of macroeconomic policy should be conducted by comparing alternative rules, i.e. strategies. But this is exactly what we do in dynamic game theory. Lucas is not this specific about the role of game theory in Lucas (1976) but is much more so in Lucas and Sargent (1981) and especially in his recent Yrjö Jahnsson Lectures [Lucas (1985)].

Kydland's and Prescott's (1977) attempt to formulate Lucas's (1976) argument in control-theoretic terms led them to conclude that the optimal control of market economy is logically impossible if the behaviour of private economic actors is "forward looking", i.e. based on dynamic optimization. The reason is that optimal macroeconomic policy is time inconsistent: the optimal plan in subsequent periods is not the continuation of the first period optimal plan over the remainder of the government's planning horizon. It is necessary to formulate policy-making in the described environment as a dynamic Stackelberg game in which the government, taking into consideration the reactions of private agents to announced policies, acts as the leader whereas the agents, behaving noncooperatively and maximizing for announced policies, act as the followers. The time inconsistency of the optimal policy follows from the fact that in such a game the leader's optimal open- or closed-loop strategy does not satisfy Bellman's principle of optimality, as was explained in section 2. Such a strategy is, therefore, credible under precommitment only. But there is no way in which the present government can commit future governments to the policy which the present policy-maker wishes them to follow, as was already explained by Phelps and Pollak (1968) in the context of economic growth. The fact that credible, time-consistent policies are usually Pareto-inferior in terms of welfare makes policy-making problematic.

The time inconsistency of optimal macroeconomic policy was independently observed by Calvo (1978), who studied monetary policy in a closed economy where agents possess rational expectations, i.e. perfect foresight. His model is not explicitly formulated as a Stackelberg game, but it has a "saddle-point" dynamic structure, which means that some of the state variables are historically predetermined while others are free to jump so as to satisfy conditions for saddlepoint stability in the same way as the follower's costate variables do in Stackelberg problems. Such "jump" variables are characteristically asset prices in forward-looking economic models. These prices, such as the exchange rate in models of the open economy, typically depend on the expected future evaluation of the system and, consequently, on the announced economic policy.

Studies on the time-inconsistency problem nowadays abound in the literature and it is impossible to review all of them here. The problem is approached via optimal control under perfect foresight in, for example, Fischer (1980), Kydland and Prescott (1980), Turnovsky and Brock (1980), Buiter (1981), Driffill (1982), Holly and Zarrop (1983), Lucas and Stokey (1983) and Stemp and Turnovsky (1984). The dynamic game aspect is more explicit in Kydland (1975), Lucas and Sargent (1981), Buiter (1983), Holly (1983), Brandsma and Hughes Hallett (1984a,b), Cohen and Michel (1984), Hillier and Malcomson (1984), Hughes Hallett (1984), Karp and Havenner (1984), Oudiz and Sachs (1984a), Backus and Driffill (1985), Jones (1985) and Miller and Salmon (1985). We have to be content here with an account of the ways suggested in the literature of dealing with the time inconsistency of optimal macroeconomic policies.

I have below classified various proposals into five broad categories:

(i) Fixed constitutional rules. The subscribers to this view [for example, Kydland and Prescott (1977, 1980) and Lucas (1985)] hold that macroeconomic policies should be formulated as constitutional rules to which future governments are also committed. I think that it is fair to say that this view is not unanimously accepted for reasons such as unwillingness to tamper with constitutions and the realization that even constitutions get amended.

(ii) Special policy instruments. As is demonstrated in Fischer (1980), Turnovsky and Brock (1980), Lucas and Stokey (1983) and Hillier and Malcomson (1984), there may exist policy instruments, such as lump-sum taxes, which make optimal policies time consistent in some dynamic problems. Such instruments, however, provide us with a problem-specific rather than a general solution to the inconsistency problem.

(iii) Loss of leadership. Buiter (1983), Holly (1983) and Backus and Driffill (1985) have suggested that the government should be deprived of the leadership role. The interaction with the private sector is then viewed as a Nash rather than a Stackelberg dynamic game. Since even open-loop Nash equilibrium strategies are time consistent (although they are not subgame perfect), the issue is resolved. The acceptance of this view would, however, mean the denial of the existence of policies which have announcement effects, such as exchange rate policies.

(iv) Time-consistent strategies. An obvious solution is to resort to time-consistent strategies only. These can be obtained by recursive methods and have been derived in Kydland (1975), Cohen and Michel

(1984), Oudiz and Sachs (1984a), Jones (1985) and Miller and Salmon (1985). The present government's leadership is preserved with respect to the private sector, but it is lost with respect to future governments, which are free to reoptimize. The latter fact constrains the present government's policy choice and, consequently, lowers welfare. Empirical work is needed before we can judge how serious this loss is.

(v) Memory strategies, threats and incentives. The time-inconsistency problem is exaggerated in the sense that, as demonstrated by Oudiz and Sachs (1984a), many time-inconsistent equilibria can be sustained by suitably defined threats even in situations where the actions of future governments cannot be bound. Such threats between governments can be formulated by means of memory strategies. As Oudiz and Sachs have shown, the compound strategy, whereby any government either plays an implicitly agreed-upon strategy if all the preceding governments have done so as well or else it plays the memoryless time-consistent strategy, is itself time consistent, subgame perfect and, in addition, Pareto-superior to the threat strategy. Being subgame perfect, the threat is credible. Time consistency does, however, impose costs since the first-best open-loop Stackelberg solution cannot usually be sustained, as has been demonstrated by Barro and Gordon (1983) in a repeated game model. Karp and Havenner (1984) have examined the case where the present government is able to commit future governments to the policies which the present government wishes them to adopt and where, in addition, it can formulate incentives or threats designed to induce the private sector to behave in the desired way. Such incentive strategies are time consistent but not subgame perfect, as was explained in section 2.

The time inconsistency of optimal macroeconomic policies is likely to remain as one of the main research topics in macroeconomics for some time. The practitioners of dynamic game theory will find research on threats, incentives and memory strategies interesting. The practical economist is struck by the lack of empirical investigations into the importance of the whole issue. Empirical work is likely to grow as well.

6. International policy coordination games

The applications of dynamic game theory surveyed in the three preceding sections were based on previous applications of optimal control theory to the corresponding problem. International policy coordination games have a different history in this respect -- they are extensions to the dynamic framework of the pioneering approach based on static noncooperative game theory and developed in a series of papers by Hamada (1974, 1976, 1979).

Hamada demonstrated that the behaviour of nations, each pursuing its own national objectives in an interdependent world, leads to an outcome which is sub-optimal (i.e. Pareto-inferior) from the viewpoint of the community of nations. There are two countries in his basic model, each of which is assumed to control domestic credit creation in a regime of fixed exchange rates so as to minimize the loss arising from the deviation of the inflation rate and the balance-of-payments position from their targets. The noncooperative Nash and Stackelberg solutions are derived; the latter is shown to be more advantageous to the leader than the former and both are demonstrated to be inferior to the Pareto-optimal joint optimization solution. Special emphasis is laid on the design of institutional "rules of the game", such as the replacement of fixed exchange rates with flexible ones, so as to reduce the welfare loss arising from the lack of cooperation between the countries. These important issues as well as other related topics have further been investigated in static settings by Johansen (1982), Jones (1983), Oudiz and Sachs (1984b) and Cooper (1985).

The lesson we learn from these theoretical exercises as well as from the reactions of individual nations to the worldwide recessions in the 1970's and early 1980's is that unilateral expansionary national economic policies may be difficult to sustain and are costly in terms of inflation and foreign borrowing. Consequently, if all countries fear unilateral expansion, then the world economy may get stuck in a low-level, noncooperative equilibrium even if all countries would like to expand. The widespread concern among politicians and economists over the lack of coordination reflects the belief that these issues are nowadays more important than they were 15 years ago and, consequently, that the welfare losses arising from noncooperation are greater than they have been in the past. The explanation is the increase in interdependence among nations which is caused by improvements in international transportation and communication. These improvements have increased both the degree of capital mobility between countries and of substitutability of foreign and home goods in aggregate demand. The empirical results of Oudiz and Sachs (1984b) are, therefore, surprising. By applying large-scale econometric models, they estimated from observed behaviour the gain of coordination between the United States, West Germany and Japan by comparing the Nash noncooperative equilibrium with the Nash bargaining solution. It turned out to be quite modest, for example, as low as one-half percentage point of GNP to the United States in each of the next few years following coordination. Certainly, more empirical work in an explicitly dynamic setting is needed before the empirical relevance of the policy coordination issue is settled.

The first dynamic game formulation of the interdependence of national macroeconomic policies is due to Myoken (1975), whose analysis is incidentally independent of Hamada's. Myoken considered a linear Keynesian two-country model in which the exchange rate is fixed and each nation controls its domestic public expenditure so as to minimize a quadratic loss function, the loss arising from deviations of the levels of international reserves and public expenditure from their national targets. He did not study the economic implications of noncooperation but was only concerned with the mathematical formulation and the open-loop Nash solution, expressed in terms of pseudoinverse matrices, of the linear-quadratic problem.

Sachs (1983) provided the first dynamic illustration of the coordination problem in the tradition of the works of Hamada and Johansen. He studied a two-country model where the floating exchange rate is determined by the current account and where a supply shock, taking the form of an increase in the price of a traded intermediate input, causes inflationary pressures. Dynamics enter through Phillips curves, and national welfare depends on domestic inflation and output. By formulating the policy coordination problem as an infinite-horizon linear-quadratic multi-stage game and by comparing its open-loop Nash solution with the Pareto-optimal joint optimization solution, Sachs demonstrated that noncooperation results in excessively contractionary national economic policies designed to export inflation through currency appreciation.

Oudiz and Sachs (1984a) have extended this model to an environment where there is forward-looking behaviour on the part of private agents so that expectations of future policy actions influence the present. This is achieved by including the capital account in the model. Assuming perfect capital mobility, so that uncovered interest arbitrage holds, the expected movements of the exchange rate depend on interest rate differentials between the two countries. Perfect foresight on the part of private agents is assumed. The exchange rate is thus not determined by past history but by the forward-looking behaviour of the asset holders. It is free to jump so as to keep the symmetrical economies on their saddlepoint paths. The problems of time consistency and credibility of national macroeconomic (monetary) policies then arise immediately.

Oudiz and Sachs compared noncooperative Nash equilibria with cooperative ones between the countries under two alternative assumptions concerning the relationship between succeeding governments in each country: (i) precommitment, in which case the countries can commit to an open- or closed-loop strategy, and (ii) time consistency, in which case no precommitment in future periods is possible. Credibility of policies is thus assumed in case (i), whereas it is achieved in case (ii) by assuming that the successive governments in both countries play a Nash game against each other in the way explained in section 2. They demonstrated numerically that in both cases noncoordination leads to overcontractionary, anti-inflation policies, relative to the social optimum, designed to export inflation. By comparing the noncooperative equilibria in case (i), where an open-loop information structure was assumed, with that of case (ii) where feedback rules applied, they came to the conclusion that inability to bind one's successors causes a bias towards more rapid inflation. It turned out to be impossible to rank cases (i) and (ii) in terms of social welfare under the noncooperative mood of play.

Miller and Salmon (1985) have performed an analysis which is similar to that of Oudiz and Sachs. They studied fiscal stabilization in a fixprice Common Market by formulating their model as an infinite-horizon linear-quadratic differential game. The forward-looking behaviour of the private sector again enters via the exchange rate between Market and the Rest of the World. They considered open-loop strategies only. The time-inconsistent (precommitment) noncooperative equilibrium between the member countries turned out to be more effective in stabilizing output than either the open-loop time-consistent equilibrium or Buiter's (1983) "loss of leadership" solution.

The dynamic games surveyed here are summarized in the table below. A general conclusion that we can draw from these as well as from the previous applications of static game theory is that the presence of an international externality results in the inefficiency displayed by noncooperative behaviour between the members of the international community. Given the importance of the coordination issue, work in this area is likely to grow fast. Even the game-theoretic models produced so far have, in my opinion, proved to be useful in interpreting what actually happened in the world economy in the 1970's and in understanding the policy discussions originating from these events. The policy-makers have also become more aware of the externality. Whether this will also be reflected in national policy-making is not self-evident; even national fiscal and monetary policies are not coordinated and may, consequently, be acting at cross purposes, as was explained in section 4. The integration of international policy coordination games with macroeconomic stabilization games would shed light on this issue.

Governments' relationship with the private sector in each country	Relationship between countries	
	Noncooperative (Nash equilibrium)	Cooperative (Pareto optimum)
No leadership	Myoken (1975) Sachs (1983) Miller & Salmon (1985)	Sachs (1983)
Stackelberg leadership: time inconsistent	Miller & Salmon(1985) Oudiz & Sachs (1984a)	Oudiz & Sachs (1984a)
Stackelberg leadership: time consistent (solved recursively)	Miller & Salmon (1985) Oudiz & Sachs (1984a)	Oudiz & Sachs (1984a)

Table 3: International policy coordination games[a]

[a] All others are linear-quadratic multi-stage games except Miller & Salmon (1985), which is a linear-quadratic differential game. The information structure is open-loop except in the time-consistent solution of Oudiz and Sachs (1984a), where feedback strategies are applied.

7. A game among sectors in an economy

If Hamada's (1974, 1976, 1979) studies have preceded the new wave of game theory models in macroeconomics, so has Pau's (1975) analysis of Danish economy as a differential game between its sectors. This pioneering application has remained unnoticed by macroeconomists and, consequently, deserves a separate treatment. There are six players in his model: the sectors of agriculture, industry, housing, transportation and other services as well as the public sector. There are altogether twenty-one control variables: investment, labour demand, and internal financing of each sector plus the public sector's additional controls consisting of imports as well as marginal taxes on wages and profits. The system is described by two state variables: foreign debt and the government's budget surplus. The system equations were derived from a nonlinear input-output model. The public sector seeks to maximize the present value of the surplus of public services while the housing sector seeks to maximize output. All other sectors maximize the present value of accumulated cash flow.

Pau's results for the years 1947-52 indicate that the open-loop Nash equilibrium of his model approximates the historical development reasonably well. It has a much better "fit" than the welfare-optimal solutions considered. In particular, the game solution seems to support an efficient defence of the agricultural labour force even though the maximization of this sector's own criterion points to a reduction of this labour force. This is interesting since subsidies to agriculture are common in industrial economies, a phenomenon for which no adequate economic theory yet exists. The introduction of economic power via dynamic games might bring more realism to economic analyses of structural change.

8. Concluding remarks

The preceding pages have, I believe, shown that dynamic game theory has indeed found its way into macroeconomics or, rather, that macroeconomists have become acquainted with a promising new tool. This acquaintance will certainly bring about many more papers, both theoretical and empirical, in the future. After the first enthusiasm has faded away, a critical appraisal is to be expected. We may here anticipate this reaction by asking if we could not have obtained the results surveyed in this paper without dynamic game theory. This question is relevant for the following reason. The demonstration of the advantages of cooperation has been the basic approach in most of the applications. Such welfare gains exist since noncooperative solutions are not in general

Pareto-optimal. To an economist this is but an example of a market failure. As markets for cooperation do not exist, it is not surprising that there exist unexploited opportunities for players to "trade" strategies which could leave all of them better-off.

We can respond to such criticism by saying that the economic consequences of the lack of cooperation are not at all self-evident and, consequently, have to be worked out. This kind of research may also offer new insights into old macroeconomic problems. An example is the interpretation, in terms of a dynamic externality, of the observed correlation between high labour costs and unemployment in a unionized economy. Research based on the comparison of noncooperative and Pareto-optimal solutions is needed as well if we are to devise more efficient economic institutions such as international monetary systems. Applications of dynamic game theory also point out limitations of existing institutions. An example is the role of government in controlling the economy. The literature on the time inconsistency of optimal policy has certainly changed our way of thinking of macroeconomic planning.

As in all applied work, an understanding of the real world is also the aim of macroeconomic applications of dynamic game theory. The literature on industrial organization shows that game theory is an efficient tool for such work. Some critics may even say that it is too efficient, the argument being that any imaginable behaviour can be explained by the aid of game theory and imagination. To prevent such views from arising in our field, we should establish a direct dialogue between the practicians and the theorists of dynamic games. As in industrial organization and microeconomics [see Binmore (1985)], such a link would provide the theorists with direct feedback on the applicability of the solution concepts. This is the final justification offered here for the applied work surveyed in this paper.

9. References

Backus, David and John Driffill (1985), "Credibility and Commitment in Economic Policy," mimeo.

Barro, R.J. and D.B.Gordon (1983), "Rules, Discretion and Reputation in a Model of Monetary Policy," Journal of Monetary Economics, vol.12, pp. 101-121.

Başar, Tamer (1985), "Stochastic Multimodelling for Teams in a Game-Theoretic Framework," in Optimal Control Theory and Economic Analysis, vol.2, G.Feichtinger (Ed.), North-Holland, Amsterdam, pp. 529-548.

Başar, Tamer and Alain Haurie (1984), "Feedback Equilibria in Stackelberg Games with Structural and Modal Uncertainties," in Advances in Large Scale Systems, vol.1, J.B.Cruz, Jr. (ed.), JAI Press, Connecticut, pp. 163-201.

Başar, T., A.Haurie and G.Ricci (1985), "On the Dominance of Capitalists' Leadership in a 'Feedback-Stackelberg' Solution of a Differential Game Model of Capitalism," Journal of Economic Dynamics and Control, forthcoming.

Başar, Tamer and Geert Jan Olsder (1982), Dynamic Noncooperative Game Theory, Academic Press, London.

Başar, Tamer and Hasan Selbuz (1979), "Closed-Loop Stackelberg Strategies with Applications in the Optimal Control of Multi-Level Systems," IEEE Transactions on Automatic Control, vol.AC-24, pp.166-178.

Binmore, K.G. (1985), "Equilibria in Extensive Games," Economic Journal (Supplement), vol.95, pp. 51-59.

Blinder, Alan S. (1983), "Issues in the Coordination of Monetary and Fiscal Policy," in Monetary issues in the 1980's, Federal Reserve Bank of Kansas City, Kansas City, pp. 3-34.

Brandsma, Andries S. and A.J. Hughes Hallett (1984a), "Economic Conflict and the Solution of Dynamic Games," European Economic Review, vol. 26, pp. 13-32.

Brandsma, Andries S. and A.J. Hughes Hallett (1984b), "Non-Causalities and Time Inconsistency in Dynamic Non-Cooperative Games," Economic Letters, vol.14, pp. 123-130.

Buhl, Hans Ulrich and Werner Machaczek (1985), "Workers' Investment and Return in a Differential Game Model," mimeo.

Buiter, Willem H. (1981), "The Superiority of Contingent Rules over Fixed Rules in Models with Rational Expectations," Economic Journal, vol.91, pp. 647-670.

Buiter, Willem H. (1983), "Optimal and Time-Consistent Policies in Continuous Time Rational Expectations Models," Technical Working Paper No. 29, National Bureau of Economic Research, Cambridge, Massachusetts.

Calvo, Guillermo A. (1978), "On the Time Consistency of Optimal Policy in a Monetary Economy," Econometrica, vol.46, pp. 1411-1428.

Case, James H. (1979), Economics and the Competitive Process, New York University Press, New York.

Chow, Gregory C. (1975), Analysis and Control of Dynamic Systems, Wiley, New York.

Clemhout, S. and H.Y. Wan, Jr. (1979), "Interactive Economic Dynamics and Differential Games," Journal of Optimization Theory and Applications, vol.27, pp. 7-30.

Cohen, Daniel and Philippe Michel (1984), "Toward a Theory of Optimal Pre-Commitment I: An Analysis of the Time-Consistent Equilibria," Working Paper No. 8412, CEPREMAP, Paris.

Committee on Policy Optimisation (1978), Report, Her Majesty's Stationery Office, London.

Cooper, Richard N. (1985), "Economic Interdependence and Coordination of Economic Policies," in Handbook of International Economics, vol. 2, R.Jones and P.Kenen (Eds.), North-Holland, Amsterdam, pp. 1195-1234.

Cruz, J.B., Jr. (1975), "Survey of Nash and Stackelberg Equilibrium Strategies in Dynamic Games," Annals of Economic and Social Measurement, vol.4, pp. 339-344.

Dockner, E., G.Feichtinger and S.Jørgensen (1985), "Tractable Classes of Nonzero-Sum Open-Loop Nash Differential Games: Theory and Examples," Journal of Optimization Theory and Applications, vol.45, pp. 179-197.

Driffill, J. (1982), "Optimal Money and Exchange Rate Policies," Greek Economic Review, vol.4, pp. 261-283.

Ehtamo, Harri and Raimo P.Hämäläinen (1985), "Construction of Optimal Affine Incentive Strategies for Linear-Quadratic Stackelberg Games," System Research Report A12, Helsinki University of Technology.

Fair, Ray C. (1978), "The Sensitivity of Fiscal Policy Effects to Assumptions about the Behaviour of the Federal Reserve," Econometrica, vol.46, pp. 1165-1179.

Faxén, Karl-Olof (1957), Monetary and Fiscal Policy under Uncertainty, Almqvist & Wiksell, Stockholm.

Fischer, Stanley (1980), "Dynamic Inconsistency, Cooperation and the Benevolent Dissembling Government," Journal of Economic Dynamics and Control, vol.2, pp. 93-107.

Hamada, K. (1967), "On the Optimal Transfer and Income Distribution in a Growing Economy," Review of Economic Studies, vol.34, pp. 295-299.

Hamada, Koichi (1974), "Alternative Exchange Rate Systems and the Interdependence of Monetary Policies," in National Monetary Policies and the International Financial System, R.Z.Aliber (Ed.), University of Chicago Press, Chicago, pp. 13-33.

Hamada, Koichi (1976), "A Strategic Analysis of Monetary Interdependence," Journal of Political Economy, vol.84, pp. 677-700.

Hamada, Koichi (1979), "Macroeconomic Strategy and Coordination under Alternative Exchange Rates," in International Economic Policy, R. Dornbusch and J.A.Frenkel (Eds.), Johns Hopkins Press, Baltimore, pp. 292-324.

Hämäläinen, Raimo P. (1978), "On the Role of Information in Decentralized Macro-Economic Stabilization," International Journal of Systems Science, vol.9, pp. 799-811.

Hammer, Jeffrey S. (1981), "Optimal Growth and Income Redistribution," Metroeconomica, vol.33, pp. 145-157.

Hillier, Brian and James M.Malcomson (1984), "Dynamic Inconsistency, Rational Expectations, and Optimal Government Policy," Econometrica, vol.52, pp. 1437-1451.

Hoel, Michael (1978), "Distribution and Growth as a Differential Game between Workers and Capitalists," International Economic Review, vol.19, pp. 335-350.

Holly, Sean (1983), "Dynamic Inconsistency and Dynamic Games in Intertemporal Optimization Models: A Resolution of the Kydland and Prescott Conundrum," Discussion Paper No. 108, Centre for Economic Forecasting, London Business School.

Holly, S. and M.B.Zarrop (1983), "On Optimality and Time Consistency When Expectations Are Rational," European Economic Review, vol.20, pp. 23-40.

Hughes Hallett, A.J. (1984), "Non-cooperative Strategies for Dynamic Policy Games and the Problem of Time Inconsistency," Oxford Economic Papers, vol.36, pp. 381-399.

Johansen, Leif (1982), "A Note on the Possibility of an International Equilibrium with Low Levels of Activity," Journal of International Economics, vol.13, pp. 257-265.

Jones, Michael (1983), "International Liquidity: A Welfare Analysis," Quarterly Journal of Economics, vol. 98, pp. 1-23.

Jones, Michael (1985), "Open Economy Monetary Policy: An Application of Dynamic Games," mimeo.

Karp, L. and A.Havenner (1984), "Toward the Resurrection of Optimal Macroeconomic Policies," in Applied Decision Analysis and Economic Behaviour, A.J.Hughes Hallett (Ed.), Martinus Nijhoff, Dordrecht, pp. 23-32.

Kendrick, David (1976), "Applications of Control Theory to Macroeconomics," Annals of Economic and Social Measurement, vol.5, pp. 171-190.

Kendrick, David (1981), "Control Theory with Applications to Economics," in Handbook of Mathematical Economics, K.J.Arrow and M.D.Intriligator (Eds.),vol.1, North-Holland, Amsterdam, pp. 111-158.

Kydland, Finn (1975), "Noncooperative and Dominant Player Solutions in Discrete Dynamic Games," International Economic Review, vol.16, pp. 321-335.

Kydland, Finn (1976), "Decentralized Stabilization Policies: Optimization and Assignment Problem," Annals of Economic and Social Measurement, vol.5, pp. 249-261.

Kydland, Finn E. and Edward C.Prescott (1977), "Rules Rather than Discretion: The Inconsistency of Optimal Plans," Journal of Political Economy, vol.85, pp. 473-493.

Kydland, Finn E. and Edward C.Prescott (1980), "Dynamic Optimal Taxation, Rational Expectations and Optimal Control," Journal of Economic Dynamics and Control, vol.2, pp. 79-91.

Lancaster, Kelvin (1973), "The Dynamic Inefficiency of Capitalism," Journal of Political Economy, vol.81, pp. 1092-1109.

Liu, Pan-Tai (1973), "Optimal Threat Strategies in Differential Games," Journal of Mathematical Analysis and Applications, vol.43, pp. 161-169.

Lucas, Robert E., Jr.(1976), "Econometric Policy Evaluation: A Critique," in The Phillips Curve and Labor Markets, K.Brunner and A.H.Meltzer (Eds.), North-Holland, Amsterdam.

Lucas, Robert E., Jr.(1985), "Models of Business Cycles," Yrjö Jahnsson Lectures, Helsinki, mimeo.

Lucas, Robert E. and Thomas J.Sargent (1981), "Introduction," in Rational Expectations and Econometric Practice, R.E.Lucas and T.J.Sargent (Eds.), Allen and Unwin, London, pp. xi-xxxvii.

Lucas, Robert E., Jr. and Nancy L.Stokey (1983), "Optimal Fiscal and Monetary Policy in an Economy without Capital," Journal of Monetary Economics, vol.12, pp. 55-93.

Marglin, Stephen A. (1976), Value and Price in a Labour-Surplus Economy, Oxford University Press, London.

Miller, Marcus and Mark Salmon (1985), "Dynamic Games and the Time Inconsistency of Optimal Policy in Open Economies," Economic Journal (Supplement), vol.95, pp. 124-137.

Mundell, R.A. (1962), "The Appropriate Use of Monetary and Fiscal Policy for Internal and External Stability," IMF Staff Papers, vol.9, pp. 70-79.

Myoken, H. (1975), "Non-zero-sum Differential Games for the Balance-of-Payments Adjustments in an Open Economy," International Journal of Systems Science, vol.6, pp. 501-511.

Nash, J.F. (1951), "Non-cooperative Games," Annals of Mathematics, vol. 54, pp. 286-295.

Neck, Reinhard (1985), "A Differential Game Model of Fiscal and Monetary Policies: Conflict and Cooperation," in Optimal Control Theory and Economic Analysis, vol.2, G.Feichtinger (Ed.), North-Holland, Amsterdam, pp. 607-632.

Neese, J.W. and R.S. Pindyck (1984), "Behavioural Assumptions in Decentralized Stabilization Policies," in Applied Decision Analysis and Economic Behaviour, A.J.Hughes Hallett (Ed.), Martinus Nijhoff, Dordrecht, pp. 251-270.

von Neumann, J. and O. Morgenstern (1944), Theory of Games and Economic Behaviour, Princeton University Press, Princeton.

Nordhaus, William D. (1975), "The Political Business Cycle," Review of Economic Studies, vol.42, pp. 169-190.

Nyblén, Göran (1951), The Problem of Summation in Economic Science, C.W.K.Gleerup, Lund.

Oudiz, Gilles and Jeffrey Sachs (1984a), "International Policy Coordination in Dynamic Macroeconomic Models," Working Paper No. 1417, National Bureau of Economic Research, Cambridge, Massachusetts.

Oudiz, Gilles and Jeffrey Sachs (1984b), "Macroeconomic Policy Coordination among the Industrial Economies," Brookings Papers on Economic Activity, 1/1984, pp. 1-64.

Papavassilopoulos, G.P. and J.B.Cruz, Jr.(1980), "Stackelberg and Nash Strategies with Memory," Journal of Optimization Theory and Applications, vol.31, pp. 253-260.

Pau, L.F. (1975), "A Differential Game among Sectors in a Macroeconomy," Automatica, vol.11, pp. 473-485.

Pau, L.F. (1979), "Research on Optimal Control Adapted to Macro- and Microeconomics," Journal of Economic Dynamics and Control, vol.1, pp. 243-269.

Phelps, E.S. and R.A.Pollak (1968), "On Second-Best National Saving and Game-Equilibrium Growth," Review of Economic Studies, vol.35, pp. 185-199.

Pindyck, Robert S. (1976), "The Cost of Conflicting Objectives in Policy Formulation," Annals of Economic and Social Measurement, vol.5, pp. 239-248.

Pindyck, Robert S. (1977), "Optimal Economic Stabilization Policies under Decentralized Control and Conflicting Objectives," IEEE Transactions on Automatic Control, vol.AC-22, pp. 517-530.

Pohjola, Matti (1983a), "Nash and Stackelberg Solutions in a Differential Game Model of Capitalism," Journal of Economic Dynamics and Control, vol.6, pp. 173-186.

Pohjola, Matti (1983b), "Workers' Investment Funds and the Dynamic Inefficiency of Capitalism," Journal of Public Economics, vol.20, pp. 271-279.

Pohjola, Matti (1984a), "Union Rivalry and Economic Growth: A Differential Game Approach," Scandinavian Journal of Economics, vol.86, pp. 365-370.

Pohjola, Matti (1984b), "Threats and Bargaining in Capitalism: A Differential Game View," Journal of Economic Dynamics and Control, vol. 8, pp. 291-302.

Pohjola, Matti (1985), "Growth, Distribution and Employment Modelled as a Differential Game," in Optimal Control Theory and Economic Analysis , vol.2, G.Feichtinger (Ed.), North-Holland, Amsterdam, pp. 581-591.

Ramsey, Frank (1928), "A Mathematical Model of Saving," Economic Journal, vol.38, pp. 543-559.

Sachs, Jeffrey (1983), "International Policy Coordination in a Dynamic Macroeconomic Model," Working Paper No. 1166, National Bureau of Economic Research, Cambridge, Massachusetts.

Schotter, Andrew and Gerhard Schwödiauer (1980), "Economics and the Theory of Games," Journal of Economic Literature, vol.18, pp. 479-527.

Selten, R. (1975), "Reexamination of the Perfectness Concept for Equilibrium Points in Extensive Games," International Journal of Game Theory, vol.4, pp. 25-55.

Shubik, Martin (1982), Game Theory in the Social Sciences: Concepts and Solutions, MIT Press.

Simaan, M. and J.B.Cruz, Jr. (1973a), "On the Stackelberg Strategy in Nonzero-sum Games," Journal of Optimization Theory and Applications, vol.11, pp. 533-555.

Simaan, M. and J.B.Cruz, Jr. (1973b), "Additional Aspects of the Stackelberg Strategy in Nonzero-sum Games," Journal of Optimization Theory and Applications, vol.11, pp. 613-626.

Stanley, Owen (1978), "Distributional Goals and Optimal Growth," Review of Economic Studies, vol.45, pp. 389-390.

Stemp, Peter J. and Stephen J.Turnovsky (1984), "Optimal Stabilization Policies under Perfect Foresight," in Applied Decision Analysis and Economic Behaviour, A.J.Hughes Hallett (Ed.), Martinus Nijhoff, Dordrecht, pp. 3-22.

Turnovsky, Stephen J. and William A.Brock (1980), "Time Consistency and Optimal Government Policies in Perfect Foresight Equilibrium," Journal of Public Economics, vol.13, pp. 183-212.

Wan, Henry Y., Jr. (1971), Economic Growth, Harcourt Brace Jovanovich, New York.

Wan, Henry Y., Jr. (1985), "The New Classical Economics - A Game-Theoretic Critique", in Issues in Contemporary Macroeconomics and Distribution, G.R.Feiwel (Ed.), MacMillan, London, pp. 235-257.

Zheng, Y.P., T.Başar and J.B.Cruz, Jr. (1984), "Stackelberg Strategies and Incentives in Multiperson Deterministic Decision Problems," IEEE Transactions on Systems, Man and Cybernetics, vol.SMC-14, pp. 10-24.

OPTIMAL STRATEGIC MONETARY POLICIES IN DYNAMIC INTERDEPENDENT ECONOMIES

Tamer Başar
Coordinated Science Laboratory
University of Illinois
1101 W. Springfield Avenue
Urbana, Illinois 61801/USA

Stephen J. Turnovsky[0/], Vasco d'Orey
Department of Economics
University of Illinois
1206 S. Sixth Street
Champaign, Illinois 61820/USA

Abstract

This paper applies the framework of dynamic game theory to the analysis of a number of issues in international policy making. First, a dynamic inflationary model is developed for two interdependent symmetric economies, where the objective of each policy maker is to trade off in an intertemporally optimal way the rate of inflation and unemployment in his economy. Then, the equilibrium is studied under a variety of behavioral assumptions. These include principally feedback Nash equilibrium, feedback Stackelberg behavior, and feedback consistent conjectural variations equilibrium, all under the feedback information pattern and with discounted objective functions defined on an infinite time horizon. These solutions are subsequently computed for different sets of numerical values assigned to some key parameters in the model, and compared with results obtained in a previous work using a static model.

1. Introduction

Recent work in international macroeconomics has emphasized the growing interdependence between economies. It has become increasingly recognized that policies implemented in one country will generate effects and policy reactions abroad and that these in turn will modify the impact of the policies in the domestic economy. Policy making in a multicountry context therefore involves strategic behavior.

Research into the analysis of strategic behavior in the context of international macroeconomic policy making began with the seminal work of Hamada (1976), who analyzed issues of monetary policy under Cournot and Stackelberg behavior. His approach was a static one and was based on a fixed exchange rate. His contribution has recently been extended by various authors including Jones (1983), Canzoneri and Gray (1985), Turnovsky and d'Orey (1985). These extensions, which remain static, include the introduction of alternative disturbances, flexible exchange rates, and the consideration of alternative strategic equilibria.

In this paper we consider the problem of strategic monetary policy making within a dynamic framework. The basic model we employ is a two country version of the standard Dornbusch (1976) model in which the policy makers in the two economies seek to optimize their respective objective functions, taken to be intertemporal quadratic cost functions defined in terms of deviations in output from its natural rate level, on the one hand, and the rate of inflation of the domestic consumer price index (CPI) on the other.

The consideration of these issues within a dynamic context is obviously important. Strategic policies, which are optimal from a short-run viewpoint, may, however, generate intertemporal tradeoffs which over time prove to be adverse. In fact, our results below will suggest this to be the case. Furthermore, the extension to a dynamic framework emphasizes new issues such as the information structure and the corresponding equilibrium concepts. We focus on three alternative equilibria, which we consider to be of interest. These are all feedback solutions in which the policies at each stage make use of current information on key economic variables such as prices and exchange rates, which under our assumptions are observable at that time. Using such information we consider: (i) feedback Nash, (ii) feedback Stackelberg, and (iii) feedback Consistent Conjectural Variations (CCV), equilibria. The first two of these are familiar, and require no further comment at this point.

The feedback CCV equilibrium is a new equilibrium concept in dynamic game theory and is a generalization of the static CCV equilibrium concept introduced recently by Breshnahan (1981), Perry (1982) and others.[1] The basic idea is that in the Nash (Cournot) equilibrium, each agent takes the behavior of his rival as given, and therefore assumes that the latter does not react to his actions. On the other hand, each agent is shown to respond in accordance with a reaction function, so that ex post, the assumption of no response is incorrect. By contrast, in the CCV equilibrium, each policy maker, in determining his own actions, correctly anticipates the response of his opponent. This equilibrium concept is therefore the strategic analogue of a rational expectations equilibrium. Our equilibrium is an extension of this concept to a feedback informational context.

The analysis is based on two symmetric economies. This has the advantage of simplifying the feedback rules, with the real money supply in each economy being adjusted to the real exchange rate. Our procedure is to derive analytical expressions for the optimal policies. However, even for the simple model we adopt, these formal expressions are extremely complex and provide only limited insight. Furthermore, for the problem with an infinite horizon, existence of equilibria in stationary policies is not guaranteed at the outset; indeed, the derivation of such existence and convergence results, even for linear-quadratic models such as those treated here, have remained as one of the challenging issues in dynamic game theory today. The main difficulty on the theoretical side is the lack of any clean monotonicity result on the cost-to-go functions arising from the three types of dynamic equilibria introduced above, thus making it impossible to utilize the general tools developed for single player infinite horizon optimization problems or infinite horizon zero-sum games in the context of nonzero-sum dynamic games. For these reasons, our analysis is carried out using numerical simulation methods. In this regard our procedure is as follows. We begin with a base set of plausible parameter values which are broadly consistent with available empirical evidence. The various dynamic equilibria corresponding to these parameter sets are computed for finite horizon games, and convergence properties of these equilibria are studied as the number of periods in the game leads to infinity. In order to determine the extent to which the results depend upon the chosen set of parameter values, we subject the solution to extensive sensitivity analysis, by allowing for sequential changes in the individual parameters. In performing our simulations, we compare the results with previous work, based on a static model and using the same parameter values. As we shall note below, the differences between the static and dynamic analyses are in may cases quite striking.

This is not the first study to apply dynamic game theory to problems of international macroeconomic policy making. Indeed the area is currently beginning to receive attention and recent work by Miller and Salmon (1985), and Oudiz and Sachs (1985), in particular, should be noted. While our study shares some features in common with these works, in particular in adopting a numerical approach, it also differs in many key respects. One of these is the consideration of alternative equilibria in this study. Also, much more detailed sensitivity analysis is conducted with the view to trying to establish patterns of behavior in the solutions.

The remainder of the paper is as follows. Section 2 outlines the model, with the derivation of the three equilibria being given in Section 3. Section 4 briefly discusses the numerical simulation procedures. Section 5 discusses in detail the behavior of the economy under the various equilibria, while the following sections reports on the sensitivity analysis. The main conclusions are reviewed in Section 7. Finally, three appendices contain the details of the arguments in Section 3.

2. The Theoretical Framework

The analysis of this paper is based on the following two-country macroeconomic model, which is a direct extension of the Dornbusch (1976) framework. It describes two identical economies, each specializing in the production of a distinct good and trading a single common bond. It assumes perfect foresight and is expressed, using discrete time, by the following set of equations

$$Y_t = d_1 Y_t^* - d_2[I_t - (P_{t+1} - P_t)] + d_3(P_t^* + E_t - P_t) \tag{1}$$

$$0 < d_1 < 1, \; d_2 > 0, \; d_3 > 0$$

$$Y_t^* = d_1 Y_t - d_2[I_t^* - (P_{t+1}^* - P_t^*)] - d_3(P_t^* + E_t - P_t) \tag{1'}$$

$$M_t - P_t = e_1 Y_t - e_2 I_t \tag{2}$$

$$e_1 > 0, \; e_2 > 0$$

$$M_t^* - P_t^* = e_1 Y_t^* - e_2 I_t^* \tag{2'}$$

$$I_t = I_t^* + E_{t+1} - E_t \tag{3}$$

$$C_t = \delta P_t + (1-\delta)(P_t^* + E_t) \tag{4}$$

$$1 > \delta > 1/2$$

$$C^* = \delta P_t^* + (1-\delta)(P_t - E_t) \tag{4'}$$

$$P_{t+1} - P_t = \gamma Y_t \tag{5}$$

$$\gamma > 0$$

$$P_{t+1}^* - P_t^* = \gamma Y_t^* \tag{5'}$$

where

- Y = real output, measured as a deviation about its natural rate level,
- P = price of domestic output, expressed in logarithms,
- C = consumer price index, expressed in logarithms,
- E = exchange rate (measured in terms of units of foreign currency per unit of domestic currency), measured in logarithms,
- I = nominal interest rate, measured in natural units,
- M = nominal money supply, expressed in logarithms.

Domestic variables are unstarred; foreign variables are denoted with asterisks. We shall also refer to these as Country 1 and Country 2, respectively.

Equations (1) and (1') describe equilibrium in the two goods markets. Output depends upon the real interest rate, output in the other country, and the relative price. The corresponding effects across the two economies are identical, with relative price influencing demand in exactly offsetting ways. The money market equilibrium conditions in the two economies are standard and are described by (2) and (2'), respectively.[2] The perfect substitutability between domestic and foreign bonds is described by the interest rate parity condition (3). Equations (4) and (4') describe the consumer price index (CPI) in the two economies. They embody the assumption that the proportion of consumption δ spent on the respective home good is the same in the two economies. We assume $1 > \delta > 1/2$, so that residents in both countries have a preference for their own good. Note that the real interest rate in (1) and (1') and the real money supplies in (2) and (2') are deflated by the output price of their respective economies. Little would be changed, except for additional detail, if the deflators were in terms of their respective CPI's. Equations (5) and (5') define the price adjustment in the two economies in terms of Phillips curve relationships, with prices responding with a one period lag to demand. On the other hand, the assumption of perfect foresight is embodied in the future price level and future exchange rate appearing in the real interest rate in (1), (1'), and the interest rate parity relationship (3).

Equations (1)-(5) describe the structure of the two economies. The policy makers in these economies are assumed to have intertemporal objective functions

$$\sum_{t=1}^{\infty} [aY_t^2 + (1-a)(C_{t+1} - C_t)^2]\rho^{t-1} \tag{6}$$

$$0 < a < 1 \quad , \quad 0 < \rho < 1 ,$$

$$\sum_{t=1}^{\infty} [aY_t^{*2} + (1-a)(C_{t+1}^* - C_t^*)^2]\rho^{t-1} \tag{6'}$$

which they seek to optimize. That is, each policy maker chooses to minimize an intertemporal cost function. The cost incurred at each point of time is quadratic, defined in terms of deviations in output from their equilibrium, natural rate, level, and the rate of inflation of the domestic cost of living. The relative weights attached to these components of the objective functions are a and 1-a, respectively. Total cost to be minimized by each policy maker is a discounted sum of the costs incurred at each period, ρ, denoting the discount rate.

Equations (1)-(5) may be solved for Y_t, Y_t^*, and $E_{t+1} - E_t$, as follows

$$Y_t = \phi_1 m_t + \phi_2 m_t^* + \phi_3 s_t \tag{7a}$$

$$Y_t^* = \phi_2 m_t + \phi_1 m_t^* - \phi_3 s_t \tag{7b}$$

$$E_{t+1} - E_t = -\beta_1 m_t + \beta_1 m_t^* + \beta_3 s_t \tag{7c}$$

where

$s_t \equiv P_t^* + E_t - P_t$ denotes the relative price (real exchange rate) at time t,

$m_t \equiv M_t - P_t$, $m_t^* \equiv M_t^* - P_t^*$ denote the real stocks of money at home and abroad, at time t,

$$\phi_1 \equiv \frac{d_2}{2}\left[\frac{1}{D} + \frac{1}{D'}\right] ; \quad \phi_2 \equiv \frac{d_2}{2}\left[\frac{1}{D} - \frac{1}{D'}\right] ; \quad \phi_3 = \frac{e_2 d_3}{D'}$$

$$\beta_1 = \frac{1 + d_1 - d_2\gamma}{D'} ; \quad \beta_2 = \frac{2e_1 d_3}{D'}$$

$$D \equiv e_2(1-d_1 - d_2\gamma) + e_1 d_2 ; \; D' = e_2(1+d_1 - d_2\gamma) + e_1 d_2$$

We assume that $1 - d_1 - d_2\gamma > 0$, implying that the IS curve of the aggregate world economy is downward sloping. It follows that

$$D' > D > 0$$

and hence

$$\phi_1 > \phi_2 > 0 \quad .$$

Taking the differences of the cost of living equations (4) at two consecutive points in time, and using (5), (5'), and (7a)-(7c), the rates of inflation of the CPI become

$$C_{t+1} - C_t = \eta_1 m_t + \eta_2 m_t^* + \eta_3 s_t \tag{8a}$$

$$C_{t+1}^* - C_t^* = \eta_2 m_t + \eta_1 m_t^* - \eta_3 s_t \tag{8b}$$

where

$$\eta_1 = \gamma[\delta\phi_1 + (1-\delta)\phi_2] - \beta_1(1-\delta)$$

$$\eta_2 = \gamma[\delta\phi_2 + (1-\delta)\phi_1] + \beta_1(1-\delta)$$

$$\eta_3 = \gamma\phi_3(2\delta-1) + \beta_2(1-\delta) \quad .$$

The optimal policy problem confronting each of the policy makers is to choose their respective money supplies to minimize their respective cost functions (6) and (6') subject to constraints (8a), (8b), (9a),(9b). Given the assumption that prices move gradually at home and abroad, we assume that both P_t and P_t^* are observed at time t. Thus it is convenient to treat the monetary control variables as being the real quantities m_t, m_t^*. Secondly, we assume that the current nominal exchange rate E_t is observed instantaneously and can therefore be monitored by the monetary authorities.[3] Thus the relative price, s_t, is observable to both policy makers at time t, and in fact the optimal monetary policies will be obtained as feedback solutions in terms of s_t. Combining equations (5),

(5'), and (7c), s_t follows the path

$$s_{t+1} = cs_t + bm_t - bm_t^* \tag{9}$$

where

$$c \equiv 1 + \beta_2 - 2\gamma\phi_3$$

$$b \equiv -(1 + d_1)/D'$$

The dynamic optimization problem faced by the two policy makers may be summarized as

$$\text{Min } J = \sum_{t=1}^{\infty} [aY_t^2 + (1-a)(C_{t+1} - C_t)^2]\rho^{t-1} \tag{10}$$

subject to

$$Y_t = \phi_1 m_t + \phi_2 m_t^* + \phi_3 s_t \tag{11}$$

$$C_{t+1} - C_t = \eta_1 m_t + \eta_2 m_t^* + \eta_3 s_t \tag{12}$$

and

$$\text{Min } J^* = \sum_{t=1}^{\infty} [aY_t^{*2} + (1-a)(C_{t+1}^* - C_t^*)^2]\rho^{t-1} \tag{10'}$$

subject to

$$Y^* = \phi_2 m_t + \phi_1 m_t^* - \phi_3 s_t \tag{11'}$$

$$C_{t+1}^* - C_t^* = \eta_2 m_t + \eta_1 m_t^* - \eta_3 s_t \tag{12'}$$

where

$$s_{t+1} = cs_t + bm_t - bm_t^* \tag{13a}$$

and

$$m_t = f_t(s_t) \ , \ m_t^* = f_t^*(s_t^*) \tag{13b}$$

and the minimization in (10) and (10') are performed over the control laws f_t and f_t^*, respectively. Since these are two coupled minimization problems, their solutions cannot be obtained independently and hence we have to resort to the framework of dynamic game theory to obtain satisfactory solutions under different modes of the decision making.

3. Derivation of Three Different Types of Noncooperative Equilibria

In this section, the solution for the dynamic game formulated in (10)-(13) will be considered under different behavioral assumptions for policy makers in each country. Specifically, we will study the equilibrium solution under the assumptions of (i) Cournot-Nash, (ii) Stackelberg, and (iii) Consistent Conjectural Variations (CCV) behavior on the part of the policy makers.

As a preliminary to the analysis of the following sections, we first substitute (11), (12) into (10), and (11'), (12') into (10') enabling us to express each country's objective function in terms of only the state variable, s_t, and the control variables of both countries, m_t, m_t^*. The resulting expressions are

$$J = \sum_{t=1}^{\infty} [Q_1 s_t^2 + 2Q_2 s_t m_t + 2Q_3 s_t m_t^* + 2Q_4 m_t m_t^* + Q_5 m_t^2 + Q_6 m_t^{*2}]\rho^{t-1} \tag{14}$$

$$J^* = \sum_{t=1}^{\infty} [Q_1^* s_t^2 + 2Q_2^* s_t m_t^* + 2Q_3^* s_t m_t + 2Q_4^* m_t m_t^* + Q_5 m_t^{*2} + Q_6^* m_t^2]\rho^{t-1} \tag{14'}$$

where

$$Q_1 = a\phi_3^2 + (1-a)\eta_3^2 = Q_1^*$$

$$Q_2 = a\phi_1\phi_3 + (1-a)\eta_1\eta_3 = -Q_2^*$$

$$Q_3 = a\phi_2\phi_3 + (1-a)\eta_2\eta_3 = -Q_3^*$$

$$Q_4 = a\phi_1\phi_2 + (1-a)\eta_1\eta_2 = Q_4^*$$

$$Q_5 = a\phi_1^2 + (1-a)\eta_1^2 = Q_5^*$$

$$Q_6 = a\phi_2^2 + (1-a)\eta_2^2 = Q_6^* \quad .$$

Together with the evolution equation for the state variable, (13a), and the control laws, (13b), the expressions for the cost functionals J and J*, as given by (14), (14'), provide a convenient framework for the application of the available theory on dynamic games to this two-country model. The game is now in recursive extensive form, which will facilitate the derivation of the equilibrium solutions using an iterative scheme. However, before going into the actual derivations, it is worthwhile to discuss first in general terms our solution method, which is common to all three types of equilibria, and to justify our general approach to the infinite horizon problem.

A. A Class of Nested Dynamic Games and Stationary Policies

Since the two-country model we have specified above involves a decision horizon of infinite length (or an infinite number of stages), some additional restrictions have to be imposed on the allowable class of control laws, so that the mathematical model and the resulting optimization problem are well defined. These restrictions, which turn out to be natural restraints on the problem, are the following:

(i) The control laws of the two players $f_t(\cdot)$ and $f_t^*(\cdot)$ are taken to be stationary, i.e., independent of the time variable t.

(ii) The state trajectory generated by these stationary control laws is required to be stable; i.e.,

$$\lim_{t\to\infty} s_t = \bar{s} \text{ for some scalar } \bar{s} \text{ independent of } s_1 \quad ,$$

where s_t is generated by

$$s_{t+1} = cs_t + bf(s_t) - bf^*(s_t) \quad , \quad t = 1,2,3, \ldots$$

and s_1 is arbitrarily chosen.

(iii) Under the chosen control laws f and f*, and for the state trajectory generated by them, the cost functions J and J* should be well defined and finite.

An equilibrium obtained under any one of the three types of behavioral assumptions to be specified later will not be acceptable unless it satisfies, or leads to the satisfaction of, these three conditions.

Our general approach to the derivation of stationary stabilization policies is first to consider a sequence of truncated (in time) nested games, obtain the corresponding equilibrium solution for each such finite-horizon game, and then to investigate the limiting behavior of these control laws as the number of stages tends to infinity. Each finite horizon game, say of duration T stages, will have a pair of cost functions given by (for a fixed T)

$$J_{T,1} = \sum_{t=1}^{T} [Q_1 s_t^2 + 2Q_2 s_1 m_t + 2Q_3 s_t m_t^* + 2Q_4 m_t m_t^* + Q_5 m_t^2 + Q_6 m_t^{*2}]\rho^{t-1} \tag{15}$$

$$J_{T,1}^* = \sum_{t=1}^{T} [Q_1^* s_t^2 + 2Q_2^* s_t m_t^* + 2Q_3^* s_t m_t + 2Q_4^* m_t m_t^* + Q_5^* m_t^{*2} + Q_6^* m_t^2]\rho^{t-1} \tag{15'}$$

and the state variable s_t will again evolve according to (13a), with s_1 arbitrarily given.

Now, for a specified equilibrium solution concept, and under the state feedback information pattern, let us assume that the above dynamic game (of duration T stages) admits a unique solution given by

$$f_{t,T}(s_t) \ , \ f_{t,T}^*(s_t) \ ; \ t = 1,\ldots,T$$

where we have shown explicit dependence upon the time horizon T. Let us consider another similar game, but with T' stages (T' > T), which also admits a unique solution (under the same behavioral assumptions), given by

$$f_{t,T'}(s_t) \ , \ f^*_{t,T'}(s_t) \quad ; \quad t = 1,\ldots,T' \quad .$$

Then, we require that the equilibrium solution adopted leads to the following "nestedness property" (NP):[4]

$$f_{T-t,T}(\cdot) = f_{T'-t,T}(\cdot) \quad ; \quad t = 0,1,\ldots,T-1 \qquad (16)$$

$$f^*_{T-t,T}(\cdot) = f^*_{T'-t,T}(\cdot) \quad ; \quad t = 0,1,\ldots,T-1 \quad . \qquad (16')$$

Hence, we have a sequence of "nested" dynamic games, defined for increasing T, which have nested equilibrium solutions. More intuitively, (16), (16') assert that the solutions are independent of the initial starting point. They are therefore simply formal statements of the familiar property of time consistency, which we will require the optimal feedback solutions to satisfy.

The nestedness property of the solution now permits us to consider the limits (for fixed $t < \infty$):

$$\lim_{T\to\infty} f_{t,T}(\cdot) \ , \ \lim_{T\to\infty} f^*_{t,T}(\cdot) \quad .$$

Let us denote these limits, if they exist, by $\bar{f}_t$ and $\bar{f}^*_t$, respectively, and assert the following three properties:

(i) $\bar{f}_t$ and $\bar{f}^*_t$ are independent of t, for t finite; i.e., they are stationary control laws;

(ii) $\bar{f}_t$ and $\bar{f}^*_t$ are stabilizing (for the state trajectory);

(iii) after $f_{t,T}$ and $f^*_{t,T}$ are substituted into J_T and J^*_T, the resulting expressions have finite limits as $T \to \infty$.

The control laws $\bar{f}$ and $\bar{f}^*$ obtained as above and with the listed properties will be defined to be the equilibrium solution of the original infinite-horizon dynamic game, under the chosen set of behavioral assumptions. We will in fact verify subsequently, through numerical simulation, that for the two-country model formulated in Section 2, such unique stationary equilibrium solutions exist under the three different types of equilibrium concepts we are considering.

B. Closed-Loop (Feedback) Nash Equilibrium Solution

The first type of equilibrium we will be addressing is the noncooperative Nash equilibrium under the so-called feedback information pattern (for both countries) as dictated by (13b).[5] Each truncated (finite-horizon) dynamic game, as described by the strictly convex cost functionals, J_T and J^*_T, is of the "linear-quadratic" type, for which the

Nash equilibrium solution is well known; see Başar and Olsder (1982). The nestedness property (16), (16') holds here, and hence the global Nash equilibrium can be obtained recursively; for this reason we would also call it the feedback Nash equilibrium. Now, for fixed T, the solution of the truncated dynamic game can be shown to be unique, and linear in the current value of the state, admitting the expressions given below in Proposition 3.1. For a proof of this result, we refer the reader to Appendix A, which utilizes the recursive technique given in Başar and Olsder (1982, Chapter 6).

Proposition 3.1: For the T-period dynamic game, the feedback Nash equilibrium solution is unique and is given by

$$m_t = f_{t,T}(s_t) = \alpha_\tau s_t \tag{17}$$

$$m_t^* = f_{t,T}^*(s_t) = \alpha_\tau^* s_t \tag{17'}$$

$$\tau \equiv T - t \; ; \; t = 1, 2, \ldots, T$$

where

$$\alpha_\tau = \frac{q_{2,\tau}q_{5,\tau}^* - q_{2,\tau}^*q_{4,\tau}}{q_{4,\tau}q_{4,\tau}^* - q_{5,\tau}q_{5,\tau}^*} \tag{18}$$

$$\alpha_\tau^* = \frac{q_{2,\tau}^*q_{5,\tau} - q_{2,\tau}q_{4,\tau}^*}{q_{4,\tau}^*q_{4,\tau} - q_{5,\tau}^*q_{5,\tau}} \tag{18'}$$

$$q_{1,\tau} = \rho c^2 \varepsilon_{\tau-1} + Q_1 \, , \quad q_{1,\tau}^* = \rho c^2 \varepsilon_{\tau-1}^* + Q_1^*$$

$$q_{2,\tau} = \rho cb \varepsilon_{\tau-1} + Q_2 \, , \quad q_{2,\tau}^* = -\rho cb \varepsilon_{\tau-1}^* + Q_2^*$$

$$q_{3,\tau} = -\rho cb \varepsilon_{\tau-1} + Q_3 \, , \quad q_{3,\tau}^* = \rho cb \varepsilon_{\tau-1}^* + Q_3^*$$

$$q_{4,\tau} = -\rho b^2 \varepsilon_{\tau-1} + Q_4 \, , \quad q_{4,\tau}^* = -\rho b^2 \varepsilon_{\tau-1}^* + Q_4^*$$

$$q_{5,\tau} = \rho b^2 \varepsilon_{\tau-1} + Q_5 \, , \quad q_{5,\tau}^* = \rho b^2 \varepsilon_{\tau-1}^* + Q_5^*$$

$$q_{6,\tau} = \rho b^2 \varepsilon_{\tau-1} + Q_6 \, , \quad q_{6,\tau}^* = \rho b^2 \varepsilon_{\tau-1}^* + Q_6^* \tag{19}$$

and

$$\varepsilon_\tau = q_{1,\tau} + 2q_{2,\tau}\alpha_\tau + 2q_{3,\tau}\alpha_\tau^* + 2q_{4,\tau}\alpha_\tau\alpha_\tau^* + q_{5,\tau}\alpha_\tau^2 + q_{6,\tau}\alpha_\tau^{*2} \tag{20}$$

$$\varepsilon_\tau = q_{1,\tau}^* + 2q_{2,\tau}^*\alpha_\tau^* + 2q_{3,\tau}^*\alpha_\tau + 2q_{4,\tau}^*\alpha_\tau\alpha_\tau^* + q_{5,\tau}^*\alpha_\tau^{*2} + q_{6,\tau}^*\alpha_\tau^2 \tag{20'}$$

$$\tau = 0, 1, 2, \ldots, T-1$$

with the boundary conditions for the q's and q*'s being

$$q_{i,0} = Q_i \ , \ q^*_{i,0} = Q^*_i \ , \ i = 1, 2, \ldots, 6 \quad .$$

The corresponding Nash equilibrium values for $J_{T,1}$ and $J^*_{T,1}$ are

$$J_{T,1} = \varepsilon_{T-1} s_1^2 \ , \ J^*_{T,1} = \varepsilon^*_{T-1} s_1^2 \quad . \tag{21}$$

We first note that the unique Nash equilibrium control laws, characterized by the two sequences $\{\alpha_\tau\}$ and $\{\alpha^*_\tau\}$, depend only on τ, the difference between the terminal time T and the current time t, representing the "time to go." Since the problem is time invariant, this implies that letting $T \to \infty$ is equivalent to letting $\tau \to \infty$, as far as the determination of the stationary equilibrium control laws are concerned; in other words, for each finite t,

$$\lim_{T\to\infty} \alpha_{T-t} = \lim_{\tau\to\infty} \alpha_\tau \equiv \bar{\alpha}$$

$$\lim_{T\to\infty} \alpha^*_{T-t} = \lim_{\tau\to\infty} \alpha^*_\tau \equiv \bar{\alpha}^*$$

whenever the limits exist.

Hence, the stationary equilibrium control laws

$$\bar{f}(s_t) = \lim_{T\to\infty} f_{t,T}(s_t) = \bar{\alpha} s_t \tag{22}$$

$$\bar{f}^*(s_t) = \lim_{T\to\infty} f^*_{t,T}(s_t) = \bar{\alpha}^* s_t \tag{22'}$$

can be obtained in principle by recursively running the algorithms (18)-(20) in forward τ-time and stopping whenever the sequences $\{\alpha_\tau\}$ and $\{\alpha^*_\tau\}$ thus generated exhibit convergence to some limits. For the two-country model this has been done for different choices of the parameter values, and convergence has been observed in each case, as to be discussed in Section 5.

In this iteration, the update equations are either (19) (with (20), (20') substituted in) or (20') (with (19) substituted in). Whenever convergence is achieved, let us denote

$$\lim_{\tau\to\infty} q^*_{i,\tau} = \bar{q}_i \ ; \ \lim_{\tau\to\infty} q^*_{i,\tau} = \bar{q}^*_i$$

$$\lim_{\tau\to\infty} \varepsilon_\tau = \bar{\varepsilon} \quad ; \ \lim_{\tau\to\infty} \varepsilon^*_\tau = \bar{\varepsilon}^*$$

Then, it readily follows from (19), (20), (20') that $\bar{\varepsilon}$ and $\bar{\varepsilon}^*$ should satisfy the highly nonlinear coupled algebraic equations

$$\bar{\varepsilon} = \bar{q}_1 + 2\bar{q}_2\bar{\alpha} + 2\bar{q}_3\bar{\alpha} + 2\bar{q}_4\bar{\alpha}\bar{\alpha}^* + \bar{q}_5\bar{\alpha} + \bar{q}_6\bar{\alpha}^*$$

$$\bar{\varepsilon}^* = \bar{q}_1^* + 2\bar{q}_2^*\bar{\alpha}^* + 2\bar{q}_3^*\bar{\alpha}^* + 2\bar{q}_4^*\bar{\alpha}^*\bar{\alpha} + 2\bar{q}_5^*\bar{\alpha}^* + \bar{q}_6^*\bar{\alpha}$$

where

$$\bar{q}_1 = \rho c^2\bar{\varepsilon} + Q_1 \ , \quad \bar{q}_1^* = \rho c^2\bar{\varepsilon}^* + Q_1^*$$

$$\bar{q}_2 = \rho cb\bar{\varepsilon} + Q_2 \ , \quad \bar{q}_2^* = -\rho cb\bar{\varepsilon}^* + Q_2^*$$

$$\bar{q}_3 = -\rho cb\bar{\varepsilon} + Q_3 \ , \quad \bar{q}_3^* = \rho cb\bar{\varepsilon}^* + Q_3^*$$

$$\bar{q}_4 = -\rho b^2\bar{\varepsilon} + Q_4 \ , \quad \bar{q}_4^* = -\rho b^2\bar{\varepsilon}^* + Q_4^*$$

$$\bar{q}_5 = \rho b^2\bar{\varepsilon} + Q_5 \ , \quad \bar{q}_5^* = \rho b^2\bar{\varepsilon}^* + Q_5^*$$

$$\bar{q}_6 = \rho b^2\bar{\varepsilon} + Q_6 \ , \quad \bar{q}_6^* = \rho b^2\bar{\varepsilon}^* + Q_6^*$$

$$\bar{\alpha} = (\bar{q}_2\bar{q}_5^* - \bar{q}_2^*\bar{q}_4)/(\bar{q}_4\bar{q}_4^* - \bar{q}_5\bar{q}_5^*)$$

$$\bar{\alpha}^* = (\bar{q}_2^*\bar{q}_5 - \bar{q}_2\bar{q}_4^*)/(\bar{q}_4^*\bar{q}_4 - \bar{q}_5^*\bar{q}_5) \quad .$$

Hence, the recursive procedure we have just outlined provides a solution to these coupled equations.

Once it is assured that the generated sequences converge, we still have to check the three conditions given in Section 3.A before declaring (22), (22') as being the Nash equilibrium solution. The first condition, stationarity of $\bar{f}_t$ and $\bar{f}_t^*$, is automatically satisfied. To check the second condition, we write down the equilibrium trajectory

$$s_{t+1} = (c + b\bar{\alpha} - b\bar{\alpha}^*)s_t \ , \ t = 1, 2, \ldots$$

$$\equiv \theta s_t$$

from which stability follows if and only if

$$|c + b(\bar{\alpha}-\bar{\alpha}^*)| < 1 \quad . \tag{23}$$

The parameter θ is the steady-state rate of convergence, and governs the rate of convergence of all variables in the two economies. Our numerical simulations indicate that this condition is also satisfied by the equilibrium solution candidate. Finally, the third condition is automatically satisfied under our hypotheses, because in view of (21),

$$\lim_{T\to\infty} J_{T,1} = \bar{\varepsilon} s_1^2 \qquad \lim_{T\to\infty} J^*_{T,1} = \bar{\varepsilon}^* s_1^2$$

both of which are finite.

Hence the conclusion is that (22), (22') is indeed the unique stationary feedback Nash equilibrium solution. This solution carries the further natural property that, in the case of stationary feedback controls, $m_t = \alpha s_t$, $m^*_t = \alpha^* s_t$, we have

$$\arg\min_{\alpha} J(m_t = \alpha s_t \ , \ m^*_t = \bar{\alpha}^* s_t) = \bar{\alpha} \tag{24}$$

$$\arg\min_{\alpha^*} J^*(m_t = \bar{\alpha} s_t \ , \ m^*_t = \alpha^* s_t) = \bar{\alpha}^* \tag{24'}$$

independently of the value of s_1. In other words, it is indeed a Nash equilibrium solution for the original infinite-horizon dynamic game.

C. Feedback Stackelberg Solution

The Nash equilibrium solution which we have considered above is a symmetric equilibrium concept in terms of the roles of the players in the game. This behavioral assumption is not always valid, especially if there is the possibility of one player (called the leader) to dominate the decision process. Such an asymmetry in the roles of the players leads to the Stackelberg solution, which admits two different definitions, global and feedback, depending upon whether the leader could enforce this policy over the entire duration of the game or only from one period to another. The latter mode of play, which corresponds to the "Feedback Stackelberg Solution," allows for a recursive derivation and satisfies the nestedness (time consistency) property introduced in Section 3.A. This is the equilibrium solution we will adopt in this subsection for our two-country model.

In the derivation of the feedback Stackelberg solution, we follow the recursive technique presented in Başar and Olsder (1982, Chapter 7), which is parallel to the derivation given in Appendix A for the Nash solution, the only difference being that now at every stage a static Stackelberg game is solved, instead of a Nash game; Appendix B elucidates this main difference in the derivation. Then, if we take Country 1 as the leader and Country 2 as the follower, the main result for a T-period dynamic game is presented as follows:

<u>Proposition 3.2</u>: For the T-period dynamic game, the feedback Stackelberg solution is unique and is given by

$$m_t = f_{t,T}(s_t) = \alpha_\tau s_t \quad , \tag{25}$$

$$m_t^* = f_{t,T}^*(s_t) = \alpha_\tau^* s_t \quad , \tag{25'}$$

$$\tau \equiv T - t \ ; \ t = 1, 2, \ldots, T$$

where

$$\alpha_\tau = \left\{ q_{2,\tau} - q_{3,\tau} \frac{q_{4,\tau}^*}{q_{5,\tau}^*} - q_{4,\tau} \frac{q_{2,\tau}^*}{q_{5,\tau}^*} + q_{6,\tau} \frac{q_{2,\tau}^*}{q_{5,\tau}^*} \frac{q_{4,\tau}^*}{q_{5,\tau}^*} \right\} \Bigg/ \left\{ \frac{2q_{4,\tau} q_{4,\tau}^*}{q_{5,\tau}^*} - q_{5,\tau} - q_{6,\tau} \left(\frac{q_{4,\tau}^*}{q_{5,\tau}^*} \right)^2 \right\} \tag{26}$$

$$\alpha_\tau^* = - \frac{1}{q_{5,\tau}^*} [q_{2,\tau}^* + q_{4,\tau}^* \ \alpha_\tau] \tag{26'}$$

and $q_{i,\tau}$, $q_{i,\tau}^*$ $i = 1, 2, \ldots, 5$, ε_τ, ε_τ^* satisfy the same equations as before, i.e., (19), (20), and (20'). The corresponding feedback Stackelberg equilibrium values for $J_{T,1}$ and $J_{t,1}^*$ are

$$J_{T,1} = \varepsilon_{T-1} s_1^2 \ , \ J_{T,1}^* = \varepsilon_{T-1}^* s_1^2 \quad . \tag{27}$$

All the observations and discussions made following Proposition 3.1 previously apply verbatim to this solution, too. In particular, we note that whenever the recursions converge,

$$\lim_{\tau\to\infty} \alpha_\tau = \bar{\alpha} \ , \ \lim_{\tau\to\infty} \alpha_\tau^* = \bar{\alpha}^*$$

where $\bar{\alpha}$ and $\bar{\alpha}^*$ satisfy

$$\bar{\alpha} = \left\{ \bar{q}_2 - \bar{q}_3 \frac{\bar{q}_4^*}{\bar{q}_5^*} - \bar{q}_4 \frac{\bar{q}_2^*}{\bar{q}_5^*} + \bar{q}_6 \frac{\bar{q}_2^*}{\bar{q}_5^*} \frac{\bar{q}_4^*}{\bar{q}_5^*} \right\} \Bigg/ \left\{ \frac{2\bar{q}_4 \bar{q}_4^*}{\bar{q}_5^*} - \bar{q}_5 - \bar{q}_6 \left(\frac{\bar{q}_4^*}{\bar{q}_5^*} \right)^2 \right\} \tag{28}$$

$$\bar{\alpha}^* = - \frac{1}{\bar{q}_5^*} \{\bar{q}_2^* + \bar{q}_4^* \bar{\alpha}\} \tag{28'}$$

and $\bar{q}_i$, $\bar{q}_i^*$, $i = 1, \ldots, 5$ are as defined earlier in Section 3.C.

The stability condition is again (23), which now uses the $\bar{\alpha}$, $\bar{\alpha}^*$'s, given above; however, there is no counterpart of the global equilibrium property (24), (24') in this context, because the feedback Stackelberg solution is <u>not</u> a global Stackelberg equilibrium.

Some numerical simulation results which illustrate the converge properties of the recursive algorithm and the stability of the resulting state trajectory are included in Section 5.

D. Feedback Consistent Conjectural Variations Equilibrium

In the Nash equilibrium, each agent assumes no response on the part of his opponent to his own actions. In fact, each policy maker will respond in accordance with his reaction curve. The Nash equilibrium is therefore consistently wrong in predicting the response of the rival. Recently, the "Consistent Conjectural Variations" (CCV) equilibrium was introduced into static game theory by Bresnahan (1981) and Perry (1982).[6] This equilibrium assumes that in choosing his own strategy, each agent correctly anticipates the response of his rival. The solution therefore corresponds to a rational expectations equilibrium. The third type of equilibrium we will be addressing here is a dynamic version of CCV.

Our generalization to dynamic games utilizes the intrinsic feedback property of the extensive form description of the two-country model, and is in spirit similar to the feedback Stackelberg solution. This dynamic equilibrium solution, which we call feedback CCV, satisfies the nestedness property. Its derivation follows a recursive pattern similar to that of the feedback Stackelberg or Nash solution, but now at each stage a static CCV solution is obtained.

The following proposition presents the feedback CCV solution for a truncated version of the two-country dynamic game model; its proof is found in Appendix C.

Proposition 3.3: For the T-period dynamic game, the feedback consistent conjectural variations equilibrium control laws are given by

$$m_t = f_{t,T}(s_t) = \alpha_\tau(x_\tau) s_t \tag{29}$$

$$m_t^* = f_{t,T}^*(s_t) = \alpha_\tau^*(x_\tau) s_t \tag{29'}$$

$$\tau \equiv T - t \; ; \; t = 1, 2, \ldots, T$$

where

$$\alpha_\tau(x_\tau) \doteq \left\{ \frac{(q_{4,\tau} + q_{6,\tau} x_\tau)(q_{2,\tau}^* + q_{3,\tau}^* x_\tau)}{q_{4,\tau}^* x_\tau + q_{5,\tau}} - q_{2,\tau} - q_{3,\tau} x_\tau \right\} \Big/ \left\{ q_{4,\tau} x_\tau + q_{5,\tau} - \frac{(q_{4,\tau} + q_{6,\tau} x_\tau)(q_{4,\tau}^* + q_{6,\tau}^* x_\tau)}{q_{4,\tau}^* x_\tau + q_{5,\tau}^*} \right\} \tag{30}$$

$$\alpha^*_\tau(x_\tau) = \left\{ \frac{(q^*_{4,\tau} + q^*_{6,\tau}x_\tau)(q_{2,\tau} + q_{3,\tau}x_\tau)}{q_{4,\tau}x_\tau + q^*_{5,\tau}} - q^*_{2,\tau} - q^*_{3,\tau}x_\tau \right\} \Big/ \left\{ q^*_{4,\tau}x_\tau + q^*_{5,\tau} - \frac{(q^*_{4,\tau} + q^*_{6,\tau}x_\tau)(q_{4,\tau} + q_{6,\tau}x_\tau)}{q_{4,\tau}x_\tau + q_{5,\tau}} \right\} \quad (30')$$

and x_τ is a solution of the quadratic equation

$$x_\tau^2 + \left(\frac{q_{5,\tau} + q_{6,\tau}}{q_{4,\tau}} \right) x_\tau + 1 = 0 \;\; ; \tau = 0, 1, 2, \ldots, T-1 \;\; . \quad (31)$$

Here, $q_{i,\tau}$, $q^*_{i,\tau}$, $i = 1,\ldots,5$; ε_t, ε^*_τ, are again determined through the recursive equations given in Proposition 3.1. The corresponding feedback CCV equilibrium values for $J_{T,1}$ and $J^*_{T,1}$ are

$$J_{T,1} = \varepsilon_{T-1}s_1^2 \;,\; J^*_{T,1} = \varepsilon^*_{T-1}s_1^2 \quad .$$

As shown in Appendix C, x_τ is the slope of the static reaction functions, which under the given symmetry assumptions is the same for both countries. Because of the relationship between the parameters of our model, the quadratic equation (31) admits generically two real solutions and hence the multiplicity of equilibria grows with the number of periods, the figure for a T-period game being 2^T. However, our numerical simulation results indicate that at each stage one solution is dominated by the other (in terms of leading to a higher incremental cost), and therefore it could be discarded; this then leads to a stagewise nondominated unique feedback CCV solution.

Again, our previous observations in connection with the feedback Nash solution in Section 3.B also hold true. The recursive scheme here involves, in addition, the computation of the solution of the quadratic equation (31) and substitution of the "dominating" solution into (30) and (31), yielding α_τ, α^*_τ, which in turn are used in (19), (20), and (20') to update on $q_{i\tau}$, $q^*_{i\tau}$, ε_τ, and ε^*_τ. If the limits

$$\lim_{\tau\to\infty} \alpha_\tau = \bar{\alpha} \;,\; \lim_{\tau\to\infty} \alpha^* = \bar{\alpha}^*$$

exist, then the stationary control laws associated with the feedback CCV solution are

$$m_t = \bar{f}(s_t) = \bar{\alpha}s_t \;\; ; \; m^*_t = \bar{f}^*(s_t) = \bar{\alpha}^*s_t$$

where $\bar{\alpha} = \bar{\alpha}(\bar{x})$ and $\bar{\alpha}^* = \bar{\alpha}^*(\bar{x})$ are given by (30) and (30'), respectively, with $q_{i,\tau}$, $q^*_{i,\tau}$, x_τ, replaced by the limit values $\bar{q}_i$, $\bar{q}^*_i$, and $\bar{x}$, respectively.

The stability Condition (23) uses the values for $\bar{\alpha}$ and $\bar{\alpha}^*$ determined above, and it has been shown numerically that it is satisfied for a wide range of the parameters of the problem; see Section 5. As in the case of the feedback Stackelberg solution, the feedback CCV solution also does not satisfy the global equilibrium property (24), (24'), satisfied by the Nash equilibrium.

4. Numerical Procedures

The parameters describing the optimal policies under the various strategic regimes are themselves complex functions of the underlying parameters of the model. Thus apart from revealing the general nature of the optimal policies, it is difficult to determine their specific properties. Moreover, one is unable to gain much insight into the general welfare implications of the different regimes. We, therefore, choose to resort to numerical simulations.

Table 1 indicates a set of base parameter values. These are chosen on the basis of reasonable empirical evidence. The elasticity of the demand for domestic output with respect to the foreign output is $d_1 = .3$; the semi-elasticity of the demand for output with respect to the real interest rate is $d_2 = .5$, while the elasticity of the demand for output with respect to the relative price is $d_3 = 1$. The income elasticity of the demand for money is $e_1 = 1$, while the semi-elasticity of money demand with respect to the nominal interest rate is .5. The share of domestic output in domestic comsumption is .6 for the two economies; the slopes of their respective Phillips curves are .75. The relative weights given to output stabilization in the objective function is $a = .75$, while the discount rate is $\rho = .9$.

While these values seem reasonable, they are arbitrary. In Part B of the table we therefore consider variants of these values, allowing the parameters to range below low values and high values. Note that since d_2, e_2, are semi-elasticities, the values of $d_2 = .5$, $e_2 = .5$, correspond to elasticities of around .03, .05, respectively.[7] Also, we have assumed previously that the share of domestic output in consumption exceeds 50%.

To consider all combinations of these parameter values would be impractical. Our approach, therefore, is to begin with the base set and introduce one parameter change at a time. Performing these changes in d_1, d_2, e_1, e_2, δ, γ, a, gives a total of 25 parameter sets. Parameter Set 1 is the base set; Sets 2-25 are obtained by substituting the corresponding values into the base set. To examine the possibility that the behavior is particularly sensitive to the discount rate ρ, we repeated the entire 25 sets for 5 different values of ρ, ranging between .8 and 1 to yield a total of 125 sets. However, since the results tended to be insensitive to ρ, we restricted further analysis to the originally chosen value of .9.

5. Alternative Equilibria: Base Parameter Set

Figures 1-3 illustrate the time paths for the equilibrium solutions corresponding to the base parameter set, described in Table 1. These have drawn for an initial unit positive shock in the relative price s, i.e., for a given initial real depreciation of the currency of Country 1.[8] The figures are drawn for a time horizon of $T = 12$ periods. The three equilibrium solutions are discussed in turn.

A. Feedback Nash

Figures 1a-1e illustrate the time paths for s_t, m_t, Y_t, $\Delta C_{t+1} \equiv (C_{t+1} - C_t)$ and the welfare costs incurred at each period, under Nash behavior. Given the symmetry of the model, the effects on the two economies are identical (in magnitude), so that the time paths for m*, Y*, ΔC* are just mirror images of those of m, y, and ΔC.

As a benchmark, suppose initially that in response to a unit increase in s, there is no response on the part of the two policy makers; that is, $m = m^* = 0$. In effect, the policy makers agree to allow the exchange rate to float freely, so that this is a kind of cooperative equilibrium. In the first instance, the positive disturbance in s raises the demand for domestic output and reduces the demand for foreign output. This leads to an increase in domestic output Y, matched by an equivalent decrease in foreign output Y*. With the real money stocks held constant in both economies, these changes in output will lead to an increase in the domestic interest rate, accompanied by a decrease in the foreign interest rate, the net effect of which is to cause the rate of exchange depreciation of the domestic currency to increase. The increase in domestic output leads to a rise in the inflation rate of domestic output. This, together with the increase in the rate of exchange depreciation, causes the rate of inflation of the overall domestic CPI to increase; the opposite occurs abroad.

Next, suppose that as in Turnovsky and d'Orey (1985), each policy maker follows a Nash strategy, using a one-period (static) objective function. In this case, if Country 1 responds to the increase in the relative price by reducing its real money stock, this mitigates the expansion in domestic output, while at the same time raising the domestic interest rate. The opposite effects occur abroad, causing the rate of exchange depreciation to increase, relative to the benchmark case of a perfectly flexible regime. This in turn leads to larger short-run variations in the rate of inflation. The increases in welfare costs associated with this increase in price variation more than offset the reduction due to lower income variation, causing the overall costs to increase. Note that this occurs despite the fact that the relative costs attached to output variation are greater. It is a reflection of the quadratic nature of the cost function which penalizes large variations more than proportionately.

Thus for Parameter Set 1, Turnovsky and d'Orey (1985) demonstrate that the simple rule of essentially no intervention can dominate other forms of strategic behavior, including Nash and other equilibria. These findings are, however, parameter sensitive, as they note. Moreover, neither the absence of intervention, nor the optimal short-run Nash policy of leaning against the wind is desirable from the viewpoint of long-run welfare maximization. Both strategies are associated with large increases in the rate of exchange depreciation (larger in the latter case), contributing to large increases in the real exchange rate, which in turn causes the fluctuations in outputs and inflation in the two countries to increase. The repetition of either strategy in each period causes the real exchange rate s to follow a divergent time path, with welfare costs ultimately increasing without limit.

By contrast, the optimal Nash policy, which minimizes the intertemporal cost function, calls for precisely the opposite response, namely, an initial real monetary expansion in Country 1, accompanied by a corresponding contraction in Country 2. These policies cause the level of output in Country 1 to now increase by more than it did in the benchmark situation. By the same token, and by the above reasoning, this causes the rate of exchange depreciation of the domestic currency, and hence the overall rate of domestic inflation, to decrease relative to the benchmark policy. Precisely the opposite effects occur abroad. The reduction in the domestic nominal rate of exchange depreciation, combined with the above movements in domestic and foreign outputs, leads to a reduction in the real exchange rate, s. This in turn leads to a mitigation in the fluctuations in outputs and inflation. As a result of implementing the second, and subsequent, stages of the optimization, the real exchange rate follows a convergent path, with steadily declining welfare costs.

For the twelve periods horizon illustrated in Figures 1.A-1.E, the coefficients of the optimal control law α, α^*, evolve as follows:

$$\alpha_\tau = -\alpha^*_\tau = .6857 \qquad \tau = 11,\dots,4$$

$\alpha_3 = -\alpha_3^* = .6856$

$\alpha_2 = -\alpha_2^* = .6873$

$\alpha_1 = -\alpha_1^* = .6439$

$\alpha_0 = -\alpha_0^* = -.9036$

The interesting point to observe is that in the last period, the policy rule switches sign. This reflects the change in optimal behavior in going from a static to an intertemporal objective function. In fact, the static analysis of Turnovsky and d'Orey (1985) is identical to the one-period-to-go solution of the present dynamic analysis. It is also of interest to note that the control law converges to its steady state ($\bar{\alpha} = .6837$, $\bar{\alpha}^* = -.6837$), within just five periods. Finally, the speed of the adjustment of the economy along the optimal trajectory is given by $\theta = .446$, implying that around 55% of the adjustment is completed within the first period.

B. Feedback Stackelberg

At each stage, the follower's response to the leader's action is given by the relationship

$$m_t^* = -[q_{2,\tau}^* s_t + q_{4,\tau}^* m_t]/q_{5,\tau}^* \quad .$$

This defines the follower's reaction function, the slope of which is $-q_{4,\tau}^*/q_{5,\tau}^*$. Being a function of τ, this changes at each stage. Using the base parameter set, Turnovsky and d'Orey (1985) show that for the one period objective, $q_4^* = .046$, $q_5^* = .305$, so that the short-run reaction curve has a negative slope equal to -.15. This means that the foreign (follower) economy responds to a unit expansion in the domestic (leader) real money supply, with a monetary contraction of .15. Turnovsky d'Orey (1985) characterize the negative slope as being a beggar-thy-neighbor world.[9] This less than proportionate response by the follower implies that the Stackelberg equilibrium lies at a point on the follower's reaction function, away from the Nash equilibrium, in the direction of the follower's Bliss point. At this equilibrium point, the leader experiences a somewhat larger increase in output, accompanied by a smaller increase in inflation, relative to the Nash equilibrium, while for the follower, the negative fluctuations in both these variables are diminished in magnitude. Furthermore, while the welfare of the leader is higher than at the Nash equilibrium, the gains to the follower are relatively larger.

Thus in the short-run Stackelberg equilibrium of the Turnovsky-d'Orey (1985) analysis, the leader engages in monetary contraction, while the follower undertakes an expansion, although the magnitudes of the respective adjustments are less than for the Nash equilibrium. For the same reasons as those given for the feedback Nash solution presented above, these responses lead to an increase in the relative price s, and cause the economy to embark on an unstable time path.

As Figure 2b shows, the appropriate initial responses become very different with an intertemporal objective function. Both the leader and the follower should now contract their respective real money stocks, with the contraction by the follower being significantly greater than in the Nash feedback case. The reason for the difference stems from the changed nature of the follower's short-run reaction function. In the initial period, we find $q_4^* = -4.481$, $q_5^* = 4.883$, so that the slope of the reaction function is now .927 and is positive.

The leader knows that if he follows the feedback Nash strategy of expanding the money supply, the follower will tend to respond in a similar fashion. This tends to exacerbate the fluctuations in output of both economies, although the more balanced adjustment means that it is likely to be accompanied by lower fluctuations in the rate of exchange depreciation (which responds to differential monetary policies), and hence in the rate of inflation of the CPI. Given that the cost function assigns greater weight to output fluctuations than to fluctuations in inflation, this is a nonoptimal situation, particularly for the leader. Accordingly, his strategy is to engage in a monetary contraction, thereby inducing an even greater contraction abroad, by the follower. The fact that the contraction is relatively greater abroad causes an appreciation of the real exchange rate, so that s_t begins to fall. This pattern of responses continues at each stage, thereby enabling the economy to follow a stable path towards equilibrium.

A consequence of the initial worldwide monetary contraction is that the initial stimulating effects of the positive shift in the relative price s on the leader economy, is largely eliminated. Indeed, in Period 1, output increases by only .06 units as compared to around .7 for the Nash equilibrium. At the same time, the monetary contraction means that the inflation of .4% under Nash becomes a deflation of .25% under Stackelberg. In the follower economy, the initial reductions in output and inflation under Nash, are even greater under Stackelberg. These comparisons become evident upon examination of Figures 1 and 2.

A striking feature of these results is the contrast in the welfares of the leader and follower between the static and dynamic games. We have already noted that for a one-period horizon, the follower is better off than the leader, with both being better off than under Nash. Now we see that over time, the leader improves his welfare vastly, though at the expense of the follower. The welfare costs under feedback Nash to both are .759. Under feedback Stackelberg, however, the leader's costs are reduced to .020, making him better off, while for the follower they rise to 2.758, making him worse off. Essentially, the fact that the game proceeds over a number of stages enables the leader to exploit his position more effectively. Basically, he is able to impose most of the burden of adjustment on the follower, forcing him to bear the bulk of the associated costs. This reversal of the relative welfares occurs even within a two period game, although the differences increase with the length of the horizon.

This finding raises serious questions of conflict in a multiperiod horizon. Obviously, in this situation neither country will agree to be the follower, raising serious doubts about the viability of the Stackelberg regime, unless there is some other mechanism whereby leadership is determined and enforced.

Finally, the convergence properties of the base parameter set can be summarized. For the 12 period horizon illustrated in Figures 2, the coefficients of the control laws α_τ, α^*_τ, evolve as follows:

$$\alpha_\tau = -.3717\ ,\ \alpha^*_\tau = -.1891 \qquad \tau = 11,\ldots,5$$

$$\alpha_4 = -.3718\ ,\ \alpha^*_4 = -.1890$$

$$\alpha_3 = -.3716\ ,\ \alpha^*_3 = -.1881$$

$$\alpha_2 = -.3493\ ,\ \alpha^*_2 = -.1778$$

$$\alpha_1 = -.1004\ ,\ \alpha^*_1 = -.1130$$

$$\alpha_0 = -.7767\ ,\ \alpha^*_0 = \ .8843 \quad .$$

In this case, the convergence of the control law to its steady state form takes 5 periods. Note again the big jump in the size of the coefficients, between the second to last and last period. While the leader should always adopt a leaning against the wind policy, the response of the follower changes qualitatively during these two periods. The speed of the adjustment of the economy, as described by θ, is .247, implying that 75% of the adjustment occurs within one period. This is considerably faster than for the feedback Nash equilibrium.

C. Feedback Consistent Conjectural Variations

The Nash equilibrium is based on the assumption that each agent presumes that his rival will not react to his actions. In the CCV solution, each policy maker correctly takes account of his opponent's reaction. In the static analysis of Turnovsky-d'Orey (1985), the reaction functions were negatively sloped, with the optimal strategy for each policy maker being to lean against the wind. That is, Policy Maker 1 should contract his real money supply in response to the real depreciation of his country's exchange rate, while Policy Maker 2 should expand his real money supply correspondingly. In the CCV solution, both policy makers are aware of this and therefore each moderates his adjustment relative to the Nash equilibrium. For Parameter Set 1, this adjustment is from -.9 to -.8 and .9 to .8, respectively. This leads to a larger increase in output accompanied by a smaller increase in the rate of inflation for Country 1, relative to the Nash equilibrium, with smaller adjustments occurring abroad.

The monetary contraction in Country 1, accompanied by the corresponding expansion in Country 2 leads to a large change in the rate of exchange depreciation of the domestic exchange rate, which in turn leads to a depreciation of the real exchange rate. Even though the magnitudes of these adjustments tend to be smaller than for the Nash equilibrium, nevertheless the time path for s, and hence for all the relevant variables in the two economies, follow time paths similar to before. Myopic optimization causes the real exchange rate to diverge, thereby generating instability and infinite welfare costs, the reasons remaining essentially as before.

As for the feedback Nash case, the optimal feedback CCV equilibrium calls for an initial monetary expansion in Country 1, accompanied by an equivalent initial contraction abroad. This is because the short-run reaction function, within the multiperiod horizon are now positively sloped for the two countries. Turnovsky and d'Orey (1985) have characterized this as being locomotive behavior, in the sense of an expansionary policy in one country encouraging an expansion in the other.

The initial monetary expansion in Country 1 is now reduced from .69 under Nash to .56, with the magnitude of the contraction abroad being reduced correspondingly. The reason is essentially the same as in the static case. Both agents know that in a locomotive world his actions will stimulate a corresponding adjustment by the other, and accordingly, each can reduce his own degree of intervention.

The qualitative pattern of adjustments is generally similar to the one for the feedback Nash equilibrium, although everything is scaled down. The magnitudes of the adjustments in output and inflation in the two economies are smaller, as are the degrees of intervention by the respective monetary authorities.

The coefficients of the feedback policies, α_τ, α^*_τ, evolve over time as follows:

$$\alpha_\tau = -\alpha^*_\tau = .5596 \qquad \tau = 11,\ldots,4$$

$$\alpha_3 = -\alpha^*_3 = .5591$$

$$\alpha_2 = -\alpha^*_2 = .5508$$

$$\alpha_1 = -\alpha^*_1 = -.4101$$

$$\alpha_0 = -\alpha^*_0 = -.7991 \quad .$$

Again the switch in the adjustment between the second to last and final periods is present. Also, as in Nash, the convergence of the control laws to their steady state form occurs within four periods. On the other hand, the speed of the adjustment of the system is now .789, which is considerably slower than in the Nash case. The intuitive reason for this is that with each agent taking full account of the adjustment of the other to his actions, has a dampening effect on his own actions, thereby slowing down the adjustment of the system.

D. Overview

These results show that, at least in the case of Parameter Set 1, all three types of equilibria suggest a sharp contrast between optimal policy with a single period objective and optimal policy within a dynamic objective function. Basically, the static analysis called for a monetary contraction for Country 1 (experiencing the positive shock in s), accompanied by an equivalent monetary expansion in Country 2. These responses tend to reduce output fluctuations, while increasing fluctuations in inflation. Given the relative weights on these in the objective functions, this is desirable for a one period horizon. However, it is not optimal over the longer run. Such policies generate increasing fluctuations in the relative price, with increasing welfare costs in the future. These can be avoided by adopting policies which generate more variation in output and less variation in inflation.

Finally, we recall that Figures 1-3 have been drawn for 12 periods. This means that in the last period, the paths may begin to diverge, due to the myopic form of the control law in that period. Since, after 11 periods of optimal dynamic control, s is by then small, such upturns may be imperceptible; see however Figure 3. The time paths for the infinite horizon case are similar, except that the values of α, α^* are the same (at their steady state values) for all periods.

6. Sensitivity Analysis

Tables 2-4 summarize key properties of the model across 28 parameter sets. These sets include the basic 25 discussed in Table 1, augmented by 3 additional sets which allow for variations in the discount rate. The last of these (Set 28) is simply the one period horizon considered by Turnovsky and d'Orey (1985), which corresponds to a discount rate of $\rho = 0$. We consider the following three aspects summarizing the equilibria:

(i) The steady state control laws, $\bar{\alpha}$, $\bar{\alpha}^*$;

(ii) The steady state rate of convergence θ;

(iii) The steady state welfare costs.

We also discuss how these respond to changes in the parameter values. Note that Set 21 ($a = 0$) and Set 25 ($a = 1$) give rise to degenerate policy games. The reason is simply that in either case, the objective function of each policy maker reduces to just one target and the two policy instruments m, m* enable each to be attained perfectly. All solutions coverge to the same, with zero welfare costs being incurred.

Given the symmetry of the model, with the exception of the Stackelberg solution, the policy rules and welfare costs to the two countries are identical, being as indicated. In the case of the Stackelberg equilibrium, the rules and the welfare of the leader and follower are reported separately. From these tables certain patterns can be observed.

A. Steady State Control Laws

Except for extreme parameter values (e.g., Sets 11, 15), the feedback Nash calls for more intensive intervention than the feedback CCV, at least for all parameter sets in which the relative weight of output in the cost function, a, exceeds .6. However, as the relative weight falls (and the weight on inflation rises), then the intensity of intervention under CCV increases and exceeds that under Nash. In virtually all cases, both the Nash and CCV solutions call for leaning with the wind. Country 1 should expand its (real) money supply in response to the real depreciation of its currency; Country 2 should contract in response to the real appreciation of its currency. By contrast, the Stackelberg leader should almost always lean against the wind, while the follower should always do so (with the exception of the degenerate case 25). Moreover, the follower should intervene with greater intensity than the leader.

B. Steady State Rate of Convergence

For all but Parameter Sets 10, 21, 25, and 28, all optimal paths converge. Parameter Set 28 is the static case, which for reasons discussed at length always leads to divergence. Parameter Sets 21 and 25 are the degenerate extremes, when the targets are always attained perfectly in each period. In this case, the divergence of s is irrelevant. It can always be accommodated by increasing adjustments in the controls m_t. m_t^*. The only genuine dynamic game in which divergence occurs is Set 10, with $d_2 = 10$. This value violates the condition for a downward sloping IS curve and hence instability is not so surprising. The problem can be seen most clearly by letting $d_2 \to \infty$, when Equations (1), (1') become

$$I_t = P_{t+1} - P_t$$

$$I_t^* = P_{t+1}^* - P_t^* \quad .$$

Combining these equations with the interest parity Condition (3), and noting the definition of s_t, we find

$$s_{t+1} = s_t$$

i.e., $\theta = 1$. It is clear from Table 3 that $\lim_{d_2 \to \infty} \theta = 1$.

With the exception of the extreme Set 7, for all other sets with $a = .75$, the values of θ under Nash, Stackelberg, and CCV, θ_N, θ_S, θ_{CCV}, respectively, satisfy

$$\theta_S < \theta_N < \theta_{CCV}$$

implying a clear ranking in the rates of convergence; Stackelberg is faster than Nash, which in turn is faster than CCV. In the latter case, the fact that each policy maker takes account of his rival's behavior induces caution and a more gradual adjustment. Furthermore, θ_{CCV} is relatively less sensitive to parameter changes than the speed of adjustment under the other forms of behavior.

C. Steady State Welfare Costs

The pattern of welfare costs is also remarkably stable and gives rise to a clear ranking among the equilibria. With the exception of the degenerate cases (Sets 21, 25) and the static case (Set 28), the ranking of the different solutions found for the base parameter set extends to all other sets. The Stackelberg leadership dominates Nash, which is superior to CCV, which in turn dominates being a Stackelberg follower. The welfare costs to the Stackelberg leader are remarkably stable across parameter sets and take him close to his Bliss point (zero costs). By contrast, the Stackelberg follower does extremely poorly, questioning the viability of this regime, relative to the alternatives. It is also interesting to note that the CCV is always dominated by Nash. This reflects the fact that CCV leads to more cautious responses and slower adjustment, thereby contributing to larger intertemporal welfare costs. Overall, the robustness of these results for the dynamic games are in sharp contrast to the rankings obtained by Turnovsky and d'Orey (1985) for the static game, which for the same parameter sets were found to be extremely parameter sensitive.

D. Sensitivity to Parameter Changes

The following more specific changes can be observed in response to parameter changes.

(i) As the degree of interdependence between the two economies, as measured by d_1, increases, the degree of intervention decreases and welfare improves. Both countries are better off with a high degree of interdependence. The rate of steady state convergence declines (θ increases) under Nash and Stackelberg, but increases slightly under CCV.

(ii) The degree of intervention decreases with the interest elasticity of the demand for output, d_2, while the rate of convergence declines. Welfare costs decline for all but the Stackelberg follower, who is made worse off.

(iii) The welfare costs and rate of convergence under CCV are all independent of the parameters characterizing the demand for money, α_1, α_2. The control laws $\bar{\alpha}$, $\bar{\alpha}^*$ do vary with these parameters. However, the impact of these on Y, Y*, and ΔE are exactly offsetting, so that these variables, and therefore the rate of convergence and welfare costs, remain insensitive to these parameter changes.

(iv) As the income elasticity of the demand for money increases, feedback Nash switches from leaning against the wind to leaning with the wind. The rate of convergence increases and welfare improves. The degree of intervention of the Stackelberg leader declines, while that of the follower increases. The rate of convergence increases, with welfare losses of the leader increasing and those of the follower declining.

(v) As the interest elasticity of the demand for money increases, feedback Nash switches from leaning with the wind to leaning against the wind. The rate of convergence declines and welfare decreases. The degrees of intervention of both Stackelberg leader and follower increase, as does the rate of convergence. The welfare costs to the leader decline, while those to the follower increase.

(vi) As the share of domestic goods in the CPI increases, intervention under Nash and CCV decline very mildly, while those of both Stackelberg players increase, again modestly. The rate of convergence in all cases declines, while the welfare costs for all but the Stackelberg leader increase gradually.

(vii) As the price responsiveness (i.e., slope of the Phillips curve) increases, all equilibria involve a decline in the rate of intervention, with faster convergence and lower welfare costs.

(viii) The equilibria are somewhat more complex functions of a, since both extremes $a = 0$, $a = 1$ lead to degenerate games with zero welfare costs. Our observations therefore are restricted to the range $.2 < a < .75$. Over this range we see that as the relative weight assigned to output variability in the objective function increases, the degree of intervention under Nash and CCV both decline. By contrast, both Stackelberg players intervene with greater intensity. The rate of convergence associated with both Nash and Stackelberg equilibria decline. In the case of CCV the convergence passes from being nonmonotonic for low values of a, to a slow gradual adjustment.

(ix) As the discount factor, ρ, increases, so that the policy makers become more far sighted (discount the future less), the control laws under both Nash and CCV call for increasing intervention. The Stackelberg follower also increases more intensively, while the intervention of the leader declines. The rate of convergence increases, and indeed for low values of ρ, (the static equilibrium being a polar case), the solutions will diverge. Welfare costs are relatively insensitive to the rate of discount, at least over the relevant range.

7. Conclusions

In this paper, we have developed dynamic strategic monetary policies using a standard two country macro model under flexible exchange rates. Three types of noncooperative equilibria have been considered, namely feedback Nash, feedback Stackelberg, and feedback Consistent Conjectural Variations.

The optimal policies have been obtained as feedback rules in which the real money supplies in the respective economies are adjusted to movements in the real exchange rate. Even for a simple model such as this, the derivation of the optimal policies is highly complex, particularly in the limiting case of an infinite time horizon. For this reason, much of our work has proceeded numerically. In carrying out our simulations, we have compared the results obtained from the present dynamic analysis with those obtained previously for the same simulation sets, but using a single period time horizon.

Many of the specific conclusions of our analysis have been noted previously. At this point, several general conclusions are worth highlighting. First, the optimal policies were found to yield convergences for all three equilibria, in the case of virtually all parameter sets. A clear ranking in the rate of convergence was obtained; feedback Stackelberg yields the fastest convergence, with feedback CCV being the slowest. The fact that convergence under feedback CCV is slower than under Nash reflects the fact that the process of taking account of his rival's actions induces caution in each policy maker, thereby slowing down the adjustment of the system.

The results indicate a sharp contrast in both the optimal policies and welfare between the previous results obtained for the short-run time horizon and the present results for the long run, thereby suggesting the importance of intertemporal and intratemporal tradeoffs. As far as welfare is concerned, while in the short run the ranking of the equilibria is highly parameter sensitive, in the long run the rankings are remarkably robust across parameter sets. Specifically, in the long run we find for each player the Stackelberg leader to be the preferred equilibrium, followed by feedback Nash, feedback CCV, and Stackelberg follower. The superiority of the Stackelberg leader suggests that it takes time for him to be able to exploit his position.

While these results are suggestive and appear promising, we should note at least two important limitations of our analysis. First, it is based on two symmetric economies, and while this is an obvious natural starting point, it clearly needs to be relaxed. Secondly, the model itself is simple in terms of minimizing the order of the dynamics; extensions in the direction of generating a richer model structure are also desirable, before the results obtained can be maintained with confidence.

The observed fact that the optimal policies obtained for truncated finite-horizon games yield convergences for all three types of equilibria, and for almost all parameter sets chosen, is suggestive of existence of a general feature shared by all classes of such models. As we have indicated earlier, there is as yet no theoretical result on the existence of equilibria (of the types considered here) for infinite-horizon dynamic games, since researchers have failed in their attempts to prove monotonicity of the cost-to-go (value) functions. The numerical results presented here, while corroborating the general expectations that the value functions are not necessarily monotonically decreasing or increasing from one stage to another, do indicate that there is in fact a monotonically converging subsequence, which is the original sequence with a few initial adjustment terms left out. Since this appears to be a general feature of the parameterized class of models adopted in this paper, a theoretical justification of convergence of finite-horizon optimal policies to a stationary infinite-horizon optimal policy may be quite tractable. In such an endeavor, one will have to work with appropriately chosen subsequences of value functions, instead of the original sequence itself. The numerical simulations conducted in this study will definitely shed light on future directions of research for a theoretical analysis of infinite-horizon dynamic games.

Table 1

Parameter Values[a/]

A. Base Set (Parameter Set 1)

$d_1 = .3,\ d_2 = .5,\ d_3 = 1,\ \alpha_1 = 1.0,\ \alpha_2 = .5$

$\delta = .6,\ \gamma = .75,\ a = .75$

B. Variants (Parameter Sets 2-25)

d_1: 0, .2, .4, .6, .8

d_2: .01, .25, 1.0, 10

e_1 = 0, 0.5

e_2 = .1, 1.0, 10

δ = .5, .75, .99

γ = .5, .1

a = 0, .2, .4, .6, 1

[a/] Since d_3 appears as a scale variable applied to s, the results are insensitive to changes in d_3 (except for a scale factor). We, therefore, do not consider changes in d_3, but instead have maintained $d_3 = 1$ throughout.

Table 2

Steady State Control Laws $\bar{\alpha}$, $\bar{\alpha}^*$[a/]

	1 Base Set	2 $d_1=0$	3 $d_1=.2$	4 $d_1=.4$	5 $d_1=.6$	6 $d_1=.8$	7 $d_2=.01$	8 $d_2=.25$	9 $d_2=1$	10 $d_2=10$
Nash	±.686	±.877	±.741	±.637	±.552	±.477	±.740	±.710	±.655	±.461
Stackelberg follower	-.372	-.894	-.514	-.253	-.068	.063	-23.64	-.832	-.155	-.015
Stackelberg leader	-1.891	-2.793	-2.141	-1.675	-1.323	-1.044	-25.12	-2.333	-1.700	-1.350
CCV	±.560	±.710	±.601	±.524	±.465	±.420	±.910	±.556	±.564	±.452

	11 $e_1=0$	12 $e_1=.5$	13 $e_2=.1$	14 $e_2=1$	15 $e_2=10$	16 $\delta=.5$	17 $\delta=.75$	18 $\delta=.99$
Nash	∓.219	±.237	±.850	±.474	±3.447	±.687	±.682	±.674
Stackelberg follower	-.452	-.407	-.022	-.815	-8.919	-.362	-.402	-.452
Stackelberg leader	-.941	-.996	-1.805	-1.993	-3.710	-1.882	-1.916	-1.955
CCV	+.251	±.155	±.760	±.309	+4.201	±.560	±.558	±.554

	19 $\gamma=.5$	20 $\gamma=1$	21 $a=0$	22 $a=.2$	23 $a=.4$	24 $a=.6$	25 $a=1$	26 $\rho=.8$	27 $\rho=1$	28 static ($\rho=0$)
Nash	±.791	±.578	±1.316	±.754	±.716	±.696	∓1	±.668	±.700	-.904
Stackelberg follower	-.391	-3.64	1.316	-.0142	-.191	-.307	-1	-.379	-.366	-.777
Stackelberg leader	-2.134	-1.656	-1.316	-1.623	-1.751	-1.840	+1	-1.876	-1.903	.884
CCV	±.658	±.460	±1.316	±1.092	±1.090	±.565	∓1	±.541	±.575	∓.799

[a/] The Nash and CCV solutions are symmetric with respect to the two countries. The upper sign relates to Country 1, the lower sign to Country 2. Thus in the base parameter set, ±.686 means that Country 1 expands its money supply, while Country 2 contracts.

Table 3

Steady State Rate of Convergence θ

	1 Base Set	2 $d_1=0$	3 $d_1=.2$	4 $d_1=.4$	5 $d_1=.6$	6 $d_1=.8$	7 $d_2=.01$	8 $d_2=.25$	9 $d_2=1$	10 $d_2=10$
Nash	.446	.379	.422	.474	.537	.613	-.025	.261	.645	1.008
Stackelberg	.247	.202	.230	.267	.318	.388	-.035	.129	.405	.930
CCV	.787	.790	.788	.786	.785	.784	-.700	.759	.831	1.011

	11 $e_1=0$	12 $e_1=.5$	13 $e_2=.1$	14 $e_2=1$	15 $e_2=10$	16 $\delta=.5$	17 $\delta=.75$	18 $\delta=.99$
Nash	.607	.485	.393	.485	.586	.444	.455	.477
Stackelberg	.383	.276	.210	.276	.361	.245	.254	.269
CCV	.787	.787	.787	.787	.787	.786	.792	.802

	19 $\gamma=.5$	20 $\gamma=1$	21 $a=0$	22 $a=.2$	23 $a=.4$	24 $a=.6$	25 $a=1$	26 $\rho=.8$	27 $\rho=1$	28 static ($\rho=0$)
Nash	.456	.442	-1.256	.261	.364	.419	5.00	.494	.407	4.739
Stackelberg	.252	.245	-1.256	.125	.192	.229	5.00	.277	.223	4.542
CCV	.794	.781	-1.256	-.652	-.644	.773	5.00	.837	.745	4.457

Table 4

Welfare Costs

	1 Base Set	2 $d_1=0$	3 $d_1=.2$	4 $d_1=.4$	5 $d_1=.6$	6 $d_1=.8$	7 $d_2=.01$	8 $d_2=.25$	9 $d_2=1$	10 $d_2=10$
Nash	.759	1.259	.882	.663	.531	.455	.456	.594	1.099	5.662
Stackelberg leader	.0202	.022	.021	.019	.017	.015	.036	.025	.014	.002
Stackelberg follower	2.758	4.772	3.258	2.367	1.810	1.457	1.711	2.230	3.782	17.13
CCV	1.266	2.177	1.494	1.086	.824	.646	.812	1.111	1.585	5.881

	11 $e_1=0$	12 $e_1=.5$	13 $e_2=.01$	14 $e_2=1$	15 $e_2=10$	16 $\delta=.5$	17 $\delta=.75$	18 $\delta=.99$
Nash	.888	.780	.735	.780	.862	.750	.787	.845
Stackelberg leader	.015	.019	.022	.019	.016	.026	.008	0
Stackelberg follower	2.896	2.777	2.740	2.777	2.865	2.714	2.897	3.144
CCV	1.266	1.266	1.266	1.266	1.266	1.256	1.303	1.379

	19 $\gamma=.5$	20 $\gamma=1$	21 $a=0$	22 $a=.2$	23 $a=.4$	24 $a=.6$	25 $a=1$	26 $\rho=.8$	27 $\rho=1$	28 static ($\rho=0$)
Nash	.719	.828	0	.305	.478	.640	0	.762	.755	.590
Stackelberg leader	.022	.018	0	.031	.035	.029	0	.019	.021	.585
Stackelberg follower	2.624	3.003	0	1.032	1.662	2.288	0	2.755	2.760	.529
CCV	1.194	1.386	0	.413	.776	1.092	0	1.257	1.274	.542

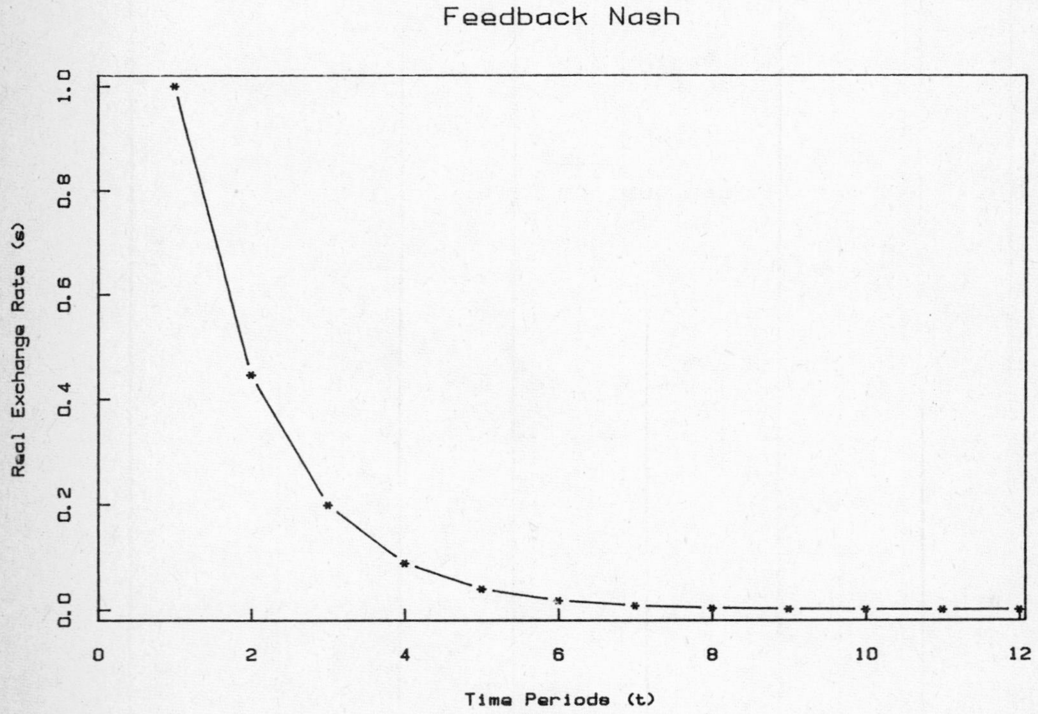

fig. 1a

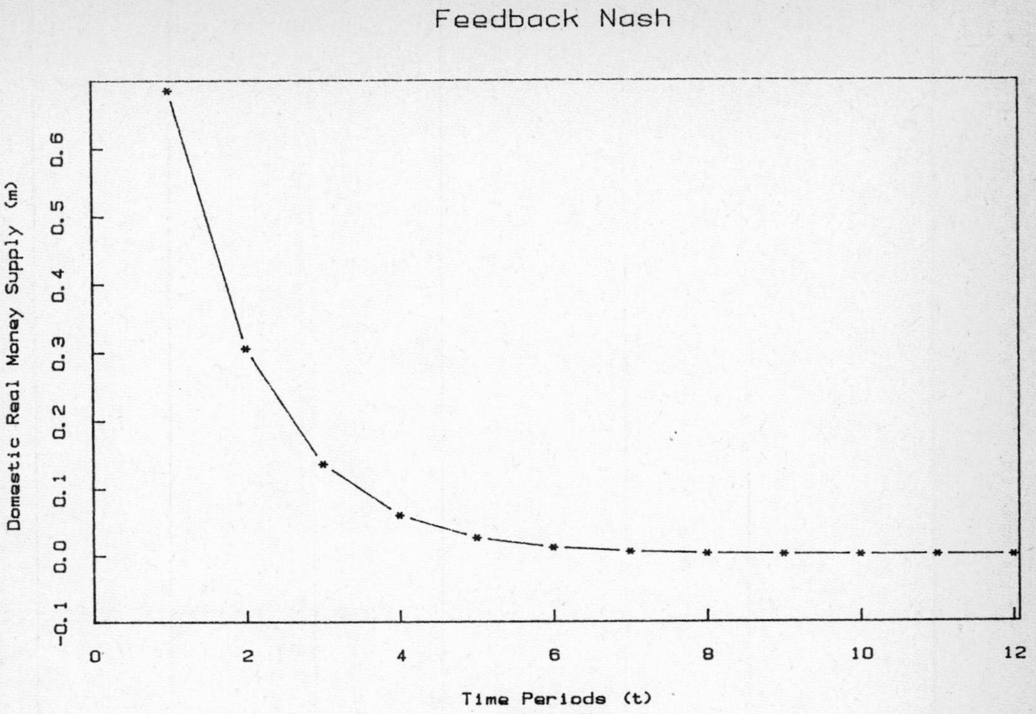

Feedback Nash
Domestic Real Money Supply (m)
-0.1
0.0
0.1
0.2
0.3
0.4
0.5
0.6
0
2
4
6
8
10
12
Time Periods (t)

fig. 1b

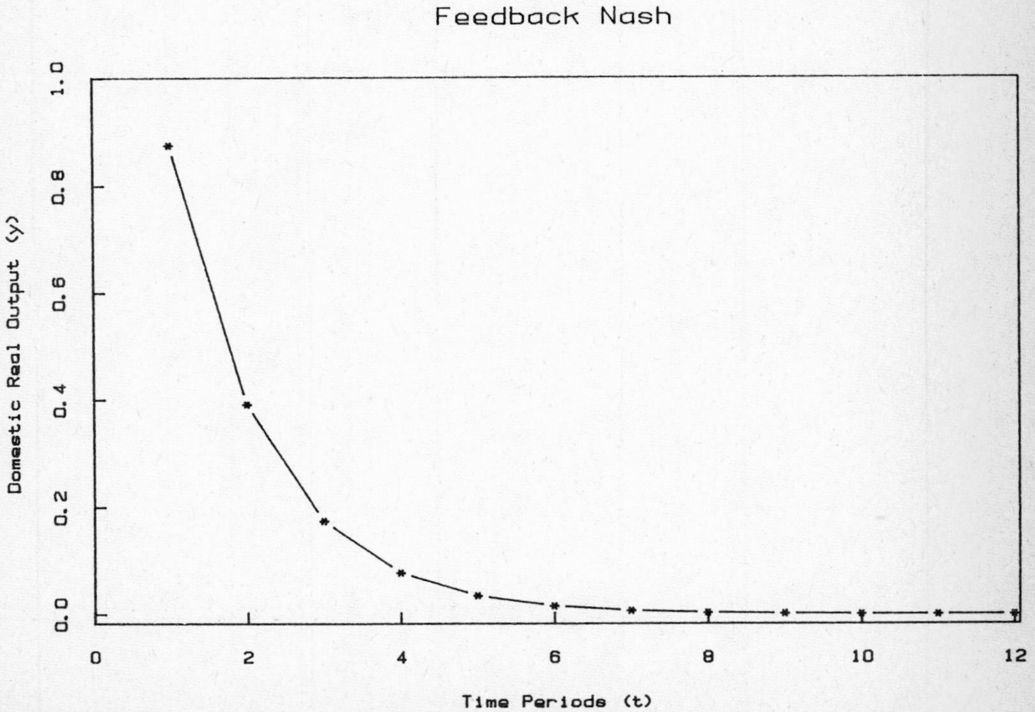

Feedback Nash
Domestic Real Output (y)
0.0
0.2
0.4
0.6
0.8
1.0
0
2
4
6
8
10
12
Time Periods (t)

fig. 1c

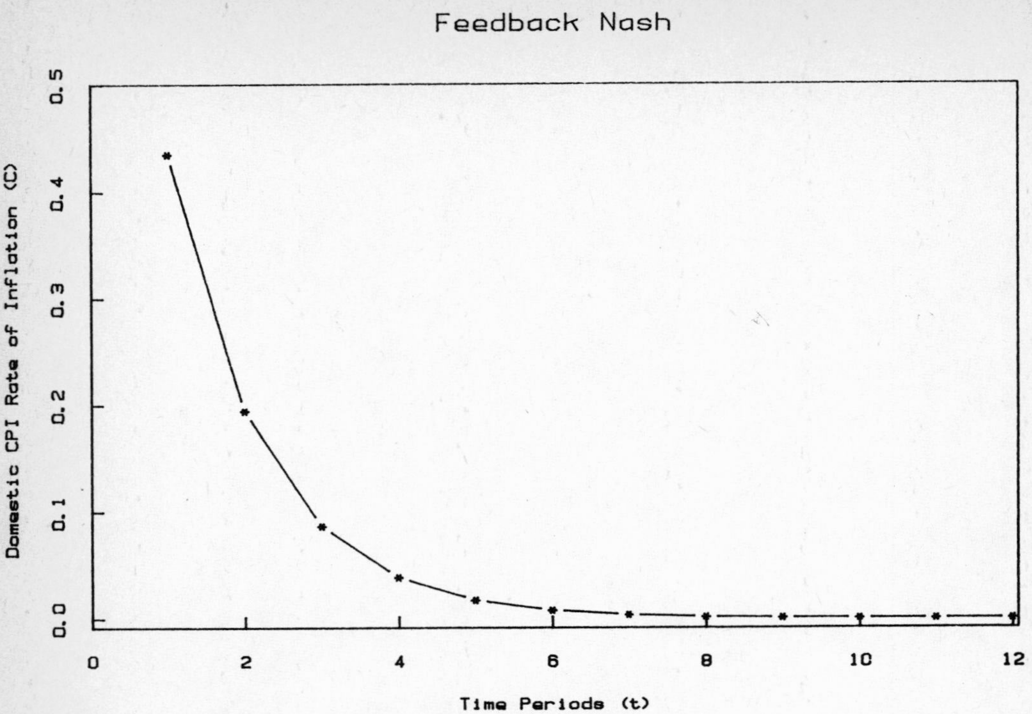
Feedback Nash
Domestic CPI Rate of Inflation (C)
0.0
0.1
0.2
0.3
0.4
0.5
0
2
4
6
8
10
12
Time Periods (t)

fig. 1d

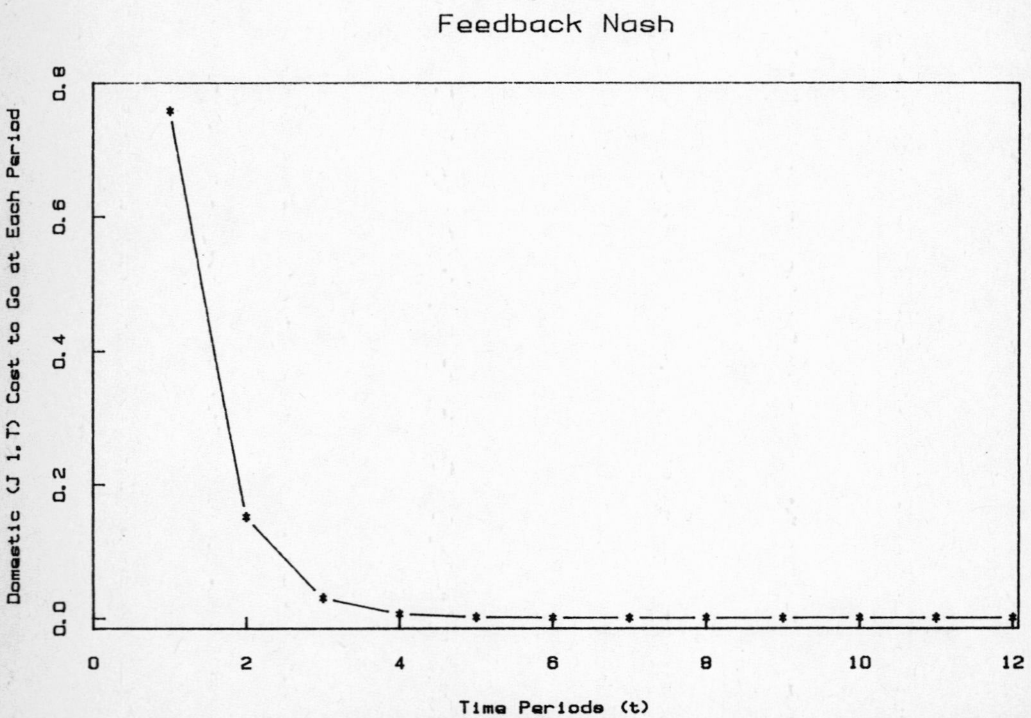
Feedback Nash
Domestic (J 1,T) Cost to Go at Each Period
0.0
0.2
0.4
0.6
0.8
0
2
4
6
8
10
12
Time Periods (t)

fig. 1e

Feedback Stackelberg

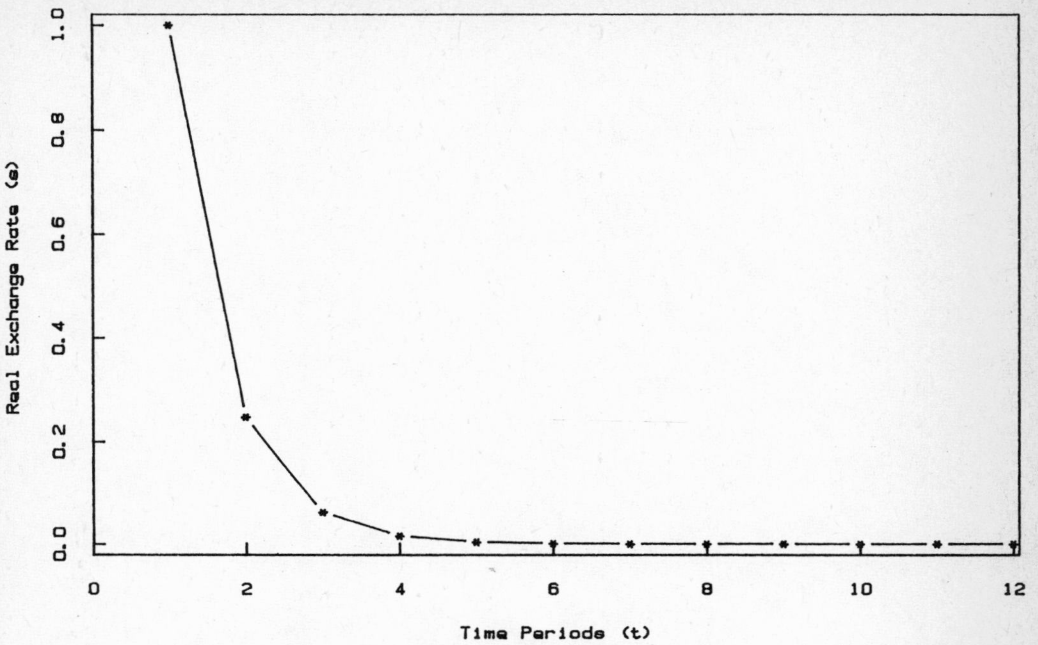

fig. 2a

Feedback Stackelberg

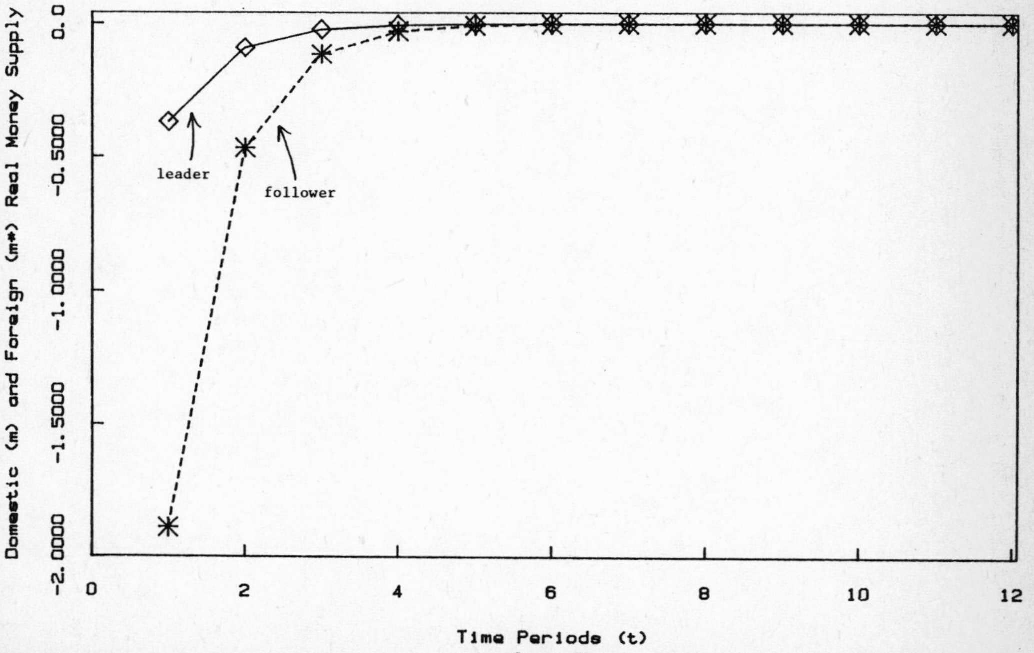

fig. 2b

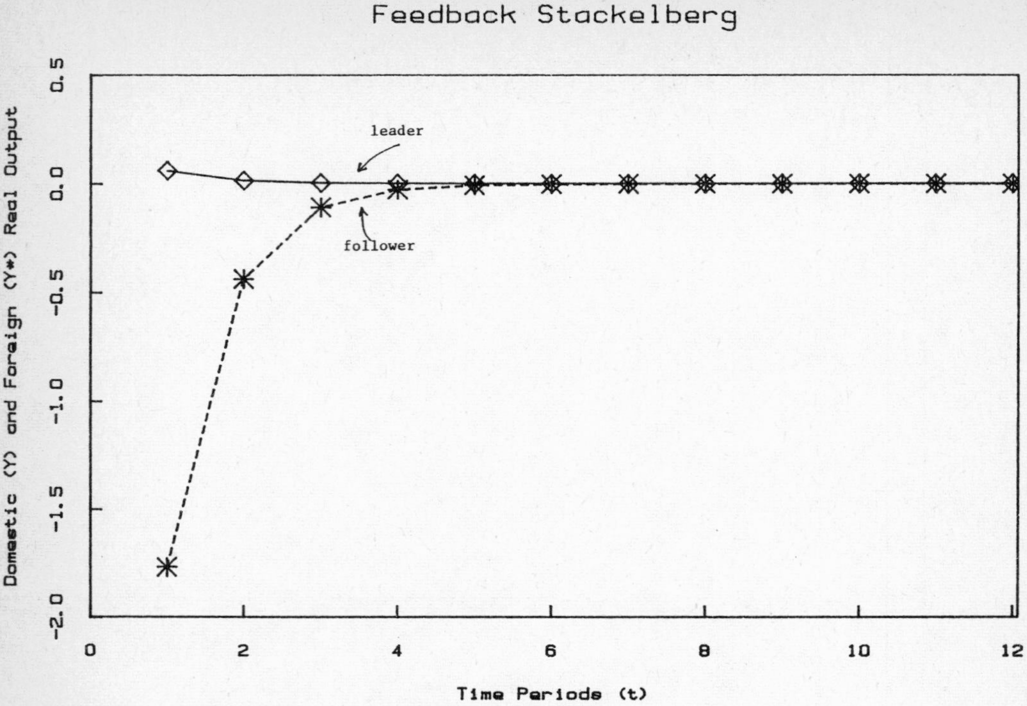

Feedback Stackelberg
leader
follower
Domestic (Y) and Foreign (Y*) Real Output
0.5
0.0
-0.5
-1.0
-1.5
-2.0
0
2
4
6
8
10
12
Time Periods (t)

fig. 2c

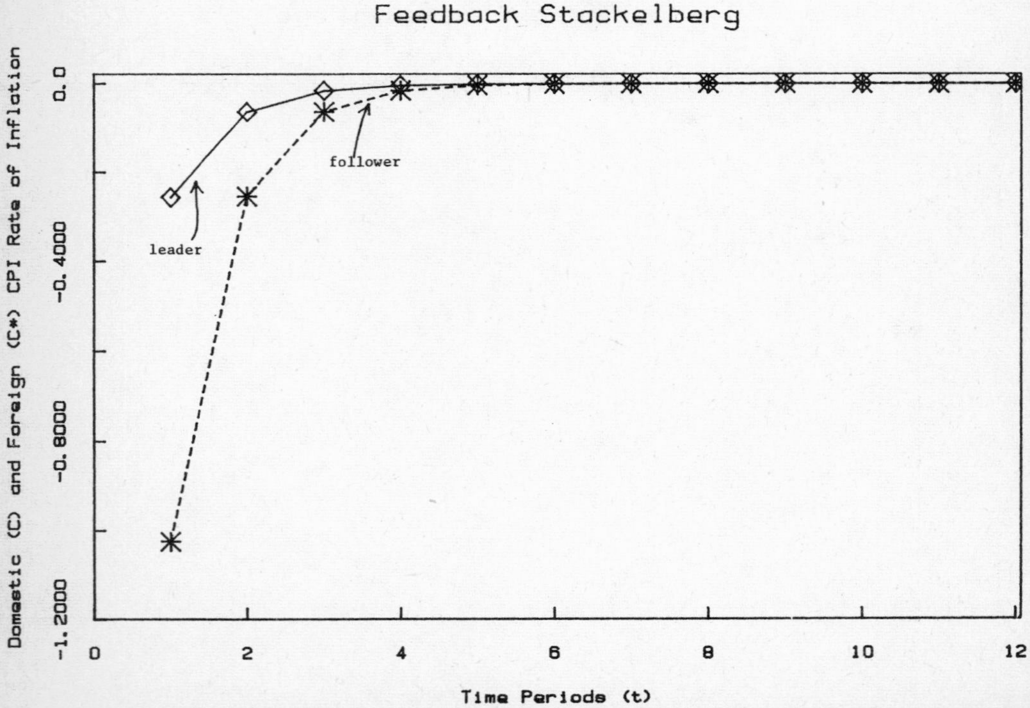

Feedback Stackelberg
follower
leader
Domestic (C) and Foreign (C*) CPI Rate of Inflation
0.0
-0.4000
-0.8000
-1.2000
0
2
4
6
8
10
12
Time Periods (t)

fig. 2d

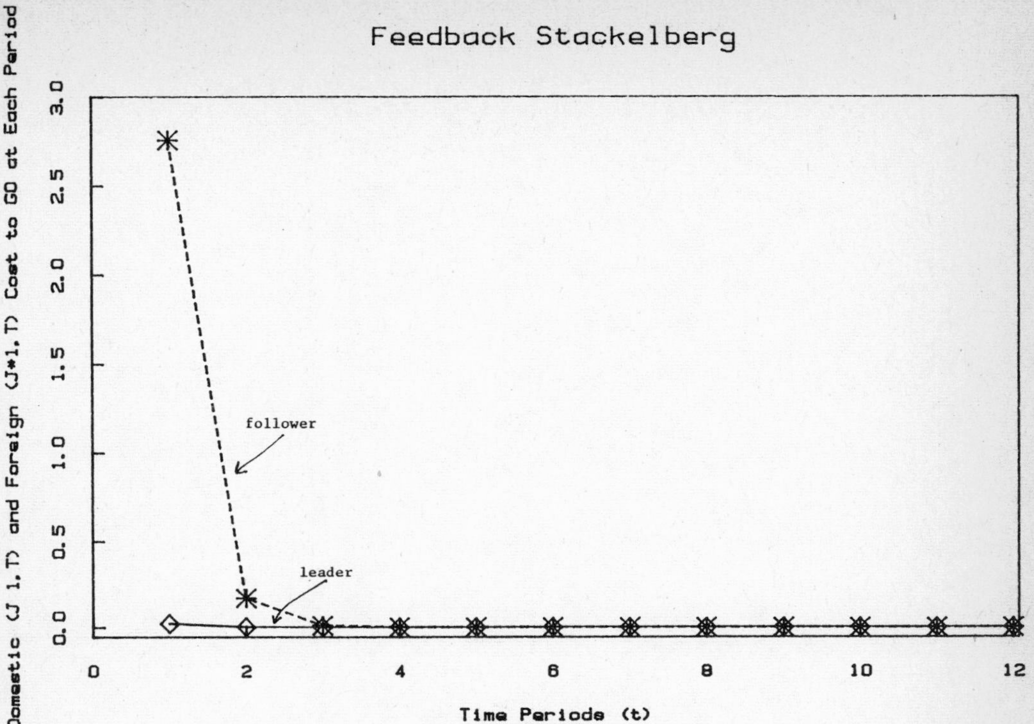
Feedback Stackelberg
Domestic (J 1, T) and Foreign (J*1, T) Cost to GO at Each Period
3.0
2.5
2.0
1.5
1.0
0.5
0.0
follower
leader
0
2
4
6
8
10
12
Time Period (t)

fig. 2e

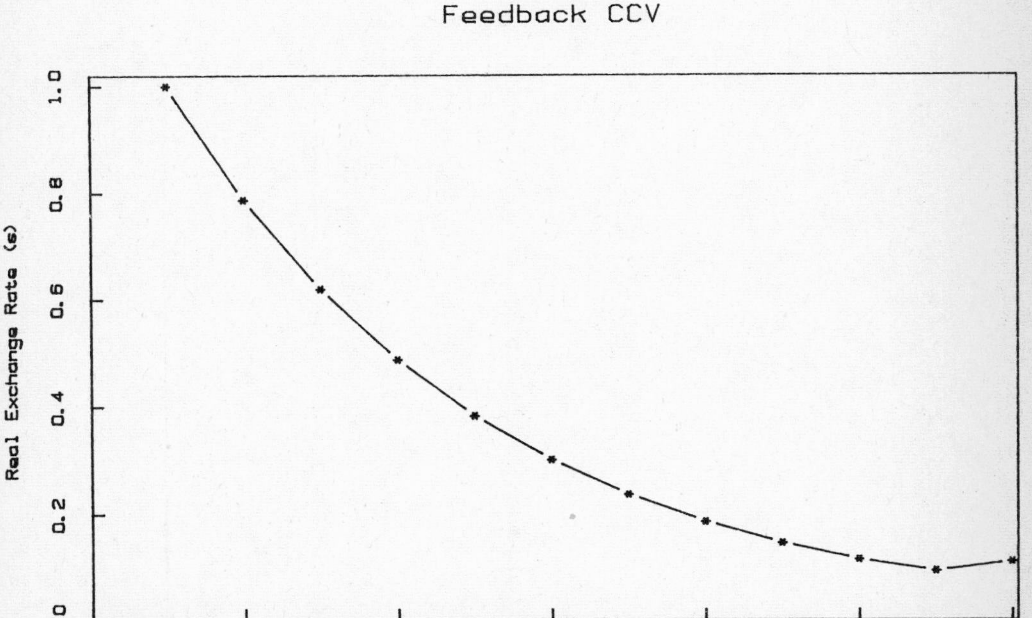
Feedback CCV
Real Exchange Rate (s)
1.0
0.8
0.6
0.4
0.2
0.0
0
2
4
6
8
10
12
Time Periods (t)

fig. 3a

Feedback CCV

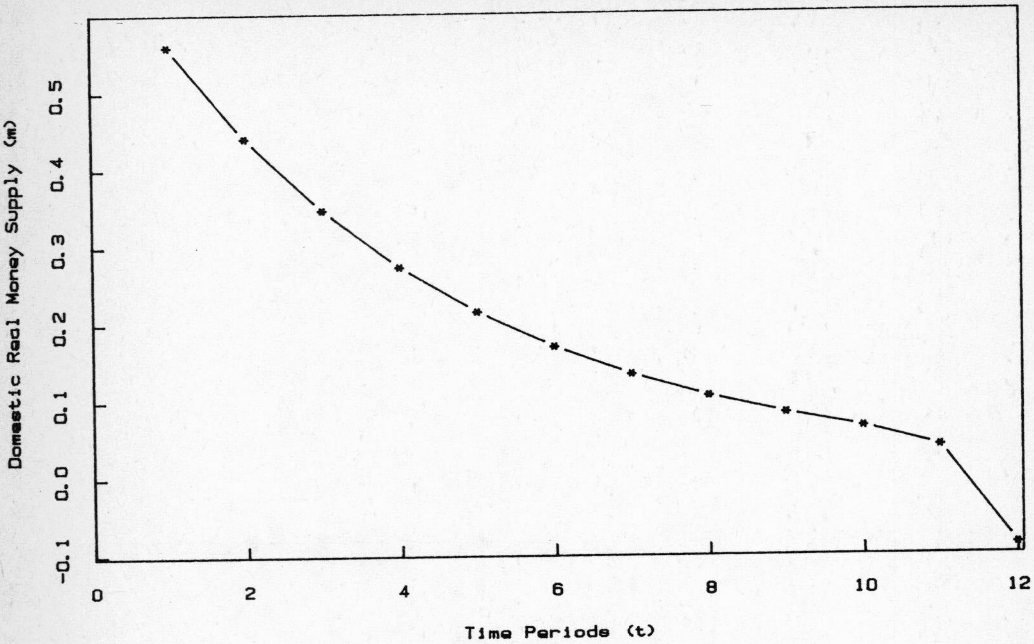

fig. 3b

Feedback CCV

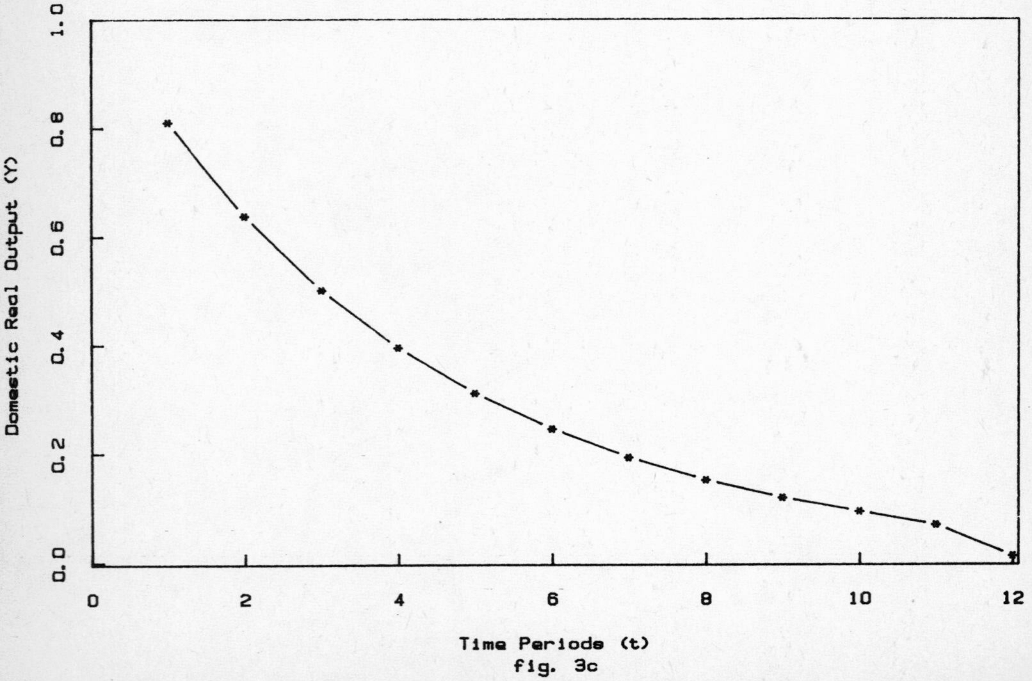

fig. 3c

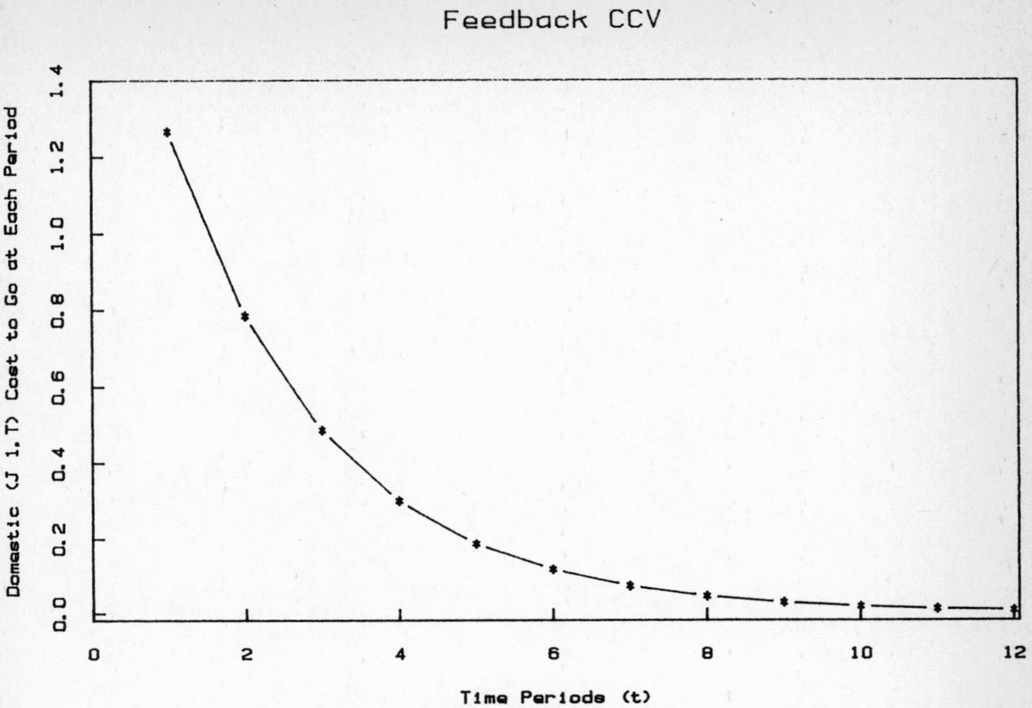
Feedback CCV
Domestic (J 1.T) Cost to Go at Each Period
0.0
0.2
0.4
0.6
0.8
1.0
1.2
1.4
0
2
4
6
8
10
12
Time Periods (t)
fig. 3e

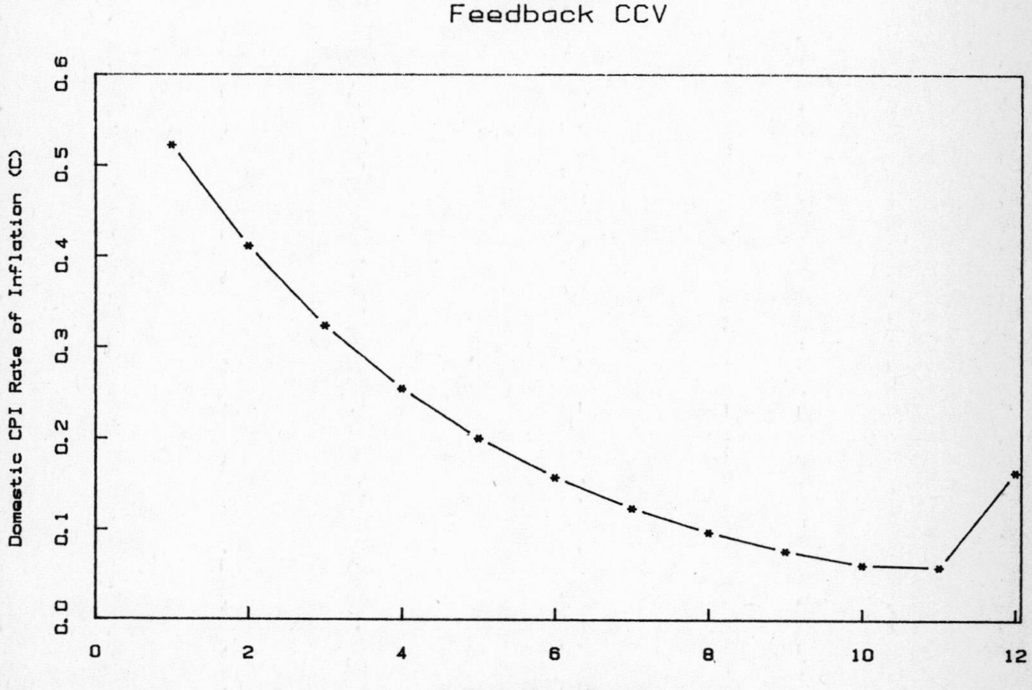
Feedback CCV
Domestic CPI Rate of Inflation (C)
0.0
0.1
0.2
0.3
0.4
0.5
0.6
0
2
4
6
8
10
12
Time Periods (t)
fig. 3d

Acknowledgement

Theoretical work of T. Başar that led to the results reported in this paper was supported in part by the U.S. Air Force under Grant AFOSR 84-0056. Research of S. J. Turnovsky and V. d'Orey were supported in part by the National Science Foundation under Grant SES-8409886.

Footnotes

0/ S. J. Turnovsky is also affiliated with the National Bureau of Economic Research.

1/ A recent paper by Hughes Hallett (1984) considers arbitrary, but not consistent, conjectural variations in a dynamic policy game framework.

2/ We maintain the usual assumption that residents of one country do not hold the currency of the other country.

3/ This assumption of the instantaneous observability of the exchange rate is a standard one in the current exchange market intervention literature.

4/ All three equilibrium concepts that we will be considering in the following sections do indeed satisfy this property, as will be elucidated later.

5/ In the one-period game, this equilibrium reduces to the usual Cournot equilibrium.

6/ See also Fershtman and Kamien (1985), Kamien and Schwartz (1983), and Başar (1985).

7/ These statements are based on values of $I = .10$, $\dot{P} = .04$. Larger values are considered in the sensitivity analysis.

8/ The initial shock in the relative price can be thought of as say the result of fiscal policies in the two economies.

9/ Note that this term is being used in a somewhat different way from its conventional usage. More commonly, a beggar-thy-neighbor world is one in which an expansionary policy in one country causes a contraction (in activity) abroad. Here we are using the term to characterize the interdependence between the adjustments in the policy instruments in the two economies, which in turn involves the slopes of the reaction functions. The same remarks apply to our usage of the term "locomotive" introduced below.

Appendix A: Proof of Proposition 3.1

We verify the result of Proposition 3.1 by utilizing Theorem 6 (p. 252) of Başar and Olsder (1982). Toward this end, we first assert that the cost-to-go functions for the two players at time period t+1 are

$$V_{\tau-1} = \rho^{t+1}\varepsilon_{\tau-1}s_{t+1}^2 \,, \; V^*_{\tau-1} = \rho^{t+1}\varepsilon^*_{\tau-1}s_{t+1}^2 \;;\; \tau = T - t \quad . \tag{A.1}$$

[Note that this is trivially true when $t = T$ ($\tau=0$), because $\varepsilon_{-1} = \varepsilon^*_{-1} = 0$.] Now, the recursive derivation leads to the relationships

$$V_\tau = \min_{m_t} [V_{\tau-1}(m_t, m^*_t) + \Delta J_t(m_t, m^*_t)] \tag{A.2}$$

$$V^*_\tau = \min_{m^*_t} [V^*_{\tau-1}(m_t, m^*_t) + \Delta J^*_t(m_t, m^*_t)] \tag{A.2'}$$

where ΔJ_t and ΔJ^*_t are the incremental costs at stage t, given by

$$\Delta J_t = J_{T,t} - J_{T,t+1} \ ; \ \Delta J^*_t = J^*_{T,t} - J^*_{T,t+1} \quad . \tag{A.3}$$

Note that (A.2)-(A.2') define a static Nash game in terms of the controls m_t and m^*_t, whose unique solution is claimed to be $m_t = \alpha_\tau s_t$, $m^*_t = \alpha^*_\tau s_t$. To prove this claim, we substitute for s_{t+1} from (13) in terms of m_t, m^*_t, s_t, which leads, in view of (A.1), to quadratic functions of m_t and m^*_t on the right-hand sides of (A.2) and (A.2'), respectively; the relevant terms in these minimands are:

$$\min_{m_t}\{\rho^{t+1}\varepsilon_{\tau-1}(As_t + Bm_t - Bm^*_t)^2 + \rho^t[(Q_5 m_t^2 + 2Q_4 m_t m^*_t + 2Q_2 s_t m_t]\}$$

$$\min_{m^*_t}\{\rho^{t+1}\varepsilon^*_{\tau-1}(As_t - Bm^*_t + Bm_t)^2 + \rho^t[Q^*_5 m^{*2}_t + 2Q^*_4 m^*_t m_t + 2Q^*_2 s_t m^*_t]\} \quad .$$

A necessary and sufficient condition for m_t and m^*_t to constitute solutions to these quadratic minimization problems is joint satisfaction of (by differentiating the first with respect to m_t and the second with respect to m^*_t):

$$\rho \ \varepsilon_{\tau-1}B(As_t + Bm_t - Bm^*_t) + Q_5 m_t + Q_4 m^*_t + Q_2 s_t = 0$$

$$\rho \ \varepsilon^*_{\tau-1}B(Bm^*_t - As_t - Bm_t) + Q^*_5 m^*_t + Q^*_4 m_t + Q^*_2 s_t = 0 \quad .$$

This set of equations admits a unique solution

$$m_t = \alpha_\tau s_t \ , \ m^*_t = \alpha^*_\tau s_t \tag{A.4}$$

where α_τ and α^*_τ are given by (18) and (18'), respectively. This completes the proof of the claim. To complete the proof of the assertion on the structure of the cost-to-go functions, we substitute (A.4) into the right-hand side of (A.2) and (A.2') [the minimization is now deleted], to obtain, in view of (20):

$$V_\tau = \rho^t \varepsilon_\tau s_t^2 \ , \ V^*_\tau = \rho^t \varepsilon^*_\tau s_t^2$$

which are the cost-to-go functions at time t, when there are $\tau = T - t$ periods to go. An inductive argument then completes the proof of the main result. □

Appendix B: Proof of Proposition 3.2

Here we use Theorem 2 of Chapter 7 of Başar and Olsder (1982). The line of argument is similar to that presented in Appendix A for the feedback Nash solution, the main difference being that the stagewise game is now of the Stackelberg type instead of being Nash. Hence, (A.2) and (A.2') in Appendix A will now be replaced by (taking Country 1 as the leader)

$$V_\tau = \min_{m_t}[V_{\tau-1}(m_t, g_t^*(m_t)) + \Delta J_t(m_t, g_t^*(m_t))] \tag{B.1}$$

$$V_\tau^* = V_{\tau-1}^*(\hat{m}_t, g_t^*(\hat{m}_t)) + \Delta J_t^*(\hat{m}_t, g_t^*(\hat{m}_t)) \tag{B.1'}$$

where $\hat{m}_t$ is the argument of the minimization in (B.1), and

$$g_t^*(m_t) = \arg\min_{m_t^*}[V_{\tau-1}^*(m_t, m_t^*) + \Delta J_t^*(m_t, m_t^*)]$$

is the optimal reaction of the follower, Country 2.

For our problem, and under assertion (A.1), g_t^* can readily be determined to be

$$g_t^*(m_t) = -(q_{2,\tau}^* s_t + q_{4,\tau}^* m_t)/q_{5,\tau}^* \quad .$$

After substitution of g_t^* into (B.1) and minimization of the resulting quadratic expression over m_t, we obtain

$$m_t = \alpha_\tau s_t$$

where α_τ is given by (26). In view of this,

$$m_t^* = g_t^*(m_t) = g_t^*(\alpha_\tau s_t) = \alpha_\tau^* s_t$$

where α_τ^* is given by (26'). Then, the left-hand sides of (B.1) and (B.2) can be evaluated to yield

$$V_\tau = \rho^t \varepsilon_\tau s_t^2 \ , \ V_\tau^* = \rho^t \varepsilon_\tau^* s_t^2 \quad ,$$

thus verifying the assertion and thereby the result of Proposition 3.2, inductively. □

Appendix C: Proof of Proposition 3.3

In the proof of Proposition 3.3, we again follow the basic line of reasoning of Appendix C, with the static equilibrium concept to be adopted being that of Consistent Conjectural Variations. The static game under consideration now is described at time t by the pair of cost functions

$$F_t(m_t, m_t^*) = V_{\tau-1}(m_t, m_t^*) + \Delta J_t(m_t, m_t^*) \quad , \tag{C.1}$$

$$F_t^*(m_t, m_t^*) = V_{\tau-1}^*(m_t, m_t^*) + \Delta J_t^*(m_t, m_t^*) \quad , \tag{C.1'}$$

which are quadratic in m_t and m_t^*. For such quadratic functions, the CCV solution is defined in terms of the relationships:

$$\frac{\partial F_t}{\partial m_t} + \frac{\partial F_t}{\partial m_t^*} \cdot \frac{dm_t^*}{dm_t} = 0 \ ; \ \frac{\partial F_t^*}{\partial m_t^*} + \frac{\partial F_t}{\partial m_t} \cdot \frac{dm_t}{dm_t^*} = 0 \tag{C.2}$$

along with two consistency conditions on the first-order response functions:

$$\frac{dm_t^*}{dm_t} \ , \ \frac{dm_t}{dm_t^*} \quad .$$

Let us assume for a moment (this will be verified subsequently) that these first-order response functions are constants, i.e.,

$$\frac{dm_t^*}{dm_t} = x_\tau^* \ ; \ \frac{dm_t}{dm_t^*} = x_\tau \quad ;$$

then, (C.2) becomes equivalent to

$$(q_{4,\tau}x_\tau^* + q_{5,\tau})m_t + (q_{4,\tau} + q_{6,\tau}x_\tau^*)m_t^* = -(q_{2,\tau} + q_{3,\tau}x_\tau^*)s_t \tag{C.3}$$

$$(q_{4,\tau}^* x_\tau + q_{5,\tau}^*)m_t^* + (q_{4,\tau}^* + q_{6,\tau}^* x_\tau)m_t = -(q_{2,\tau}^* + q_{3,\tau}^* x_\tau)s_t \quad , \tag{C.3'}$$

which justifies the assumption made on $\frac{dm_t^*}{dm_t}$ and $\frac{dm_t}{dm_t^*}$, that is that they are constants. Now, consistency in these derivatives dictates the following relationships:

$$x_\tau = -\,(q_{4,\tau} + q_{6,\tau}x^*)/(q_{4,\tau}x^* + q_{5,\tau})$$

$$x_\tau^* = -\,(q_{4,\tau}^* + q_{6,\tau}^* x_\tau)/(q_{4,\tau}^* x_\tau + q_{5,\tau}^*) \quad ,$$

which involve two quadratic equations, one for x_τ and another one for x_τ^*. Since we are dealing with a symmetric two-country model, an iterative argument proves that $x_\tau = x_\tau^*$, where x_τ satisfies

$$q_{4,\tau}x_\tau^2 + (q_{5,\tau} + q_{6,\tau})x_\tau + q_{4,\tau} = 0 \quad ,$$

which is precisely (31). Solving for m_t and m_t^* from (C.3) and (C.3') we obtain

$$m_t = \alpha_\tau s_t \ , \ m_t^* = \alpha_\tau^* s_t \quad ,$$

where α_τ and α_τ^* are given by (30) and (30'), respectively. Finally, substituting this solution into (C.1) and (C.2), we arrive at

$$F_t(\alpha_\tau s_t, \alpha_\tau^* s_t) = \rho^t \varepsilon_\tau s_t^2 \equiv V_\tau$$

$$F_t^*(\alpha_\tau s_t, \alpha_\tau^* s_t) = \rho^t \varepsilon_\tau^* s_t^2 \equiv V_\tau^* \quad ,$$

thereby completing the proof by making use of the standard inductive argument. □

References

Başar, Tamer (1985), "A Tutorial on Dynamic and Differential Games," this volume.

Başar, Tamer and Geert Jan Olsder (1983), Dynamic Noncooperative Game Theory, Academic Press, New York.

Bresnahan, T. F. (1981), "Duopoly Models with Consistent Conjectures," American Economic Review, vol. 71, pp. 934-945.

Canzoneri, M. and J. A. Gray (1985), "Monetary Policy Games and the Consequences of Noncooperative Behavior," International Economic Review, to appear.

Dornbusch, R. (1976), "Expectations and Exchange Rate Dynamics," J. Political Economy, vol. 84, pp. 1161-1176.

Fershtman, Chaim and Morton I. Kamien (1985), "Conjectural Equilibrium and Strategy Spaces in Differential Games," in Optimal Control Theory and Economic Analysis 2, G. Feichtinger, edt., pp. 569-580.

Hamada, K. (1976), "A Strategic Analysis of Monetary Interdependence," J. Political Economy, vol. 84, pp. 677-700.

Hughes-Hallett, A. J. (1984), "Non-Cooperative Strategies for Dynamic Policy Games and the Problem of Time Inconsistency," Oxford Economic Papers, vol. 36, pp. 381-399.

Jones, M. (1983), "International Liquidity: A Welfare Analysis," Quarterly Journal of Economics, vol. 98, pp. 1-23.

Kamien, M. I. and N. L. Schwartz (1983), "Conjectural Variations," Canadian Journal of Economics, vol. 16, pp. 191-211.

Miller, M. H. and M. Salmon (1985), "Policy Coordination and Dynamic Games," in W. H. Buiter and R. C. Marston (eds.), International Economic Policy Coordination, Cambridge University Press, Cambridge, U.K.

Oudiz, G. and J. Sachs (1985), "International Policy Coordination in Dynamic Macroeconomic Models," in W. H. Buiter and R. C. Marston (eds.), International Economic Policy Coordination, Cambridge University Press, Cambridge, U.K.

Perry, M. K. (1982), "Oligopoly and Consistent Conjectural Variations," Bell J. of Economics, vol. 13, pp. 197-205.

Turnovsky, Stephen J. and Vasco d'Orey (1985), "Monetary Policies in Interdependent Economies: A Strategic Approach," presented at USJF-SSRC Conference, Tokyo, March.

OPTIMAL DYNAMIC PRICING IN AN OLIGOPOLISTIC MARKET: A SURVEY*

Steffen Jørgensen
Institute of Theoretical Statistics
Copenhagen School of Economics and Business Administration
10 Julius Thomsens Plads
DK-1925, Frederiksberg C (Copenhagen) Denmark

Abstract

The article deals with some important issues in relation to the determination of optimal pricing policies in an oligopolistic market. This problem has been approached by using different bodies of research, e.g. economic theory, marketing science and game theory. However, many models are still inadequate in their treatment of the dynamics of pricing as well as the problems of competitive interactions.

We give a statement of the actual and potential contributions from the different areas of research mentioned and review a series of models which offers prescriptions for the pricing manager in a dynamic, oligopolistic environment.

> *"Oligopoly theory began with Cournot, more than 140 years ago. Judging from many intermediate textbooks on price theory, one might think it ended with him too"*
>
> James W. Friedman
> "Oligopoly Theory"

1. INTRODUCTION

This article considers a series of issues related to the determination of optimal dynamic pricing policies in an oligopolistic market. The problem of determining optimal prices in general has given rise to a long series of contributions in economic and related theories. A well

*This work was supported by NATO Research Grant No. 121/84.

known result is, for example, that the price must be set to equate marginal costs and revenues for a static monopolist. Another approach to optimal pricing is found in the areas of business pricing and marketing where, until recently, check-list and rule-of-thumb procedures have been prevailing. A well known concept here is that of mark-up pricing.

A common characteristic of most approaches to optimal pricing appears to be that neither the dynamic aspects of decision making nor the effects of actual or potential competition have been, in general, satisfactorily modelled in the context of a mathematical model. Thus, some models are fairly elaborate in the dynamics but competition is often assumed away or taken as exogenous. Game theory offers a promising avenue for handling competition but in many of these models the market dynamics seems to be inadequately modelled.

In the last two decades a considerable body of research has been developed in optimal control and differential games. It might be conjectured that differential game theory will prove useful in achieving the goal of building models that are better capable of capturing the essential characteristics of the dynamics as well as the competitive aspects of optimal pricing in oligopoly.

Recently, a growing interest in applying differential game theory to the problems of dynamic competitive pricing has been observed. These models deal with quite a large range of problems in optimal pricing; new product pricing, potential entry of rivals, the effects of cost dynamics (experience curve) and so on. This paper will provide a review of this literature which is important from a managerial as well as a theoretic point of view.

The plan for the paper is as follows: in Section 2 we state the objectives of pricing models and describe the major characteristics of the pricing environment. Also we investigate in some detail the potentials of various areas of research: business pricing models, economics, marketing and game theory. After a brief treatment of basic concepts of game theory we deal with some developments in oligopoly theory. We conclude the section with a few remarks on market structures and the problem of potential entry into a market. Section 3 surveys a series of papers dealing with monopolistic and oligopolistic dynamic pricing models. Most of this work is cast in the framework of optimal control theory or differential games and we assume that the reader is familiar with these theoretical developments. In Section 4 we summarize our findings and state some general remarks and guidelines for further research.

At this instant it is in order to draw attention to some other review articles in related areas: Nagle (1984) surveys the economic foundations for pricing while Monroe and Della Bitta (1978) and Rao (1984) report on pricing research in marketing. The use of game theory in modelling competition is the subject of Moorthy (1984). Surveys of differential games applications in advertising and in management science are found in Jørgensen (1982b) and Feichtinger and Jørgensen (1983), respectively. Finally, innovation diffusion models, which play an important role in pricing of new products, are reviewed in articles by Mahajan and Muller (1978), Mahajan and Peterson (1984) and Kalish and Sen (1985).[1]

2. BASIC CONCEPTS AND PROBLEMS IN PRICING

What are the objectives, or purposes, of a pricing model? Monroe and Della Bitta (1978) state that they are fourfold:

- to describe the pricing environment
- to explain pricing behavior
- to predict the outcome of pricing
- to prescribe pricing decisions.

The models under survey all incorporate two or more of these elements. The most elaborate model which we will encounter, the dynamic game theoretic oligopolistic pricing model, contains a description of the pricing situation in terms of a specific model and intends to prescribe pricing policies for each oligopolist. Hereby, also the outcome of the competitive pricing process is predicted. The explanatory purpose is considered as of minor importance. What will be of a certain interest to us in what follows is to look at the literature from the point of view of the four objectives.

To provide a sound description of the pricing environment we need models that cope with reality, making simplifications but with careful and explicit justification. Hence, already in the descriptive phase there is a need for empirical work, an aspect which, however, has been almost neglected in the research under review, We shall have more to say about this question later on. In order to describe the pricing situation it is evident that we must know the major characteristics of the pricing environment. Here the following elements are vital (see also Jeuland and Dolan (1982)):

---

[1]A review of the diffusion literature dealing with competition, by R.J. Dolan, A.P. Jeuland and E Muller is forthcoming in J. Wind and V. Mahajan (eds.), Advances in Product and Marketing Strategy, Vol. II, Innovation Diffusion and Growth Models.

1) Demand and cost interdependencies exist between products. Because of such interrelations, pricing of a given product cannot be treated independently of other products in the line. These remarks apply to a single firm. Considering the firm as an agent in a market it is also obvious that interdependencies to other firms' products must be taken into account, unless the firm finds itself in a position where it can disregard such relations. However, in too many cases, interdependencies have simply been assumed, by the model builder, not to exist. The main reason for this is, of course, mathematical convenience. The greater part of the literature considers the single product monopoly, thus avoiding the problems of interrelations.

2) Demand conditions for a given product are unstable over time and are normally not known deterministically. The level of demand changes over time because of changes in wealth per household, the number of households, consumers' tastes, or the entry or exit of competing brands. Even with a market of constant size, demand may change because buyers change their expectations or their stocks (Telser (1972)). Thus, if price expectations are derived from past prices, then current demand depends on current and past prices. For durable goods, the demand becomes dynamic since a given stock yields services for more than just one time period. An important branch of the literature, to which we shall return in Section 3, concerns the dynamics of new product diffusion.

3) Costs change over time because of changes in produced volume and due to experience effects (cost learning). Inflation is another source of time variation of costs. Especially the experience effect has been extensively explored in recent research work. Learning on the part of a producing firm means that unit costs decrease as experience (accumulated volume) increases. The idea originated in the early sixties; see, for instance, Kalish (1983).

4) The issue of competition is central since most markets are intermediate cases between pure competition and absolute monopoly. Hence, inherent in the pricing situation is a need for consideration of competitive reactions in a established market as well as the possible entry of rivals into the market. As already mentioned, one of the major weakness of the models so far proposed is the neglection of this problem; in most cases it is assumed away or treated in an inadequate ad hoc matter.

5) Price sometimes may convey some information on the quality of experience goods such that the prices, at which previous purchases were made, in a sense position the item. Hence, if a firm has build up a reputation for quality then it possibly can reap some benefits from this

by charging a higher price. The idea of price as an information medium about product quality originated in the fourties; we shall not pursue it in detail here.

6) Pricing cannot be considered isolated from the determination of the other strategic variables in the firms' marketing mix. Here, especially the simultaneous determination of prices and advertising has received attention; we will return to this work in Section 3. The question of how price and advertising interact is of considerable interest, not only to the marketing manager but also because of its consumer welfare implications. This has given rise to a series of contributions which is notable for a high content of empirical work.

7) In practice, firms normally do not have a single, unique price. There are quantity discounts, two-part tariffs or discounts to special groups of customers. Also, trade-in allowances and credit terms make the pricing policy non-unique. In the greater part of the literature, however, price is treated as a single variable. Another question of practical interest is that changes are normally not costless (example: catalogs). Hence it may be appropriate to introduce an adjustment cost for changing the price.

8) From a model-building point of view we need to know that kind of good we consider. Thus, consumer goods are traditionally divided into durables and non-durables, in connection with a distinction between new products and established products. The question of repeat/no repeat purchases should be taken into account too. In the present paper we consider mostly consumer goods but some models of natural resource pricing are also of interest. The distinction between non-differentiated (homogeneous) goods and differentiated goods should be kept in mind. In the case of homogeneous goods there is (at least in principle) only one market price.

9) Finally we mention the problem of pricing in a vertical channel where we must deal with complicated interactions between manufacturer(s), retailer(s) and final consumers. This problem has received very little interest in the literature, when cast in a dynamic game theoretic framework, but we shall report on a few recent attempts in that area.

We conclude this description of some features of the pricing environment by noting that we will not deal with public service pricing. There is a considerable body of research in this field, mainly economics oriented, but we can disregard it by agreeing on considering the pricing problem from the point of view of the marketing manager in a privately owned firm.

If one looks at the pricing problem from the viewpoint of such a manager, then it is natural to ask what the literature can offer in relation to the goals of description, explanation, prediction and prescription. Of course, no clear cut answers can be provided but it seems worthwhile to investigate in some detail the contributions and potentials of different lines and areas of research work. First, it is almost trivial to observe (Monroe and Della Bitta (1978), Simon (1982)) that price theory and pricing research have won only little recognition in actual business practice. Some of the reasons for this (sad) state of affairs are that managers are reluctant to implement the models developed in the literature because they are either (i) too mathematical sophisticated (managers are not interested in mathematics and there is often a communication barrier between manager and researcher) or (ii) too simple (unrealistic), neglecting dynamic and competitive aspects. Another reason is that some models offer only little or no guidance at all. Many models are dominated by a classical economic approach to pricing theory, as opposed to marketing or business price theory. (The meaning of these labels will be made more clear in the following). Furthermore, as already mentioned, a large part of the models lacks empirical foundation and verification. Monroe and Della Bitta (1978, p. 426) note, for instance, on the important problem of dynamics;

'Perhaps a major limiting aspect of the current pricing models is the lack of dynamism. Only three models recognize the need to develop pricing strategies over a relevant time period and to allow for market dynamics; all other models are static'

Things are, however (and fortunately), improving. Six years later Rao (1984, p. 45) notes that

'Recent years have witnessed an intense amount of activity on models for pricing products over time. Almost invariantly this research relates to new products since dynamic issues are most important in that area. The existing knowledge on life cycle, experience curves, and consumer processes of adoption and diffusion has been integrated into this stream of research'

In what follows we will distinguish four areas of pricing research, each offering advice to the pricing manager. The categorization suggested is not exhaustive and overlappings certainly occur but it provides a rough guideline when going through the literature.

A: Business pricing models

This area is characterized by being to a great extent verbal (i.e. non-quantitative) although prices, sales and costs essentially are quantitative phenomena. Possible it originated with the works of Dean, Oxenfeldt and others in the fifties and offers an approach to pricing which claims to take into account costs, market segmentation, buyer response, target markets and so forth. Typically, it attempts to design a flowchart or checklist showing how these various relevant factors should be included in the decision process. The main objective is to establish (i) a base price, i.e. a long-term pricing strategy and (ii) a structure of (tactical) discounts (Rao (1984)). As to the latter price promotions, these are well known means to increase sales temporarily for frequently purchased consumer goods. There is a rich literature in this area, concerning such issues as the optimal amount of price off, the duration and number of times of such offers etc. See Monroe and Della Bitta (1978), Rao (1984). Dynamic and competitive elements are by and large ignored. At the textbook level of business pricing theory, managerial recommendations are often trivial and useless. A few samples (Duncan, Hollander and Savitt (1983)) will exemplify the point:

'There are three pricing alternatives: price at the competitors' level, price below the competitors' level, and price above the competitors' level' (p. 397)

and

'The ideal markdown is one that is just enough to sell the merchandise under consideration. That is the best policy; however, applying it to specific situations is difficult' (p. 420).

Nevertheless, some business pricing authors are well aware of the need for more sophisticated machinery. In for example Hague (1971) a very elaborate pricing checklist is developed but it is recognized that (Hague (1971, p. 106)):

'Only some kind of mathematical model can handle the complex relationships that usually exist in oligopoly pricing. What is more, such a model would have to allow for the view which any given firm took of the way in which its competitors would react to changes in its own pricing or marketing policy'

Later on, however, Hague expresses some doubt about how far techniques like game theory can help the firm to predict the events to follow a price change in an oligopoly, but suggests that a watch should be kept on developments in that field since they could prove important. After having read the present survey article, the reader is asked to make his own opinion about the truth of this statement.

Summarizing on business pricing models we will say that what is offered is a very detailed (realistic) description of the pricing situation and its ingredients but the prescriptions are generally too vague to offer effective guidance. There is also a lack of a theoretical framework for analysis; what remains looks more or less like a morass of flowcharts, checklists, rules-of-thumb and routine procedures.

B: Economic theory

In the theory of market mechanisms (market equilibrium theory) there is a great volume of scientific work, the most outstanding contributors being Walras, Marshall, Hicks, Samuelson and Arrow (see e.g. Grubbström (1972)). A main characteristic which distinguishes this field from others is the concern with market equilibria and the mechanisms that lead to these equilibria. For example, there is a set of behavioral dynamic equations, underlying the market mechanism, which describes the adjustment of prices, the formation of equilibria in different markets, and the collective behavior of the economic agents that constitute the market. This area of research also focuses on the explanation of firms' behavior and studies the rationality and welfare implications of different 'price policies' in alternative competitive and regulatory contexts. The economic theory of competitive market equilibria attempts to describe and explain how markets behave, also assessing the welfare implications of such behavior. It does not attempt, in general, to prescribe how a firm should set its prices in an optimal way.

Other branches of economics have more to contribute in relation to normative pricing. Classical economic results, as the Amoroso-Robinson formula (marginal cost = marginal revenue) or the Evans (1924) model of dynamic monopoly, are still of importance when designing optimal pricing policies. Furthermore, which seems somewhat paradoxical, the economic industrial organizations literature appears to be well ahead of marketing theory (see Paragraph C below) with respect to the richness of pricing issues under consideration. Problems in bundling (example: book clubs), price discrimination between market segments, nonlinear pricing (decreasing unit price as the size of the box increases) and two-part prices all have their origin in the economic literature and have been studied in detail there. Quite a few of these problems are also encountered in the business pricing literature (Paragraph A above) but there they are mostly dealt with in a non-quantitative way.

In summary, although economics deals with rather general entities and appears to abstract from those features that may be of greatest interest from an optimal pricing viewpoint, the usefulness of economic theory is evident: it rests in its ability to identify the factors that are relevant to the decision problem and it contributes a long series of important concepts and insights: see Nagle (1984) for a further discussion of these issues.

C: Marketing theory

Recent marketing science literature on pricing typically aims at developing price strategies for the firm, utilizing concepts and insights from economic demand and cost theory, marketing theories of consumer behavior and a number of other branches of research, for instance, optimal control theory and game theory. It doesn't seem quite unjustified to say that the marketing approach to pricing is the most 'hybrid' of the ones under consideration. This is, of course, not a disadvantage as long as the constructs borrowed from other disciplines are theoretically as well as empirically sound, and are brought into use within the marketing context in an appropriate way. However, as the review of the literature will demonstrate, there are some cases where concepts and results elsewhere developed have been incorporated into a marketing model in an ad hoc or not easily justifiable fashion. The prescriptive (not to mention the descriptive) value of such models is therefore limited. Since the review of marketing pricing models will be one of the main areas of this paper we postpone a further treatment of this body of research to Section 3.

D: Game theory

The potential contributions of (noncooperative) game theory to marketing models (including pricing) are surveyed by Moorthy (1984) who, in particular, focusses on competitive situations. Essential to all such situations is a certain degree of interdependence and some conflicts of interest between the firms in a market. Interdependencies in time and among firms arises in different ways (cf. Section 2); here we shall treat it more formally. Following Friedman (1977, Ch. 5) consider a market with M firms such that firm i ($i=1,\dots,M$)[2] quotes price p_{it} and has profit function $F_i(\underline{p}_t)$ in period t; $t=1,\dots,T$. Here $\underline{p}_t$ denote the M-vector of prices $(p_{1t},\dots,p_{Mt})$. The total present value profits of

[2]A list of symbols is given at the end of the article.

firm i are given by

$$J^i = \sum_{t=1}^{T} a_i^{t-1} F_i(\underline{p}_t)$$

where a_i is a discount factor. First we note that this model is stationary in the sense that if $t \neq t'$ and $\underline{p}_t = \underline{p}_{t'}$, then $F_i(\underline{p}_t) = F_i(\underline{p}_{t'})$ is implied for all i. Time-dependence occurs if, for example, F_i is a function of $\underline{p}_t$ as well as past prices. This could be the case for durable goods. Situations where time-dependence occurs must of course be treated by a dynamic model. In addition to time-dependence, a truly competitive situation will involve time-dependent behavior, modelled e.g. by reaction functions $p_{it} = g_i(\underline{p}_{t-1})$. Note that this concerns the 'mood of play' of the firms, and is a separate issue apart from the time-dependence mentioned above. Note that if F_i in period t depends on actions on both current and past periods (i.e. non-stationarity) then time-dependence is structural and will prevail no matter how the firms choose to act.

Noncooperative game theory seeks to predict/prescribe the behavior of rational (e.g. utility maximizing) firms that compete in a market. The firms are intelligent in the sense that they recognize that the other firms are rational. (A game may have irrational players as long as we can describe properly such irrationality). The game is described by its rules which are, in broad terms, (i) the number of players, (ii) a feasible set of actions for each player, (iii) a utility function for each player, (iv) a strategy (i.e. a contingent plan of action) for each player, (v) an information structure. The rules are what is common knowledge to all players and if items (i)-(v) are known by all, then the players are said to have complete information. A game of perfect information is one where every player at every instant (stage) knows the actions of the other players earlier in the game.

The 'solution' of the game which is most often used is the Nash equilibrium (NE). In a NE no player wishes to unilaterally alter his strategy and hence it is a best-response to the other players' Nash strategies. The NE is appealing because of its property of self-fulfilling expectations and it also constitutes a self-enforcing agreement since there are no incentives to break the agreement unilaterally. In the next section we shall report on pricing problems where the NE has been applied. In this connection it is important to realize that game theory as such cannot be used as a straightforward 'technique' (like e.g. differential calculus) to provide precise solutions for a pricing problem. But it can yield useful insights into a problem even if the 'solution' itself may seem unreasonable. The difficulties arise because game theoretic analysis demands a precise description of the problem environment, a demand which may not be easily accomodated. Also, solutions are often nonunique and further elaborations (e.g. refinements of the equilibrium concept) may be needed to single out an equilibrium. Finally, game theory is, by construction, an extreme theory, based on high-order intelligence and rationality, assumptions that may not be satisfied in reality (see also Moorthy (1984)).

Why is there a need to study oligopoly models? Judging from the amount of literature in the areas of pure competition and absolute monopoly one should think that these market structures were the most important, from the point of view that they were also encountered in a majority of cases in reality. The fact is that a very large percentage of the GNP's in private-enterprise industrialized countries is produced by (multiproduct) firms, operating in oligopolistic markets, that is, in markets that are neither monopolies nor atomistic competition. What sets oligopoly apart from pure competition and monopoly is that oligopolistic firms are strategically linked to one another. In monopoly or pure competition the decision problem facing the firm is 'simple' since in the former it is alone in the market and in the latter the interdependencies with other firms are negligible.

Oligopoly theory deals with the fact that the actions of any firm may have considerable, and noticeable, consequences for the other firms. The theory is usually said to originate with the writings of Cournot around 1840: later studies were made by Bertrand, Bowley, Edgeworth and Stackelberg. This research was static although part of it shows some concern with multiperiod aspects, in terms of e.g. conjectural variations, reactions functions and the leader-follower problem. However, none of the models were explicitly dynamic although Cournot and others attempted to understand dynamic behavior. But they really did not leave the single-period setting (Friedman (1982)). Quite remarkably, oligopoly theory, until recently, evolved without addressing the role of time: oligopolistic markets were analyzed statically, or at best, conversationally dynamically.

In the past 15-20 years a considerable amount of work has been done, with a clear inspiration from the early pioneers, cf. Friedman (1977, 1983a). One category of models involves lagged responses where a firm does not know the current actions of its competitors, prior to making its own decision. Another category of models assumes that firms can respond instantaneously to any change of price made by another firm but there are costs for adjusting price. A third class of models is more closely linked with the game theoretic approach. For extensive surveys of these branches of oligopoly theory, see Friedman (1977, 1982, 1983a).

It seems correct to say that recent advances in obtaining a better understanding of oligopolistic pricing stem from two primary sources: noncooperative game theory and dynamic economics. Here, game theory has contributed to the modelling and understanding of the strategic interactions, inherent in oligopoly, whereas dynamic economics, with its roots in dynamic monopoly theory, has contributed with models and tools of importance for the analysis of the dynamics of oligopoly. Recently, also marketing science has contributed to oligopoly theory, the most outstanding contributions being perhaps those in new product diffusion. In this area, game theory, dynamic economics and marketing theory have been brought together in a seemingly fruitful and promising collaboration.

We shall close this section with a few remarks on some specific market structures, particularly interesting for the study of oligopoly pricing, and see how they have been treated in the literature. Also the problem of entry into an existing industry will be dealt with in some detail since it forms an interesting 'intermediate' case between monopoly and oligopoly. In the literature two related models have been dealt with extensively:

- Monopoly
- Monopoly with potential entrant(s)

to which obviously also

- Oligopoly (duopoly)

should be related. But research in the latter area is much more sparse. Interesting, but till now not adequately studied, is the case of entry into an oligopolistic market where the situation is 'doubly competitive': M firms, in an established market, face potential entry of competitors number M+1,M+2,... In contrast hereto, the standard case is the one where a monopolist anticipates single (or multiple) entry. Under certain circumstances, the oligopoly facing entry can be represented by the case of a monopoly facing entry, namely if we allow for implicit collusion. (Note that noncooperative theory, strictly speaking, does not allow explicit agreements). But it is possible to think about a noncooperative equilibrium which allows competitors to collude, implicitly, by threatening to punish cheaters. There is an interesting literature on this subject: because of space limitations we confine our interest to the non-collusive case.

Whereas in essence oligopoly theory deals with actual competition between firms in a certain market, the literature on entry treats the case of potential competition. The work on the latter subject started around 1950 with researchers as Bain and Sylos-Labini. Two main points of criticism have been raised against the major part of the entry literature. First, many models are static, but entry is intrisically a dynamic process and must be studied within a dynamic model. Analyzing entry by using a single-period model is not the study of entry at all (Friedman (1983a)). In static entry theory, what in fact is determined is the (largest) number of firms which can coexist with non-negative profits, once the market is in long run equilibrium. Assumptions are as elsewhere in static theory: instantaneous adjustments, no adjustment costs, and so forth. Later developments have tried to remedy some of the shortcomings of static modelling by introducing e.g. stochastic elements and dynamics. However, an essential feature which have been retained in most models, is that the entrant is not an explicit decision maker. A few exceptions exist; note also that the standard approach can be defended if the number of firms is so large that gamelike individual behavior tends to be unimportant. But in the majority of models, decisions on whether (and when) to enter are described by various ad hoc rules. Some examples will be given below. The basic question is here whether the proposed (ad hoc) entry rules are consistent with an optimizing strategy on behalf of the entrant, realizing that there is no reason to believe that the entrant should be less intelligent than the existing firm(s).

A concept which has won widespread reputation in the entry literature is that of a limit price. The argument states that the established firm (the monopolist) can set a sufficiently low price (the limit price) which will prevent entry. Cast in its original framework the problem may not be very interesting: the only operative question which remains is whether or not the monopolist will set the limit price (Friedman (1983a)). One objection to the limit pricing approach is why the entrant should expect the current price of the monopolist to have any informational value as to the price established after entry. The conventional wisdom asserts that the preentry price acts as an information source to the entrant such that, for example, low pricing by the established firm signals low (marginal) costs. Hence, the entrant is supposed to infer some lacking information (on profitability) from the pre-entry behavior of the monopolist.

This kind of reasoning has given rise to other arguments (than limit pricing) for entry prevention: for instance, the established firm may signal to potential entrants through having excess capacity, large advertising expenditures, inventories or other special investments in the pre-entry period. Also economies of scale and irreversibility of investments have been considered; see, for example, Spence (1977). These instruments are supposed to be chosen in a strategic way such that entry is discouraged. In the case of irreversible investments, the established firm commits itself in advance which may serve as a (credible) threat. Thus, excess capacity (for instance) allows the established firm to expand output and lower price, when threatened by entry, thereby reducing the prospective profits of the entrant. If there are cost experience effects, it may be important to obtain low costs prior to rival entry (Bass and Rao (1983)).

The question of such barriers to entry is well known and has received considerable interest with regard to its managerial and welfare implications.

Let us finish this section by stating some of the key issues of the entry problem and noting that most of them still await a satisfactory answer, in terms of an optimal dynamic strategy for both the monopolist and the entrant:

- How does the current policy of the monopolist affect entry?
- Can the established firm pursue a policy which will delay or even prevent entry?
- How should such a strategy be designed optimally?
- What it the entrant's optimal (agressive) strategy?

3. A REVIEW OF THE LITERATURE

3.1. PRELIMINARIES

The purpose of this section is to review a series of contributions to pricing theory. Since our main interest lies in dynamic models of oligopolistic competition we shall disregard that line of research which deals with static models, unless the results of such analysis have important implications for the study of the dynamic problem. Also, quite a few papers treat markets where goods are homogenous, i.e. they are regarded by the consumers as perfect substitutes. The decision problem is then one of quantity-setting rather than pricing. Of course this approach is of minor relevance to the pricing manager facing a market with differentiated products but we shall refer occasionally to this literature because of game theory's relevance for the price setting problem. The same arguments as those applied to the static and homogenous goods models are also valid for monopoly models. We shall, however, go into some more detail in the review of the latter models since many dynamic oligopolistic models are more or less straightforward extensions of their monopoly counterparts and, moreover, some results from dynamic monopolies seem to carry over to dynamic oligopolies. An interesting question here is whether such results tend to confirm a suspection that oligopolists should behave 'as if they were monopolists' or the similarities arise because of improper (too simplistic) modelling of the competitive interdependencies between oligopolists.

Because of its historical interest we briefly present the Evans (1924) model for a dynamic monopoly. Let demand and price at time t be denoted by q(t) and p(t), respectively. A cost function is given by C(q) where C is quadratic. (Here, and in the sequel we omit the time argument when no confusion can arise). Letting a dot over a variable denote the time derivatives the dynamics are given by

$$q = ap + b\dot{p} + d \tag{3.1}$$

where $a < 0$, $b, d > 0$ are constant. The monopolist's decision problem is to determine a differentiable price path to maximize

$$J = \int_0^T (pq - C)dt$$

subject to (3.1) and p(0), p(T) given. The problem can be solved by using calculus of variations which yields a trajectory p, depending on t in an exponential fashion. The problem is treated in detail by Miller (1979). Tintner (1937) generalized the dynamics to $q = f(p,\dot{p})$ and had a general cost function. He also introduced second order derivatives in f, i.e. $q = f(p,\dot{p},\ddot{p})$ but appears to be in error in the analysis of the Euler equation (Grubbström (1972)). Note that the model (3.1) assumes a certain amount of sluggnishness on the part of consumers' reactions to price changes, i.e. a consumer expectation element is inherent in the model. Supply, on the other hand, is supposed to adjust instantaneously to demand. Also note that in an optimal control formulation, price is the state variable (i.e. $\dot{p} = g(p,q)$) and q the control.

A related calculus of variations model for a monopoly is proposed by Telser and Graves (1972) who specify the dynamics as

$$p = f(t) - q - a_1\dot{q} - a_2\ddot{q} \tag{3.2}$$

where $\dot{f} > 0$ if the consumers increase in number and wealth over time. The economic motivation for (3.2) does not, however, seem quite clear.

The Evans model was extended by Roos (1925) to the case of two (identical) duopolists under the same assumptions on demand and costs as in Evans (1924). This problem has recently been revisited by Fershtman and Kamien (1984) who consider two identical duopolists producing a homogeneous good. The dynamics are given by (defining $q = q_1 + q_2$)

$$\dot{p} = s(d - q + ap)$$

i.e. $a = -1$ and $s = -1/b$ in (3.1). Main subjects of the paper are to study the relationship between the Nash equilibrium of the dynamic game and the static Cournot equilibrium (obtained for $s \to \infty$) as well as the implications of different information structures (open-loop versus closed-loop).

3.2. DIFFUSION MODELS

A diffusion model describes the adoption rate and sales of a (new) product, focusing on the consumer adaption process. In recent work the cost experience curve notion has been incorporated into these models. Hence there are learning effects on both demand and cost side. Most applications have dealt with durable goods where each adopter represents one unit of sales; there have been a smaller number of applications for nondurables where, in contrast, each adopter generates a stream of sales. In most cases repeat sales have been ignored; for exceptions see Jeuland and Dolan (1982) and Mahajan et al. (1983).

As previously mentioned, reviews of diffusion model literature are found in Mahajan and Muller (1978), Mahajan and Peterson (1984) and Kalish and Sen (1984). Jeuland (1981) gives a review of some of the approaches that have been used to incorporate price into diffusion models.

It seems correct to say that the current stream of research in diffusion models originated with the Bass (1969) model. Let $x(t)$ denote the number of adopters and let a,b be nonnegative constants. The Bass (1969) model is

$$\dot{x} = (a+bx)(N-x) \ . \tag{3.3}$$

From this simple model for the evolution of the number of adopters a long series of extensions/modifications has originated. Obviously the model is unfit for optimal price planning since x evolves independently of price but before we address this question let us briefly note that Easingwood et al. (1983) propose (3.3) be changed to a nonuniform version by substituting bx^{ε} for bx in (3.3); $\varepsilon \geq 0$. This remedies some shortcomings of the Bass (1969) model. For example, the new specification allows for a nonsymmetrical diffusion curve. The model only considers first purchases but has been extended to include also repeat purchases by Mahajan et al. (1983).

Robinson and Lakhani (1975) were the first to incorporate price into (3.3). They multiplied the right-hand side by an exponential price term:

$$\dot{x} = (a+bx)(N-x)e^{-\eta p} \qquad \eta = \text{const.} > 0 \tag{3.4}$$

and also included cost experience, i.e. marginal costs decrease when cumulative sales increase. In this dynamic monopoly model they found that the optimal price is first increasing, then decreasing. Also it turned out that the optimal dynamic price is always lower than the myopic price (the optimal price for the corresponding static problem). These results have been verified in a number of later developments and seem to be quite robust. The validity of the results can, however, be questioned since the analysis was based on a numerical example. Also the discount rate (r) used in the calculations was remarkably high (r=0.4). In the computations, three different types of optimal policies were compared with respect to the corresponding total present value profits:

- myopic optimal price
- optimal constant price
- dynamic optimal price

This kind of comparison has been used elsewhere, as we shall see later on.

Jeuland and Dolan (1982) extend the Bass (1969) and Robinson and Lakhani (1975) models to include repeat purchases. Let $x_1(t)$ denote the number of adopters (triers) and $x_2(t)$ the total cumulative sales (including both trial and repeat sales). The number of triers follows the Robinson-Lakhani model with a power function price term:

$$\dot{x}_1 = (a+bx_1)(N-x_1)p^{-\eta} \tag{3.5}$$

and cumulative sales evolve according to

$$\dot{x}_2 = \dot{x}_1 + \beta x_1 \, p^{-\eta} \quad . \tag{3.6}$$

In (3.6) the second term on the right-hand side models the repeat sales component. For durables we can but $\beta \doteq 0$ if the horizon (T) is short. The model includes cost experience and the monopolist seeks a pricing policy which maximizes total present value profits on [0,T]. Jeuland and Dolan (1982) show that in a myopic case ($r = \infty$) price should be decreased, following the decrease in costs. This result has also been obtained in a number of other models and is seemingly quite robust. For zero discounting (i.e. a far-sighted manager) there are three different policies:

- increasing price followed by a decreasing price (cf. Robinson and Lakhani (1975)). This policy emerges for durables when the imitation effect (parameter b) is important.
- If the parameter b is small (i.e. imitation effect unimportant) then price should be decreased (skimming price policy).
- For nondurables with frequent repeat purchases (e.g. a grocery item) the parameter β is large and the policy is to increase price (penetration price policy).

In the case of a positive (but finite) discount rate only numerical results were obtainable. The tendency is that the three general shapes above are encountered in this case, too. In an earlier work, Dolan and Jeuland (1981) also consider both durables and nondurables. The model is a variant of (3.4), cost experience is included but repeat sales are not explicitly modelled. For a static demand function (where the right-hand side of the evolution equation only depends on p) price should be decreased, following the cost decrease, and the dynamic optimal price is always below the myopic price. If there are demand side dynamics then a penetration policy is optimal if the repeat rate is dominant. For durables and zero discount rate the same results as in Jeuland and Dolan (1982) are obtained.

In Teng and Thompson (1985) a durable good is considered with sales evolution given by (3.5). The model incorporates cost experience and the result obtained by Robinson and Lakhani (1975), and later articles, namely a penetration policy followed by a skimming policy, is confirmed for $\eta < 1$.

Leaving aside for a moment the stream of research that followed Bass (1969) let us note that Bass (1980) proposes a monopoly model where the dynamics are exogenous and modelled by a time function. For a durable good demand (sales) is given by

$$\dot{x} = h(t)\ f(p)$$

where h(t) is an exogenous life cycle and f(p) is a power function, cf. (3.5). Hence the demand curve shifts only as a function of time, not as a function of previous sales. The life cycle h(t) could possibly be interpreted as representing effects of competition that are likely to appear soon after introduction (Kalish and Sen (1985)). Bass (1980) assumes that the monopolist maximizes current profits which leads to the well known static pricing rule of Amoroso-Robinson where price will decrease over time. This finding (which we observe also in other models) is consistent with many consumer durable technological innovations and Bass provides some empirical evidence for a range of products, for instance, refrigerators, air conditioners and dishwashers.

Bass and Bultez (1982) try to remedy the myopic optimizing behavior assumed in Bass (1980). For a dynamic, optimal solution it is shown that the price is decreasing and always lower than the myopic price. In contrast to Robinson and Lakhani (1975), Bass and Bultez (1982) report that there are only slight differences in optimal discounted profits when price is myopically determined as opposed to a true dynamic strategy. Such comparisons should, however, be taken with caution since the results were obtained in numerical examples based on relatively large discount factors. Also it may be because the experience rate and other factors 'dominate' the model such that long-run optimization does not yield a substantial advantage in profits compared to myopic optimization.

Dockner (1984a, 1985) extends the Robinson-Lakhani model (and Dolan and Jeuland (1981)) to a duopoly. Considering durables, let $x_i(t)$ denote the accumulated sales of firm i, i=1,2. The state equations are

$$\dot{x}_i = f^i(p_1,p_2)(N-x_i-x_j) \qquad i,j=1,2;i\neq j \tag{3.7}$$

where p_i is the price of firm i. Compared to the models so far encountered, it is assumed in (3.7) that imitation effects are small which permits us to set b=0 in (3.4). Hence diffusion takes place only because of the innovation effect. In (3.7) the signs of the first and second order derivatives of functions f^i satisfy reasonable assumptions. Dockner looks for a Nash equilibrium in open-loop controls, $p_i(t,x_{io},x_{jo})$ which means that the players commit themselves at the start of the game to use time functions, not strategies that depend on the current state also. In Dockner (1984a) functions f^i are specified as $f^i = \exp(p_j-p_i)$ and for zero discounting it turns out that the player with the lowest marginal cost will have an advantage, in the sense that his price is the lowest (and is decreasing). The market share of this player will increase. The general formulation (3.7) is treated in Dockner (1985) but only for the less interesting case where f^i is independent of p_j. For zero discounting it is shown that prices are decreasing over time due to the saturation effect. In summary the result (decreasing price) already known from the monopoly case is confirmed in this duopoly model. This is, however, not very surprising since the competitive interaction between the players is weak; the duopolists are only interrelated through the x_j term in (3.7). Also, the game is played with open-loop controls which is somewhat unsatisfactory, from a game theoretic as well as from a managerial point of view. In practice, a firm will know its market share and will normally also have the possibility of observing the opponent's market share; there is no reason to believe that a firm should disregard such knowledge when designing its pricing policy. Playing the game with feedback strategies $p_i(x_i,x_j,t)$, and taking f^i to be linear in prices, reveals that the feedback solution (found by a dynamic programming approach) is degenerate. It only depends on t and is hence constant with respect to state (x_i,x_j). Also from a research point of view this is an interesting feature; other examples of the property are Reinganum (1982), Fershtman (1985).

An oligopoly extension of the Bass (1969) model is Erickson (1983a) where the sales rate of firm i (i=1,...,M) for a durable evolves according to

$$\dot{x}_i = (a+bx)(N-x)f^i \tag{3.8}$$

where $x = \sum_{i=1}^{M} x_i$ and

$$f^i = k - k'\left[p_i + \gamma(p_i - \bar{p})\right] , \tag{3.9}$$

$\bar{p}$ being the average of $p_1,\ldots,p_M$. Note in (3.8) that the evolution of sales of firm i involves a function of total (cumulative) sales of all firms. Another specification of functions f^i could be proposed:

$$f^i = k_i - k_i' p_i + \sum_{j=1}^{M} \gamma_{ij}(p_j - p_i) \qquad j\neq i \ ; \ \gamma_{ij}=\gamma_{ji} \tag{3.10}$$

where $\gamma_{ij}(p_j - p_i)$ is that portion of the market gained from (lost to) firm j owing to a favorable (unfavorable) price differential. Note that in (3.9) gains/losses are not allocated to a specific competitor since p_i is only compared to $\bar{p}$. The specification (3.9) has also been used by Wolf and Shubik (1978) in a static model (with advertising). Erickson (1983a) looks for an open-loop Nash equilibrium and obtains his results by numerical analysis. He finds that prices are lowered with greater experience (as we have seen it in other models) and that increased competition (i.e. number of firms increasing) can reduce prices if the products are interdependent. If not, prices can actually be raised through increased competition.

Thompson and Teng (1984) establish a durable goods model with dynamics given by a mixture of the Bass (1969) the Ozga and the Vidale-Wolfe models. As to the latter, see the survey paper by Sethi (1977). The model has been critisized as being unrealistic by Jeuland (1981). As in the Robinson-Lakhani model the right-hand side of the dynamics contains a multiplicative exponential price term. For a monopolist, numerical calculations yield reasonable results when comparing myopic, optimal constant and optimal dynamic policies (cf. Robinson and Lakhani (1975), Bass (1980), Bass and Bultez (1982)). The authors were, however, unable to prove anything about the time paths of the optimal dynamic pricing policy. Turning to the case of an oligopolistic market the authors (again) refrain from solving the general problem but choose to consider a market with a single price which is determined by the largest competitor (a price leader). In a numerical example it turns out that this firm should decrease its price, following the cost decrease due to experience.

In all diffusion models reviewed so far, the total market potential was assumed to be constant; price only affects the customers through the adoption effect. Mahajan and Peterson (1978, 1982) and Jørgensen (1978) argue that total potential, N, varies as a result of the firm's (firms') marketing efforts and exogenous factors such as increasing number and wealth of households. The idea to consider N a function of price probably originated with Seglin (1963) and Chow (1967). Some applications to the monopoly case now exist, mostly based on the Bass (1969) model. Assume that total market N is inversely related to price, p. Then the Bass (1969) model becomes

$$\dot{x} = (a+bx)(N(p)-x) \tag{3.11}$$

with $N' < 0$.

Feichtinger (1982a) and Jørgensen (1983) consider a nondurable where each adopter buys at a constant rate, regardless of price. This assumption is somewhat limiting (Kalish and Sen (1985)) since price thereby only determines the number of potential adopters. Feichtinger (1982), who generalizes Jørgensen (1983), takes N(p) as concave decreasing and shows that the price of a monopolist should be smoothly increased if the initial sales rate, x_0, is lower than the long-run (equilibrium) sales rate, x^*. The results are obtained by using a phase diagram method and are only valid inside a certain neighborhood of x^*. Taking N(p) to be linear, and assuming constant marginal costs,

Jørgensen (1983) also obtains a penetration policy which is piecewise constant and therefore may be more appealing to managers.

Kalish (1983) also considers a durable good with dynamics

$$\dot{x} = h(x)(N(p)-x)$$

which is a slight generalization of (3.11) and concludes that a decreasing price is the most likely one since early adopters are willing to pay a higher price. Thereafter price should be gradually decreased to reach additional segments of the market. This corresponds to what has been observed in practice for e.g. pocket calculators. The conclusions of Kalish (1983) are somewhat weakened by the fact that in one case he takes $h(x)$ = constant (i.e. we have (3.11) for $b = 0$; the case of no imitation effect) while in another case he assumes $h' < 0$. This corresponds to supposing a negative word of mouth effect which may not be appropriate. (See Mahajan, Muller and Kerin (1984) for a treatment of negative information effects in an advertising model.) In the more interesting case, $h' > 0$, no uniform answers can be given but a penetration policy is recommended, at least on an initial interval (cf. Feichtinger (1982), Jørgensen (1983)).

The models with a price-dependent total potential assume a homogenous population in the sense that consumers do not differ with respect to their evaluations of the product. The concept of a reservation price, V, has recently been brought into use to relax this assumption. The reservation price is simply the maximum amount of money the buyer will pay for the product and represents the value of the product (to the customer) in monetary terms. The notion of a reservation price has been used by Jeuland (1981) and Kalish (1984) in the context of an optimal pricing model with diffusion-type dynamics. Let N_o be the size of the market potential at zero price and f a density function for the number of persons in each segment of the market. Then market potential N is given by

$$N(p) = N_o \int_{\rho \geq p} f(\rho)d\rho \quad . \tag{3.12}$$

Another feature included by Jeuland (1981) and Kalish (1984) is customer uncertainty about the new product's performance which leads the customers to discount their valuation of the product. The Jeuland (1981) and the Kalish (1984) models treat discounting due to uncertainty different and they also differ in their modelling of information diffusion and the timing of adoption. Hence comparisons are difficult; both between the two models and also toward the other literature on price-dependent market potentials. However, Jeuland (1981) confirms the result of Jørgensen (1983) that the product should be introduced at a low price and after some time price should be raised to a regular (steady state) price. This holds as long as the diffusion effect is sufficiently strong. The Kalish (1984) model is more elaborate than most of the models so far surveyed. He assumes that there are two steps in the adoption process: awareness (through advertising and word of mouth) and adoption (which occurs if the buyer is informed (aware) and $V \geqq p$). Let x denote the sales rate for a nondurable (or accumulated sales for a durable). The first part of the dynamics is given as

$$\dot{x} = k \left[N(p/U(x/N_o))I - x\right]$$

where I is the number of individuals aware of the innovation and U is a utility function, acting as the discount factor due to uncertainty about product performance. The second part of the dynamics is an equation for the evolution of awareness: $\dot{I} = g(I,x,A)$ where A represents advertising. Incorporating cost experience, Kalish (1984) obtains, in reasonable special cases, that the optimal price of a monopolist should be decreasing (monotonically) over time for a durable good. This holds unless early adopters have a strong effect on increasing future demand; if this should be the case the policy is altered to using a low (but increasing) price followed by a decreasing price path. For nondurables and no cost experience price should be lowest at the introduction and than monotonically increased to a steady state level. This results again confirms the finding of Feichtinger (1982) but within the context of a richer model. Ignoring the awareness part of the model (i.e. putting I = 1 (full awareness)) the Kalish (1984) results can be compared to Robinson and Lakhani (1975) and Mahajan and Peterson (1978).

Erickson (1983b) treats (3.11) for a durable and takes N as a power function in p. The model includes cost experience and attempts to model competition by letting the market share, say, S of the price leader be given by

$$S = (\sigma_o \, p^{\sigma_1} + 1)^{-1} \qquad \sigma_1 > 1 \quad .$$

Thus, share does not decline sharply with price until price is 'large enough'. Note, however, that this kind of modelling competition is unsatisfactory since competitors are purely exogenous. In a numerical example Erickson (1983b) demonstrates that the price (of the leader) should be decreased due to N's price sensitively, cost experience and 'competitive pressure'.

Yoon and Lilien (1985) consider a monopolist who introduces a product and anticipates future competition. (For the 'entry problem', see also Section 3.3 below). During the monopoly period the sales dynamics are given by (3.11) with b=0, i.e. a pure innovation process. In the duopoly period, i.e. after entry of the rival, the dynamics are specified as in (3.11) but with the term bx replaced by a price differential term: $\gamma(p_j - p_i)$, cf. (3.10). A serious modelling problem emerges in connection with the term N(p) in (3.11). Denoting the monopolist and the rival prices by p_1 and p_2, respectively, is is assumed without any justification that $N = N(p_2)$ in the duopoly period. Also it is assumed that througout the game $p_2 < p_1$ which is not at all obvious.

Recently attempts have been made to unify the models and results scattered in various papers. As we have seen above, in most cases a particular structure (functional form) of the model is employed. Clarke, Darrough and Heineke (1982) and Kalish (1983) were the first to pose the monopoly optimal pricing problem in greater generality. Consider the durable goods case and let x denote cumulative sales. General sales and cost functions are given by

$$\dot{x} = q(x,p) \tag{3.13}$$

and

$$C = C(x,q) \tag{3.14}$$

where C is total cost. Note that C depends on x (experience) as well as q (current output). Clarke et al. (1982) specify two functional forms for total cost C:

$$C = c_o + m(x)\,h(q) \qquad m' < 0\,,\quad h' > 0 \quad \text{(scaling)}$$

and

$$C = c_o + m_1(x) + h_1(q) \qquad m_1' < 0\,,\quad h_1' > 0 \quad \text{(translation)}\,.$$

Kalish considers only the case $C = C(x)$. For the case where $q_x = 0$, the 'static demand' case, Clarke et al. (1982) obtain

(a) price is (continuously) decreasing if C is (scaling)
(b) Price is (continuously) increasing if C is (translation).

It is interesting to note that the result in (a) but not in (b) is confirmed by Kalish (1983). The result in (a) was obtained earlier by Jeuland and Dolan (1982) for a particular specification of C(x) and also by Spence (1981). The latter considered, however, the somewhat extreme case of zero discounting. The result (a) holds in a slightly more general case than $\dot{x} = q(p)$, namely the case where $\dot{x} = f(t)q(p)$, see Bass and Bultez (1982), Kalish (1983). Returning to the general case (3.13), Clarke et al. (1982) and Kalish (1983) consider a multiplicative separable specification:

$$\dot{x} = f(x)g(p) \tag{3.15}$$

which implies that demand elasticity is independent of experience x. For constant marginal costs and $f'' < 0$ (which holds, for example, in the Bass (1969) model) Kalish (1983) shows that if $f'(x_o) > 0$ and $f'(x(T)) < 0$, i.e. initially there are positive effects of additional adopters on future sales, then the pricing policy is to introduce at a low but increasing price and at some instant start to decrease the price, a result we have noted a couple of times before. Clarke et al. (1982) obtain a similar pricing rule for the model (3.15). It is worthwhile noticing that in the no discounting case the results can be strengthened. For the dynamics given by (3.15), Kalish (1983) shows that

$$f'(x) \gtrless 0 \quad \Rightarrow \quad \dot{p} \gtrless 0 \quad ,$$

i.e. positive (negative) diffusion effects imply increasing (decreasing) price. (See also Teng and Thompson (1985, Section 3.2) where the same result is obtained in a nondurables model with $\dot{x} = kx\,\exp(-\eta p)$ which is a special case of (3.15)). Let us also note a recent attempt to explain why monopolistic prices may exhibit a considerable volatility. Wirl (1985) considers a nondurable good with dynamics given by (3.13) and assumes constant marginal costs. For $q_{pp} > 0$ and at least for some x_o (which may hold in reasonable cases) there is no optimal policy but a kind af chattering control is recommended, i.e. price should be changes frequently and discontinuously. However, it might be conjectured that this type of policy would not emerge if adjustment costs (for changing the price) were taken into consideration or if the dynamics were non-autonomous, i.e. (3.13) had the form q(x,p,t).

The problem of price adjustment costs has not received very much attention in the control literature although it has some managerial relevance. First, it can be argued (Aizenman (1984)) that customers attach some value to price stability: incomplete information induces buyers to cater to firms with relatively stable prices and avoid those firms which change prices often and by considerable amounts. See, however, Wirl (1985). Second, direct (and considerable) costs can be related to the very act of changing prices; this is important in the case of e.g. catalogs.

In relation to the problem of when and by how much to change a price the issue of inflation is of course important. Here, stochastic models are used by Sheshinski and Weiss (1977) and Aizenman (1984) to capture the fact that inflation cannot be perfectly foreseen. Tapiero (1974), Sheshinski and Weiss (1977) and Aizenman (1984) focus on the problem of designing a pricing policy which can quide the manager concerning the frequency and magnitude of price changes. All three papers include a fixed cost of price change; Aizenman (1984) and Tapiero (1974) (in a diffucion model) also include a cost which depends on the percentage change of price. The basic problem is to determine (i) a sequence of prices that are to remain constant during finite intervals, and (ii) a sequence of switching instants at which price adjustments are made. Note that essentially two types of control problems are involved: a control problem with parameters to determine optimal price levels (for fixed switching instants) and a subsequent switching time optimization. A feasible pricing policy becomes a step-function which may be more appealing to managers than the smooth policies usually derived in theoretical work. The papers quoted all deal with a monopoly case and as such they are not in the focus of this survey but the 'step-function' approach to optimal pricing should be carried over to the multiplayer context although considerable analytical difficulties surely well emerge.

Dockner and Jørgensen (1985) consider a multiplayer extension of Clarke et al. (1982) and Kalish (1983). Let x_i denote accumulated sales of firm i (i=1,...,M) and let the dynamics be given by

$$\dot{x} = f^i(x_1,\dots,x_M,p_1,\dots,p_M) \quad . \tag{3.16}$$

Looking for an open-loop Nash equilibrium the authors derive a multiplayer dynamic Amoroso-Robinson relation which for M=1 reduces the well known monopoly solution (see, for example, Kalish (1983)); for M=2 an analogous result was obtained by Bürk (1976). With static demand functions, i.e. f^i only depends on $(p_1,\dots,p_M)$ optimal prices are decreasing for the case of positive discount rates and cost learning. This result corresponds to what have been observed in monopolistic counterparts;

see e.g. Kalish (1983). If the oligopolists are 'uncoupled' in the sense that

$$\dot{x}_i = g^i(p_i)h^i(p_1,\ldots,p_{i-1},p_{i+1},\ldots,p_M) \qquad (3.17)$$

then the results are similar to those obtained by Kalish (1983) for the one-player case. Hence, under the specification (3.17) each oligopolist 'behaves as if he were a monopolist'. For the linear demand functions involving a price-differential term (see also (3.10) and Eliashberg and Jeuland (1984))

$$\dot{x}_i = a_i - b_i p_i + \sum_{j=1}^{M} \gamma_{ij}(p_j - p_i) \quad ; \quad \gamma_{ij} = \gamma_{ji} \geq 0 \qquad (3.18)$$

optimal prices are again decreasing in the positive discounting but no cost experience case. Furthermore, price levels (and the rates of price decrease) are higher in the substitution case ($\gamma_{ij} > 0$) than in the no substituting case ($\gamma_{ij} = 0$).

Introducing demand learning also (but still in a separable fashion) changes the evolution equation into

$$\dot{x}_i = H^i(x_i)q^i(p_1,\ldots,p_M) \qquad (3.19)$$

and in the case with cost learning but zero discount rates then

$$\dot{p}_i \gtrless 0 \quad \text{if} \quad H^i_{x_i} \gtrless 0 \quad \text{for all } i \;.$$

This result was obtained for the monopoly case by Kamien and Schwartz (1981, p. 119) and Kalish (1983, Th. 2). Note that the result is only valid when <u>all</u> firms are subject to either positive diffusion effects ($H^i_{x_i} > 0$) or negative diffusion effects ($H^i_{x_i} < 0$). The 'mixed' cases where $H^i_{x_i}$ is positive for some firms, negative for other, can be treated, however, if the price-separability assumption (3.17) is invoked also.

Dockner and Jørgensen (1985) also consider two cases without cost learning where the first case combines the linear demand functions (3.18) with a Bass (1969) diffusion model, (3.3), for the total industry experience. (See also Erickson (1983a)). The second case deals with a model where the evolution of sales of a particular firm only depends on the price of that firm but also on the vector $(x_1,\ldots,x_M)$ of cumulative volumes.

Wernerfeldt (1984) obtains steady state optimal price for an open-loop Nash differential game models with market share dynamics. Let S_i denote the market share of firm i (i=1,...,M). The evolution equations are given by

$$\dot{S}_i = g(S_1,\ldots,S_M,p_1,\ldots,p_M) \quad ,$$

see also Dockner and Jørgensen (1985), Eq. (3.16). His main concern is, however, not to characterize the optimal dynamic price paths but to study the existence and stability properties of (symmetric as well as asymmetric) steady state equilibria.

An oligopoly model which also fits into the general formulation (3.16) is proposed by Feichtinger and Dockner (1985). Let S_i denote the market share of the i'th firm; the dynamics are given by

$$\dot{S}_i = - g_i(p_i)S_i + \frac{1}{M-1} \sum_{j=1}^{M} g_j(p_j)S_j \qquad j \neq i \tag{3.20}$$

where function $g_i(p_i)$ is zero for $p_i \leq \tilde{p}_i$ (const.) and convex increasing for $p_i > \tilde{p}_i$. Hence, for p_i sufficiently large, customers are 'driven away' from firm i. Note that the model is such that customers are not 'attracted to' firm i by its low price since g_i only depends on p_i. This is a major weakness of the model, compared to e.g. (3.18). The authors are aware of this and suggest an alternative formulation including a price-differential term, but this model turns out to be intractable. Note, in (3.20), that customers that are 'pushed away' from firm i are allocated evenly among the other M-1 firms. Choosing a power function for g_i an open-loop Nash solution implies, for sufficiently large (small) salvage values of terminal market share, that prices p_i should be decreased (increased) which seems intuitively clear. However, for certain combinations of terminal salvage values, also nonmonotonous price paths are possible. The Feichtinger and Dockner (1985) model was propably motivated by similar approaches in monopolistic models, for instance, the Phelps and Winter (1971) model which we shall discuss in Section 3.4.

It is also of interest to note some other approaches to dynamic oligopolistic pricing. Simon (1982) presents an alternative to the game theoretic equilibrium determination approach by relying on managerial judgements. Thus, the manager is (i) supposed to predict (the expected) competitive prices for the current time period; then he optimizes taking these prices as given. Next, the manager (ii) reconsiders his original estimates of competitors' prices, assuming that the prices in (i) will in fact be realized. For nondurable goods, dynamic response functions are used to model sales rates being dependent on absolute price and price relative to competitors as well as various nonprice factors. Relative prices are specified in the well known way:

$$\text{relative price of firm } i = (p_i - \bar{p})/\bar{p}$$

where $\bar{p}$ is a (market share) weighted average of competitors' prices. Maximizing present value profits leads to a dynamic version of the Amoroso-Robinson pricing rule (for this, see, for example, Spremann (1975) Kalish (1983)).

Spence (1981), Bass and Rao (1983), Fudenberg and Tirole (1983a) and Reynolds (1985) all consider homogeneous goods, that is, there is a common market price, p, determined by an inverse demand function. Here the oligopolists are quantity-setters rather than price-settes. Although these models may not be of major interest from the pricing manager's point of view, we shall review them briefly since they contain ideas and approaches that may prove useful for the development of models of price-setting oligopolists. Let

$$q_i = \text{output of firm } i \quad ; \quad Q = \sum_{i=1}^{M} q_i = \text{total industry output}$$

$$x_i = \text{cumulative output of firm } i \quad ; \quad X = \sum_{i=1}^{M} x_i = \text{total cumulative industry output}$$

Bass and Rao (1983) take a general inverse demand function

$$p = g(X,Q,t) \tag{3.21}$$

while Spence (1981) uses the simple model $p = g(X)$. Fudenberg and Tirole (1983a) and Reynolds (1985) choose $p = g(Q)$. All authors (except Reynolds (1985)) incorporate cost experience into their models. In an open-loop Nash equilibrium (Bass and Rao (1983)) each firm seeks to determine q_i such that present value profits are maximized subject to $\dot{x}_i = q_i$. Spence (1981) considers both open-loop and closed-loop Nash solutions while Reynolds (1985) determines Nash feedback strategies. A conclusion obtained by both Spence (1981) and Bass and Rao (1983), the latter in a numerical calculation for a duopoly with the simple model $p = g(Q)$, is that a very small (high) cost learning rate tends to yield optimal dynamic paths close to the myopically optimal paths. (see also Clarke and Dolan (1984)).

The Fudenberg and Tirole (1983a) model is interesting from a game theoretic point of view. They consider two types of equilibria:

- A perfect equilibrium which requires that each firm correctly anticipates how the future actions of its rivals depend on their future costs (and thus on current output). Hence the firms have 'rational expectations' which prevent them, among other things, from making threats they would not like to carry out.

- A precommitmant equilibrium (which is an open-loop equilibrium): here each firm believes that the future cost structure of the industry does not influence the rivals' future output rates. However, this kind of equilibrium is inconsistent with an emphasis on a truly competitive strategy.

Although the model is relatively simple (a two-period model) and price-setting behavior is not the main focus, there seems to be some promise in this game theoretic approach when it comes to proper modelling and analysis of oligopolistic pricing policy.

3.3. COMPETITIVE FRINGE AND NEW ENTRY

Dynamic formulations of the problem of entry of competitors into anestablished market, controlled by a monopolist (or a cartel) probably originated around 1970. Pashigian (1968) suggested a very simple model where the evolution of the monopolist's sales depends only on time. In a footnote he proposed an extension which leads to the Gaskins (1971) model. Since many extensions have been made of the latter, we whall present it briefy here. It is based on the limit price notion (Bain (1949)) where the limit price, p_L, is the highest price the established seller can set without inducing entry. The total market demand is given by f(p), where p is the established firm's price, and the level of rival sales is denoted by x; the residual demand of the established firm is $q(p,t) = f(p) - x$. Thus, the net effect of rival entry is to shift laterally the established firm's residual demand curve. Gaskins (1971) postulates the following dynamics for 'the rate of rival entry'

$$\dot{x} = k(p - p_L) \qquad k = \text{constant} > 0 \qquad (3.22)$$

and solves an infinite horizon optimal control problem for the established firm, assuming constant marginal costs. It is, however, easy to show that the results are valid also for any convex cost function. The main results are as follows: the optimal dynamic price is below the myopic price such that (denoting the steady state level of x by x*)

$$\text{if } x_o \gtrless x^* \quad \text{then p is} \begin{Bmatrix} \text{(low and) increasing toward} \\ \text{(high and) decreasing toward} \end{Bmatrix} p_L \quad \text{and}$$

$$\text{rivals are} \begin{Bmatrix} \text{driven out of the market} \\ \text{entering the market} \end{Bmatrix}$$

Jacquemin and Thisse (1972) extended the Gaskins model by introducing different expressions for entry and exit rates (note that entry and exit are modelled symmetrically in the Gaskins model). They also allowed the established firm to buy up rivals, at a cost. On the right-hand side of (3.22) a term is subtracted, reflecting the effects of such expenditures. These modifications change the optimal pricing policy of the established firm such that p does not tend to p_L.

De Bondt (1977) and Feichtinger (1983) offer another generalization of Gaskins (1971), by replacing (3.22) with

$$\dot{x} = g(p - p_L) \tag{3.23}$$

where function g satisfies $g(p_L) = 0$ and $g' > 0$. Also a general convex cost function is employed. Feichtinger (1983) truncates the horizon by including a salvage value term into the objective functional of the established firm. In De Bondt (1977) and Feichtinger (1983) the results of Gaskins (1971) are confirmed and no essential new insights are provided.

Shupp (1977) suggests a model along the same lines as the Gaskins model and its extensions. In a market with homogeneous goods, M established firms act collusively, each having an equal share of the residual demand. The rate of entry is also here governed by an ad hoc rule, namely by a weighted sum of long-run profit margin and short-run profit margin. Since (i) the M established firms act collusively and the products are homogeneous and (ii) entrants are not modelled as explicit decision makers, the problem turns into an optimal control problem to determine a single market price, p. As seen elsewhere, there is an inverse relationship between p and the fringe's sales level, x. Also in Gilbert and Goldman (1978) ad hoc assumptions on entry behavior are utilized. A monopolist controls a stock of resource and entry occurs (i) if monopoly reserves fall below a critical value or, alternatively (ii) depending on the current market price. In the first case, under an assumption that demand before entry is independent of what happens after entry, pre-entry price should be high (above the monopoly level) if the reserves are large enough. In the second case entrants act as myopic price takers and enter if price exceeds some lower limit. Also here, the pre-entry price is higher than the pure monopolistic price.

In addition to the Gaskins (1971) paper, another approach to modelling the entry problem originated around 1970. Kamien and Schwartz (1971) model the probabilistic entry of a firm but are only concerned with the established firm's pre-entry pricing policy; after entry the established firm's profits are assumed to be constant. This implies an unrealistic assumption: the entrant considers only current profits (price) of the established firm (see (3.24)) below) when deciding whether or not to enter. The entrant pays no attention to his own prospecspective profits after entry. As mentioned, the same is true for the established firm. Let $F(t)$ denote the probability that entry has occured by time t ('the entry rate'). Then $\dot{F}/(1-F)$ is the (instantaneous) conditional probability of entry at time t, given that entry has not yet occured. Kamien and Schwartz (1971) assume that

$$\frac{\dot{F}}{1-F} = g(p) \tag{3.24}$$

where function g is convex increasing. Hence the model uses the conventional argument that entry rate increases for p increasing. Note that only with some difficulty this can be interpreted in the usual way (that current price signals future profitability) since the entrant's profits are of no concern. The established firm solves the optimal control problem

$$\max_{p} \int_{0}^{\infty} \exp(-rt)\left[R_1(p)(1-F) + R_2F\right]dt \tag{3.25}$$

where R_2 = constant. R_1 and R_2 are the profits before and after entry, respectively. The optimal pricing policy is simply to keep p at a constant value which is less than the monopoly price but higher than the limit price. Hence, in this model, it is more profitable to delay entry than to preclude entry altogether. A minor modification of (3.24) is suggested in Kamien and Schwartz (1981) where a fixed time delay is included by replacing $p(t)$ by $p(t-\tau)$.

The Kamien-Schwartz approach to modelling entry is clearly unsatisfactory and should only be seen as a first attempt. Perhaps the most important contribution of Kamien and Schwartz (1971) it the introduction of uncertainty through an ingenious formulation of the state equation, allowing for a treatment as a deterministic control problem. This 'trick' has been used in a series of later applications in optimal control and differential games, see, for instance, Kamien and Schwartz (1981), Feichtinger (1982c), Reinganum (1982).

The model (3.24) assumes that the entrants react only to current price and not to other factors; in a sense, entrants are treated as a homogeneous neutral group. To relax the homogenity assumption, Bourguignon and Sethi (1981) assume that

$$\dot{F}/(1-F) = g(p)h(F)\ , \tag{3.26}$$

that is, the conditional probability of entry depends also on the current rate of entry. Note that the price effect and the effect of current entry are separated. Three groups of entrants are identified:

(i) neutral ($h'=0$), (ii) aggressive, who hasten to enter when F is high ($h'>0$), and (iii) cautious, who do the opposite ($h'<0$). Advertising, A, is also included in the model. The dynamics (3.26) are specialized into

$$\dot{F} = f(p,A)(1-F)^n$$

such that cases (ii) and (iii) are obtained for $n<1$ and $n>1$, respectively. Depending on the relationship between F and some limit values, different rules (stay-out, forbid entry, etc.) are obtained. However, the results appear somewhat inconclusive.

All the above models of the entry problem suffer from the same deficiency: the problem is seen only from the point of view of the established firm which solves an optimal control problem under various ad hoc assumptions on the behavior of the potential entrants. The latter are not rational, optimizing agents.

A first attempt to incorporate the competitive fringe as active decision makers in a dynamic model was made by Lieber and Barnea (1977) who studied the case of an established firm (a cartel) exploiting a stock of exhaustible resource and facing competition from a fringe, producing a substitute good. With a notation already employed, let total market demand be given by f(p) where p is the established firm's price, let x denote fringe output and let y denote the established firm's remaining stock of resource. Then $q(p,t) = f(p) - x$ is the sales function of the established firm and its stock of resource evolves according to $\dot{y} = - q(p,t)$. The competitive fringe invests in production capacity (equal to x) and uses investment expenditures at a rate of u. Assuming no depreciation, a second state equation is given by $\dot{x} = u$.

Lieber and Barnea (1977) choose a linear demand function f(p), constant marginal costs of production and a convex investment cost function c(u). Being unable to solve the two-player Nash differential game they turned the problem into an optimal control problem for the established firm by assuming that the fringe behaves as though price p were forever constant. An open-loop Nash solution of the Lieber-Barnea problem was obtained by Jørgensen (1982a) and Dockner (1984), the latter for a formulation with more general demand and cost functions. In Dockner and Jørgensen (1984a) also the Stackelberg and Pareto differential games solutions were determined. It turns out that the fringe, regardless of the solution concept used, always increases capacity whereas the established firm decreases its price (except in a subcase of the Pareto solution.

Hoel (1983) studies a resource problem similar to that in Lieber and Barnea (1977) and puts an upper limit on the fringe's investment rate. However, due to the linear structure of the fringe's optimization problem, investment in substitute capacity becomes a control variable of the monopolist and hence the problem is turned into an optimal control problem for the monopolist who determines the rate of resource extraction as well as the investment rate.

In the last ten years a considerable amount of literature has been published on the effects of the supply-side market structure on the pattern of exploitation of natural resources. We shall report briefly on these developments. The problem of a cartel (monopoly) facing competitive fringe suppliers has already been mentioned (Lieber and Barnea (1977) and others; see above). In this area there are also some interesting results by Lewis and Schmalensee (1980a,b). We note two different approaches to modelling the resource extraction problem:

- A monopolist (or a stable cartel) controls the major part of the total market and faces competition from a fringe of many (small) suppliers, each too small to influence the going market price in a noticeable way. The fringe firms take price as beyond their control and choose output rates to maximize profits. The monopolist chooses the price to maximize his profits subject to fringe supply behavior. This approach, as already has been noted, has been applied in more or less sophisticated versions.

- In a resource market there are a few suppliers, each of importance, which means a truly oligopolistic market. Here the amount of literature is much more modest.

In Lewis and Schmalensee (1980b) a duopoly with a monopolist and a fringe is considered. A stationary demand function is given, relating market price to total market sales; the latter being the sum of monopolist and fringe sales. Depending on the elasticity of demand, in a Nash open-loop equilibrium the price decreases, increases or is constant but fringe supplies are eventually exhausted. An interesting case of incomplete information is also considered where the fringe does not know the monopolist's initial stock of resource. But the best strategy of the latter is to be honest and announce his actual initial stock!

In Lewis and Schmalensee (1980b, Section 4) an M-firm oligopoly model is presented. Analysis of this problem is also the focus of Lewis and Schmalensee (1980a). In an open-loop Nash equilibrium each firm chooses an output path leading to a monotonically increasing market price. But, as mentioned, the main interest in this line of research is not to prescribe individual price policies but to prove existence of output equilibrium and to characterize their properties.

Two papers, both with a strong empirical content, are Hnyilicza and Pindyck (1976) and Cremer and Weitzman (1976). The former considers an optimal control problem of determining the OPEC oil price. Looking at the OPEC as a two-part cartel (of saver and spender countries) a Pareto-optimal solution is obtained for price and for the allocation of total output between the two groups. Cremer and Weitzman (1976) view the behavior of OPEC as a pricing monopolist sharing the world oil market with a competitive sector. The purpose is to predict what oil prices would be if OPEC members cooperated in rational action to maximize present value discounted profits. Also the competitive fringe acts like rational profit-maximizers rather than following some (ad hoc) behavioral rule. An unrealistic feature of the model is, however, that OPEC announces all future prices and the fringe takes those prices as given in their production optimization problem. See also the Lieber and Barnea (1977) approach mentioned above.

Recently some attempts have been made to model the entry problem in a more satisfactory way. Erickson (1983c, pp. 1-2) correctly notes that

"Two aspects of the entry/reaction situation in particular need to be treated. One is that the situation needs to be approached in a multiplayer context.... The decisions and actions of the entering and reacting competitors need to be considered jointly if either are to be effective. The other important aspect that needs to be consicered is that the entry/reaction process is a dynamic one".

Erickson (1983b) develops a rather elaborate model for entry of firm number M+1 into a market already having M competitors. The dynamics are developed in terms of market shares, $S_i(i=1,\dots,M,M+1)$ such that, for the established firms

$$\dot{S}_i = \gamma\left[(1-d_i)\tilde{S}_i - S_i\right] \qquad i=1,\dots,M \tag{3.27}$$

where $\tilde{S}_i$ is firm i's share prior to entry and d_i is the fraction of $\tilde{S}_i$ which will be lost to firm M+1, ultimately. This fraction depends on the difference between p_i and p_{M+1}:

$$d_i = \beta_{io} + \beta_{i1}(p_i - p_{M+1}) \ . \tag{3.28}$$

Note that $\tilde{S}_i$ is assumed to be constant which means that no dynamic competition goes on prior to entry. Further firm i only loses customers to firm M+1, not to any other of the established firms. The author looks for an open-loop Nash equilibrium for all M+1 firms but has to resort to a numerical solution with data from the US automobile industry facing entry of e.g. Japanese cars. Hence the conclusions are limited to this special application. It turns out that Nash prices are generally higher than actual prices which could be anticipated since the model only deals with competition between domestic manufacturers on the one side and import on the other side.

Another approach to the entry problem is Feichtinger (1982c) who takes the starting point in the Kamien and Schwartz (1971) model, see (3.24)-(3.25), but assumes both the established firm and the entrant to be explicit decision makers. As before, price of the established firm (p) influences its pre-entry profits, R_1, and the entry rate. The latter depends also on the R&D expenditures, u, which are the control of the entrant. Hence (3.24) is modified to

$$\dot{F}/(1-F) = kpu \ ,$$

assuming linearity in both controls. The performance index for the established firm is (omitting the terminal salvage value)

$$J^1 = \int_0^T \exp(-r_1 t)\left[R_1^1(p)(1-F) - K_1\dot{F} + R_2^1 F\right]dt \qquad (3.29)$$

see also (3.25). For the entrant the payoff is

$$J^2 = \int_0^T \exp(-r_2 t)\left[R_1^2(u)(1-F) - K_2\dot{F} + R_2^2 F\right]dt \ . \qquad (3.30)$$

Equation (3.29) corresponds to (3.24) apart from the middle term in the brackets, $- K_1\dot{F}$, which is negative and represents a one-shot loss of profits for the established firm incurred by the entry of the rival. In (3.30) the term $- R_1^2(u)$ is the R&D expenses of the entrant prior to entry whereas the term $- K_2\dot{F}$ is a one-shot gain obtained by entry. As in the Kamien-Schwartz model, post-entry profits (R_2^i) are constant. Feichtinger (1982c) looks for en open-loop Nash equilibrium and has to simplify by disregarding discounting and putting $R_2^i = 0$. Especially the latter assumption is, of course, highly unrealistic. Despite of the simplifications it is only possible to conclude about the control u which will increase. The price p remains on the whole indeterminate but is (as expected) lower than the static price.

Milgrom and Roberts (1982) also study the entry problem in a model where both the established firm and the entrant are rational maximizers, using the limit price notion. The conventional wisdom of limit pricing, as already noted, asserts that a low pre-entry price (below the short-run maximizing level) will prevent entry. The authors rightly note that in most of the literature the analysis has been concentrated on the decision problem facing the established firm, taking as given the limit-pricing assumption. Milgrom and Roberts (1982) introduce incomplete information about the unit costs of the other firm; information on these costs is relevant to both firms' post-entry behavior. The relationship assumed in earlier literature, that a low price tends to discourage entry, emerges endogeneously in a Nash equilibrium of the Milgrom-Roberts model. The model is a simple two-period model and the goods are homogeneous, i.e. there is a single market price. Two types of equilibria must be considered:

- 'pooling' where observing the established firm's output, q, does not provide any information to the entrant

- 'separation' where observing q allows the value of the established firm's unit costs to be inferred correctly.

In the latter equilibrium limit pricing will not deter entry, relative to a complete information case (in which no limit pricing will occur for this particular model). The Milgrom-Roberts model offers an interesting game theoretic approach to the limit pricing phenomenon but it is somewhat unrealistic to assume that firms learn about one another's unit costs as soon as entry has occured. Also a two-period model appears to be substantially less general than an infinite horizon model but with only <u>one</u> entrant (and no exit) any model, despite the length of the horizon, gets a kind of two-period character.

The model of Shupp (1977), see above, has been modified in Shupp (1985) to incorporate both firms as rational decision makers in a differential game. Demand evolution is described by linear functions involving a price-differential term, see (3.10) and also Yoon and Lilien (1985). A numerical solution is provided; the results are in general reasonable but due to the arbitrariness in the assignment of parameter values, the results should be taken with caution.

Some recent papers on the entry problem, but more oriented toward 'classical' game theory are Friedman (1977) who explicitly considers the two distinct stages: pre-entry where the monopolist chooses price and investments, taking into account that his investments (not the price) may affect the plan of the entrant, and post-entry where a duopoly situation is prevailing. The paper also discusses the problems of exit. Dixit (1980) and Fudenberg and Tirole (1983b) study the strategic importance of investments as a means to deter entry; the former in a two-period game, the latter in a differential game. For some general remarks or strategic entry deterrence see Salop (1979). Flaherty (1980) revisits the Bain suggestion that entry can be prevented by limit pricing and demonstrates that this holds in a simple open-loop Nash differential game model with output rates as the controls.

Two recent studies with relation to the entry problem also deserve to be mentioned, Hauser and Shugan (1983) consider a firm which tries to adjust its price and other strategic variables to defend its position in an existing market from attack by a competitive new product. A rather sophisticated (but static) model of consumer behavior is used but the problem is viewed only from the side of the established (defending) firm. Under certain assumptions on consumer tastes and market segmentation it turns out that defensive profits can be increased by decreasing price which is a type of policy frequently observed for package goods. Clarke and Dolan (1984) focus on pricing strategies for an innovating monopolist who faces competition at some known time where a rival enters and the market is a duopoly for the rest of a given planning period. The authors use simulation to assess the effects of three different policies:

- myopic pricing, i.e. the monopolist maximizes current period profits in each oeriod. Let this price by p_m.
- skimming, i.e. initial price above p_m.
- penetration, i.e. initial price below p_m.

Buyer behavior is modelled by a diffusion type mechanism based on reservation prices for the monopolist's and the entrant's products. The kind of consumer learning assumed is, however, not easily understood. Also the behavioral assumptions of firms' reactions are subject to criticism. In the pre-entry period the monopolist is supposed to use a myopic pricing rule; after entry, also myopic pricing is assumed and such that the monopolist acts as a leader in the Stackelberg sense or, alternatively, the entrant simply matches the monopolist's price. Hence both players are myopic decision makers and the entrant is placed in a passive role. However, there is nothing inherent in the model which yields such asymmetry between the players. Let us also note that the use of simulation implies a trade-off between more richness in modelling and lacking generality of conclusions.

In the case where the entrant imitates the monopolist's price the latter acts as a price leader. This problem has received a fair amount of attention in the literature and we shall offer some general comments. Price leadership is normally thought of as a situation in an M-firm market where a particular firm, most often the largest, takes the initiative to price changes. After such a change, the other (smaller) firms quickly follow with parallel price changes. Such behavior can be taken as an example of implicit collusion and in order to work it demands (at least) that the rival firms' actions are observable and there is some alignment of interests, for instance such that all firms are oriented toward long-run profits. Hence no firm has an interest in engaging in short-term strategic pricing. When analyzing price leadership it is of importance to determine the conditions (i) under which leadership emerges and (ii) what determines who will be the leader. As to the latter question, traditional Stackelberg-type analyses fail to give an answer since a firm acts as the leader simply by assumption. However, leadership may not be a chosen role and from game theoretic studies it is known that there are cases where, for example, no firm wants to lead or both firms wish to do so, see Basar (1973). Hence additional machinery is needed for an adequate analysis of the leadership problem.

3.4. PRICING AND OTHER STRATEGIC VARIABLES

The problem of the simultaneous determination of price, advertising, quality, and other strategic variables has concerned economics and marketing researchers for quite a long time. We have seen above that the problem of optimal pricing in a dynamic competitive environment causes serious problems in the modelling as well as the analytical phase; these problems are of course accentuated when we try to deal with the question of determining an optimal marketing mix in a dynamic multiplayer context. Historically it seems right to start with the static monopoly model for optimal price, advertising and quality by Dorfman and Steiner (1954).[3] Also in the static context, Lambin et al. (1975) studied optimal marketing mix in an oligopoly and obtained 'Dorfman' Steiner' type equilibrium conditions. However, their model is not truly competitive since one firm essentially acts as a monopolist taking into account the behavioral responses of the other firms when designing its optimum marketing mix.

In a dynamic model, Phelps and Winter (1970) considered a firm which enjoys some monopoly power with respect to its current customers but the firm cannot maintain forever a price above the going market price without losing its customers to other firms. The market structure

---

[3] The result has been extensively quoted in the literature as the 'Dorfman-Steiner Theorem' but was in fact established ten years before by the Danish economist, Professor Børge Barfod. Due to limited circulation of the journal in which he published the result, and the general turbulence of war time, Barfod's contribution remained virtually unknown until recently. See Jørgensen (1981).

is a mixture of pure competition and monopoly, not quite easily understood. Denote by S the market share of the firm in question and p its price. Let $\bar{p}$ be the constant average price of all other firms. The dynamics are given by

$$\dot{S} = f(p,\bar{p})S \qquad (3.31)$$

where function f is such that S decreases whenever $p > \bar{p}$. The firm under consideration seeks to determine a pricing policy such that present value profits over an infinite horizon are maximized. It is shown that the optimal price, as expected, is lower than the myopic price. The model has severe limitations, which was also noted by the authors; Phelps and Winter (1970, p. 336). Taking the model for what it is, Luptacik (1982) and Feichtinger (1982b) analyze a version including advertising. On the right-hand side of (3.31) a concave advertising effectiveness function, g(A), is added. The most interesting conclusion of this extension is that optimal price and optimal advertising 'work' in the same direction. For example, increasing advertising should be accompanied by a decreasing price policy such that both instruments stimulate sales. This kind of synergism has been noted also in the marketing literature, see Kalish (1984, p. 22) and Rao (1984, p. 51). Rao reports on an econometric study of the eyeglasses market in the US where price were substantially lower in those states where advertising of eyeglasses was allowed (and undertaken) than in those states where it was forbidden. A survey of a large number of brands in several product categories, sold in supermarkets, showed that manufacturer advertised brands were sold at lower retail margins than unadvertised brands. In a test-market experiment (household cleaning product, snack food, speciality food) Eskin and Baron (1977) obtained this kind of negative interaction between price and advertising. Thus a low price/high advertising and a high price/low advertising strategy produced substantially higher profits than introductory marketing plans with low (high) price and low (high) advertising.

Dockner, Feichtinger and Sorger (1985) study a general price-advertising model with dynamics

$$\dot{x} = f(x,p,A) \qquad (3.32)$$

which could be regarded as an extension of the Clarke et al. (1982) and Kalish (1983) general pricing models; see Section 3.2. Dockner et al. (1985) obtain optimal pricing and advertising strategies for various multiplicative separable versions of (3.32). Also cases where the total market depends on p or A, respectively, are investigated. Note that the multiplicative structure implies that the price elasticity of demand is independent of the advertising rate.

Another approach to simultaneous determination of price and advertising takes its starting point in the seminal paper by Nerlove and Arrow (1962). The idea behind the model is simple and originates from optimal capital theory. Advertising is supposed to build up a stock of goodwill, G, which, however, depreciates because of forgetting, switching to other brands and so on. The dynamic equation for the evolution of G is

$$\dot{G} = A - \delta G \qquad \delta = \text{constant} > 0 . \qquad (3.33)$$

The monopoly model (3.33) has been widely used and extended in various directions; see the survey paper by Sethi (1977). Spremann (1981) includes the Nerlove-Arrow model in a larger (monopoly) model with demand learning and market share depreciation. The sales dynamics have some resemblance with the Teng and Thompson (1985) durable goods model. The main objective of the Spremann (1981) study is to compare the dynamically optimal pair (p,A) with that of a myopic firm.

A dynamic model for the simultaneous determination of price and advertising is also found in Spremann (1985) for a monopolistic firm. Spremann (1985) uses the Nerlove-Arrow dynamic advertising goodwill model as his first state equation and introduces a variable, L(t), called 'reputation', in the demand function. Demand, q(t), depends on price, goodwill stock and reputation. The latter evolves according to a second state equation

$$\dot{L} = h(p_o/p)q - \delta L$$

where function h is such that $h(p_o) = 0$ and $h'<0$; p_o is the price which corresponds to a fixed level of quality. The firm seeks to determine optimal price and advertising.

Feichtinger, Luhmer and Sorger (1985) assume that buyers build up a 'price image' of a store as a measure of the value that the buyer gets for his money. This price image is regarded as a sort of capital stock in which the firm invests by charging low prices. This approach resembles the 'goodwill' of Nerlove and Arrow (1962), 'brand loyalty' of Clemhout and Wan (1974), and others. The firm's problem is the same as in Spremann (1985).

Proceeding to some multiplayer models let us note the study by Clemhout and Wan (1974) who model optimal pricing in an oligopoly.

Demand functions are given by $q_i = q_i(p_i)$ and sales, x_i, are proportional to demand: $x_i = v_i q_i$ where v_i is an artifact termed 'clientele', denoting what firm i can sell when price equals marginal cost. Introducing G_i as brand loyalty, the clientele of firm i depends on G_i and G_j:

$$v_i = G_i - s_{ij} G_j + K_i \quad . \qquad (s_{ij}, K_i > 0 \text{ and constant})$$

Brand loyalty evolves in a Nerlove-Arrow-type fashion (Nerlove and Arrow (1962))

$$\dot{G} = x_i - \delta_i G_i \quad .$$

It is shown that a Nash-optimal pricing policy is penetration and increasing competition (i.e. increasing the parameter s_{ij}) tends to lower prices.

Thépot (1983) considers optimal advertising, pricing and investment in a duopoly with Nerlove-Arrow-type dynamics for the evolution of the firms' production capacities and their goodwill stocks. In an open-loop Nash equilibrium the pricing policies of the duopolists depend on the degree of influence, the advertising goodwill of one firm has on the sales of the other. If there is (roughly) the same influence then prices should be kept constant such that the firms engage in pure advertising competition. If there is an asymmetry between the firms such that, for example, Firm 2 has an advantage in terms of goodwill cross-elasticity, then Firm 1 should decrease its price to some steady state level while Firm 2 responds with advertising, keeping its price fixed. In the extreme case of very strong asymmetry (i.e. Firm 2 has an overwhelming advantage) then Firm 1 should not advertise at all but responds with price policy only, as described above.

Gaugusch (1984) assumes an extreme form of asymmetry between two firms. In a duopolistic market, Firm 1 uses only advertising (and has a constant price) whereas Firm 2 manipulates its price but does not engage in advertising. The dynamic equations for the evolution of the sales rates are only marginally connected to other marketing models but include linear terms of the type $p_i - p_j$. In an open-loop Nash equilibrium the pricing rule of Firm 2 depends on the salvage value terms, as noted also for other models with fixed planning periods.

Returning to the Nerlove-Arrow model we note that Friedman (1983b) studies an M-firm oligopoly with advertising goodwill and looks for a Nash solution in open-loop controls, being the output rates, not the price. An explanation for this choice is provided (and needed since the products are differentiated). Closed-form solutions are obtainable for a symmetric model with quadratic profit functions but analysis of the steady state prices turns out to be difficult due to conflicting effects of output and goodwill. However, for $M \to \infty$, steady state price tends to marginal cost such that conventional competitive effects are predominating. Fershtman et al. (1983) study an advertising goodwill duopoly with uncoupled Nerlove-Arrow dynamics. Let (p_1,p_2), (A_1,A_2) and (G_1,G_2) denote prices, advertising expenditures, and goodwill stocks, respectively, of the two players. The sales of Firm 1, say, x_1, depends on goodwill stocks and prices in the following way:

$$x_1 = \left\{ \frac{G_1}{N} \left(1 - \frac{G_2}{N}\right) q_1(p_1) + \frac{G_1}{N} \frac{G_2}{N} \hat{q}_1(p_1,p_2) \right\} N$$

where N denotes the number of potential buyers. The purchase rates, q_1 and $\hat{q}_1$, respectively, are specified as

$$q_1(p_1) = (\alpha_1 + \alpha_2)(1 - kp_1)$$

$$\hat{q}_1(p_1,p_2) = \alpha_1(1 - kp_1) + \gamma(p_j - p_i)$$

whereby it is assumed that (each) firm i has two markets: a monopoly with demand function q_i and a duopoly demand function $\hat{q}_i$. Note that for $p_i = p_j$ the two firms simply share the market according to the weights α_i. The method of analysis resembles that of Nerlove and Arrow (1962): for every t and for a given pair of goodwill stocks, the firms compete via the prices. The resulting payoffs are functions of (G_1,G_2) and the firms engage in dynamic competition via their investments in goodwill, i.e. via their advertising expenditures. Hence prices are adjusted instantaneously and depend only on (G_1,G_2); p_i is a feedback control. Maximizing present value profits on an infinite horizon yields, under certain concavity and boundedness conditions, the existence of a (nonunique) Nash equilibrium for all values of initial goodwill. There is an expansion period if both goodwill stocks increase, due to high levels of advertising, whereas prices decrease (cf. the synergy effect mentioned above). If goodwill stocks evolve in different directions then the movement of prices cannot be ascertained and there may by cyclical solutions. However, focusing on solutions that indeed approach a stationary equilibrium (i.e. $A_i^* = \delta_i G_i^*$) the model exhibits nice properties. It can be shown that the dynamical system converges to a stationary equilibrium for $t \to \infty$, even if it does not start there. For all initial goodwill levels there exists a Nash equilibrium solution converging to the stationary point, which does not depend on the initial stocks of goodwill. This question of dependence on initial goodwill stocks (initial values of the state variables) is of some importance. Consider the market for personal computers where firms like IBM, Apple and Texas Instruments can be assumed to have different (initial) goodwill levels due to different previous activities. The question is then whether this will give a strategic advantage.

Dockner and Feichtinger (1985) analyze a Nash open-loop differential game where demand, x_i, evolves according to the adjustment process

$$\dot{x}_i = k_i[f^i(p_1,\ldots,p_M,A_1,\ldots,A_M) - x_i] \qquad k_i = \text{const.} > 0 \qquad (3.34)$$

where f^i represents an instantaneous 'equilibrium demand'. The dynamics (3.34) were proposed by Schmalensee (1972) for a single firm model. Different generalizations of the 'Dorfman-Steiner theorem' are obtained and a certain interest is confined to the question whether an advertising strategy based on a constant percentage of sales could be optimal.

Another area of pricing theory where price is to be set in conjunction with other decision variables of the firm, is pricing in production-inventory systems. Here the pricing policy can play an important role in smoothing demand which is of interest to the production manager. Pekelman (1974) was probably the first to introduce pricing explicitly in a dynamic production-inventory model. Let y denote a firm's inventory level at time t, w its production rate and f(p,t) the sales rale. Then the well known dynamics for inventory evolution are

$$\dot{y} = w - f(p,t) \quad . \qquad (3.35)$$

Feichtinger and Hartl (1985) analyze the optimal control problem of determining an optimal pair (p,w) for a single firm seeking to maximize present value profits over a fixed horizon. Production costs as well as inventory/shortage costs are included. It is shown that p and w work 'synergistically' on y, i.e. they influence y in the same direction. It is, for example, not optimal to compensate an increase in w by a decrease in p in order to stimulate demand.

The production-inventory problem is also interesting in a multiplayer context. However, no extensions have yet been made for the general case of M producers, using differential game theory. Also the price line problem (a firm produces n interrelated products) has not been sufficiently analyzed. The latter problem has obvious managerial importance, for instance in relation to the concept of loss leader pricing.

Recently optimal control theory and differential games have been applied to the problem of determining optimal prices, production and ordering in a vertical channel. For a survey of new developments in channel pricing literature, see Rao (1984, Section 8). Eliashberg and Steinberg (1984) and Jørgensen (1986) address the following problem. Consider a simple two-member channel with a manufacturer supplying a retailer who, in turn, sells to the final consumers. The manufacturer must choose a production rate and a price toward the retailer while the latter must select a purchasing policy and a price toward the final consumers. Both firms carry inventories and the dynamics of the model are given by straightforward modifications of (3.35). Costs of production, ordering and inventory holding (shortage) are introduced. The solution approach differs: Jørgensen (1986) looks for a Nash (open-loop) equilibrium while Eliashberg and Steinberg (1984) apply a sequential solution of the Stackelberg type. However, they do not solve the game by applying the necessary conditions of Simaan and Cruz (1973). Instead, the retailer solves an optimal control problem taking the manufacturer's price as a parameter. This yields an implied (derived) demand function which the manufacturer faces (the retailer's ordering rate as a function of the manufacturer's price). The manufacturer maximizes his profits over the horizon which yields controls that thereafter can be substituted into the retailer's reaction function. In Jørgensen (1986) the manufacturer always quotes his maximal price (as a result of the model's linear structure) while Eliashberg and Steinberg (1984) obtain a more sophisticated pricing policy for the manufacturer. Under certain conditions a retailer policy of increasing price followed by decreasing price is obtained in both articles. Again, because of the model's structure, Jørgensen (1986) obtains for the production and purchasing policies bang-bang solutions with singular segments whereas these policies are more 'smooth' in Eliashberg and Steinberg (1984). Both models, being simple, open up for several extensions/modifications. Let us briefly note that it can be assumed that the manufacturer controls the retailer's selling price (resale price maintenance) or, perhaps more interesting, the consequences of cooperation (vertical integration) can be analyzed by determining the Pareto-optimal set. Then a bargaining scheme (Nash, Kalai-Smorodinsky etc.) could be applied to single out a solution. Also the effects of threats and cheating could be studied in the cooperative solution.

4. CONCLUSIONS

In this section we start by stating the basic conclusions of the research surveyed in Section 3. For monopolistic dynamic diffusion models the optimality conditions now are well established; a summary is given in Kalish and Sen (1985, Table 2) to which the reader also is referred. The factors that are most important for the shape of the pricing policy are the following:

(i) Type of good: durable/nondurable.

(ii) Cost structure: cost experience/no cost experience.

(iii) Discounting: zero interest rate/positive (but finite) interest rate.

(iv) Carry over effects: positive/zero/negative.

where a positive (negative) diffusion, or carry over, effect refers to the fact that $f_x > 0$ ($f_x < 0$) in any diffusion model $\dot{x} = f(x,p)$. There are three basic shapes of the optimal pricing policy of a monopolist:

(a) Skimming, i.e. price is gradually decreased over the planning period. This type of policy occurs for cost experience alone (i.e. with static demand, $f_x = 0$) or for a typical durable good. Results on this type of policy have been obtained by e.g. Spence (1981), Dolan and Jeuland (1981), Jeuland and Dolan (1982), Bass and Bultez (1982), Clarke et al. (1982) (but with the reverse conclusion if cost is additive), Kalish (1983, 1984).

(b) Penetration, i.e. price is increased over the planning period. This policy is typical for products with positive diffusion effects and no cost experience. Results on this type of pricing strategy are found in e.g. Dolan and Jeuland (1981), Jeuland and Dolan (1982), Jeuland (1981), Feichtinger (1982), Jørgensen (1983), Kalish (1983, 1984).

(c) Penetration followed by skimming, i.e. price is first to be increased, then decreased on a final interval. This kind of policy emerges typically for separable demand functions, $f(x,p) = g(x)h(p)$ where the initial diffusion effect is sufficiently strong and interest rate is low. Hence the pricing policy in a sense follows the product life cycle. Results on this type of strategy are reported in e.g. Dolan and Jeuland (1981), Jeuland and Dolan (1982), Robinson and Lakhani (1975), Clarke et al. (1982), Kalish (1983, 1984), Teng and Thompson (1985).

In addition to these results it has often been verified that the optimal dynamic price is lower than the optimal myopic price (Robinson and Lakhani (1975), Dolan and Jeuland (1981), Bass and Bultez (1982) and several others).

It should be kept in mind that all these results depend on the assumption that customers do not speculate in future price changes; consumers only react to current price. To relax this assumption we could consider to incorporate the ideas of early monopoly models, cf. Section 3.1.

Oligopolistic diffusion models show decreasing durables prices due to experience (Dockner and Jørgensen (1985), Erickson (1983a), Thompson and Teng (1984)) as in the monopoly case. Penetration (skimming) strategies emerge if there are positive (negative) diffusion effects (Dockner and Jørgensen (1985)). This result also carries over from the one-player case but the increase (decrease) in oligopolistic prices is faster than that of monopoly price. Some multiplayer models show that increased competition tends to lower prices (Erickson (1983a), Clemhout and Wan (1974)); also a lack of product interdependence induces oligopolistic firms to act as monopolists (Erickson (1983a), Dockner and Jørgensen (1985)).

Summarizing on oligopolistic diffusion models we have to conclude that the amount of additional knowledge, relative what we already know about the monopoly case, does not seem to be substantial. We are inclined to maintain the hypothesis that oligopolistic pricing <u>does differ</u> from monopolistic pricing but the models so far applied have not been sophisticated enough in their modelling of the strategic interrelations of the competiting firms to detect these differences. Of course it is possible to cast doubt on the monopoly results as well; the ones we are comparing with. However, the optimality conditions for the monopoly case with dynamic demand and cost conditions seem well developed and confirmed in several studies. See Clarke et al. (1982), Kalish (1983) and Kalish and Sen (1985).

On the problem of entry we first note that in most cases the models are of the type: an optimal control problem is solved for a monopolist facing entry where the entrant's behavior is modelled in an ad hoc fashion. The entrant is treated as a passive, non-optimizing agent. Also we note that the 'limit pricing' literature is rich in models for entry behavior but these models remain ad hoc assumptions since the empirical support for any particular one is weak or absent (Jeuland and Dolan (1982)). In the dynamic entry literature several streams of research can be indentified, one emerging from the Gaskins (1971) study, another from Kamien and Schwartz (1971). These studies, and later modifications model the entry problem as a one-player case and do not seem to have shed very much light on the entry problem in terms of the strategic interdependencies between the established firm and the entrant. A commonly reported result is that price of the established firm and output of the competitive fringe is inversely related, see Gaskins (1971), Shupp (1977), Feichtinger (1983), Jørgensen (1982a), Dockner (1984b), Dockner and Jørgensen (1984a). A third line of research is concerned with the problem of a price-setting monopoly facing competitive fringe, as in Lieber and Barnea (1977) and later works. The focus is here on determining an optimal price of the monopolist or optimal outputs for all competitors. Recent attempts have been made to model the entry problem with rational, maximizing agents, cf. Friedman (1979), Feichtinger (1982c), Milgrom and Roberts (1982), Erickson (1983c), Clarke and Dolan (1984), Shupp (1985), Yoon and Lilien (1985). No unifying principles are seen to emerge here. For example, Erickson (1983c) and Shupp (1985) only report on numerically obtained results, the Feichtinger (1982c) and Yoon and Lilien (1985) analysis is incomplete, the Milgrom and Roberts (1982) model is very simple (but holds some promise) while the Clarke and Dolan (1984) study, using simulation, supposes an unrealistic degree of myopism and asymmetry.

Recent work on the dynamic optimal marketing mix problem has mainly been concerned with the simultaneous determination of price and advertising, based on the advertising goodwill model of Nerlove and Arrow (1962). See Thépot (1983), Friedman (1983b), Fershtman et al. (1983). Also, channel problems have been analyzed in a dynamic multiplayer context; Eliashberg and Steinberg (1984) and Jørgensen (1986). These types of problems are considerably more complicated (both in the modelling and the analytical phase) than the pure pricing problem and no general conclusions can be drawn from the small amount of research so far done.

As noted above, the major part of the pricing models so far proposed has tried to escape the difficult problem of modelling properly the dynamics and interdependencies of an oligopolistic market. As to the latter various approaches have been proposed:

- a newly introduced product in the pre-entry period
- a price-leader situation
- more er less sophisticated Stackelberg-type followership
- multiplayer modelling but with weak competitive interdependencies.

Also the problem of empirical validation has been, on the whole, neglected. Most of the research under review did not focus on testing the models with real data although it is in pricing (as elsewhere) important to stress the empirical aspects of modelling. Here it seems that research in pricing is not so well developed as, for instance, advertising where the number of empirical studies is much larger.

There appear to be two alternative paths to follow in future work on dynamic oligopolistic pricing:

(1) Build more 'realistic' models that are better suited for applications. Such models will, inevitably, be much more complex and call for large amounts of research effort in the modelling and analytical phases. With almost certainty it will be impossible to derive nice closed-form prescriptive solutions for such models and one has to resort to 'optimal' policies found by numerical optimization and simulation. Here it is essential that the model represents reality with a high degree of precision since the model yields policies in terms of numbers. We should also note that such models cannot provide an overall qualitative insight, i.e. no general propositions can emerge from it. (Strictly speaking, all what one learns from such a model is about the specific case run on the computer.)

(2) The other alternative is to establish small (i.e. highly simplified) models that are analytically tractable. Then the analytical solutions obtained may give some insights into the direction and the form (i.e. the general qualitative nature) of optimal policies. Here we should notice that the relevant question to pose about the assumptions underlying such a model is not whether the assumptions are 'realistic' from a descriptive point of view, but whether they yield a satisfactory approximation for the specific purpose. However, with regard to (i) the diffusion models for new products and also (ii) the modelling of multiplayer interdependencies, it seems advisable, in the light of the presentation in Section 3, that future modelling tries to introduce (i) richer processes of consumer choice at the individual level and (ii) more 'game theoretic' thinking to catch the interrelations between firms.

It is fair to note that recent attempts have been made along both lines of research ((1) and (2) above), and work seems to be in good progress. Papers are forthcoming, in increasing numbers, dealing with the long-avoided competitive problem. This problem is attacked using different approaches, for example,

- judgmental models (e.g. Simon (1982))
- Simulation or numerical optimization (e.g. Clarke and Dolan (1984), Thompson and Teng (1984))
- 'classical' game theory (e.g. Fudenberg and Tirole (1983a))
- differential games (e.g. Dockner and Jørgensen (1985)).

Here we shall not go into the strengths and weaknesses of these various approaches but only note that the differential game approach seems to offer a promising framework for future analysis since it explicitly and directly considers the two critical (and much neglected) aspects of market behavior: dynamics and competition. But future applications of differential game theory will no doubt benefit from borrowing from the other approaches, especially 'classical' game theory. Thus, looking at the differential game models of oligopolistic pricing here surveyed, it is the belief of the author that we are on the right track but to cope with the interdependencies of oligopoly, more emphasis should perhaps be put on 'game', less emphasis on 'differential'. Shubik (1982a, p. 62) states that

"Mathematically the theory of differential games draws upon the fields of differential equations, dynamical systems, the calculus of variations, and especially control theory ... This mix of technical disciplines has tended to attract a separate class of mathematical specialists from those attracted to the general body of game theory, and their work often reveals a lack of awareness of basic gametheoretic issues and ideas".

5. REFERENCES

Aizenman, J. (1984), "Optimal Price Adjustment with Time Dependent Costs," Working Paper No. 1319, National Bureau of Economic Research, Cambridge, MA.

Bain, J. (1949), "A Note on Pricing in Monopoly and Oligopoly," American Economic Review, Vol. 39, pp. 448-464.

Başar, T. (1973), "On the Relative Leadership Property of Stackelberg Strategies," Journal of Optimization Theory and Applications, Vol. 11, pp. 655-661.

Bass, F.M. (1969), "A New Product Growth Model for Consumer Durables," Management Science, Vol. 15, pp. 215-227.

Bass, F.M. (1980), "The Relationship Between Diffusion Rates, Experience Curves and Demand Elasticities for Consumer Durable Technological Innovations," Journal of Business, Vol. 53, No. 3, Part 2, pp. 51-67.

Bass, F.M. and A.V. Bultez (1982), "A Note on Optimal Strategic Pricing of Technological Innovations," Marketing Science, Vol. 1, No. 4, pp. 371-378.

Bass, F.M. and R.C. Rao (1983), "Equilibrium Dynamic Pricing of New Products in Oligopolies: Theory and Evidence," Working Paper No. 10-8-83, University of Texas at Dallas.

Bourguignon, F. and S.P. Sethi (1981), "Dynamic Optimal Pricing and (Possibly) Advertising in the Face of Various Kinds of Potential Entrants," Journal of Economic Dynamics and Control, Vol. 3, No. 2, pp. 119-140.

Bondt, R.R. de (1977), "On the Effects of Retarded Entry," European Economic Review, Vol. 9, pp. 361-371.

Bürk, R. (1976), "A Note on Dynamic Duopoly and the Amoroso-Robinson Relation," Zeitschrift für Nationalökonomie, Vol. 36, pp. 389-395.

Clarke, D.G. and R.J. Dolan (1984), "A Simulation Analysis of Alternative Pricing Strategies for Dynamic Environments," Journal of Business, Vol. 57, No. 1, Part 2, pp. 179-209.

Clarke, F.H., M.N. Darrough and J.M. Heineke (1982), "Optimal Pricing Policy in the Presence of Experience Effects," Journal of Business, Vol. 55, pp. 517-530.

Chow, G.C. (1967), "Technological Change and the Demand for Computers," American Economic Review, Vol. 57, pp.1117-1130.

Clemhout, S. and H.Y. Wan (1974), "Pricing Dynamics: An Intertemporal Oligopoly Model and Limit Pricing," Paper presented at the Econometric Society North America Winter Meeting, San Francisco.

Cremer, J. and M.L. Weizman (1976), "OPEC and the Monopoly Price of World Oil," European Economic Review, Vol. 8, pp. 155-164.

Dixit, A. (1980), "The Role of Investment in Entry-Deterrence," The Economic Journal, Vol. 90, March, pp. 95-106.

Dockner, E. (1984a), "Optimale Preisbildung unter Dynamischer Nachfrage: Die Nash-Lösung eines Differentialspiels," in Operations Research Proceedings 1983, H. Steckhan et al. (Eds.), Springer-Verlag, Berlin, pp. 592-598.

Dockner, E. (1984b), "Optimal Pricing of a Monopoly Against a Competitive Producer," Optimal Control Applications & Methods, Vol. 5, No. 4, pp. 345-352.

Dockner, E. (1985), "Optimal Pricing in a Dynamic Duopoly Game Model," Zeitschrift für Operations Research, Vol. 29, Issue 2, Series B, pp. 1-16.

Dockner, E. and G. Feichtinger (1985), "Dynamic Advertising and Pricing in an Oligopoly: A Nash Equilibrium Approach," Paper presented at the 7th Annual Conference on Economic Dynamics and Control, London, June.

Dockner, E. and S. Jørgensen (1984a), "Cooperative and Non-cooperative Differential Game Solutions to an Investment and Pricing Problem," Journal of the Operational Research Society, Vol. 35, No. 8, pp. 731-739.

Dockner, E. and S. Jørgensen (1985), "Optimal Pricing Strategies for New Products in Dynamic Oligopolies," Working Paper, University of Economics, Vienna/Copenhagen School of Economics and Business Administration, Copenhagen.

Dockner, E., G. Feichtinger and G. Sorger (1985), "Interaction of Price and Advertising under Dynamic Conditions", Working Paper, University of Economics and Technical University, Vienna.

Dolan, R.J. and A.P. Jeuland (1981), "Experience Curves and Dynamic Demand Models: Implications for Optimal Pricing Strategies", Journal of Marketing, Vol. 45, pp. 52-62.

Dorfman, R. and P.O. Steiner (1954), "Optimal Advertising and Optimal Quality", American Economic Review, Vol. XLIV, pp. 826-836.

Duncan, D.J., S.C. Hollander and R. Savitt (1983), Modern Retailing Management, R. Irwin, Homewood, Ill.

Easingwood, C.J., V. Mahajan and E. Muller (1983), "A Nonuniform Influence Innovation Diffusion Model of New Product Acceptance", Marketing Science, Vol. 2, pp. 273-296.

Eliashberg, J. and A.P. Jeuland (1982), "New Product Pricing Strategies Over Time in a Developing Market: How Does Entry Affect Prices", Working Paper 82-021, Center for Research in Marketing, University of Chicago.

Eliashberg, J. and A.P. Jeuland (1983), "The Impact of Competitive Entry in a Developing Market Upon Dynamic Pricing Strategies", Working Paper, University of Pennsylvania.

Eliashberg, J. and R. Steinberg (1984), "Marketing-production Decisions in Industrial Channels of Distribution", Working Paper, The Wharton School and Columbia University.

Erickson, G.M. (1983a), "Dynamic Pricing in Oligopolistic New Product Markets", Working Paper, University of Washington, Seattle.

Erickson, G.M. (1983b), "The Separate Effects of Competitive Entry, Price Sensitivity and the Learning Curve on the Dynamic Pricing of New Durable Products", Working Paper, University of Washington, Seattle.

Erickson, G.M. (1983c), "Market Entry and Optimal Price Reaction: A Differential Game Approach", Working Paper, University of Washington, Seattle.

Erskin, G.J. and P.H. Baron (1977), "Effects of Price and Advertising in Test-market Experiments", Journal of Marketing Research, Vol. 14, pp. 499-508.

Evans, G.C. (1924), "The Dynamics of Monopoly", American Mathematical Monthly, Vol. 31, pp. 77-83.

Feichtinger, G. (1982a), "Optimal Pricing in a Diffusion Model With Concave Price-dependent Market Potential", Operations Research Letters, Vol. 1, pp. 236-240.

Feichtinger, G. (1982b), "Saddle Point Analysis in a Price-advertising Model", Journal of Economic Dynamics and Control, Vol. 4, pp. 319-340.

Feichtinger, G. (1982c), "Ein Differentialspiel für den Markteintritt einer Firma", in Operations Research Proceedings, B. Fleischmann et al. (Eds.), Springer, Berlin, pp. 636-644.

Feichtinger, G. (1983), "Optimale Dynamische Preispolitik bei Drohender Konkurrenz", Zeitschrift für Betriebswirtschaft, Vol. 53, pp. 156-171.

Feichtinger, G. and E. Dockner (1985), "Optimal Pricing in a Duopoly: A Non-cooperative Differential Games Solution", Journal of Optimization Theory and Applications, Vol. 45, pp. 199-218.

Feichtinger, G. and R. Hartl (1985), "Optimal Pricing and Production in an Inventory Model", European Journal of Operational Research, Vol. 19, pp. 45-56.

Feichtinger, G. and S. Jørgensen (1983), "Differential Game Models in Management Science", European Journal of Operational Research, Vol. 14, pp. 137-155.

Feichtinger, G., A. Luhmer and G. Sorger (1985), "Price Image Strategy: An Optimal Control Problem", Research Report No. 74, Institute for Econometrics and Operations Research, Technical University, Vienna.

Fershtman, C. (1985), "Identification of Classes of Differential Games for which the Open Loop is a Degenerated Feedback Nash Equilibrium", Working Paper, Economics Department, The Hebrew University, Jerusalem.

Fershtman, C. and M.I. Kamien (1984), "Price Adjustment Speed and Dynamic Duopolistic Competitors", Working Paper, Northwestern University, Evanston, Ill.

Fershtman, C., V. Mahajan and E. Muller (1983), "Advertising, Pricing and Stability in Oligopolistic Markets for New Products", Working Paper No. 83-804, Southern Methodist University, Dallas, Tx.

Flaherty, M.T. (1980), "Dynamic Limit Pricing, Barriers to Entry, and Rational Firms", Journal of Economic Theory, Vol. 23, pp. 160-182.

Friedman, J.W. (1977), Oligopoly and the Theory of Games, North-Holland, Amsterdam.

Friedman, J.W. (1979), "On Entry Preventing Behavior and Limit Price Models of Entry" in Applied Game Theory, S.J. Brans et al. (Eds.), Physica-Verlag, Würzburg, pp. 236-253.

Friedman, J.W. (1982), "Oligopoly Theory" in Handbook of Mathematical Economics, Vol. II, K.J. Arrow and M.D. Intriligator (Eds.), North-Holland, Amsterdam, pp. 491-534.

Friedman, J.W. (1983a), Oligopoly Theory, Cambridge University Press, Cambridge.

Friedman, J.W. (1983b), "Advertising and Oligopolistic Equilibrium", Bell Journal of Economics, Vol. 14, pp. 464-473.

Fudenberg, D. and J. Tirole (1983a), "Learning-by-doing and Market Performance", Bell Journal of Economics, Vol. 14, pp.522-530.

Fudenberg, D. and J. Tirole (1983b), "Capital as a Commitment: Strategic Investments to Deter Mobility", Journal of Economic Theory, Vol. 31, pp. 227-250.

Gaskins, D.W. (1971), "Dynamic Limit Pricing: Optimal Pricing Under Threat of Entry", Journal of Economic Theory, Vol. 3, pp. 306-322.

Gaugusch, J. (1984), "The Non-cooperative Solution of a Differential Game: Advertising versus Pricing", Optimal Control Applications and Methods, Vol. 5, pp. 353-360.

Gilbert, R.J. and S.M. Goldman (1978), "Potential Competition and the Monopoly Price of an Exhaustible Resource", Journal of Economic Theory, Vol. 17, pp. 319-331.

Glaister, S. (1974), "Advertising Policy and Returns to Scale in Markets Where Information is Passed between Individuals", Economica, Vol. 41, pp. 139-156.

Grubbström, R.W. (1972), Economic Decisions in Space and Time, Business Administration Studies, Gothenburg.

Hague, D.C. (1971), Pricing in Business, George Allen and Unwin, London.

Hauser, J.R. and S.M. Shugan (1983), "Defensive Marketing Strategies", Marketing Science, Vol. 2, pp. 319-360.

Hnyilicza, E. and R.S. Pindyck (1976), "Pricing Policies for a Two-part Exhaustible Resource Cartel", European Economic Review, Vol. 8, pp. 139-154.

Hoel, M. (1983), "Resource Extraction when there is a Limit on the Level of Investment in Substitute Capacity", Memorandum No. 11, Institute of Economics, University of Oslo.

Jacquemin, A.P. and J. Thisse (1972), "Strategy of the Firm and Market Structure: An Application of Optimal Control Theory" in K. Cowling (Ed.) Market Structure and Corporate Behavior, Gray-Mills, London, pp. 63-84.

Jeuland, A.P. (1981), "Parsimonious Models of Diffusion of Innovation, Part B: Incorporating the Variable of Price", Working Paper, University of Chicago, Graduate School of Business.

Jeuland, A.P. and R.J. Dolan (1982), "An Aspect of New Product Planning: Dynamic Pricing" in Market Planning Models, A.A. Zoltners (Ed.), North-Holland, Amsterdam.

Jørgensen, S. (1978), "Optimal Price and Advertising Policies for a New Product", Paper presented at a workshop on "Model Building and Operations Research Applications in Marketing", European Institute for Advanced Studies in Management, Brussels.

Jørgensen, S. (1981), "En Note om Dorfman-Steiner Teoremet", Nationaløkonomisk Tidsskrift, Vol. 119, pp. 409-413.

Jørgensen, S. (1982a), "A Differential Game Solution to an Investment and Pricing Problem", Paper presented at "Tenth Optimization Days", Montreal.

Jørgensen, S. (1982b), "A Survey of Some Differential Games in Advertising", Journal of Economic Dynamics and Control, Vol. 4, pp. 341-369.

Jørgensen, S. (1983), "Optimal Control of a Diffusion Model of New Product Acceptance with Price-dependent Total Market Potential", Optimal Control Applications and Methods, Vol. 4, pp. 269-276.

Jørgensen, S. (1986), "Optimal Production, Purchasing and Pricing: A Differential Game Approach", European Journal of Operational Research, Vol. 23, pp.

Kalish, S. (1983), "Monopolist Pricing with Dynamic Demand and Production Cost", Marketing Science, Vol. 2, pp. 135-160.

Kalish, S. (1984), "A New Product Adoption Model with Price, Advertising and Uncertainty", Working Paper, University of Rochester.

Kalish, S. and S.K. Sen (1985), "Diffusion Models and the Marketing Mix for Single Products" in Advances in Product and Marketing Strategy, II, Innovation Diffusion and Growth Models, J. Wind and V. Mahajan (Eds.), pp.

Kamien, M.I. and N.L. Schwartz (1971), "Limit Pricing and Uncertain Entry", Econometrica, Vol. 39, pp. 441-454.

Kamien, M.I. and N.L. Schwartz (1981), Dynamic Optimization: The Calculus of Variations and Optimal Control in Economics and Management, North-Holland, London.

Lambin, J.J., P.A. Naert and A. Bultez (1975), "Optimal Marketing Behavior in Oligopoly", European Economic Review, Vol. 6, pp. 105-128.

Lieber, Z. and A. Barnea (1977), "Dynamic Optimal Pricing to Deter Entry under Constrained Supply", Operations Research, Vol. 25, pp. 696-705.

Lewis, T.R. and R. Schmalensee (1980a), "On Oligopolistic Markets for Nonrenewable Natural Resources" Quarterly Journal of Economics, Vol. XCV, pp. 475-491.

Lewis, T.R. and R. Schmalensee (1980b), "Cartel and Oligopoly Pricing of Non-replenishable Natural Resources" in Dynamic Optimization and Mathematical Economics, P.T. Liu (Ed.), Plenum Press, New York, pp. 133-156.

Luptacik, M. (1982), "Optimal Price and Advertising Policy under Atomistic Competition", Journal of Economic Dynamics and Control, Vol. 4, pp. 57-71.

Mahajan, V. and E. Muller (1979), "Innovation Diffusion and New Product Growth Models in Marketing", Journal of Marketing, Vol. 43, pp. 55-68.

Mahajan, V. and R.A. Peterson (1978), "Innovation Diffusion in a Dynamic Potential Adopter Population", Management Science, Vol. 24, pp. 1589-1597.

Mahajan, V. and R.A. Peterson (1982), "Erratum to: Innovation Diffusion in a Dynamic Potential Adopter Population", Management Science, Vol. 28, p. 1087.

Mahajan, V. and R.A. Peterson (1984), "Innovation Diffusion: Models and Applications", Working Paper No. 84-112, Southern Methodist University, Dallas, Tx.

Mahajan, V., E. Muller and R.A. Kerin (1984), "Introduction Strategy for New Products with Positive and Negative Word-of-Mouth" Management Science, Vol. 30, pp. 1389-1404.

Mahajan, V., S. Sharma and J. Wind (1983), "An Approach to Repeat-Purchase Diffusion Analysis", Working Paper No. 83-106, Southern Methodist University, Dallas, Tx.

Milgrom, P. and J. Roberts (1982), "Limit Pricing and Entry under Incomplete Information: An Equilibrium Analysis", Econometrica, Vol. 50, pp. 443-459.

Miller, R.E. (1979), Dynamic Optimization and Economic Applications, McGraw-Hill, New York.

Monroe, K.B. and A.J. Della Bitta (1978), "Models for Pricing Decisions", Journal of Marketing Research, Vol. 15, pp. 413-428.

Moorthy, K.S. (1984), "Using Game Theory to Model Competition", Working Paper, Yale School of Management, New Haven, CT.

Nagle, T. (1984), "Economic Foundations for Pricing", Journal of Business, Vol. 57, pp. 3-38.

Nerlove, M. and K.J. Arrow (1962), "Optimal Advertising Policy under Dynamic Conditions", Economica, Vol. 39, pp. 129-142.

Pashigian, B.P. (1968), "Limit Price and the Market Share of the Leading Firm", Journal of Industrial Economics, Vol. 16, pp. 165-177.

Pekelman, D. (1974), "Simultaneous Price-production Decisions", Operations Research, Vol. 22, pp. 788-794.

Phelps, E.S. and S.G. Winter (1971), "Optimal Price Policy under Atomistic Competition" in Microeconomic Foundations of Employment and Inflation Theory, E.S. Phelps et al. (Eds.), MacMillan, New York.

Rao, V.R. (1984), "Pricing Research in Marketing: The State of the Art", Journal of Business, Vol. 57, pp. 39-60.

Reinganum, J.F. (1982), "A Class of Differential Games for Which the Closed-loop and Open-loop Nash Equilibria Coincide", Journal of Optimization Theory and Applications, Vol. 36, pp. 253-262.

Reinganum, J.F. and N.L. Stokey (1985), "Oligopoly Extraction of a Common Property Natural Resource: The Importance of the Period of Commitment in Dynamic Games", International Economic Review, Vol. 26, pp. 161-173.

Reynolds, S.S. (1985), "A Differential Game Approach to Oligopolistic Interdependence", Working Paper, Department of Economics, University of Arizona, Tucson, Az.

Robinson, V. and C. Lakhani (1975), "Dynamic Price Models for New Product Planning", Management Science, Vol. 21, pp. 1113-1132.

Roos, C.F. (1925), "A Mathematical Theory of Competition", American Journal of Mathematics, Vol. 47, pp. 163-175.

Salop, S.C. (1939), "Strategic Entry Deterrence", American Economic Review, Vol. 69, No. 2, pp. 335-338.

Schmalensee, R. (1972), The Economics of Advertising, North-Holland, Amsterdam.

Seglin, L. (1963), "How to Price New Products", Chemical Engineering, September, pp. 181-184.

Sethi, S.P. (1977), "Dynamic Optimal Control Models in Advertising: A Survey", SIAM Review, Vol. 19, pp. 685-725.

Sheshinski, E. and Y. Weiss (1977), "Inflation and Costs of Price Adjustment", Review of Economic Studies, Vol. XLIV (2), No. 137, pp. 287-303.

Shubik, M. (1980), Market Structure and Behavior, Harvard University Press, Cambridge, MA.

Shubik, M. (1982), "Game Theory Models and Methods", in Handbook of Mathematical Economics, Vol. I, K.J. Arrow and M.D. Intriligator (Eds.), North-Holland, Amsterdam, pp. 285-330.

Shubik, M. (1982a), Game Theory in the Social Sciences. Concepts and Solutions, The MIT Press, Cambridge, Mass.

Shubik, M. and M.J. Sobel (1980), "Stochastic Games, Oligopoly Theory, and Competitive Resource Allocation", in Dynamic Optimization and Mathematical Economics, P.T. Liu (Ed.), Plenum Press, New York, pp. 89-100.

Shupp, F.R. (1977), "Dynamic Limit Pricing in a Mature Market", in Mathematical Economics and Game Theory, Essays in Honor of Oskar Morgenstern, Springer Lecture Notes in Economics and Mathematical Systems, 141, pp. 435-445.

Shupp, F.R. (1985), "Limit Pricing in a Mature Market: A Dynamic Game Approach", Paper presented at the 7th Annual Conference on Economic Dynamics and Control, London, June.

Simaan, M. and J.B. Cruz (1973), "On the Stackelberg Strategy in Nonzero-sum Games", Journal of Optimization Theory and Applications, Vol. 11, pp. 613-626.

Simon, H. (1982), "Pricestrat - An Applied Strategic Pricing Model for Nondurables", in Marketing Planning Models, A.A. Zoltners (Ed.), North-Holland, Amsterdam, pp. 23-41.

Spence, A.M. (1977), "Entry, Capacity, Investment and Oligopolistic Pricing", Bell Journal of Economics, Vol. 8, pp. 534-544.

Spence, A.M. (1981), "The Learning Curve and Competition", Bell Journal of Economics, Vol. 12, No. 1, pp. 49-70.

Spremann, K. (1975), "Optimale Preispolitik bei Dynamischen Deterministischen Absatzmodellen", Zeitschrift für Nationalökonomie, Vol. 35, pp. 63-73.

Spremann, K. (1981), "Hybrid Product Life Cycles and the Nerlove-Arrow Theorem", Working Paper, University of Ulm, W. Germany.

Spremann, K. (1985), "The Signalling of Quality by Reputation", in Optimal Control Theory and Economic Analysis 2, G. Feichtinger (Ed.), North-Holland, Amsterdam, pp. 235-252.

Takayama, A. (1974), Mathematical Economics, Dryden Press, Hinsdale, Ill.

Tapiero, C.S. (1974), "Optimum Price Switching", International Journal of Systems Science, Vol. 5, pp. 83-96.

Telser, L.G. (1972), Competition, Collusion and Game Theory, MacMillan, London.

Telser, L.G. and R.L. Graves (1972), Functional Analysis in Mathematical Economics, The University of Chicago Press.

Teng, J.T. and G.L. Thompson (1985), "Optimal Strategies for General Price-advertising Models", in Optimal Control Theory and Economic Analysis 2, G. Feichtinger (Ed.), North-Holland, Amsterdam, pp. 183-195.

Thépot, J. (1983), "Marketing and Investment Policies of Duopolists in a Growing Industry", Journal of Economic Dynamics & Control, Vol. 5, No. 4, pp. 387-404.

Thompson, G.L. and J.-T. Teng (1984), "Optimal Pricing and Advertising Policies for New Product Oligopoly Models", Marketing Science, Vol. 3, No. 2, pp. 148-168.

Tintner, G. (1937), "Monopoly Over Time", Econometrica, Vol. 5, pp. 160-170.

Wernerfelt, B. (1984), "Consumers with Differing Reaction Speeds, Scale Advantages and Industry Structure", European Economic Review, Vol. 24, pp. 257-270.

Wirl, F. (1985), "Stable and Volatile Prices: An Explanation by Dynamic Demand", in Optimal Control Theory and Economic Analysis 2, G. Feichtinger (Ed.), North-Holland, Amsterdam, pp. 263-278.

Wolf, G. and M. Shubik (1978), "Market Structure, Opponent Behavior and Information in a Market Game", Decision Sciences, Vol. 9, pp. 421-428.

Yoon, E. and G.L. Lilien (1985), "New Product Pricing Strategies in Monopoly-duopoly Markets: An Extension of the Eliashberg-Jeuland Model", Working Paper, College of Business Administration, Pennsylvania State University.

References Added in Proof

Geroski, P.A., L. Philips and A. Ulph (1985), "Oligopoly, Competition and Welfare: Some Recent Developments", Journal of Industrial Economics, Vol. 33, No. 4, 369-386.

Harrington, J.E. (1984), "Noncooperative Behavior by a Cartel as an Entry-deterring Signal", Rand Journal of Economics, Vol. 15, No. 3, pp. 426-433.

LIST OF SYMBOLS

M = number of firms

i,j = indices; i,j=1,...,M

t = current time

T = terminal time

r = discount rate

q,Q = quantity, output, demand

x,X = {cumulative sales (number of adopters) / sales rate}

S = market share

N = max(x) or max(X)

p = price

$\bar{p}$ = average price

p_m = myopic price

p_L = limit price

V = reservation price

C = total cost function

c_o = fixed cost

J = payoff functional

A = advertising rate

u = investment or R&D expenditures

w = production rate

G = goodwill or brand loyalty

I = number of persons aware of an innovation

L = reputation

v = clientele

y = stock of resource, inventory

f,F,g,h,H,m,R,U = functions

a,b,d,n,k,K,s,α,β,γ,δ,ε,η,σ,τ = parameters

DYNAMIC ADVERTISING AND PRICING IN AN OLIGOPOLY: A NASH EQUILIBRIUM APPROACH

Engelbert Dockner
Institute of Economic Theory and Policy
University of Economics
A-1090, Augasse 2-6, Vienna Austria

Gustav Feichtinger
Institute for Econometrics and Operations Research
University of Technology
A-1040, Argentinierstraße 8, Vienna Austria

Abstract

A general dynamic oligopolistic price-advertising model is formulated and open-loop Nash solutions are derived. As a main result a generalisation of the well known Dorfman - Steiner - Theorem to heterogenous oligopoly markets is presented. Furthermore a detailed discussion of long run equilibrium solutions is given. For an important special case of the general model formulation it is shown that the optimal advertising policies are constant over time and constitute degenerated feedback solutions.

1. Introduction

It is an empirical fact (see e.g. Schmalensee (1972)) that advertising strategies of many firms acting in different markets (monopoly, oligopoly) are based on a constant percent of sales rule. In their pioneering paper Dorfman and Steiner (1954) were among the first in giving a theoretical foundation to that phenomenon, but for the static monopoly case only. Their result states that a monopolist facing a price and advertising dependent demand function will advertise until the ratio of dollar advertising to dollar sales is equal to the ratio of advertising elasticity of demand to price elasticity of demand (Dorfman - Steiner - Theorem). Schmalensee (1972) and many others (Eeckhoudt (1972), Jacquemin (1973), Teng and Thompson (1985), Dockner et al. (1985)) generalized that result to a dynamic framework, but also treated the monopoly case. Lambin et al. (1975), however, generalized the Dorfman - Steiner - Theorem to the static oligopoly case. But there is still a lack to extend it to a dynamic oligopoly setting.

The present paper is an attempt to fill this gap. It analyzes optimal advertising and pricing strategies of firms acting in a market with few sellers and differentiated products (heterogeneous oligopoly) and states conditions under which a constant percent of sales advertising rule is consistent with rational firm behavior (in the sense of profit maximization) also for the dynamic oligopoly case. It should be noted that Schmalensee (1972) treats a dynamic oligopoly model, too, but he only considers the question of optimal advertising policies and assumes a constant price for all firms (monopoly price). The aim of our paper is to study the case of oligopolistic price and advertising competition where we assume that the firms own price and advertising rate are the instruments under the firms control to influence equilibrium demand of the products. Thus, we are focusing on the question of price and advertising determination in industries selling heterogeneous products and analyze it by using a dynamic analytic model. See, however, Schmalensee (1976) for an argument that price competition is relatively rare in markets with differentiated products.

In order to construct analytical modles of oligopoly markets it is necessary to make assumptions on the behavior of the firms due to actions of their competitors, i.e. to make assumptions on their reaction functions. According to the theory of differential games and the solution concepts available we choose the Nash equilibrium approach which corresponds to the "classical" Cournot assumption in the case of a homogeneous oligopoly market (quantity setting instead of price setting). As Schmalensee (1976) pointed out there are some arguments for justifying this assumption in the non price competition case, which are still valid in the case of price and advertising competition. There is at least a rather technical argument: a Cournot (Nash) like reaction pattern leads to more or less "tractable" models of oligopoly competition.

The paper is organized as follows: in Section 2 the dynamic oligopoly model is presented and the assumptions are stated. Section 3 starts with a discussion of the necessary optimality conditions and is followed by some immediate conclusions. Here a generalization of the well known Dorman - Steiner - Theorem for dynamic oligopolies is presented. In Section 4 we characterize the long run equilibrium solutions and give economic interpretations in terms of long run elaticities, whereas Section 5 covers a result concerning the global asymptotic stability of these solutions. In Section 6 we briefly present an interesting special case of our general model and Section 7 concludes the paper.

2. The model

We now formulate the dynamic oligopoly model. Let $N \geq 2$ be the number of firms producing a differentiated product. Assume that at every moment of time there is an equilibrium demand of player i, $f^i(p_1, \ldots, p_N, a_1, \ldots, a_N)$, depending on the prices p_i set by the oligopolists and their advertising rates a_i. We suppose that for i = 1, ..., N

$$f^i_{p_i} < 0, \; f^i_{p_j} > 0 \quad \text{for } j \neq i \tag{1a}$$

$$f^i_{a_i} > 0, \; f^i_{a_i a_i} < 0, \; f^i_{a_j} < 0 \quad \text{for } j \neq i \tag{1b}$$

Further we assume that the determinants of the matrices M_a and M_p defined by

$$M_a = \begin{bmatrix} f^1_{a_1 a_1} & \ldots & f^1_{a_1 a_N} \\ \cdot & & \cdot \\ \cdot & & \cdot \\ \cdot & & \cdot \\ f^N_{a_1 a_N} & \ldots & f^N_{a_N a_N} \end{bmatrix} \qquad M_p = \begin{bmatrix} f^1_{p_1} & \ldots & f^1_{p_N} \\ \cdot & & \cdot \\ \cdot & & \cdot \\ \cdot & & \cdot \\ f^N_{p_1} & \ldots & f^N_{p_N} \end{bmatrix} \tag{1c}$$

have the sign

$$\text{sign}(\det M_a) = \text{sign}(\det M_p) = \text{sign}(-1)^N \tag{1d}$$

Thus, in the case of N = 2 we have $\det M_a > 0$, $\det M_p > 0$ (cf. Thépot (1983)).

The assumptions (1ab) are classical ones implying that advertising expenditures are subject to decreasing returns. Assumption (1d) states that a firm's price change (advertising variation, respectively) has a higher impact on its equilibrium demand than on that of the competitors (i.e. the "direct" effects of a price (advertsising) variation are globally stronger than the "indirect" ones). Notice that for example in a two player model $f^i_{p_i} + f^i_{p_j} < 0$ implies $\det M_p > 0$.

The actual demand of the i-th firm is denoted by s_i. Actual demand is not generally equal to equilibrium demand because of costs of change or costs of breaking habits (cf. Schmalensee (1972), p. 26). It moves towards f^i (which depends on the prices and advertising rates) by the simple adjustment mechanism

$$\dot{s}_i = \alpha_i[f^i(p_1, \ldots, p_N, a_1, \ldots, a_N) - s_i] \; . \tag{2}$$

Here, α_i is a positive constant adjustment coefficient of player i. Moreover the production costs $c_i(s_i)$ are assumed to be convex with

$$c_i(0) = 0, \; c_i'(0) = 0, \; c_i'(s_i) > 0 \text{ for } s_i > 0, \; c_i''(s_i) > 0 \tag{3}$$

Finally, k_i are the constant unit costs of advertising, and r_i denotes the discount rate of the i-th firm in the oligopoly.

Player i faces the problem of choosing the time paths of p_i and a_i so as to maximize the present value of the stream of profits

$$J_i = \int_0^\infty e^{-r_i t}[p_i s_i - c_i(s_i) - k_i a_i]dt \tag{4}$$

under the system dynamics (2), where the initial state $s_i(0) = s_{io} \geq 0$ is given. It should be noted that Fershtman and Kamien (1984) solved a similar duopoly model to the one described by (1) - (4). Instead of dealing with a heterogeneous market they discuss a homogeneous one and focus primarily on the price adjustment speed of the unique market price. Moreover for a general survey on oligopolistic pricing models and related topics we refer the reader to Jørgensen (1985).

3. Optimality Conditions

To calculate open-loop Nash solutions for the differential game defined in Section 2, we define the current - value Hamiltonian for player i (cf., e.g. Başar and Olsder (1982)):

$$H^i = p_i s_i - c_i(s_i) - k_i a_i + \sum_{j=1}^{N} \lambda_j^i \alpha_j (f^j - s_j)$$

The adjoint variable λ_j^i can be interpreted as the shadow price of the state variable s_j as assessed by player i. From now on unless otherwise stated we restrict ourselves to the case of N = 2 firms.

Necessary conditions for an open-loop Nash equilibrium are given by the adjoint equations (see (5)) and the Hamiltonian maximizing conditions (see (6)).

$$\begin{aligned} \dot{\lambda}_i^i &= r_i \lambda_i^i - H_{s_i}^i = (r_i + \alpha_i)\lambda_i^i - p_i + c_i' \\ \dot{\lambda}_j^i &= r_i \lambda_j^i - H_{s_j}^i = (r_i + \alpha_j)\lambda_j^i \quad \text{for } j \neq i \end{aligned} \tag{5}$$

It turns out that the costate variables λ_j^i are redundant in the sense of Dockner et al. (1985), i.e. $\lambda_j^i = 0$ for $j \neq i$. Thus, we get by defining $\lambda_i = \lambda_i^i$

$$H^i = p_i s_i - c_i(s_i) - k_i a_i + \lambda_i \alpha_i (f^i - s_i).$$

The maximizing conditions for interior solutions are

$$H_{p_i}^i = s_i + \lambda_i \alpha_i f_{p_i}^i = 0 \tag{6a}$$

$$H^i_{a_i} = - k_i + \lambda_i \alpha_i f^i_{a_i} = 0 \qquad (6b)$$

To get a maximum of the Hamiltonians with respect to p_i and a_i we assume that the second order conditions are met. Thus we have to impose further that

$$f^i_{p_i p_i} < 0 \quad \text{and} \quad f^i_{p_i p_i} f^i_{a_i a_i} - (f^i_{a_i p_i})^2 > 0$$

holds, i.e. the demand functions are jointly concave in (p_i, a_i). Wirl (1985) studies the implications of concave and convex price-dependent demand functions respectively but for the monopoly case. It turns out that convex demand functions lead to volatile prices (i.e. a "zig-zag" policy). The second order maximization conditions do not, however, guarentee that we get optimal solutions for the differential game defined above. Rather the sufficient conditions have to be satisfied (see Leitmann and Schmitendorf (1978)). But for our problem formulation it is easy to verify these conditions.

From (1) and (6a) or (6b), respectively, we get the result that

$$\lambda_i \geq 0 \text{ for } t \in [0, \infty) \qquad (7)$$

i.e. an additional unit of sales of a firm is positively assessed by that firm which makes economic sense. Defining $\pi_i = - f^i_{p_i} p_i / f^i$ as the price elasticity of equilibrium demand of firm i, and $\omega_i = f^i_{a_i} a_i / f^i$ as the advertising elasticity of equilibrium demand of firm i we get by combination of (6a) and (6b)

$$\alpha_i \lambda_i = \frac{a_i k_i}{f^i_{a_i} a_i} = - \frac{p_i s_i}{f^i_{p_i} p_i} \qquad (8)$$

which leads us to

Theorem 1 (Dorfman - Steiner - Theorem): Firm i will advertise until the ratio of advertising expenditures to revenue is equal to the ratio of advertising elasticity of equilibrium demand to price elasticity of equilibrium demand, i.e.

$$\frac{a_i k_i}{p_i s_i} = \frac{\omega_i}{\pi_i} \qquad (9)$$

Theorem 1 implies for the case of a constant elasticity ratio (ω_i / π_i) a defense for the advertising policy based on a percent of sales rule. To study optimal price and advertising strategies in more detail we specify equilibrium demand functions as

$$f^i(p_i,p_j,a_i,a_j) = b_i - p_i^{\gamma_i} + p_j^{\mu_i} + a_i^{\upsilon_i} a_j^{-\varphi_i} \tag{10}$$

where b_i, γ_i, μ_i, υ_i and φ_i are positive constants. Demand specification (10) implies that marginal demand with respect to the price of the own firm is independent of all other marketing instruments, which is a rather restrictive assumption. According to (1a-d) the following parameter constraints have to be satisfied (cf. Thépot (1983)).

$$\gamma_i > 1; \mu_i \geq 0 \tag{11a}$$

$$0 < \upsilon_i < 1; \varphi_i \geq 0 \tag{11b}$$

$$\Delta = (1-\upsilon_1)(1-\upsilon_2) - \varphi_1\varphi_2 > 0 \tag{11c}$$

Substitution of (10) into the optimality conditions (6ab) yields

$$s_i - \lambda_i \alpha_i \gamma_i p_i^{\gamma_i - 1} = 0 \tag{12a}$$

$$- k_i + \lambda_i \alpha_i \upsilon_i a_i^{\upsilon_i - 1} a_j^{-\varphi_j} = 0 \tag{12b}$$

From (12ab) we get by use of the implicit function theorem that $p_i = p_i(s_i,\lambda_i)$ and $a_i = a_i(\lambda_i,\lambda_j)$ with

$$\partial p_i/\partial s_i > 0, \quad \partial p_i/\partial \lambda_i < 0 \tag{13}$$

$$\partial a_i/\partial \lambda_i > 0, \quad \partial a_i/\partial \lambda_j < 0 \tag{14}$$

(13) states that (i) as long as sales of firm i are increasing (decreasing) (i.e. equilibrium demand is higher (lower) than actual demand) the price of that firm has to be increased (decreased) to reach equilibrium demand; (ii) as long as future sales of firm i are increasingly (decreasingly) valued by itself the price has to be decreased (increased) which makes economic sense. (14) states that as long as future sales of firm i are increasingly (decreasingly) valued by itself advertising has to be increased (decreased). (13) and (14) together yield the following

Theorem 2: Under the assumptions (10) and (11) the optimal price and advertising strategy of firm i is characterized by the following relationships

$$\frac{df^i}{d\lambda_i} > 0 \tag{15}$$

$$\frac{df^i}{ds_i} < 0 \tag{16}$$

The proof follows immediately from (10),(11), (13) and (14).

These are the expected results: when sales of firm i are more highly valued by itself the optimal strategies have to be set to increase them. When actual sales of firm i are increasing (decreasing) the optimal strategies have to decrease (increase) equilibrium demand to reach actual demand. This is a generalization of the results known from the monopoly case (Schmalensee (1972)) to oligopolistic markets.

To get deeper insights in the dynamic interactions of prices and advertising rates we differentiate (12) with respect to time and obtain

$$(\gamma_i - 1)\frac{\dot{p}_i}{p_i} = \frac{\dot{s}_i}{s_i} - \frac{\dot{\lambda}_i}{\lambda_i} \tag{17a}$$

$$\frac{\dot{a}_i}{a_i} = (1/\Delta)((1-\upsilon_i)\frac{\dot{\lambda}_i}{\lambda_i} - \varphi_i\frac{\dot{\lambda}_j}{\lambda_j}) \tag{17b}$$

For $s_i > f^i$ it holds in the case of $p_i > c_i'$ and $(p_i - c_i')/p_i < 1/\dot{\pi}_i$ that

$$\frac{\dot{\lambda}_i}{\lambda_i} > (r_i + \alpha_i) - \alpha_i\pi_i[1 - \frac{c_i'}{p_i}] > 0. \tag{18}$$

Thus we have established that as long as actual demand for both firms is higher than equilibrium demand the prices have to be decreased, i.e.

$$\dot{s}_i < 0 \implies \dot{\lambda}_i > 0 \implies \dot{p}_i < 0. \tag{19}$$

This result is again a generalization of the monopoly case. For the case of $s_i < f^i$ and s_i very small the opposite is likely to occur; i.e.

$$\dot{s}_i > 0 \implies \dot{\lambda}_i < 0 \implies \dot{p}_i > 0. \tag{20}$$

The results of (19) and (20) allow for the following interpretation. Whenever actual demand is higher (lower) than equlibrium demand actual sales are decreasing (increasing) according to the adjustment mechanism (2) and the corresponding shadow prices are increasing (decreasing). Thus, to reach equilibrium demand prices have to be decreased (increased). The results of the corresponding advertising strategies are not uniform however. In the case of a constant elasticity ratio they are put together in the following Corollary.

Corollary 1: For the case of a constant elasticity ratio ω_i/π_i

$$\text{(i) } \dot{s}_i < 0 \text{ and } \dot{p}_i < 0 \Longrightarrow \dot{a}_i < 0$$

$$\text{(ii) } \dot{s}_i > 0 \text{ and } \dot{p}_i > 0 \Longrightarrow \dot{a}_i > 0$$

holds.
The proof follows immediately from (9).

The results of Corollary 1 can be interpreted as follows: as long as equilibrium demand of firm i is lower than actual demand and prices are decreasing to stimulate equilibrium demand, advertising expendiutres can be reduced. This implies that the firms should concentrate on price policy rather than on the advertising strategy. In the reverse case, if actual demand is lower than equilibrium demand and prices are increasing advertising expenditures have to be increased. Now firms have to concentrate on advertising rather than on pricing policies. These results seem to be opposite to the ones of Theorem 2 but are consequences of the constant elasticity ratio.

So far we have studied optimal solution patterns and marketing and competition interactions. In the following Section we turn to determine long run equilibrium solutions and to interpret them economically.

4. Characterization of the Long Run Equilibrium Solution

To study long run equilibrium solutions we compute the steady state of system (2) and (5)

$$\dot{s}_i = 0 \Longleftrightarrow s_i^\infty = f^i \qquad (21a)$$

$$\dot{\lambda}_i = 0 \Longleftrightarrow \lambda_i^\infty = \frac{p_i^\infty - c_i'}{r_i + \alpha_i}. \qquad (21b)$$

Substitution of (21ab) into the maximization conditions (6ab) yields

$$f^i + \frac{\alpha_i}{r_i + \alpha_i}(p_i - c_i')f^i_{p_i} = 0. \qquad (22)$$

From (22) we get by use of the elasticities defined above

$$p_i^\infty = \frac{\pi_i \alpha_i/(r_i + \alpha_i)}{\pi_i \alpha_i/(r_i + \alpha_i) - 1}\, c_i' \qquad (23)$$

(23) is an Amoroso - Robinson - type relation which says that the long run optimal price is higher than the marginal costs. If we rearrange (23) we get

$$\frac{\alpha_i}{r_i+\alpha_i}\frac{(p_i^\infty-c_i^!)}{p_i^\infty}=\frac{1}{\pi_i} \tag{24}$$

If we interpret $(p_i^\infty-c_i^!)/p_i^\infty$ according to Lerner's degree of monopoly power as a measure of oligopoly power of firm i (cf. Lerner (1934)), condition (24) states that the long run degree of oligopoly power of firm i is equal to the reciprocal value of the price elasticity of equilibrium demand:

$$L^i=\frac{\alpha_i}{r_i+\alpha_i}\left[\frac{p_i^\infty-c_i^!}{p_i^\infty}\right]=\frac{1}{\pi_i} \tag{25}$$

(25) states that the higher the elasticity π_i will be the lower is the long run degree of oligopoly power ceteris paribus. It is important to notice that if equilibrium demand of firm i is given as

$$f^i(p_i,p_j,a_i,a_j)=g^i(p_i)h^i(p_j,a_i,a_j) \tag{26}$$

(i.e. multiplicatively separable) and marginal costs are constant, then the optimal long run oligopolistic equilibrium price coincides with the corresponding monopoly price. Thus each oligopolist acts in the long run like a monopolist.

Now let us turn to the analysis of long run advertising strategies. Using (21) and (6b) we get

$$k_i=\frac{\alpha_i}{r_i+\alpha_i}(p_i^\infty-c_i^!)f_{a_i}^i. \tag{27}$$

Rearranging (27) yields by the use of the advertising elasticity of demand, ω_i,

$$\frac{a_i^\infty k_i}{p_i^\infty f^i}=\frac{\alpha_i}{r_i+\alpha_i}\frac{(p_i^\infty-c_i^!)}{p_i^\infty}\omega_i, \tag{28}$$

i.e.

$$\frac{a_i^\infty k_i}{p_i^\infty f^i}=L^i\omega_i \tag{29}$$

(29) gives rise to the following interpretation: in the long run the ratio of advertising to sales is equal to the product of the degree of oligopoly power and the advertising elasticity of equilibrium demand.

Thus, an increase of advertising activities relatively to sales results in a higher degree of oligopoly power, ceteris paribus, which in turn implies using (25) a lower price elasticity of demand. Thus "heavy" advertising leads to a reduction of equilibrium priceelasticity of demand, ceteris paribus.

5. Global Stability Results for Equilibrium Solutions

In this Section we treat the global stability properties of Nash equilibrium solutions given by the necessary optimality conditions (2),(5) and (6). We show by using a theorem developed by Haurie and Leitmann (1984) that all uniformly bounded solutions converge to the unique steady state solution defined by (21). According to Haurie and Leitmann (1984) we use vector Ljapunov functions to derive this global stability result. To simplify the proofs we again treat the case of N = 2 players. By the use of the implicit function theorem we get from the maximizing conditions (6) that

$$p_i = \tilde{p}_i(s_1,s_2,\lambda_1,\lambda_2) \tag{30a}$$

$$a_i = \tilde{a}_i(s_1,s_2,\lambda_1,\lambda_2) \tag{30b}$$

Thus, the modified Hamiltonian dynamic system is the differential equation system in $(s_1,s_2,\lambda_1,\lambda_2)$ given by

$$\begin{aligned}
\dot{s}_1 &= \alpha_1[f^1(\tilde{p}_1,\tilde{p}_2,\tilde{a}_1,\tilde{a}_2) - s_1] \\
\dot{s}_2 &= \alpha_2[f^2(\tilde{p}_1,\tilde{p}_2,\tilde{a}_1,\tilde{a}_2) - s_2] \\
\dot{\lambda}_1 &= (r_1+\alpha_1)\lambda_1 - \tilde{p}_1 + c_1' \\
\dot{\lambda}_2 &= (r_2+\alpha_2)\lambda_2 - \tilde{p}_2 + c_2'
\end{aligned} \tag{31}$$

It is easy to verify that system (31) possesses a unique steady state solution, wich we characterized in the preceeding saction. We now transform the solution $z = (p_1^\infty,p_2^\infty,a_1^\infty,a_2^\infty)$ into $z' = (0,0,0,0)$. From the theory of Hamiltonian dynamical systems we know that the canonical system of an optimal controlproblem can never be stable. All that can be expected is the saddle-point "stability". Here we prove that the dynamical modified Hamiltonian system (31) has the saddle-point property. We state the result in the form that all uniformly bounded solutions of system (31) converge to the steady state z (or z'), i.e. there exists a global manifold such that all solutions emanating from this manifold converge to the steady state.

Theorem 3: Under the assumptions (10) and (11) system (31) has a unique stationary state. Moreover all bounded state and costate solutions corresponding to open-loop Nash equilibria must converge to $(p_1^\infty, p_2^\infty, a_1^\infty, a_2^\infty)$

The proof is a straight forward application of Lemma 6.1 of Haurie and Leitmann (1984) using the same vector valued Ljapunov function.

The result of Theorem 3 is not surprising since it is a consequence of the adjustment mechanism (2) which constitutes a stable system.

6. An Important Special Case

In this Section we consider the case where equilibrium demand is only a function of advertising. Thus we suppress the price dependency and study only optimal advertising strategies. This can be justified by an argument of Schmalensee (1976) who writes that "it is a generally accepted 'stylized fact' that price competition is relatively rare in markets with few sellers and differentiated products" (Schmalensee (1976), p. 493). We make a second assumption by considering a constant market price and constant marginal costs. Through these assumptions we obtain the following advertising differential game with

$$\dot{s}_i = \alpha_i [f^i(a_1, \ldots, a_N) - s_i] \tag{32}$$

$$s_i(0) = s_{io} \text{ given}$$

as the state equations and

$$J_i = \int_0^\infty e^{-r_i t} [m_i s_i - k_i a_i] dt \tag{33}$$

as the objective functions. m_i is the difference between constant price and constant marginal production cost. For a general survey of oligopolistic advertising models see Jørgensen (1982).

Studying problem (32), (33) in more detail it turns out that the game is state separable and therefore according to (5) qualitatively solvable, i.e. the Nash equilibrium solutions are governed by a differential equation system in the controls only. To get deeper insights into the qualitative behavior of optimal advertising solutions we therefore derive that differential equation system and discuss it.

According to (32) and (33) the maximizing conditions (6) and the adjoint equations (5) are independent of the current state. By differentiation of (6b) with respect to time and substitution of (6b) into (5) we get the differential equation system in the controls a_i

$$\frac{k_i f^i_{a_i a_i}}{\alpha_i f^i_{a_i}} \dot{a}_i + \frac{k_i}{\alpha_i f^i_{a_i}} \sum_{\substack{j=1 \\ i \neq j}}^{N} f^i_{a_i a_j} \dot{a}_j = - f^i_{a_i} \left[\frac{(r_i + \alpha_i) k_i}{\alpha_i f^i_{a_i}} - m_i \right] \qquad (34)$$

The following Theorem characterizes the optimal solutions of system (34)

Theorem 4: Under the assumptions $r_i = r$, $\alpha_i = \alpha$ for all i, system (34) is completely unstable and the characteristic roots of the linearized system are given by $l_i = r + \alpha$. The optimal strategies are constant and given by the steady state solution of system (34).

The proof of Theorem 4 is a straight forward application of Proposition 5.2 in Dockner et al. (1985).

Theorem 4 is an interesting result because it characterizes optimal advertising solutions which are constant over the planning period $[0,\infty)$. In Section 3 we have characterized optimal advertising policies which are based on a constant percent of sales rule. It is obvious that for the constant solution given by Theorem 3 the following holds

$$\frac{a_i k_i}{p_i f^i} = \frac{m_i \alpha_i}{p_i (r_i + \alpha_i)} \omega_i \qquad (35)$$

which means that this solution is also based on a constant percent of sales rule according to equilibrium demand f^i. Thus we have established a second argument for justifying the empirical advertising rule mentioned in the introduction. Furthermore the solutions given by Theorem 4 constitute feedback solutions in the sense that the closed-loop (feedback) solitions are degenerated and coincide with the open-loop solutions. It should be noted that the advertising model studied by Leitmann and Schmitendorf (1976) also possesses these properties.

7. Conclusions

In this paper we studied optimal advertising and pricing strategies for a firm acting in a market with few sellers and differentiated products. A dynamic oligopolistic model was formulated and open-loop Nash solutions derived. The model was interpreted as a generalization of the advertising differential game considered by Schmalensee (1972). As a key result it turned out that empirical observed advertising strategies based on a constant percent of sales rule are consistent with rational firm behavior in oligopolistic markets, i.e. a generalization of the well known Dorfman - Steiner - Theorem was obtained. As a general rule we established the result that optimal policies should be set in a way such that equilibrium demand is increased (decreased) whenever actual sales of the firm considered are higher (lower) than equilibrium demand.

In a special example we discussed conditions under which constant advertising strategies are optimal even for the case of no constant elasticity ratio. Trivially this solutions were also based on a constant percent of sales rule. According to the stability properties of the dynamic system it was shown that each bounded optimal solution converges to the steady state solution of the pseudo - Hamiltonian system.

Acknowledgement

We would like to thank Steffen Jørgensen and Henry Y. Wan, Jr. for valuable comments.

8. References

Başar, T. and G.J. Olsder (1982), Dynamic Noncooperative Game Theory, Academic Press, London.

Dockner, E., G. Feichtinger and S. Jørgensen (1985), "Tractable Classes of Nonzero-Sum Open-Loop Nash Differential Games: Theory and Examples Journal of Optimization Theory and Applications, vol. 45, pp.179-197.

Dockner, E., G. Feichtinger and G. Sorger (1985), "Interaction of Price and Advertising under Dynamic Conditions," Working Paper, University of Economics and Technical University, Vienna.

Dorfman, R. and P.O. Steiner (1954), "Optimal Advertising and Optimal Quality," American Economic Review, vol. 4, pp.826-836.

Eeckhoudt, L.R. (1972), "The 'Dorfman Steiner' Rule," Zeitschrift für Nationalökonomie, vol.32, pp.487-491.

Fershtman, C. and M.I. Kamien (1984), "Price Adjustment Speed and Dynamic Duopolistic Competitors," Discussion Paper No. 620S, Northwestern University, Easton, Illinois.

Haurie, A. and Leitmann (1984), "On the Global Asymptotic Stability of Equilibrium Solutions for Open-Loop Differential Games," Large Scale Systems, vol. 6, pp.107-122.

Jacquemin, A.D. (1973), "Optimal Control and Advertising Policy," Metro-Economica, vol. 25, pp.200-207.

Jørgensen, S. (1982), "A Survey of some Differential Games in Advertising," Journal of Economic Dynamics and Control, vol. 4, pp.341-369.

Jørgensen, S. (1985), "Optimal Dynamic Pricing in an Oligopolistic Market: A Survey," this volume.

Lambin, J., P.A. Naert and A. Bultez (1975), "Optimal Marketing Behavior in Oligopoly," European Economic Review, vol. 2, pp.105-128.

Leitmann, G. and H. Stalford (1972), "Sufficiency for Optimal Strategies in Nash Equilibrium Games," in Techniques of Optimization, A.V. Balakrishnan (Ed.), Academic Press, New York.

Leitmann, G. and W.E. Schmitendorf (1978), "Profit Maximization through Advertising: A Nonzero-Sum Differential Games Approach," IEEE Transaction on Automatic Control, vol. AC-23, pp.645-650.

Lerner, A.P. (1934), "The Concept of Monopoly and the Measurement of Monopoly Power," Review of Economic Studies, vol. 1, pp.157-176.

Lévine, J. and J. Thépot (1982), "Open-Loop and Closed-Loop Equilibrium in a Dynamic Duopoly," in Optimal Control Theory and Economic Analysis, G. Feichtinger (Ed.), North-Holland, Amsterdam.

Schmalensee, R. (1972), The Economics of Advertising, North-Holland, Amsterdam.

Schmalensee, R. (1976), "A Model of Promotional Competition in Oligopoly," Review of Economic Studies, vol. 43, pp.493-508.

Thépot, J. (1983), "Marketing and Investment Policies of Duopolists in a Growing Industry," Journal of Economic Dynamics and Control, vol. 5, pp.387-404.

Teng, J.T. and G.L. Thompson (1985), "Optimal Strategies for General Price-Advertising Models," in Optimal Control Theory and Economic Analysis, vol. 2, G. Feichtinger (Ed.), North-Holland, Amsterdam.

Wirl, F. (1985), "Stable and Volatile Prices: An Explanation by Dynamic Demand," in Optimal Control Theory and Economic Analysis, vol. 2, G. Feichtinger (Ed.), North-Holland, Amsterdam.

GAME THEORY MODELS OF FISHERIES MANAGEMENT - A SURVEY

Veijo Kaitala
Systems Analysis Laboratory
Helsinki University of Technology
Otakaari 1, 02150 Espoo, Finland

Abstract

A survey of the literature dealing with the multi-agent exploitation of fishery resources is presented. The most common problems of fishery management include competitive exploitation of open-access fishery resources, non-cooperative and cooperative or bargaining approaches to resource management. This survey concentrates on papers which deal with dynamic game and control theory problems of resource modelling and bargaining.

1. Introduction

Mathematical modelling has long traditions in the analysis and design of fish resource exploitation (for extensive lists of references, see e.g. the books of Clark (1976), or Mirman and Spulber (1982)). The optimal control approach to resource exploitation has been developed by Clark (1976, 1980), and others. There is in the literature a growing interest in the use of multiagent decision making theory in dynamic fishery management problems.

This paper reviews the most common multi-agent decision making models in fishery management. The problems include competitive exploitation of open-access fishery resources, non-cooperative and cooperative or bargaining approaches to resource management. Most of the papers deal with the non-cooperative mode of decision making (Chiarella et al., 1984; Clark, 1980; Fischer, 1981; Hämäläinen and Kaitala, 1982; Kaitala and Hämäläinen, 1981; Kemp and Long, 1980; Levhari and Mirman, 1980; Mirman, 1979). Dynamic bargaining models have so far received minor attention (Munro, 1979, 1982a). The topics of equilibrium agreements have previously been considered in the literature on resource exploitation by Hämäläinen et al. (1984, 1985), Kaitala et al. (1985), and Kaitala (1985).

The paper is organized as follows. The deterministic models of the fisheries' dynamics and the decision criteria of the harvesting agents are introduced in Section 2. Section 3 reviews the competitive and rational expectations approaches to model decision making in open-access fisheries. Non-cooperative restricted access fishery models are discussed in Section 4. The issues of dynamic bargaining and cooperative harvesting of resources are reviewed in Section 5.

Literature on the economics of renewable resources has been reviewed by Munro (1982b), Spulber (1982), and Andersen and Sutinen (1984). Survey papers on differential game models in management science and economics have been published by e.g. Clemhout and Wan (1979), Feichtinger and Jørgensen (1983), Jørgensen (1984, 1985), and Pohjola (1985).

2. Resource and decision dynamics

2.1. Resource dynamics

We consider the problem of multi-agent fishery management. The resource dynamics is described by a deterministic differential equation model of the form

$$\dot{x}(t) = F(x(t)) + G(x(t)) - \sum_{i=1}^{N} h_i(t),\ x(0) = x_o, \tag{1}$$

where $x^T = (x_1,\ldots,x_n) \in R_+^n$ is the state variable representing the stock of n substocks of fish in different fishing grounds. $F^T = (F_1,\ldots,F_n)$ represents the growth function of the fishery, and $G^T = (G_1,\ldots,G_n)$ describes the interdependence of the subfisheries on each other. The growth rate F_j of each substock j is assumed to depend on the substock x_j, only. We further consider the concave growth functions for which $F_j(0) = F_j(K_j) = 0$, $K_j > 0$, $F_j'(0) > 0$, $F_j''(x_j) < 0$, $x_j \in (0,K_j)$, where K_j is the carrying capacity of subfishery j. For example, the growth function of the Schaefer or logistic form (Schaefer, 1957)

$$F_j(x_j) = r_j x_j (1-x_j/K_j),$$

where r_j is an intrinsic growth rate, satisfies these conditions. The harvest rate of agent i is denoted by $h_i = (h_{i1},\ldots,h_{in})$, $i = 1,\ldots,N$. Agent i does not necessarily have access to all subfisheries. Usually the harvest rate is assumed to be bilinear in the stock, x_j, and the fishing effort, E_{ij},

$$h_{ij}(t) = q_j E_{ij}(t) x_j(t),\ i = 1,\ldots,N,\ j = 1,\ldots,n, \tag{2}$$

where q_j is the catchability coefficient in fishery j. The catchability coefficient is a scaling factor which depends on the measure of the fishing effort (daily man hours, size of the fleet, etc.).

The agents represent countries, independent fishing fleets of different nationalities, or enterprises. The number of agents in a fishery, N, is determined by the assumptions on the access to the fishery. The three important fisheries are open-access common property fishery, sole-owner fishery (N = 1), and restricted entry common property fishery ($N > 1$ fixed).

The instantaneous net revenue or utility flow to an agent i from a fishery, $L_i(x,E_i)$, depends on the stock, $x(t)$, and the fishing effort, $E_i(t)$. There are two cases frequently encountered in the literature: a) the net revenue flow from the fishery is of the form

$$L_i(x,E_i) = \sum_{j=1}^{n} (p_{ij}x_j - c_i)E_{ij}, \tag{3}$$

where c_i is a unit cost of an effective fishing effort $(q_j = 1)$, and the demand function of the fish, $p_{ij} = p_{ij}(h_1,\ldots,h_n)$, is of finite or infinite elasticity, and b) the utility $U_i(h_i)$ from the consumption of fish is concave in the harvest, h_i.

2.2 Optimality in infinite horizon optimization

In the case of one decision maker in a restricted access fishery the problem of rationality becomes one of optimal control. In resource economics optimization, problems are traditionally formulated over infinite time horizons. This approach is dominant in the literature of fishery economics, too (see e.g. Clark, 1976; Mirman and Spulber, 1982; Andersen and Sutinen, 1984). The possibility to consider the performance criteria which grow without limit is enabled by relaxing the definition of optimality (see e.g. Haurie, 1982).

Let $A(x_o)$ denote the set of trajectories x emanating from the initial state x_o. An admissible fishing effort E is a piecewise continuous function from $[0,\infty)$ to a fixed subset U of $\mathbb{R}^n$, which generates a non-negative trajectory x as a solution of Equation (1). Now define for each admissible fishing effort E a net revenue for an agent as follows:

$$J^T(x_o,E) \triangleq \int_0^T e^{-st}L(x,E)dt, \quad T > 0,$$

where $s \geq 0$ is the discount rate of the agent. (The subindex i

has been dropped for notational simplicity.)

Definition 2.1. An admissible fishing effort E^* generates a strongly optimal trajectory $x^* \in A(x_o)$ if $\lim_{T\to\infty} J^T(x_o,E^*)$ exists and is finite and if for any other admissible fishing effort E the following holds:

$$\lim_{T\to\infty} \{J^T(x_o,E^*) - J^T(x_o,E)\} \geq 0.$$

This is the ordinary optimality concept applied in optimal control problems. An extension of this definition, the main motivation of which is the use of zero discount rates, is as follows.

Definition 2.2. An admissible fishing effort E^* generates an overtaking optimal trajectory $x^* \in A(x_o)$ if, for any other admissible fishing effort E, the following holds:

$$\liminf_{T\to\infty} \{J^T(x_o,E^*) - J^T(x_o,E)\} \geq 0.$$

Clearly, strong optimality implies overtaking optimality. The latter solution concept of overtaking optimality permits the analysis of infinite time horizon game and optimization problems even when the revenue integrals diverge. The definitions of optimality can be repeated for all choices of admissible control functions. The set U of admissible values of the control functions can in particular be time or state dependent. Overtaking optimality can be applied to open-loop (Nash) equilibrium solutions of infinite horizon differential games in a standard way (for further mathematical properties and examples in resource management, see Haurie and Leitmann, 1984; Hämäläinen et al., 1984, 1985; Kaitala et al., 1985; Kaitala, 1985).

3. Open-access to fishery resources

One basic and extensively analyzed concept in fishery economies is that of the open-access common-property fishery. An unregulated fishery, such as high sea fishery, is open to the exploitation of the resources by anyone and at any time. This situation leads to competitive behaviour between fishermen.

When the entry of the harvesting agents to a fishery is completely free, individual decisions are based on myopic optimization (Gordon, 1954; Clark, 1976, 1980). Each agent maximizes instantaneous utility or net revenue flow. Myopism reflects the assumption that a harvesting agent is unwilling or unable to utilize information about the total number of agents and their harvesting strategies, or about the fish resource dynamics. Clark (1976) noted that myopic behaviour coincides with optimizing under an infinite discount rate. One more explanation for myopic harvesting is that an agent believes that his individual harvest rate has no practical effect on the fish stock. In an open-access fishery, the number of competitive agents increases until the net revenue flows of the agents dissipate (Gordon, 1954; Clark, 1976). Bionomic equilibrium results when entry and exit in the fishery stabilize and long-term stock equilibrium is reached.

The efficiency of an open-access competitive fishery is compared with the socially efficient fishery (Gordon, 1954; Smith, 1969; Clark, 1976). One common conclusion is that regulation is needed to correct the misallocation of resources resulting from open-access to the fishery.

An extension to the analysis of open-access fisheries is provided by models predicting the rate of entry and exit of harvesting agents in the fisheries. In these models, instantaneous optimization with respect to the fishing effort is not included, and the fishing effort is defined by the total number of harvesting agents or by the size of the fishing fleet. Changes in the fleet size occur through the entry and exit decisions of agents. Their decisions are based on myopic or rational expectations as to the net revenues or profits to be obtained from the fishery (Smith, 1969; Berck and Perloff, 1984).

4. Non-cooperative restricted access fisheries

Clark (1980) applied the theory of non-cooperative Nash equilibrium solutions of N-person nonzero-sum differential games to model the exploitation of resource in a limited-access single stock fishery. In such a fishery, N producers (N fixed) have unrestricted rights to exploit the resources. For simplicity, in this section the results will be presented for two-person games only.

The dynamics of the resource is described by the model given by (1) ($x(t) \in R_+$, and $G(x) \equiv 0$). Each agent maximizes the present value of the economic rent from the fishery

$$J_i(E_1,E_2) = \int_0^\infty e^{-s_i t} L_i(x(t),E_i(t))dt, \ i = 1,2,$$
$$0 \leq E_i(t) \leq E_{i\ max},$$

where $L_i(.,.)$ is of the linear form (3), the price of fish is fixed, and $s_i > 0$ is the discount rate of agent i. The Nash equilibrium solution concept assumes full information, i.e. the agents know the resource dynamics (1), (2) and each other's decision criterion (3). Furthermore, we will assume that each control E_i will be chosen as a function of the current state and time. Then, the Nash equilibrium solution consists of a pair of feedback control strategies[1] (E_1^N, E_2^N) such that

$$J_1(E_1^N, E_2^N) \geq J_1(E_1, E_2^N) \quad \text{for all } E_1,$$

$$J_2(E_1^N, E_2^N) \geq J_2(E_1^N, E_2) \quad \text{for all } E_2.$$

This solution is an equilibrium, because there is no temptation for any agent to deviate unilaterally from this solution. Thus the equilibrium strategy is a safe strategy for each agent in the sense that if one realizes his equilibrium strategy, then the rational co-player will certainly have no incentive to deviate from his equilibrium strategy. This solution, under the feedback information pattern, is also called the Feedback Nash equilibrium, and it satisfies the time consistency property (see (Başar, 1985) for further elaboration on this point).

The "safe" equilibrium solution does not in this case appear to be very attractive for the less efficient agent. (Agent 2 is the less efficient one, i.e. $x_2^\infty > x_1^\infty$, where $x_i^\infty = c_i/(p_i q_i)$, i = 1,2, is the usual bionomic equilibrium for agent i. Thus, agent 1 is able to gain economic rent on lower stock levels than agent 2.) Let x_1^* denote the sole owner optimal (steady state) stock level for agent 1. The feedback Nash equilibrium solution, where the fishing efforts are functions of the state x(t), is specified as follows:

$$E_1^N(x) = \begin{cases} E_{1\,max} & x > \min(x_1^*, x_2^\infty) \\ F(x)/(q_1 x), & x = \min(x_1^*, x_2^\infty) \\ 0 & x < \min(x_1^*, x_2^\infty) \end{cases}$$

$$E_2^N(x) = \begin{cases} E_{2\,max} & , x > x_2^\infty \\ 0 & , x < x_2^\infty \end{cases} \tag{4}$$

[1] In general, strategies are classified on the basis of the information available to the players as follows (Başar and Olsder, 1982): open-loop, feedback, and closed loop (memory) strategies. In the open-loop case the strategies are chosen as time functions over the time horizon of the game. In a feedback information structure only the current value of the state, x(t), is available to the player. When the player has access to state information with memory, the strategies are closed loop or memory strategies. When the player is not committed to his announcement, a cheating strategy is also possible (Hämäläinen, 1981).

If $x_1^* < x_2^\infty$, agent 1 will operate on his sole owner optimum. If $x_1^* > x_2^\infty$, agent 1 will operate on the level which deters the entry of agent 2 to the fishery. In any case, the less efficient agent 2 is eliminated by his competitor. Moreover, when the two agents in the fishery are equally efficient, the non-cooperative feedback Nash behaviour results in a total dissipation of the economic net revenue flow. These results can be extended to the case of N agents.

Fischer (1981) showed that the solution of the feedback form (4) is also a feedback Nash solution for a game with $L_i(x,E_i) = R_i(x)E_i$, where $R_i(x)$ is a continuous concave function of x, and $R_i(x^\infty) = 0$.

In the divided fishery model there are two neighbouring fishing zones, the substocks of which are biologically interdependent (Kemp and Long, 1980; Kaitala and Hämäläinen, 1981; Hämäläinen and Kaitala, 1982). The harvesting agents have unrestricted rights to the resource exploitation in their own zone but no access to the neighbouring zone. (Such a divided fishery exists, for example, in the Gulf of Finland, where the Finnish and Soviet fleets exploit the resources in their own coastal zones.) The dynamics of the divided restricted-access fishery is as follows:

$$\begin{aligned} \dot{x}_1(t) &= F_1(x_1(t)) - h_{11}(t) - d(x_1(t) - x_2(t)) \\ \dot{x}_2(t) &= F_2(x_2(t)) - h_{22}(t) - d(x_2(t) - x_1(t)), \end{aligned} \tag{5}$$

where $F_1(.)$ and $F_2(.)$ are natural growth functions, and d is a diffusion coefficient. The natural growth of the fish stock in an area depends on the size of the fish stock in that area only. The interdependence of the two substocks is due to the diffusion, which is proportional to the difference in the stock sizes. The development of the model is presented by Hämäläinen and Kaitala (1982).

In the paper by Kaitala and Hämäläinen (1981), the fishing fleets of two coastal countries share unrestricted access to the fishery in a gulf. Then the countries declare restricted entry fishing zones (Eq. (5)). Necessary conditions for open-loop Nash equilibria result in two-point boundary value problems, which are solved numerically. Examples show that the division of the fishery results in less intensive harvesting and higher biomass levels in both zones. A less efficient country benefits economically from the division of the resources. This result also suggests that coastal countries establish restricted entry fishing zones when they are not able to compete with more efficient fishing fleets.

Hämäläinen and Kaitala (1982) provide an analysis that is a divided fishery counterpart of harvest game model of Clark (1980). The two countries have three options in their choice of policy variables: stock level, harvest rate, and fishing effort. It should be noted that the fishing effort is in practice the only implementable control variable. The term "policy variable" is used in the sense that the optimal strategies are designed using these variables as decision-making tools. (The rational reaction of a country depends on the policy variable chosen by the neighbouring country.) Numerical experiments show that the countries are able to maintain relatively large fish populations in their zones in spite of non-cooperation. Moreover, the weaker the interdependence between the substocks, the better is the result for the countries and the closer the solution is to a Pareto-optimal solution. Thus, two equally efficient countries can avoid total rent dissipation by splitting the fishery.

5. Cooperative resource exploitation and bargaining

One condition for an acceptable agreement in multi-agent resource management is that the agreement about the joint exploitation of the resource satisfies Pareto-efficiency. A Pareto-efficient agreement cannot be made better for both of the agents by any other agreement. In other words, either a change in the agreement gives the same total net return for both of the agents, or one or both of the agents lose by deviating from the agreement. The formal definition of Pareto-efficiency is as follows (Leitmann, 1974): A pair of control strategies (E_1^*, E_2^*) constitutes a Pareto-efficient agreement if and only if, for any other pair (E_1, E_2) either

$$J_i(E_1,E_2) = J_i(E_1^*,E_2^*),\ i = 1,2,$$

or for $i = 1$ or 2, $J_i(E_1,E_2) < J_i(E_1^*,E_2^*)$.

One way to obtain a Pareto-efficient solution is to optimize the joint scalar decision criterion $J(E_1,E_2) = a_1 J_1(E_1,E_2) + a_2 J_2(E_1,E_2)$ subject to (1), (2), where the weights a_1, a_2 are constants $0 < a_1$, $a_2 < 1$, $a_1 + a_2 = 1$). The solution of this problem is Pareto-efficient under some regularity conditions on the objective functions (Leitmann, 1974).

Mirman (1979) and Levhari and Mirman (1980) presented a feedback Nash equilibrium solution for a special log-linear discrete time game. They showed that the steady state utility flows from the consumption of fish for two competitive countries are lower than in cooperative exploitation of the resources. (Cooperation here means Pareto-optimality with equal weights.)

Chiarella et al. (1984) studied a general continuous-time model of a fishery to which several utility maximizing countries share access. They state conditions under which non-cooperative open-loop solutions coincide with cooperative solutions. An essential assumption is that the utility flow $U_i(h_1,\ldots,h_i,\ldots,h_N)$ is concave in h_{ij}, $j=1,\ldots,n$. Theorem 1 of Chiarella et al. (1984) states that "If U_i is a function of h_i only, and has an infinite slope at the origin, then there exists an equilibrium trajectory, which is Pareto-optimal." In other words, when an open-loop biomass yield of fish determines the utilities of the harvesting countries, there is nothing better than to harvest non-cooperatively. This result is concerned with open-loop Nash equilibrium solutions only. A similar result was independently obtained by Kaitala et al. (1985). In particular they studied the problem of how to negotiate an agreement when the number of Pareto-optimal equilibrium solutions is infinite.

Kemp and Long (1980) showed that when the agents in a divided fishery are symmetrical, and when the utility flow does not depend on the stock, the symmetric Nash equilibria are Pareto-optimal. Chiarella et al. (1984) extended this result to the case where the interdependence between the substocks is of the nonlinear form.

There are different bargaining schemes available in the literature dealing with static games (Nash, 1950; Kalai and Smorodinsky, 1975; Roth, 1979). A bargaining scheme can also used in dynamic cooperative games to pick a single Pareto-optimal solution to represent the outcome of bargaining. For example, the well-known bargaining scheme proposed by Nash (1950) determines the agreement as the solution of the following problem

$$\max_{(E_1,E_2)\in U_1\times U_2} (J_1(E_1,E_2)-y_1)(J_2(E_1,E_2)-y_2),$$

$$y_i = J_i(E^{SQ},E^{SQ}), \quad i=1,2,$$

subject to (1), (2), where E^{SQ}, $i=1,2$, denote the disagreement strategies in the case where no agreement is reached (the status quo). (In the case of a dynamic game J_i, $i=1,2$, is a mapping from appropriate decision spaces (e.g. open-loop or feedback control functions) to real line.) The resulting constant weights a_1,a_2 are called the bargaining weights.

The Nash bargaining scheme satisfies the six axioms of Pareto-optimality, feasibility, rationality, symmetry, and independence of irrelevant alternatives and of linear transformations (for discussion of these properties, see e.g. Roth, 1979). The axiom of independence of irrelevant alternatives was criticized by Kalai and Smorodinsky (1975). They proposed a new scheme which satisfies the axiom of individual monotonicity but which cannot be extended to N-person cooperative games (N > 2) (Roth, 1979). No empirical studies on the axiomatic bargaining seem to have appeared in fisheries management literature.

Munro (1979) investigated the joint management of transboundary resources by two countries. The problem formulation in that paper is the same as in the paper of Clark (1980), with the exception that the countries were assumed to cooperate. The Nash bargaining scheme is applied and the non-cooperative Nash feedback solution is considered as the disagreement policy. An essential assumption made by Munro (1979) is that the countries negotiate a binding agreement. Problems that arise between the countries through different social discount rates, fishing effort costs, and consumer tastes are studied under the following three forms of agreement: the shares from the total harvests of the countries are fixed or time variant, and side payments between the countries are permitted. The first two cases of different discount rates or fishing effort costs will not cause any major difficulties when side payments are allowed. A special model of different consumer tastes is, however, shown to lead to non-convex optimization and multiple equilibria.

In a recent paper Munro (1982a) examined the problem of processing sector and harvesting sector as a bilateral monopoly problem in the bargaining framework. In this problem the monopsonized processing sector is confronted with the monopolized harvesting sector. Both sides have an incentive to negotiate on cooperation, since failure to cooperate leads to losses for both. Integration of the two sectors is argued to occur (Munro, 1982a), although agreements are assumed be binding. In particular, social desirability of the bilateral monopoly harvesting of resources is studied.

Hämäläinen et al. (1984, 1985) provide an analysis of bargaining solutions for infinite time horizon fishery games where the agreements are not binding. This situation is very common in international fisheries management where the resource exploitation is based on recommendations rather than on tight agreements. In a dynamic game setting a Pareto-optimal unbinding agreement in most cases leaves the temptation for each agent to deviate unilaterally from the agreed policy during the remaining period. This means that the agreement is not an equilibrium agreement.

One immediate question is whether the agents can do anything to prevent cheating. It is sometimes realistic to assume that cheating can be detected after a finite time period. One idea that has recently appeared in the control theory literature is to use threats to eliminate the temptation to cheat (Tolwinski, 1982; Haurie and Tolwinski, 1981). An effective and credible threat of punishment should cheating be detected prevents the co-harvester from cheating.

The purpose of punishment (which is announced in advance as following cheating) is to guarantee that the total utility from the game cannot be increased by cheating. Thus the temptation to cheat disappears and the Pareto-optimal agreement obtains an equilibrium property. This equilibrium solution also dominates the non-cooperative equilibrium solutions (status quo). For this reason it has been emphasised in the literature that the purpose of the agents is by no means to enter a situation where the punishments are implemented.

The idea of threat supported agreements was tested extensively in fishery games by Hämäläinen et al. (1984, 1985). The Kalai-Smorodinsky bargaining scheme was applied to obtain bargaining solutions. The choice of the bargaining scheme does not, however, have any effects on the results obtained, and consequently the analysis could have been carried out by applying any other bargaining scheme available. Open-loop equilibrium solutions were considered as status quo policies. (The characterization and computation of open-loop equilibrium solutions of infinite time horizon differential games is a difficult mathematical problem. A review of this topic is given in Kaitala (1985).) The problems of current interest which were not solved completely include perfectness of equilibria (i.e. how to incorporate the possibility of repeated cheating), credibility of threats (punishment hurts all the agents), and the selection of the status quo. We end this section with a short discussion on the status quo.

The status quo is applied should no agreement be reached. Open-loop equilibrium is not, however, the only possible choice. For example, in the papers by Haurie and Tolwinski (1981), Tolwinski (1982), and Munro (1979, 1982a) status quo is described through feedback equilibria and mini-max threat policies. In high sea fisheries, a natural status quo is unregulated open-access harvesting.

Even if only open-loop equilibria are considered as status quo policies, the problem of the non-uniqueness of disagreement behaviour still remains. It is clear from the results obtained by Clark (1980), Hämäläinen and Kaitala (1982), and Kaitala and Hämäläinen (1981) that a change in the property rights or control variables also changes the status quo and hence the outcome of the bargaining process. A natural solution would be to choose a game the solution of which dominates the solutions of the other games. But as the results of Hämäläinen and Kaitala (1982) suggest, such an equilibrium choice does not usually exist. For example, Hämäläinen and Kaitala (1982) have not been able to identify a game the solution of which dominates the solutions of the other games.

It may also happen in a disagreement situation that the agents solve independently different games, and the resulting solution does not usually provide an equilibrium strategy pair. Such a disagreement situation would not be safe for the players. One condition for obtaining a safe disagreement solution is for each agent to solve and implement the solution of the same Nash game. Thus a succesful non-cooperation requires mutual communication and cooperation, too.

6. Conclusion

In this paper we have surveyed the applications of game theory and bargaining models to fishery management problems. The few papers on stochastic fishery games and game theory studies of regulation and incentives have not been included in this survey (for the first topic, see (Sobel, 1982), and for a short review on the two latter topics, see (Kaitala, 1985)). Several issues of multilateral resource exploitation still need further theoretical elaboration. Besides the topics mentioned above, these include e.g. applications of closed-loop solution concepts to resource game and bargaining problems, and time consistency and equilibrium properties of agreements.

The need for multi-agent fishery management models arises from the recent development of the practice and jurisdiction of international marine resource exploitation. This development has been reported in the Law of the Sea (1983). The main aim of the law is to rationalize the utilization of international marine resources and to encourage countries to cooperate. Game theory interpretation of this law without doubt deepens our insight into the duties of international resource organizations and fishing countries.

7. References

Andersen, P. and J.G. Sutinen (1984), "Stochastic Bioeconomics: A Review of Basic Methods and Results," Marine Resource Economics, vol.

1, pp.117-136.

Başar, T. (1985), "A Tutorial on Dynamic and Differential Games," this volume.

Başar, T. and G.J. Olsder (1982), Dynamic Noncooperative Game Theory, Academic Press, New York.

Berck, P. and J.M. Perloff (1984), "An Open-Access Fishery with Rational Expectations," Econometrica, vol. 52, pp. 489-506.

Chiarella, C., M.C. Kemp, N.V. Long and K. Okuguchi (1984), "On the Economics of International Fisheries," International Economic Review, vol. 25, pp. 85-92.

Clark, C.W. (1976), Mathematical Bioeconomics: The Optimal Management of Renewable Resources, Wiley-Interscience, New York.

Clark, C.W. (1980), "Restricted Access to Common-Property Fishery Resources: A Game Theoretic Analysis," in Dynamic Optimization and Mathematical Economics, P. Liu (Ed.), Plenum Press, New York.

Clemhout, S. and H.Y. Wan, Jr. (1979), "Interactive Economic Dynamics and Differential Games," Journal of Optimization Theory and Applications, vol. 27, pp. 7-30.

Feichtinger, G. and S. Jørgensen (1983), "Differential Game Models in Management Science," European Journal of Operational Research, vol. 14, pp. 137-155.

Fischer, T.R. (1981), "An Hierarchical Game Approach to Fishery Resource Management," IEEE Transactions on Systems, Man, and Cybernetics, vol. SMC-11, pp. 216-222.

Gordon, H.S. (1954), "Economic Theory of a Common-Property: The Fishery," Journal of Political Economy, vol. 62, pp. 124-142.

Hämäläinen, R.P. (1981), "On the Cheating Problem in Stackelberg Games," International Journal of Systems Science, vol. 12, pp. 753-770.

Hämäläinen, R.P., A. Haurie and V. Kaitala (1985), "Equilibria and Threats in a Fishery Management Game," Optimal Control Applications & Methods, (in press).

Hämäläinen, R.P., A. Haurie and V. Kaitala (1984), "Bargaining on Whales: A Differential Game Model with Pareto Optimal Equilibria," Operations Research Letters, vol. 3, pp. 5-11.

Hämäläinen, R.P. and V. Kaitala (1982), "A Game on the Choice of Policy Variables in a Dynamic Resource Management Game," Proc. 21st IEEE Conference on Decision and Control, vol. 1, Orlando, Florida.

Haurie, A. (1982), "Stability and Optimal Exploitation over an Infinite Time Horizon of Interacting Populations," Optimal Control Applications & Methods, vol. 3, pp. 241-256.

Haurie, A. and G. Leitmann (1984), "On the Global Asymptotic Stability of Equilibrium Solutions for Open-Loop Differential Games," Large Scale Systems, vol. 6, pp. 107-122.

Haurie, A. and B. Tolwinski (1981), "Acceptable Equilibria in Dynamic

Bargaining Games," in System Modelling and Optimization, Proc. 10th IFIP Conference, Drenic, R.F. and F. Kozin (Eds.), New York.

Jørgensen, S. (1984), "Differential Game Models in Management Science: A Survey," pp. 578-591, in Operations Research Proceedings 1983, Berlin, Heidelberg, Springer-Verlag.

Jørgensen, S. (1985), "Optimal Dynamic Pricing in an Oligopolistic Market: A Survey," this volume.

Kaitala, V. (1985), Game Theory Models of Dynamic Bargaining and Contracting in Fisheries Management, Helsinki University of Technology, Ph.D. dissertation.

Kaitala, V. and R.P. Hämäläinen (1981), "A Differential Game Model of the Non-Cooperative Management of an International Fishery," Proc. First International Conference Applied Modelling and Simulation, vol. V, pp. 183-186, Lyon, France, September 7-11.

Kaitala, V., R.P. Hämäläinen and J. Ruusunen (1985), "On the Analysis of Equilibria and Bargaining in a Fishery Game," in Optimal Control Theory and Economic Analysis 2, G. Feichtinger (Ed.), North-Holland, Amsterdam, New York, Oxford.

Kalai, E. and M. Smorodinsky (1975), "Other Solutions to Nash's Bargaining Problem," Econometrica, vol. 43, pp. 513-518.

Kemp, M.C. and N.V. Long (1980), "Resource Extraction under Conditions of Common Access," in Exhaustible Resources, Optimality, and Trade, Kemp, M.C. and N.V. Long (Eds.), North-Holland, Amsterdam, New York, Oxford.

The Law of the Sea (1983). United Nations Convention on the Law of the Sea with Index and Final Act of the Third United Nations Conference of the Law of the Sea, New York, UN, 262 pp.

Leitmann, G. (1974), Cooperative and Non-Cooperative Many Players Differential Games, Springer-Verlag, Vienna.

Levhari, D. and L.J. Mirman (1980), "The Great Fish War: An Example Using a Dynamic Cournot-Nash Solution," Bell Journal of Economics, vol. 11, pp. 322-334.

Mirman, L.J. (1979), "Dynamic Models of Fishing: A Heuristic Approach," in Control Theory in Mathematical Economics, Liu, P.T. and J.G. Sutinen (Eds.), New York, Marcel Decker.

Mirman, L.J. and D.F. Spulber (Eds.) (1982), Essays in the Economics of Renewable Resources, North-Holland, Amsterdam, New York, Oxford.

Munro, G.R. (1979), "The Optimal Management of Transboundary Renewable Resources," Canadian Journal of Economics, vol. 12, pp. 355-376.

Munro, G.R. (1982a), "Bilateral Monopoly in Fisheries and Optimal Management Policy," in Essays in the Economics of Renewable Resources, Mirman, L.J. and D.F. Spulber (Eds.), North-Holland, Amsterdam, New York, Oxford.

Munro, G.R. (1982b), "Fisheries, Extended Jurisdiction and the Economics of Common Property Resources,", Canadian Journal of Economics, vol. 15, pp. 405-425.

Nash, J. (1950), "The Bargaining Problem," Econometrica, vol. 18, pp. 155-162.

Pohjola, M. (1985), "Applications of Dynamic Game Theory to Macroeconomics," this volume.

Roth, A.E. (1979), Axiomatic Models of Bargaining, Springer-Verlag, Berlin.

Schaefer, M.B. (1957), "Some Considerations of Population Dynamics and Economics in Relation to the Management of Marine Fisheries," Journal of Fisheries Research Board of Canada, vol. 14, pp. 669-681.

Smith, V.L. (1969), "On Models of Commercial Fishing," Journal of Political Economy, vol. 77, pp. 181-198.

Sobel, M.J. (1982), "Stochastic Fishery Games with Myopic Equilibria," in Essays in the Economics of Renewable Resources, Mirman, L.J. and D.F. Spulber (Eds.), North-Holland, Amsterdam, New York, Oxford.

Spulber, D.F. (1982), "A selective survey," in Essays in the Economics of Renewable Resources, Mirman, L.J. and D.F. Spulber (Eds.), North-Holland, Amsterdam, New York, Oxford.

Tolwinski, B. (1982), "A Concept of Cooperative Equilibrium for Dynamic Games," Automatica, vol. 18, pp. 431-447.

COMMON-PROPERTY EXPLOITATIONS UNDER RISKS OF RESOURCE EXTINCTIONS*

S. Clemhout
and
H. Wan, Jr.
Cornell University
Ithaca, New York 14853/USA

Abstract

For a renewable resource under the random hazards of extinction, a variational correspondence principle is introduced to show under what conditions, joint optimization can increase both the resource stock in stasis and the survival prospect of the resource. The analysis is independent of the assumption of particular function forms.

1. Introduction

It is well-known that in the absence of property rights, the exploitation of renewable biological resources (e.g., marine life) causes a divergence between the private and the public interests. Under Laissez Faire, the outcome is often the untimely depletion or extinction of the species in question. Thus, overfishing leaves a breeding stock too small to survive or thrive.

To be sure, species do become extinct due to random events of nature. Nevertheless, human activity may precipitate the incipient trends, and under common property tenure, the results deviate from the social optimum. To devise policy remedies for modifying individual behavior, it is essential to understand precisely the costs and benefits of all parties concerned.

This paper focuses upon the "long run" which is favored by economists. By "long run" we mean a state of affairs neither affected by the initial stock as dictated by history, nor associated with any "planned extinction" for any species at any date.

---

*We acknowledge helpful discussions with M. Majumdar, L. Olsen, R.E. Schuler, and M. Yano. Thanks are due to A. Haurie, who first suggested we consider jump processes during our work on Clemhout and Wan (1985a). We claim full property rights over any mistakes and shortcomings in the final product.

Regarding this "long-run" concept, four topics will be examined:

1. Whether the notion "long run" can be meaningfully defined where extinction may happen at any instant, with its probabilistic timing partially controlled by the interactions of rational agents.
2. What economic interpretations can be given to the "long-run" resource level, if it can be defined.
3. Which factors decide this "long run" resource level and how would rational agents behave during any transition toward that level.
4. Most importantly, when can the "stability" property of the long run positions be utilized to compare the equilibrium resource levels associated with the noncooperative and cooperative solutions.

Section 2 provides a bird's eye view of the related literature and how this study supplements past results. Section 3 addresses our first topic: the meaning of the "long run" in our context. Section 4 sets up the model, transforms it into a deterministic analog with state-dependent discount rate and derives an analytic characterization of the stationary stock. Section 5 addresses the second issue: how to interpret the equilibrium condition for the long run stock. A ready application is to compare models with state-dependent and fixed discount rates, regarding the sensitivity of the stationary stock to parametric functional variations. Section 6 addresses the third issue: properties of the equilibrium policy off the stationary path. Section 7 addresses our final topic: the comparison between the cooperative and noncooperative solutions. Section 8 provides some concluding remarks.

2. Relationship to Previous Works

The problem of common property was noted by Hotelling (1930) for exhaustible resources and elaborated by Gordon (1954) in a fishery model, which made no explicit reference to time.[1] Related works may be found in Clark (1976) and Das Gupta (1982). The interaction among the interested parties has been modeled as dynamic games with closed-loop strategies, first by Levhari and Mirman (1980) in a multi-stage version, and by Clark (1980) as a differential game.

---

[1] Among the examples of Dales (1968), those concerning the Medieval commons, high seas, and free ways are all essentially time-less in that the supply of services in the future is unaffected by the resource utilization in the present. The analysis of Worcester (1968) also focuses upon such issues. Clearly in the case of petroleum reserves and fisheries, the intertemporal linkage of supplies is crucial.

The present paper is part of a larger study about the conservation of economically exploited species, under common property tenure. In Clemhout and Wan (1985a), we first discussed the advantages of models specified in continuous time and closed-loop strategies, and then presented a multi-species model perturbated by random shocks as white noises. That paper shares with Levhari and Mirman (1980) and Clark (1980) two common features: (a) particular functional forms are adopted, and (b) under the equilibrium evolution, no species becomes extinct in finite time.

By contrast, Clemhout and Wan (1985b) studied a deterministic, single species model by phase diagrams: no specific functional form was assumed. The main result is that the noncooperative equilibrium evolution can be consistent with extinction in finite time: the extinction is "planned", by all players, in a sense.

The present study takes a different tack: extinction may be caused by nature, through sudden, random shocks. The instant probability for extinction varies inversely with the resource level; the latter is influenced by economic agents in their dynamic interactions. There can never be guaranteed survival (of the resource) in perpetuity. There may be equilibrium trajectories where the resource stays at some constant level until its sudden demise.[2] Such a formulation seems to be consistent with current discussions of species extinction in biology.[3] It also reveals that public policy decisions are choices among a spectrum of feasible options, and not between moral absolutes.

We adopt here a differential game with a jump process.[4] A differential game is an n-coupled control model, where the equilibrium policy for any player is optimal for him with all other players using their

---

[2] Conversely, in the present framework, there can be "planned extinction" in finite time, unless a random demise happens first. One requirement for this outcome is the relaxation of Assumption 3 below.

[3] The causes of species extinction is often a matter of dispute, e.g, see Officer and Drake (1983) on the Cretaceous-Tertiary extinctions, and Martin and Klein (1984) on the Quarternary-Holocene extinctions. Clearly, many waves of extinction predate the appearance of Homo Sapiens. On the other hand, overkill by human-beings probably have played some role in the more recent instances of extinction. The views of Vereschagin and Baryshnikov (ch. 22) and Klein (ch. 25) on the mammalian extinctions in Siberia and Africa in Martin and Klein (1984) appear to be quite convincing on this latter point.

[4] A discussion of controlled jump process can be found in Pliska (1975).

equilibrium policies. A policy prescribes actions according to available information. This latter forms part of the state description. A jump process involves three questions at each instant: (i) whether there is any shock, (ii) if yes, whether the species survives the shock, and (iii) if yes again, which direction of change takes place. The probabilities for all these three cases may depend upon the state and the players' actions. Clemhout and Wan (1985a and b) may be subsumed as special cases here.

3. The "Long Run" and its Meaning

As previously stated, our principal concern here is about the "long-run" equilibrium which has always preoccupied economists. In a deterministic, stationary environment, and under suitable conditions, the "turnpike theorems" hold over a sufficiently long time horizon. For many purposes, properties about the "turnpike" supply all the answers desired. However, ours is a stochastic environment. Randomness enters not just through shocks perturbing the system, as in Clemhout and Wan (1985a), but more intrinsically through random truncations which may cut the horizon short. If, for example, the "half-life" of a particular marine species is only a decade or two, under equilibrium revolution, is it meaningful to apply the "long-run" concept which apparently hints at infinite durations?

Since a differential game is an n-coupled control model it suffices here to consider the problem of intertemporal optimization for an individual, who maximizes his expected payoff over the potentially infinite horizon. Having set up the necessary conditions for a maximum, we then inquire whether there exists any steady-state solution. In general, this implies an invariant probability distribution for the state variable and an optimal policy which prescribes specific controls at each state. In the limit (or, degenerate) case, we may have a single steady-state level for the state variable. This level is what we <u>define</u> as the "long run" position. Until the moment of sudden demise, the state variable will either behave as a random variable as governed by some invariant distributions, or stay at a constant value. Hence, formally speaking, the concept of a "long run" position will be well defined.

In contrast, how meaningful is this "long-run" concept must be decided case by case. We shall first assume that the steady-state is <u>locally stable</u>, or else, matters may never even approximate what is in the mind of the literary economists. Does the equilibrium trajectory have a "fair chance" to enter some "small neighborhood" of the steady-state, and stay there for "sufficiently long time" before extinction happens (as it is bound to, with a probability approaching 1, at some finite future time)? Clearly, this depends partly on the model, and partly on the researcher's judgement, considering terms such as "fair chance", "small neighborhood", and "sufficiently long time". In case some intuitively obvious answer is beyond reach, one must invoke some computationally oriented model (e.g., Sobel (1982)).

An increased risk (of resource extinction) can affect the "long-run" approach in two ways: (a) it erodes the meaningfulness of the "long-run" position, as seen above, and (b) it undermines any stability of the optimal stationary solution. Intuitively, under risky situations, individuals have less incentive to conserve. More technically, it is known that the higher the "discount rate" the less likely one can guaranty "global asymptotical stability" in models with a constant discount rate and an n-dimensional state vector. To be sure, the specific model in this paper has a state dependent discount rate and a single state variable, so that the relevance of the above result is unknown. (Interested readers may refer to Cass and Shell (1976) for known results.)

In this explorative study, we shall concentrate exclusively on the essence: the only uncertainty considered is whether the resource stock survives, not how it thrives. Then, the expected payoff of each individual is simply equivalent to the discounted utility stream with a varying instantaneous discount rate, which varies inversely with the level of the stock. Consequently, we can study a stochastic model from its deterministic analog.

4. The Model, the Equilibrium and Some Sensitivity Analysis

Consider a simple model where N similar individuals harvest a single type of renewable resource under common property tenure. Natural shocks may occur between instant t and instant $t + \Delta$, with probability $\theta\Delta + o(\Delta)$, where $\Delta > 0$ is a small number and $\theta > 0$. Such an event, once it occurs, has a probability $g(x)/\theta > 0$ of wiping out this resource which exists at t, and a probability $1 - g(x)/\theta$ of having no effect (x is the resource level).[5]

We adopt:

Assumption 1. $g(x)$ is a positive, strictly decreasing, twice differentiable function, defined for all $x \geq 0$.

[5] For such heuristic interpretations, one may refer to Kushner (1971) and Merton (1971).

Set f(x) as the "recruitment function", so that should the resource survive, the evolution of the stock is represented by the equation:

$$\dot{x} = f(x) - \Sigma_{i=1}^{N} c_i \quad , \ x(0) \text{ given,} \tag{1}$$

where c_i is the harvest rate of individual i.

We adopt:

> <u>Assumption</u> <u>2</u>. $f(x) \geq 0$ at all $x \in [0,\bar{x}]$, for some $\bar{x} > 0$, $f(0) = 0 = f(\bar{x})$ and $f(\cdot)$ is concave, and twice differentiable.

All N individuals are assumed to have the same von Neumann-Morgenstern utility index, $u(c_i)$, about which we adopt:

> <u>Assumption</u> <u>3</u>. $u(0) = 0 < u'(\cdot)$, $0 > u''(\cdot)$, $u(\cdot)$ being twice differentiable. Also $u'(0) = \infty$.

Define T as the instant of extinction of the resource stock (T is a "Markovian time"), then the payoff for individual i is:

$$E_T \int_0^T u[c_i(t)]dt = \int_0^\infty \exp\left[-\int_0^T g[x(s)]ds\right] g[x(T)] \int_0^T u[c_i(t)]dt \, dT$$

where $\exp\left[-\int_0^T g[x(s)]ds\right]g[x(T)]dT$ is the probability of the extinction occurring between T and T + dT.

Changing the order of integration: the above expression is shown to be:

$$\int_0^\infty u[c_i(t)]\left(\int_t^\infty \exp\left[-\int_0^T g[x(s)]ds\right]g[x(T)]dT\right)dt$$

$$= \int_0^\infty u[c_i(t)] \int_t^\infty \left[-d\left(\exp\left[-\int_0^T g[x(s)]ds\right]\right)\right]dt$$

$$= \int_0^\infty \exp\left[-\int_0^t g[x(s)]ds\right]u[c_i(t)]dt \tag{2}$$

after taken into account that the eventual extinction is certain, i.e.,

$$\exp\left[-\int_0^\infty g[x(s)]ds\right] = 0.$$

We focus upon the symmetric solutions under both the cooperative and the noncooperative equilibria, with all individuals having the same harvest rates all the time.

Specifically, the cooperative solution corresponds to:

Problem C

$$\text{Max} \int_0^\infty \exp\{-\int_0^t g[x(s)]ds\}\, u[c_i(t)]dt \qquad (3)$$

s.t.

$$\dot{x} = f(x) - Nc_i, \qquad x(0) \leq \bar{x} \text{ is given,}$$

and the noncooperative solution corresponds to:

Problem N

$$\text{Max} \int_0^\infty \exp\{-\int_0^t g[x(s)]ds\}\, u[c_i(t)]dt \qquad (4)$$

s.t.

$$\dot{x} = [f(x) - (N-1)\,\Gamma(x)] - c_i$$

$$\text{with:} \quad \Gamma[x(t)] = c_i(t) \qquad (5)$$

These are formally equivalent to deterministic models with state-dependent discount rates.

In (5), the equilibrium concept is specified as closed-loop Nash. Closed-loop strategies are much more appropriate than open-loop strategies in game theory as seen from Clemhout and Wan (1985a).

In the tradition of the economic literature, we make "long-run comparisons" between the stationary resource levels for Problems C and N. Such a comparison becomes meaningful under:

The "Long-Run" Hypothesis

There exist from Problems C and N, equilibrium stationary solutions which are asymptotically stable in the relevant sense.

By stationary we mean constant x and c_i over the horizon [0,T], till the sudden termination of the resource stock. By equilibrium we mean no player alone can improve his payoff by adopting a different decision rule than the equilibrium rule which implies the particular stationary values of x and c_i. By asymptotic stability in the relevant sense we mean that for Problem N (resp. C), if the initial x-value is the steady-state level for Problem C (resp. N) the equilibrium trajectory will converge to the steady-state level for Problem N (resp. C).

The characterization of the equilibrium stationary solution calls for the familiar optimal control exercise below.

To simplify notations, we first define two functions:

$$F(x) = \begin{cases} f(x) & \text{for Problem C} \\ f(x) - (N-1)\Gamma(x) & \text{for Problem N,} \end{cases} \qquad (6)$$

$$U(c) = \begin{cases} u(c/N) & \text{for Problem C} \\ u(c) & \text{for Problem N.} \end{cases} \qquad (7)$$

and define:

$$(x(t),\ c(t)) \equiv (x^*,\ c^*) \qquad (8)$$

as the asymptotically stable <u>equilibrium</u> <u>stationary</u> <u>solution</u> in question. Note that for Problem C (resp. N), the symbol c now stands for the aggregate (resp. individual) harvest rate. Define further:

$$g^* = g(x^*), \qquad h(x) = g(x) - g^*$$

and note that if the maximands in (3) or (4) are multiplied by a positive constant $e^{q(o)}$, (x^*, c^*) remains the asymptotically stable optimal stationary solution. Now introduce further the variable:

$$q(t) = \int_t^\infty h[x(s)]ds$$

so that,

$$\exp[q(o)]\ \exp\{-\int_o^t g[x(s)]ds\} = e^{-g^*t}\ e^{q(t)}, \quad q(\infty) = 0.$$

To derive the first order necessary conditions for the equilibrium, a discounted Hamiltonian can then be set up for Problems C and N:

$$H = e^q U(c) + \lambda[F(x)-c] + \mu[-h(x)]$$

with the maximum principle:

$$e^q U'(c) = \lambda, \qquad (9)$$

together with:

$$\begin{aligned} \dot{x} &= F(x) - c \qquad , x(o) \text{ given} \\ \dot{q} &= - h(x) \\ \dot{\lambda} &= g^*\lambda - F'(x)\lambda + h'(x)\mu \\ \dot{\mu} &= g^*\mu - e^q U(c). \end{aligned} \tag{10}$$

Equating the left-hand side of (10) to zero, we have:

$$\begin{aligned} F(x^*) &= c^* \\ h(x^*) &= 0 \\ g^* - F'(x^*) &= - h'(x^*)\mu^*/\lambda^* \\ \mu^* &= U(c^*)/g^* \end{aligned} \tag{11}$$

By (9),

$$U'(c^*) = \lambda^*. \tag{12}$$

Using the facts that:

$$h'(x^*) = g'(x^*), \qquad g^* = g(x^*)$$

we obtain, by rearrangement, from (10) and (11),

$$g(x^*) - F'(x^*) = - \frac{g'(x)}{g(x^*)} \Big/ \frac{U'(F(x^*))}{U(F(x^*))} \tag{13}$$

which characterizes the equilibrium/stationary solution for x^*.

5. Interpretation of the Stationary Solution

We have an equivalent form to (13), i.e.,

$$g(x^*) = G(x^*) \tag{14}$$

where,

$$G(x) = F'(x) - \frac{g'(x)\ U[F(x)]}{g(x)\ U'[F(x)]}$$

For the conventional case of a fixed discount rate, $g'(x) \equiv 0$, so that

$g(x^*) = F'(x^*)$, representing the usual equivalence between the discount rate and the own rate of interest, at the equilibrium. The left-hand side, g, stands for the "cost" of maintaining a resource at the margin, in the relative sense. Against this, on the right-hand side is the "benefit" of having that resource level, again at the margin and measured relatively, as a "rate of interest", i.e., $G(x) = F'(x)$. In the present case, the "benefit" term represents both the productive and the conservative uses of the resource. The former is $F'(x)$, and the latter term may be interpreted as follows. The instantaneous utility stream at the equilibrium is $U[F(x^*)]$, and the reduction of the extinction risk provides an instantaneous rate of advantage $-g'U$, in "util" terms. This may be converted to physical terms of $-g'U/U'$, so that the capitalized expression is $-g'U/U'g$. The inclusion of this latter term makes it justifiable to maintain a larger resource level than what is traditionally the case.

A consequence of a state-dependent discount rate is that the change of origin for the instantaneous utility function, U, has effect in the present model, but not the traditional models, e.g., the Ramsey model.

More specifically, the equilibrium stock x^* in a model with a state-dependent discount rate is more sensitively dependent upon the "basic building blocks" of the model than a fixed discount model. By the "basic building blocks" we mean the triplet of functions (U, F, g). From (13), or (14), we can summarize the situation below.

Table 1
Determinants of x^*

	Models with State-dependent discount rate	Models with fixed discount rate
Utility Function		
Value U	Yes	No
Slope U'	Yes	No
Production Function		
Value F	Yes	No
Slope F'	Yes	Yes
Discount Function		
Value g	Yes	Yes
Slope g'	Yes	___

We have now set the stage for "comparative dynamic analysis" under parametric function change. The use of this approach is broader than most of us realize. Later, our comparison between the cooperative and noncooperative solutions is also conducted under this framework after some reformulation.

To prepare for such analysis, we now define,

$$\kappa(x) = [-g'(x)/g(x)]\ U(F(x)) - [g(x) - F'(x)]\ U'(F(x))$$

as the "net marginal benefit" of increasing the "stationary stock". The above discussion motivates the adoption of:

<u>Assumption</u> <u>4.</u> $\kappa(x) = 0$ iff $x = x^*$ and $\kappa'(x^*) < 0$

Assumption 4 may be regarded as an implication of some joint restrictions on the triplet $(U(\cdot), F(\cdot), g(\cdot))$. For illustration, introduce:

<u>Assumption</u> <u>4a</u>
(i) $G(o) > g(o)$.
and
(ii) $G(\cdot)$ is concave and $g(\cdot)$ is convex.

We can establish the result:

(C) If $G(x^*) = g(x^*)$, Assumptions 1 and 4A then imply Assumption 4.

<u>Proof</u>

Set $D(x) = G(x) - g(x)$, and define x^{**} to be the smallest $x \in (o, x^*]$ with $D(x) = 0$. Now, $D(o) > 0$ and $D''(x) < 0$ for all $x \geq 0$.

By the Mean Value Theorem, $D'(x^{**}) = \frac{D(x^{**}) - D(0)}{\rho x^{**}} < 0$ for some $\rho \varepsilon (0, 1)$. The concavity of D then implies:

$D'(x) < 0$ for all $x > x^{**}$.

Thus, for all $x > x^{**}$,

$$D(x) = 0 + \int_{x^{**}}^{x} D'(y)dy < 0.$$

Hence, $D(x^*) = 0$ implies that

$$x^* = x^{**}$$

is the only root for the equation $D(x) = 0$.

See the example in Section 7 for illustration.

Other sets of conditions can also be found to imply Assumption 4.

6. Off the Stationary Path

We now study the adjustment process when the stock of resource differs from its equilibrium stationary level, seeking means to characterize and analyze the player's decision rule of $c_i = \Gamma(x)$.

For quantitative characterization, we first take the logarithmic time derivative of (9) and use (10) and (9) in succession, to obtain in (10) a dynamic equation for c in lieu of λ:[6]

$$\dot{c} = \frac{U'(c)}{U''(c)} (g - F') + \frac{h'\mu}{U''} e^{-q} \qquad (15)$$

The optimal trajectory lies within the two dimensional stable manifold for the following autonomous system:

$$\dot{x} = F(x) - c \qquad x(\infty) = x^*$$

$$\dot{q} = - h(x) \qquad q(\infty) = 0$$

$$\dot{c} = \frac{U'(c)}{U''(c)} \{g(x) - F'(x) + \frac{h'(x)}{U'(c)} \mu e^{-q}\} \qquad c(\infty) = F(x^*)$$

$$\dot{\mu} = g^*\mu - e^{q}U(c) \qquad \mu(\infty) = U[F(x^*)]/g^*.$$

The initial position is decided both by the given value x(o) and an initial transversality condition on the triplet $[q(o), c(o), \mu(o)]$.

Alternatively, by using the integrating factor e^{-g^*t}, one can solve for μ to obtain: $\mu(t) = \int_t^\infty \exp[-g^*(s-t)+q]\, U(c)ds$. Use this result and

---

[6] Thus,

$$U''\dot{c}/U' = h + \dot{\lambda}/\lambda$$
$$= h + g^* - F' + h' \mu/\lambda \text{ (by(10))}$$

which is equivalent to: $(g - F') + h' \mu e^{-q}/U'$

the definition $q = \int_t^\infty h[x(s)]ds$ in (15), one obtains the system of integro-differential equations for adjustment,

$$\dot{x} = F(x) - c$$
$$\dot{c} = (U'/U'')\{g - [F' - \frac{g'}{U'} \int_t^\infty \exp(-\int_t^\infty g[x(s')]\, ds')\, U[c(s)]ds]\}$$

These necessary conditions for optimality imply a unique c(o) for each given x(o). Starting from other values of c, the system would not approach the desired asymptotic values (x*, F(x*)), i.e., the optimal stationary solution.

We note that at the optimal stationary solution, $\dot{x} = o = \dot{c}$, the last equation becomes equivalent to (13) or (14). Likewise, a positive constant value for g would reduce the term of iterated integrals in the last equation to zero, and our model to the familiar Ramsey model.

Qualitatively, one ought not take for granted that the familiar features in the Ramsey model carry over automatically. A case in point is the monotonicity of the decision rule for harvest, i.e., the property:

(M) $\Gamma(\cdot)$ is a monotonically increasing function near the asymptotically stable optimal stationary solution: $\Gamma'(x^*) > 0$

This is a property which can be guaranteed by an additional requirement:

Assumption 5. $F'(x^*) > 0$

This requirement, the positive productivity of the equilibrium resource stock is a "natural" under the traditional postulate of a fixed time-preference rate. It has to be separately included here as a postulate. The reason is quite obvious, when we reflect upon the interpretation of (14).

The resource stock plays a dual role in this model: (1) The growth rate of the stock starts to be positive and then decreases (with crowding). (2) A larger stock may reduce the instant probability of extinction ("safety in numbers"). Thus, at equilibrium, the growth rate F'(x*) may well be negative. We can now state and prove:

Proposition 1

Under the above assumptions, there is a neighborhood of x* over which $\Gamma'(x^*) \geq 0$.

Proof

Suppose the proposition is not true: $\Gamma'(x^*) < 0$. We then have $F'(x^*) - \Gamma'(x^*) = \eta$, for some $\eta > 0$. Now, by our state equation:

$$\dot{x}(t) = F(x(t)) - \Gamma(x(t))$$

$$= [F(x^*) - \Gamma(x^*)] + (x(t) - x^*)(F'(x^*) - \Gamma'(x^*)) + o(x(t) - x^*)$$

$$= 0 + \eta\,(x(t) - x^*) + o(x(t) - x^*),$$

with

$$(1/2)|x(t) - x^*|\,\eta < |\dot{x}| < (3/2)|x(t) - x^*|\,\eta$$

if

$$|x(t) - x^*| < \varepsilon,$$

for some $\varepsilon > 0$.

But since $x(t) \to x^*$, there exists $t_o > 0$ such that, $t > t_o$ then $|x(t) - x^*| < \varepsilon$. This means, for $t > t_o$, $|\dot{x}(t)| = \frac{d}{dt}|x(t) - x^*| > (\eta/2)|x(t) - x^*|$.

Thus, $|x(t) - x^*| > |x(t_o) - x^*| \exp\{(\eta/2)(t - t_o)\}$ which contradicts $x(t) \to x^*$.

The need for Assumption 5 can be illustrated intuitively in Figures 1 and 2 below. Figure 1 is implied by Assumption 5, and Figure 2 is ruled out by that postulate. Figure 1 has a "conventional" phase diagram, known since Koopmans (1965). For (x^*, c^*) to be a "stationary solution", $\dot{c}$ must agree in sign with $\dot{x}$ along the stable arms of the phase portrait. The dotted line in Figure 2 presents the pathological case of $\dot{c}$ having an opposite sign versus $\dot{x}$ at the stationary solution along the stable arms. That is, $\Gamma'(x^*) < 0$, so that property (M) becomes lost to us.

7. A Comparison Between the Noncooperative and Cooperative Solutions

We shall now compare the magnitudes of x^*_C and x^*_N, making use of Proposition 1 and Assumption 4, where x^*_C and x^*_N are the solutions to Problems C and N respectively. First, we recall the definitions of $F(\cdot)$ and $U(\cdot)$, so that we have the characterization conditions:

Figure 1:

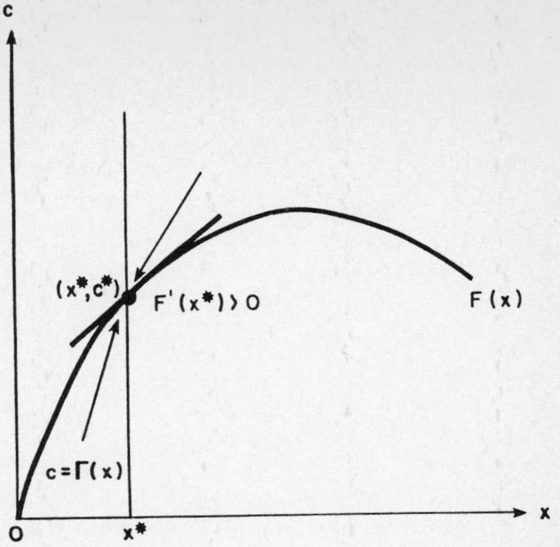

Normality Ensured

Figure 2:

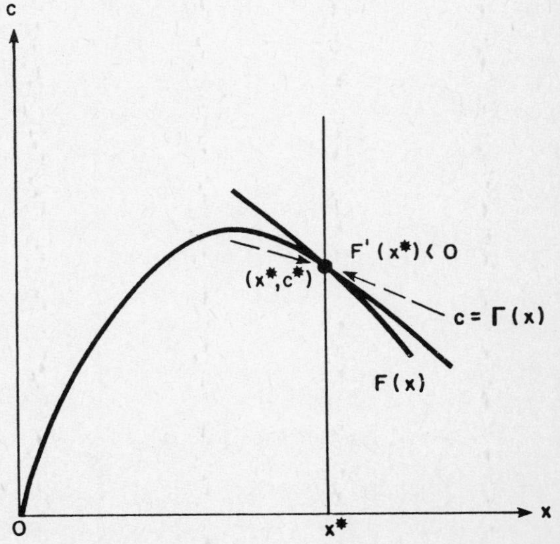

Pathology to be Excluded

$$0 = -u[f(x^*_C)/N]\, g'(x^*_C)/g(x^*_C) - [g(x^*_C) - f'(x^*_C)]\, u'[f(x^*_C)/N]/N$$

and

$$0 = -u[f(x^*_N) - (N-1)\Gamma(x^*_N)]\, g'(x^*_N)/g(x^*_N)$$

$$- [g(x^*_N) - f'(x^*_N) + (N-1)\Gamma'(x^*_N)]u'[f(x^*_N) - (N-1)\Gamma(x^*_N)]$$

Since at an equilibrium,

$$\frac{f(x^*)}{N} = f(x^*) - (N-1)\Gamma(x^*)$$

and since

$$u' > 0,$$

we can rearrange the above two conditions into:

$$0 = -\frac{g'(x^*_C)/g(x^*_C)}{u'[f(x^*_C)/N]/u[f(x^*_C)/N]} - \frac{g(x^*_C) - f'(x^*_C)}{N} = L(x^*_C), \tag{18}$$

and

$$0 = -\frac{g'(x^*_N)/g(x^*_N)}{u'[f(x^*_N)/N]/u[f(x^*_N)/N]} - \frac{g(x^*_N) - f'(x^*_N)}{N} \tag{19}$$

$$- (N-1)\{\frac{g(x^*_N)}{N} - [\frac{f'(x^*_N)}{N} - \Gamma'(x^*_N)]\}$$

$$= L(x^*_N) - M(x^*_N),$$

where:

$$L(x) = \kappa(x)/u'[f(x)/N]$$

$$M(x) = \frac{N-1}{N}\{g(x) + [N\Gamma'(x) - f'(x)]\}.$$

Now,

$$Nr' - f' = r' - [f'-(N-1)r']$$

$$= r' - F'$$

which is positive at x_N^*, by Figure 1 where the stable arms form a steeper angle than the slope of F at x_N^*. Since $g(x) > 0$ at all $x \geq 0$,

$$M(x_N^*) > 0.$$

In view of Assumption 4, we can construct Figure 3, which demonstrates graphically,

Figure 3:

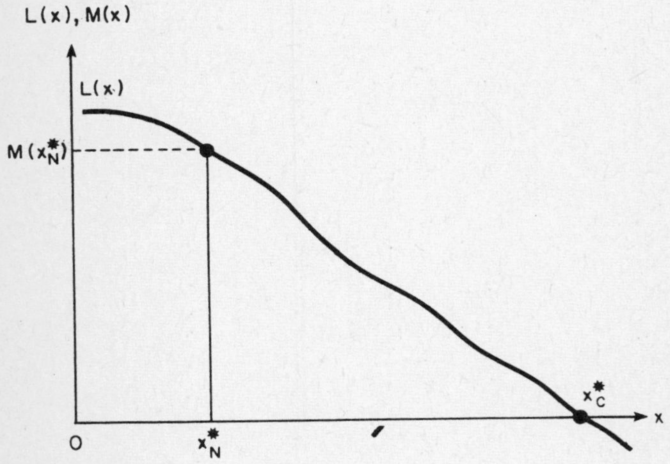

Stationary Stocks for Cooperative and Noncooperative Solutions

Proposition 2

$x^*_N < x^*_C$.

The derivation sketched above can obviously be made rigorous.

Corollary

The instantaneous probability for extinction is higher when the resource is exploited under a noncooperative stationary solution than under a cooperative stationary solution:

$$g(x^*_N) > g(x^*_C).$$

Although our attention is focused upon the optimal stationary solution, the determination of that solution, for the noncooperative equilibrium, depends upon that solution being asymptotically stable. We have taken this stability property as given. All sufficient conditions for stability which are known today are of the curvature requirement type.[7] These are inapplicable in view of our state-dependent discount rate. Of course, cases exist in our problem for which global asymptotic stability is evidently assured. For example, consider the $g(\cdot)$ function as nearly a positive constant function as one likes, say, $\sup_x\{g+|g'|/g\} < \varepsilon$. Eventually, global asymptotic stability should obtain.

To illustrate the key concepts above, we present a partially worked out example.

Example

Suppose that:

$$g(x) = \beta e^{v-x}, \qquad U(c) = c^{1/2}, \qquad F(x) = x(1-x).$$

It is straightforward to find that:

$$\kappa(x) = -U[F(x)]g'(x)/g(x) - [g(x) - F'(x)]\, U'[F(x)]$$

$$= x^{1/2}(1-x)^{1/2} - [\beta e^{v-x} - (1-2x)]\,(1/2)\, x^{-1/2}\,(1-x)^{-1/2}$$

---

[7] For instance, the results of Cass and Shell (1976), Brock and Scheinkerman (1976) and Rockafellar (1976).

$$=(1-2x^2 - \beta e^{v-x})/[2x^{1/2}(1-x)^{1/2}]$$

Case (i) $\beta = 7/8$, $v = 1/4$.

One may verify that $x^* = 1/4$, $g(x^*) = 7/8$, and both Assumptions 4 and 5 are satisfied: $\kappa'(x^*) = -1/4\sqrt{3}$, $F'(x^*) = 1/2$.

Case (ii) $\beta = 1/3$, $v = 2/3$.

Here $x^* = 2/3$, $g(x^*) = 1/9$. Also, $\kappa'(x^*) = -23/6\sqrt{2}$, $F'(x^*) = -1/3$.

Thus, Assumption 4 is satisfied, but not Assumption 5. Figure 4, upper panel portrays,

$$F'(x) + [-g'(x)/g(x)]/[U'(x)/U(x)] = 1 - 2x^2$$

and

$$g(x) = \beta e^{v-x}$$

for both cases (i) and (ii) in order to determine the respective values of x^*. The aligned lower panel presents the recruitment function $F(x) = x(1-x)$, so that its slopes at the stationary values in both cases are readily shown.

The above example satisfies Assumption 4a if $\beta e^v < 1$.

The above example incorporates simple, easily computable functions in order to illustrate the concepts underlying the definition of a stationary solution and Assumptions 4 and 5. Whether these stationary solutions are asymptotically stable equilibrium values, in fact, whether they are at equilibrium at all, have not been numerically verified.

8. Concluding Remarks

At the end of an exploratory study, it seems appropos to offer some observations which may be of some use for other researchers.

1. Samuelson (1947) proposed the "correspondence principle", utilizing stability conditions to aid comparative statics. Our present work clearly is inspired by his example, with two variations: (a) our "stability property" pertains to optimal programmes of rational agents and "real time", and (b) our comparison is among equilibrium stationary paths under different "institutional" arrangement.

Figure 4:

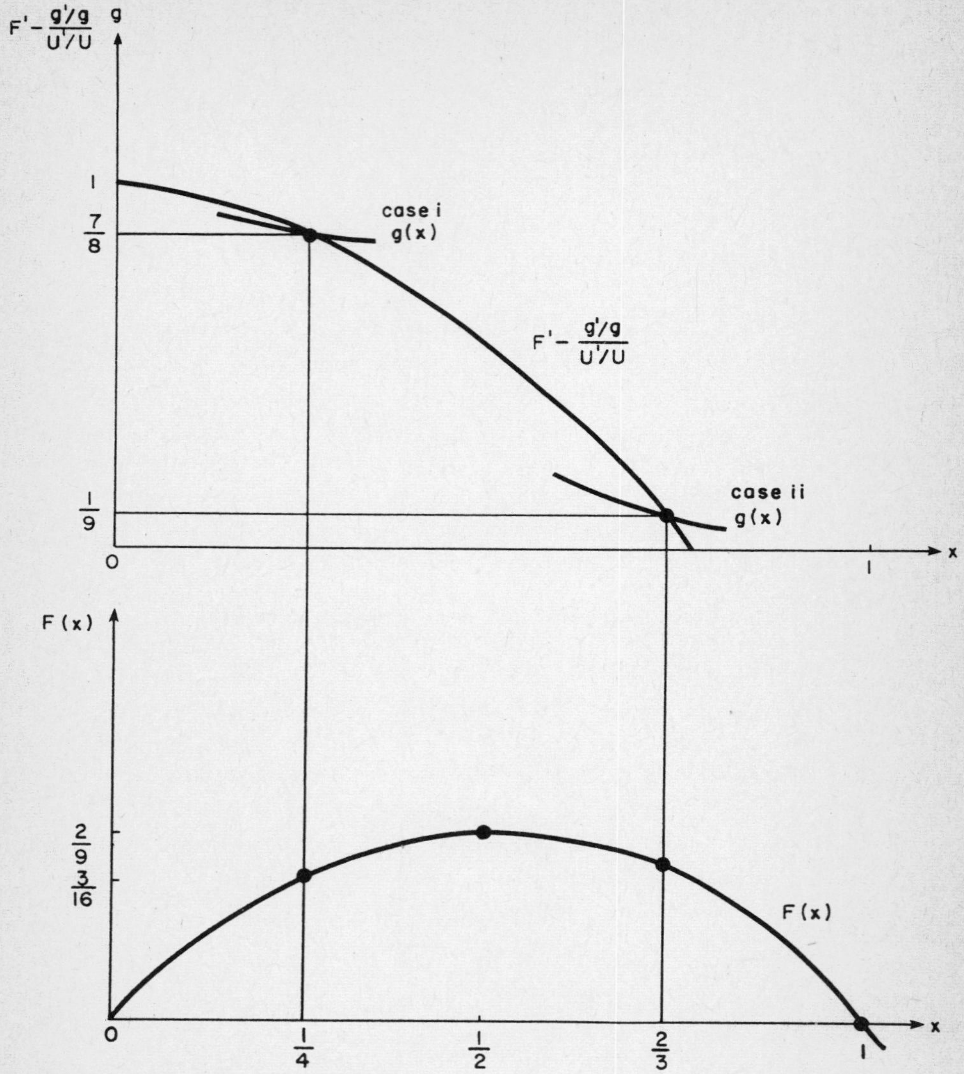

Stationary Stocks and Rates of Recruitment

2. Dorfman, Samuelson and Solow (1958) introduced the turnpike concept to capture the neo-classic tradition about the "long run". In such models, the horizons are usually of known length, be it finite or infinite. Our experimentation here is to apply the turnpike concept to the jump-process, with state-dependent probabilities for termination. This also corresponds to the biological notion of "stasis", with extinctions as "punctuations". All that is left out is the initiation of the process.

3. Isaacs (1965) and Case (1969) pioneered the study of differential games. Despite its fast growth, differential game has been criticised (including Clemhout and Wan, 1979) for assuming special functional forms. These criticisms are largely mitigated by the recent use of methods like phase diagram to solve certain types of differential games (Clemhout and Wan, 1985b).[8] Additionally, in this study we have demonstrated that by a combination of analytic and graphic methods we can tackle others. Special functional forms need not be assumed in either case.

9. References

Brock, W.A. and J.A. Scheinkman (1976), "Global Asymptotic Stability of Optimal Control Systems with Applications to the Theory of Economic Growth," Journal of Economic Theory, pp. 164-190.

Case, J.H. (1967), "Toward a Theory of Many Player Differential Games," SIAM Journal of Control, pp. 1-19.

Cass, D. and K. Shell (1976), "The Structure and Stability of Competitive Dynamic Systems," Journal of Economic Theory, pp. 31-70.

Clark, C.W. (1973), "Profit Maximization and the Extinction of Animal Species," Journal of Political Economy, pp. 950-961.

Clemhout, S. and H. Wan, Jr. (1979), "Interactive Economic Dynamics and Differential Games," Journal of Optimization, Theory and Applications, pp. 7-30.

________ (1985a), "Resource Exploitation and Ecological Degradation as Differential Games," in Journal of Optimization, Theory and Applications, pp. 471-481.

________ (1985b), "Cartelization Conserves Endangered Species?" in Optimal Control Theory and Economic Analysis 2, G. Feichtinger (Ed.), North Holland, Amsterdam.

---

[8] Several applied mathematics fields (including "partial differential equations," itself) do not yet have a "completely general" theory. Yet they do make important contributions to applications in the physical sciences.

__________ (1987), Differential Game, The New Palgrave: A Dictionary of Economic Theory and Doctrine, New York: The Macmillan Press Ltd.

Dales, J.H. (1968), "Land, Water and Ownership," Canadian Journal of Economics, pp. 791-804.

Das Gupta, P. (1982), The Control of Resources, Oxford: Basil Blackwell.

Dorfman, R., P.A. Samuelson and R.M. Solow (1958), Linear Programming and Economic Analysis.

Gordon, H.S. (1954), "The Economic Theory of Common Property Resources: The Fishery," Journal of Political Economy, pp. 131-141.

Isaacs, R. (1965), Differential Games, New York: John Wiley.

Koopmans, T.C. (1963), "On the Concept of Optimal Growth, in Pontificiae Academiae Scientiarum Scripta Varia," Study Week on the Econometric Approaches to Development Planning, Amsterdam: North Holland.

Kushner, H.J. (1971), Introduction to Stochastic Control, New York: Holt, Reinhart and Winston.

Levhari, D. and L.J. Mirman (1980), "The Great Fish War: An Example Using a Cournot-Nash Solution," The Bell Journal of Economics, pp. 322-334.

Martin, P.S. and R.G. Klein (1984), Quarternary Extinctions, A Prehistoric Revolution, Tuscon, AZ: The University of Arizona Press.

Merton, R.C. (1971), "Optimal Consumption and Portfolio Rules," Journal of Economic Theory, pp. 373-413.

Officer, C.B. and C.L. Drake (1983), "The Cretaceous - Tertiary Transition," Science, pp. 1383-1390.

Pliska, S.R. (1975), "Controlled Jump Processes," Stochastic Processes and Their Applications, pp. 259-282.

Rockafellar, T. (1976), "Saddlepoints of Hamiltonian Systems in Convex Lagrange Problems Having as Non-Zero Discount Rate," Journal of Economic Theory, pp. 71-113.

Samuelson, R.A. (1948), The Foundations of Economic Analysis, Cambridge, MA: Harvard University Press.

Sobel, M.J. (1982), "Stochastic Fishery Games With Myopic Equilibria," in Essays in the Economics of Renewable Resources, L.J. Mirman and D.F. Spulber, (Eds.), Amsterdam: North Holland.

Worcester, D. (1969), "Pecuniary and Technologial Externalities, Factor Rents and Social Costs," American Economic Review, pp. 873-885.

Vol. 157: Optimization and Operations Research. Proceedings 1977. Edited by R. Henn, B. Korte, and W. Oettli. VI, 270 pages. 1978.

Vol. 158: L. J. Cherene, Set Valued Dynamical Systems and Economic Flow. VIII, 83 pages. 1978.

Vol. 159: Some Aspects of the Foundations of General Equilibrium Theory: The Posthumous Papers of Peter J. Kalman. Edited by J. Green. VI, 167 pages. 1978.

Vol. 160: Integer Programming and Related Areas. A Classified Bibliography. Edited by D. Hausmann. XIV, 314 pages. 1978.

Vol. 161: M. J. Beckmann, Rank in Organizations. VIII, 164 pages. 1978.

Vol. 162: Recent Developments in Variable Structure Systems, Economics and Biology. Proceedings 1977. Edited by R. R. Mohler and A. Ruberti. VI, 326 pages. 1978.

Vol. 163: G. Fandel, Optimale Entscheidungen in Organisationen. VI, 143 Seiten. 1979.

Vol. 164: C. L. Hwang and A. S. M. Masud, Multiple Objective Decision Making – Methods and Applications. A State-of-the-Art Survey. XII, 351 pages. 1979.

Vol. 165: A. Maravall, Identification in Dynamic Shock-Error Models. VIII, 158 pages. 1979.

Vol. 166: R. Cuninghame-Green, Minimax Algebra. XI, 258 pages. 1979.

Vol. 167: M. Faber, Introduction to Modern Austrian Capital Theory. X, 196 pages. 1979.

Vol. 168: Convex Analysis and Mathematical Economics. Proceedings 1978. Edited by J. Kriens. V, 136 pages. 1979.

Vol. 169: A. Rapoport et al., Coalition Formation by Sophisticated Players. VII, 170 pages. 1979.

Vol. 170: A. E. Roth, Axiomatic Models of Bargaining. V, 121 pages. 1979.

Vol. 171: G. F. Newell, Approximate Behavior of Tandem Queues. XI, 410 pages. 1979.

Vol. 172: K. Neumann and U. Steinhardt, GERT Networks and the Time-Oriented Evaluation of Projects. 268 pages. 1979.

Vol. 173: S. Erlander, Optimal Spatial Interaction and the Gravity Model. VII, 107 pages. 1980.

Vol. 174: Extremal Methods and Systems Analysis. Edited by A. V. Fiacco and K. O. Kortanek. XI, 545 pages. 1980.

Vol. 175: S. K. Srinivasan and R. Subramanian, Probabilistic Analysis of Redundant Systems. VII, 356 pages. 1980.

Vol. 176: R. Färe, Laws of Diminishing Returns. VIII, 97 pages. 1980.

Vol. 177: Multiple Criteria Decision Making-Theory and Application. Proceedings, 1979. Edited by G. Fandel and T. Gal. XVI, 570 pages. 1980.

Vol. 178: M. N. Bhattacharyya, Comparison of Box-Jenkins and Bonn Monetary Model Prediction Performance. VII, 146 pages. 1980.

Vol. 179: Recent Results in Stochastic Programming. Proceedings, 1979. Edited by P. Kall and A. Prékopa. IX, 237 pages. 1980.

Vol. 180: J. F. Brotchie, J. W. Dickey and R. Sharpe, TOPAZ – General Planning Technique and its Applications at the Regional, Urban, and Facility Planning Levels. VII, 356 pages. 1980.

Vol. 181: H. D. Sherali and C. M. Shetty, Optimization with Disjunctive Constraints. VIII, 156 pages. 1980.

Vol. 182: J. Wolters, Stochastic Dynamic Properties of Linear Econometric Models. VIII, 154 pages. 1980.

Vol. 183: K. Schittkowski, Nonlinear Programming Codes. VIII, 242 pages. 1980.

Vol. 184: R. E. Burkard and U. Derigs, Assignment and Matching Problems: Solution Methods with FORTRAN-Programs. VIII, 148 pages. 1980.

Vol. 185: C. C. von Weizsäcker, Barriers to Entry. VI, 220 pages. 1980.

Vol. 186: Ch.-L. Hwang and K. Yoon, Multiple Attribute Decision Making – Methods and Applications. A State-of-the-Art-Survey. XI, 259 pages. 1981.

Vol. 187: W. Hock, K. Schittkowski, Test Examples for Nonlinear Programming Codes. V. 178 pages. 1981.

Vol. 188: D. Bös, Economic Theory of Public Enterprise. VII, 142 pages. 1981.

Vol. 189: A. P. Lüthi, Messung wirtschaftlicher Ungleichheit. IX, 287 pages. 1981.

Vol. 190: J. N. Morse, Organizations: Multiple Agents with Multiple Criteria. Proceedings, 1980. VI, 509 pages. 1981.

Vol. 191: H. R. Sneessens, Theory and Estimation of Macroeconomic Rationing Models. VII, 138 pages. 1981.

Vol. 192: H. J. Bierens: Robust Methods and Asymptotic Theory in Nonlinear Econometrics. IX, 198 pages. 1981.

Vol. 193: J. K. Sengupta, Optimal Decisions under Uncertainty. VII, 156 pages. 1981.

Vol. 194: R. W. Shephard, Cost and Production Functions. XI, 104 pages. 1981.

Vol. 195: H. W. Ursprung, Die elementare Katastrophentheorie. Eine Darstellung aus der Sicht der Ökonomie. VII, 332 pages. 1982.

Vol. 196: M. Nermuth, Information Structures in Economics. VIII, 236 pages. 1982.

Vol. 197: Integer Programming and Related Areas. A Classified Bibliography. 1978 – 1981. Edited by R. von Randow. XIV, 338 pages. 1982.

Vol. 198: P. Zweifel, Ein ökonomisches Modell des Arztverhaltens. XIX, 392 Seiten. 1982.

Vol. 199: Evaluating Mathematical Programming Techniques. Proceedings, 1981. Edited by J.M. Mulvey. XI, 379 pages. 1982.

Vol. 200: The Resource Sector in an Open Economy. Edited by H. Siebert. IX, 161 pages. 1984.

Vol. 201: P. M. C. de Boer, Price Effects in Input-Output-Relations: A Theoretical and Empirical Study for the Netherlands 1949–1967. X, 140 pages. 1982.

Vol. 202: U. Witt, J. Perske, SMS – A Program Package for Simulation and Gaming of Stochastic Market Processes and Learning Behavior. VII, 266 pages. 1982.

Vol. 203: Compilation of Input-Output Tables. Proceedings, 1981. Edited by J. V. Skolka. VII, 307 pages. 1982.

Vol. 204: K.C. Mosler, Entscheidungsregeln bei Risiko: Multivariate stochastische Dominanz. VII, 172 Seiten. 1982.

Vol. 205: R. Ramanathan, Introduction to the Theory of Economic Growth. IX, 347 pages. 1982.

Vol. 206: M.H. Karwan, V. Lotfi, J. Telgen, and S. Zionts, Redundancy in Mathematical Programming. VII, 286 pages. 1983.

Vol. 207: Y. Fujimori, Modern Analysis of Value Theory. X, 165 pages. 1982.

Vol. 208: Econometric Decision Models. Proceedings, 1981. Edited by J. Gruber. VI, 364 pages. 1983.

Vol. 209: Essays and Surveys on Multiple Criteria Decision Making. Proceedings, 1982. Edited by P. Hansen. VII, 441 pages. 1983.

Vol. 210: Technology, Organization and Economic Structure. Edited by R. Sato and M.J. Beckmann. VIII, 195 pages. 1983.

Vol. 211: P. van den Heuvel, The Stability of a Macroeconomic System with Quantity Constraints. VII, 169 pages. 1983.

Vol. 212: R. Sato and T. Nôno, Invariance Principles and the Structure of Technology. V, 94 pages. 1983.

Vol. 213: Aspiration Levels in Bargaining and Economic Decision Making. Proceedings, 1982. Edited by R. Tietz. VIII, 406 pages. 1983.

Vol. 214: M. Faber, H. Niemes und G. Stephan, Entropie, Umweltschutz und Rohstoffverbrauch. IX, 181 Seiten. 1983.

Vol. 215: Semi-Infinite Programming and Applications. Proceedings, 1981. Edited by A.V. Fiacco and K.O. Kortanek. XI, 322 pages. 1983.

Vol. 216: H.H. Müller, Fiscal Policies in a General Equilibrium Model with Persistent Unemployment. VI, 92 pages. 1983.

Vol. 217: Ch. Grootaert, The Relation Between Final Demand and Income Distribution. XIV, 105 pages. 1983.

Vol. 218: P. van Loon, A Dynamic Theory of the Firm: Production, Finance and Investment. VII, 191 pages. 1983.

Vol. 219: E. van Damme, Refinements of the Nash Equilibrium Concept. VI, 151 pages. 1983.

Vol. 220: M. Aoki, Notes on Economic Time Series Analysis: System Theoretic Perspectives. IX, 249 pages. 1983.

Vol. 221: S. Nakamura, An Inter-Industry Translog Model of Prices and Technical Change for the West German Economy. XIV, 290 pages. 1984.

Vol. 222: P. Meier, Energy Systems Analysis for Developing Countries. VI, 344 pages. 1984.

Vol. 223: W. Trockel, Market Demand. VIII, 205 pages. 1984.

Vol. 224: M. Kiy, Ein disaggregiertes Prognosesystem für die Bundesrepublik Deutschland. XVIII, 276 Seiten. 1984.

Vol. 225: T.R. von Ungern-Sternberg, Zur Analyse von Märkten mit unvollständiger Nachfragerinformation. IX, 125 Seiten. 1984

Vol. 226: Selected Topics in Operations Research and Mathematical Economics. Proceedings, 1983. Edited by G. Hammer and D. Pallaschke. IX, 478 pages. 1984.

Vol. 227: Risk and Capital. Proceedings, 1983. Edited by G. Bamberg and K. Spremann. VII, 306 pages. 1984.

Vol. 228: Nonlinear Models of Fluctuating Growth. Proceedings, 1983. Edited by R.M. Goodwin, M. Krüger and A. Vercelli. XVII, 277 pages. 1984.

Vol. 229: Interactive Decision Analysis. Proceedings, 1983. Edited by M. Grauer and A.P. Wierzbicki. VIII, 269 pages. 1984.

Vol. 230: Macro-Economic Planning with Conflicting Goals. Proceedings, 1982. Edited by M. Despontin, P. Nijkamp and J. Spronk. VI, 297 pages. 1984.

Vol. 231: G.F. Newell, The M/M/∞ Service System with Ranked Servers in Heavy Traffic. XI, 126 pages. 1984.

Vol. 232: L. Bauwens, Bayesian Full Information Analysis of Simultaneous Equation Models Using Integration by Monte Carlo. VI, 114 pages. 1984.

Vol. 233: G. Wagenhals, The World Copper Market. XI, 190 pages. 1984.

Vol. 234: B.C. Eaves, A Course in Triangulations for Solving Equations with Deformations. III, 302 pages. 1984.

Vol. 235: Stochastic Models in Reliability Theory. Proceedings, 1984. Edited by S. Osaki and Y. Hatoyama. VII, 212 pages. 1984.

Vol. 236: G. Gandolfo, P.C. Padoan, A Disequilibrium Model of Real and Financial Accumulation in an Open Economy. VI, 172 pages. 1984.

Vol. 237: Misspecification Analysis. Proceedings, 1983. Edited by T.K. Dijkstra. V, 129 pages. 1984.

Vol. 238: W. Domschke, A. Drexl, Location and Layout Planning. IV, 134 pages. 1985.

Vol. 239: Microeconomic Models of Housing Markets. Edited by K. Stahl. VII, 197 pages. 1985.

Vol. 240: Contributions to Operations Research. Proceedings, 1984. Edited by K. Neumann and D. Pallaschke. V, 190 pages. 1985.

Vol. 241: U. Wittmann, Das Konzept rationaler Preiserwartungen. XI, 310 Seiten. 1985.

Vol. 242: Decision Making with Multiple Objectives. Proceedings, 1984. Edited by Y.Y. Haimes and V. Chankong. XI, 571 pages. 1985.

Vol. 243: Integer Programming and Related Areas. A Classified Bibliography 1981–1984. Edited by R. von Randow. XX, 386 pages. 1985.

Vol. 244: Advances in Equilibrium Theory. Proceedings, 1984. Edited by C.D. Aliprantis, O. Burkinshaw and N.J. Rothman. II, 235 pages. 1985.

Vol. 245: J.E.M. Wilhelm, Arbitrage Theory. VII, 114 pages. 1985.

Vol. 246: P.W. Otter, Dynamic Feature Space Modelling, Filtering and Self-Tuning Control of Stochastic Systems. XIV, 177 pages. 1985.

Vol. 247: Optimization and Discrete Choice in Urban Systems. Proceedings, 1983. Edited by B.G. Hutchinson, P. Nijkamp and M. Batty. VI, 371 pages. 1985.

Vol. 248: Plural Rationality and Interactive Decision Processes. Proceedings, 1984. Edited by M. Grauer, M. Thompson and A.P. Wierzbicki. VI, 354 pages. 1985.

Vol. 249: Spatial Price Equilibrium: Advances in Theory, Computation and Application. Proceedings, 1984. Edited by P. T. Harker. VII, 277 pages. 1985.

Vol. 250: M. Roubens, Ph. Vincke, Preference Modelling. VIII, 94 pages. 1985.

Vol. 251: Input-Output Modeling. Proceedings, 1984. Edited by A. Smyshlyaev. VI, 261 pages. 1985.

Vol. 252: A. Birolini, On the Use of Stochastic Processes in Modeling Reliability Problems. VI, 105 pages. 1985.

Vol. 253: C. Withagen, Economic Theory and International Trade in Natural Exhaustible Resources. VI, 172 pages. 1985.

Vol. 254: S. Müller, Arbitrage Pricing of Contingent Claims. VIII, 151 pages. 1985.

Vol. 255: Nondifferentiable Optimization: Motivations and Applications. Proceedings, 1984. Edited by V.F. Demyanov and D. Pallaschke. VI, 350 pages. 1985.

Vol. 256: Convexity and Duality in Optimization. Proceedings, 1984. Edited by J. Ponstein. V, 142 pages. 1985.

Vol. 257: Dynamics of Macrosystems. Proceedings, 1984. Edited by J.-P. Aubin, D. Saari and K. Sigmund. VI, 280 pages. 1985.

Vol. 258: H. Funke, Eine allgemeine Theorie der Polypol- und Oligopolpreisbildung. III, 237 pages. 1985.

Vol. 259: Infinite Programming. Proceedings, 1984. Edited by E.J. Anderson and A.B. Philpott. XIV, 244 pages. 1985.

Vol. 260: H.-J. Kruse, Degeneracy Graphs and the Neighbourhood Problem. VIII, 128 pages. 1986.

Vol. 261: Th.R. Gulledge, Jr., N.K. Womer, The Economics of Made-to-Order Production. VI, 134 pages. 1986.

Vol. 262: H.U. Buhl, A Neo-Classical Theory of Distribution and Wealth. V, 146 pages. 1986.

Vol. 263: M. Schäfer, Resource Extraction and Market Structure. XI, 154 pages. 1986.

Vol. 264: Models of Economic Dynamics. Proceedings, 1983. Edited by H.F. Sonnenschein. VII, 212 pages. 1986.

Vol. 265: Dynamic Games and Applications in Economics. Edited by T. Başar. IX, 288 pages. 1986.